JOURNAL FOR THE STUDY OF THE OLD TESTAMENT SUPPLEMENT SERIES
185

Sheffield Academic Press

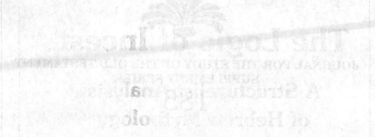

The Logic of Incest

JOURNAL FOR THE STUDY OF THE OLD TESTAMENT
SUPPLEMENT SERIES
185

A Structural Analysis
of Hebrew Mythology

Editor
David J.A. Clines

Seth Daniel Kunin

Executive Editor
John Jarick

Editorial Board
Richard J. Coggins, Alan Cooper, Tamara C. Eskenazi,
J. Cheryl Exum, John Goldingay, Robert P. Gordon,
Norman K. Gottwald, Andrew D.H. Mayes, Carol Meyers,
Patrick D. Miller

Sheffield Academic Press

The Logic of Incest

A Structuralist Analysis of Hebrew Mythology

Seth Daniel Kunin

Journal for the Study of the Old Testament
Supplement Series 185

Copyright © 1995 Sheffield Academic Press

Published by
Sheffield Academic Press Ltd
Mansion House
19 Kingfield Road
Sheffield, S11 9AS
England

Typeset by Sheffield Academic Press
and
Printed on acid-free paper in Great Britain
by Bookcraft
Midsomer Norton, Somerset

British Library Cataloguing in Publication Data

A catalogue record for this book is available
from the British Library

ISBN 1-85075-509-4

CONTENTS

Acknowledgments   7
List of Figures   9
Abbreviations   10
Introduction   11

Chapter 1
MYTH AND THEORY   19

Chapter 2
ISRAELITE 'IDEALIZED' ETHNOGRAPHY   49

Chapter 3
ABRAHAM   62

Chapter 4
ISAAC   94

Chapter 5
JACOB   112

Chapter 6
JOSEPH AND HIS BROTHERS   135

Chapter 7
CREATION   162

Chapter 8
THE STRUCTURE OF GENEALOGIES IN GENESIS   178

Chapter 9
THE STRUCTURE OF RABBINIC THOUGHT (A)   205

Chapter 10
THE STRUCTURE OF RABBINIC THOUGHT (B) 231

Chapter 11
THE STRUCTURE OF HEBREW THOUGHT 257

Bibliography 282
Index of References 292
Index of Authors 296

ACKNOWLEDGMENTS

My thanks are due to the many people who assisted me in both the writing of, and the development of the concepts found in this book. Dr Stephen Hugh-Jones supervised my PhD research which is the basis of this book. He was always available to discuss my work. Rabbi Dr Nicholas De Lange also gave me useful advice regarding my analysis of rabbinic texts. I would also like to thank Rabbi Dr Jonathan Magonet for his comments on the biblical chapters. Dr Graham Davies also provided useful comment and criticism. I am also indebted to Dr Carolyn Kunin and Rabbi David Kunin for their ongoing support and suggestions. Thanks are also due to Diana Lipton and Paula Aarons who patiently proofread several versions of the book. I would also like to express my deep appreciation to Professor Neil Gillman and Professor Robert Murphy who helped me develop my theoretical approach. I would also like to convey my continuing appreciation to the Laws, conversations and debates with them led to the genesis of this work. I also thank the ORS without whose support I could not have embarked on my research. My research was also funded by a grant from the Memorial Foundation for Jewish Culture. I am grateful to Sheffield Academic Press for their willingness to publish this book.

LIST OF FIGURES

Figure
1. Map of Judah under Persian Rule   51
2. Israelite Rules of Incest   60
3. *Wife/Sister 2*   84
4. Israel in Egypt   85
5. Structural Comparison of *Wife/Sister 2* and Israel in Egypt   85
6. Strucural Elements of Genesis 22   101
7. Illustration of the Structure of Genesis 22   101
8. Structural Elements of Genesis 37   101
9. Illustration of the Structure of Genesis 37   102
10. Comparison of the Structures of Genesis 22 and Genesis 37   102
11. The Sons of Jacob   142
12. Jacob's Blessings   159
13. Ideological History of Nations Genealogically Close to Israel   195
14. Ideological History of Nations Genealogically Distant
        from Israel   197
15. Ideological History of Israel and the Nations   198
16. Genealogical and Ideological Relations   202
17. Diachronic Levels of Hebrew Mythology   207
18. Diachronic Development of Key Mythemes   253
19. Structural Equations for Horizontal Oppositions   259
20. Synchronic Development of the Sacrifice Mytheme   260
21. Structural Equation of Vertical and Horizontal Oppositions   261
22. The Mythemes Found in the Four Textual Strata   270
23. Structure of Israelite Geography   275

ABBREVIATIONS

BDB	F. Brown, S.R. Driver and C.A. Briggs, *Hebrew and English Lexicon of the Old Testament*
BHS	*Biblia hebraica stuttgartensia*
HR	*History of Religions*
JAAR	*Journal of the American Academy of Religion*
JANESCU	*Journal of the Ancient Near Eastern Society of Columbia University*
JBL	*Journal of Biblical Literature*
JCS	*Journal of Cuneiform Studies*
JNES	*Journal of Near Eastern Studies*
JSOT	*Journal for the Study of the Old Testament*
USQR	*Union Seminary Quarterly Review*
VT	*Vetus Testamentum*
ZAW	*Zeitschrift für die alttestamentliche Wissenschaft*

INTRODUCTION

This book examines Hebrew mythology from a structuralist perspective. The approach is based on the theoretical and methodological apparatus of Claude Lévi-Strauss (1963, 1966, 1976, 1985, 1988),[1] modified in terms of suggestions by E. Leach (1961, 1969), Leach and Aycock (1983), D. Sperber (1975), T. Turner (1977, 1985) and R. Wagner (1981), and new modifications of structuralist theory developed during this research. I apply this theoretical and methodological approach to Hebrew mythological texts. The texts examined here were written over a two-thousand-year period between the eighth century BC and the thirteenth century AD. Four diachronically distinct levels of transformation are analyzed: Genesis (redacted in the fifth century BC), *Genesis Rabbah* (edited in the fourth century AD), *Pirke deRabbi Eliezer* (edited in the eighth century AD) and the compilations (edited between the eleventh and thirteenth century AD).

Five interrelated questions are examined. (1) Can structuralist theory be applied usefully to societies conscious of history and change (and are there any societies which do not have historical consciousness)? (2) What is the relationship between continuity and transformation as a mythological tradition develops diachronically? (3) What role does diachronic development within a myth play in relation to its underlying structure? (4) What is the synchronic structure of Israelite (i.e., biblical) myth? (5) Are there identifiable patterns of transformation and continuity between biblical myth and the three diachronically distinct levels of rabbinic myth.

The first three questions which relate to structuralist theory are examined in detail in Chapter 1, which discusses the theoretical approach

---

1. The methodology for the interpretation of myth employs the three rules suggested by Lévi-Strauss:

1. A myth must never be interpreted on one level only.
2. A myth must never be interpreted individually.
3. A group of myths must never be interpreted alone, but by reference: (a) to other groups of myths; and (b) to the ethnography of the societies in which they originate (1976: 65).

underlying this analysis. The first question is tied to a basic distinction in Lévi-Strauss's work between 'hot' and 'cold' societies (i.e., societies that perceive themselves as changing or static respectively) (see §1.3). Although in his early work Lévi-Strauss suggested that 'hot' societies were not amenable to structuralist analysis (1966: 233-34), in a recent work he appears to have modified this opinion (1985: 219-34). It is suggested below that the two types of societies should be regarded as having alternative strategies for dealing with time, rather than being distinct and mutually exclusive types. It is suggested further that all societies are ranged between the two ideal types with none being completely 'hot' or 'cold'.[1]

The second question is of greater significance and is the basis for one of the primary innovations of this dissertation. In his *Mythologiques*,[2] Lévi-Strauss focuses on the transformations of myth between communities in geographic proximity (1969a, 1973, 1978, 1981). As Sperber suggests (1979: 42), it is likely that Lévi-Strauss replaces diachronic transformation with geographic transformation owing to the nature of the societies he studied (i.e., lacking indigenous written mythologies). Had diachronic material been available, it would have been the best medium for studying transformations in structure.

The material analyzed in this book offers an opportunity for diachronic analysis, focusing on transformation through time rather than space. Within the biblical text itself there are at least four diachronic levels. The biblical myths are the foundation for literally hundreds of texts written at later diachronically distinct and datable periods. Seven texts, including Genesis, spanning the full two-thousand-year period are examined here. These texts reveal both consistent patterns of transformation and consistency at the level of underlying structure. The consistency revealed may be due, in part, to the myths being part of a single set based on a common matrix, rather than immutable structures (see Lévi-Strauss 1981: 627).

Underlying structure is used in respect to three different levels.[3] The most basic level ($s^{(1)}$) is that deriving from biological structures of the brain, this level has no direct relation to the meaning of the myth. The level $s^{(1)}$ is common to all human beings. The second level ($s^{(2)}$) is that

1.   See the discussion in Turner 1988: 239-46.
2.   Lévi-Strauss 1969a, 1973, 1978 and 1981 are collectively titled *Mythologiques*.
3.   This is a model to facilitate discussion. It is not suggested that underlying structure actually can be divided into discrete categories.

of matrix or set. Although this level also has no direct relation to meaning, the myths (and other structured elements) at a particular synchronic moment will be structured by this matrix (and will transform within the possibilities it creates). The third level ($s^{(3)}$), is that of mytheme. It is on this level that we find meaning attached to structure. At any time a community will have many such structures. This book is primarily interested in examining $s^{(2)}$ and $s^{(3)}$ on a synchronic level (i.e., the biblical text), and examining the transformations in the two types of structure on the diachronic level.

The third question is tied to the synthesis of Lévi-Strauss's approach and the modifications suggested by T. Turner (1977). Lévi-Strauss was primarily concerned with static synchronic structures which could be categorized and analyzed independently of their narrative placement within a myth. Turner suggests that diachronic development of structure is also significant. He shows that there is often a progressive development within structural elements in a specific myth and that this development is fundamentally tied to the structural meaning of the text. Turner often analyzes such development to the detriment of synchronic structures. The biblical and rabbinic materials suggest that the two elements should be viewed as complementary, rather than as mutually exclusive methods of analysis.

The final two questions can be regarded as ethnographic. They are concerned with understanding the mind or culture which created Israelite myth, and examining the relationship between biblical culture and rabbinic culture. The first of these questions (i.e., regarding biblical structure) is examined in Chapters 3 through 8. Chapters 3 through 7 present detailed analysis of all the myths of Genesis. This analysis differs from all previous anthropological analyses, structuralist or otherwise, because it examines every text, revealing a comprehensive picture of Israelite myth as introduced in Genesis. All previous analyses (see below) have examined individual texts or small groups of texts outside the context of the system as a whole. This comprehensive analysis is in line with structuralist theory, which suggests that a large body of myths must be analyzed to discover a clear view of the underlying structure (both $s^{(2)}$ and $s^{(3)}$).

Throughout the discussions of biblical myth, and occasionally in respect to the midrashic material, I provide summaries of the myths. The summaries are not the texts that have been analyzed. In all cases the original version of the myth in its original language is the source of exegesis. The summaries are provided to help the reader understand the narrative elements of the myth (see Lévi-Strauss 1981: 632). Where possible the reader should refer to the original text.

Chapter 8 addresses a subsidiary question: is the structure ($s^{(2)}$) that is found in Israelite myth also found in biblical genealogies (non-narrative material)? The analysis reveals that the genealogies are characterized by the same underlying structure. The genealogies are characterized by a structural pattern that is exactly the opposite of that suggested by anthropologists and biblical scholars.

Chapters 9 and 10 provide the final diachronic layers of the myth. Five different midrashic texts are closely analyzed both synchronically (in terms of their own structures) and diachronically in relation to each other and to the biblical text. The analysis highlights interesting patterns of transformation which can be charted through the diachronic development. It also reveals that certain structural relations remain consistent in all the texts discussed.

Only a small selection of rabbinic material is presented. It should not be thought that these were the only texts analyzed; all texts in the five midrashic books were analyzed. For reasons of space, however, only those texts which contained significant structural elements are discussed in full. Those texts that contained only small structural fragments, repeated material already discussed or were structurally inert are not presented. (See Chapter 9 for examples of fragmentary and inert texts.)

Throughout the analysis of the biblical texts, reference is made to the work of other structuralists who have analyzed individual biblical texts.[1] The most substantial of these previous analyses, that of Edmund Leach (1969, 1970) Leach and Aycock (1983) and T. Prewitt (1990) are discussed in relation to specific points throughout the thesis (for the primary discussions of their work see below: §§1.11 and 6.1).[2]

One problem found in Leach's analysis (and also found in several other analyses) should be highlighted from the outset. Leach relies solely on English translations. Such translations theoretically could transform

---

1.   I make little reference to non-anthropological structuralists. For the most part they are concerned with surface structure rather than underlying structure and thus their analyses are not analogous to that attempted here. Some of the more interesting literary structuralist (and non-structuralist) analyses of the Bible are: Bar-Efrat 1979; Fisch 1973, 1982; Jobling 1978, 1986; Polzin 1977; and White 1979.

2.   Terry Prewitt's analysis of the Bible is only partially concerned with structuralist analysis. It also includes sections on semiotics and hermeneutics. The one section which is consciously structuralist, 'Structuralist Hermeneutics', is concerned with literary surface structure rather than underlying structure.

the structures of the myths into new variations mirroring the world of the translator rather than the community from which the myth was taken. Language, too, is intimately related to underlying structure.[1] This is especially true of Hebrew. Biblical usage of verbs, for example, is directly tied to Israelite perception of time. Grammatically, perfect and imperfect verbs can reverse their temporality with the addition of a single letter, making them functionally identical. Also, in the biblical and rabbinic understanding of time, past and future are functionally interchangeable. Both of these elements are tied to a concentric understanding of time and space.

The biblical text also makes use of puns which often emphasize or reveal the structural oppositions; these usually are lost in translation. Equally, puns found in translation are often the product of poor transliteration and can lead to mistaken associations (see, for example, Emerton's discussion of Leach [Emerton 1976: 88] and Prewitt 1990: 133 n. 4] in which he confuses הרן [Abraham's brother spelled with a ה] with חרן [a city in Mesopotamia spelled with a ח]).

Michael Carroll's (1985) article offers cogent criticisms of Leach's analysis of the early chapters of Genesis. His own suggestions for a structure of Genesis, however, have several flaws. His first structural principle is the reversal of the structure of Genesis. One problem with Carroll's work is his initial focus upon Cain as a culture hero, when in fact Cain is rejected by the myth. Carroll's structural principle emphasizes devaluation of close kinship, which leads to separation and creation of a new cultural element. He misses the fact that only the rejected brother is finally devalued and separated, ultimately the chosen son and the family are united or reunited. Carroll mistakes segments of the system for the system as a whole.

The work of Mary Douglas (1966, 1975) is referred to, especially in Chapter 11 which extends the analysis of myth to other cultural spheres. Initially, she did not analyze food taboos in the context of Israelite culture as a whole. In *Implicit Meanings*, as discussed in Chapter 11,

---

1. This is in line with my understanding of structuralist theory rather than that of Lévi-Strauss. In *The Naked Man* he suggests that even though the original language is helpful in understanding a myth, it is not an absolute requirement (1981: 644). I suggest that when a myth is translated and borrowed by someone from a different culture, the structures must, by definition, be transformed to fit the needs of the society of the translator or borrower. Structure is not an artifact. It is a 'living' transforming 'entity' which fits (and creates) the needs of the society in which it exists.

Douglas extends her analysis to broader cultural spheres. In general, the overall structure discussed in this book is consistent with her analysis of Israelite food taboos.

Several other anthropological analyses are also briefly discussed in the context of the myths they examine. The most interesting of these is the work of Pitt-Rivers (1977). The primary problem of his work, one also found in Prewitt, lies in two assumptions: that texts in the Bible necessarily contain relics of past cultural forms and that narrative order is the same as diachronic order of composition. Both assumptions must be seriously questioned.[1] A second problem with his work lies in his categorization of text. He suggests that a text should be considered myth if it contains fantastic material but 'historic' if it does not. As discussed below (§1.7), texts that contain fantastic material can be shown to have identical mythical structure to those which do not.

The major distinction, however, between the approach applied in this book and that of Pitt-Rivers lies in the way the biblical text is viewed. Due to his definition of mythology (by which a large part of the biblical text is not considered myth), Pitt-Rivers accepts much of the text as depicting (or reflecting) ethnographic reality. As this book considers the biblical text to be mythological in nature, it views the 'ethnographic reality' of the Bible differently. Due to the nature of the material studied, it is probably impossible to determine which of these approaches is closer to the 'truth'.

The two final analyses are functionalist interpretations of individual biblical texts. It should be noted that Leach's work is also consciously functionalist (Leach and Aycock 1983: 1). The functionalist element in his approach is most apparent in his emphasis on the conscious use of structure rather than the unconscious role which is analyzed here. Schapera (1985) discusses the myth of Cain and its relation to the biblical concept of murder. His analysis is interesting particularly because it relies on several biblical texts to support its argument. In a similar vein, Leonard Mars (1984) examines the myth of Onan. The only serious problem with their approach (as opposed to specific arguments) is that of transformation within myth. In the absence of external data it is difficult to take narrative descriptions at face value. Although I confine my own interpretation to structuralist analysis, I recognize that the biblical text works on many levels and would be usefully analyzed from a variety of perspectives (see Lévi-Strauss 1976: 65, see p. 11, above).

---

1. See §1.7 for a detailed discussion of Pitt-Rivers' analysis.

My research differs in several important ways from previous structuralist analyses of biblical material. My approach is holistic in as true a sense as possible; myths are discussed in context. All the myths of Genesis and the genealogies are analyzed in the original language. The structural principles presented are a synthesis of the overall structural elements found in all the myths.

This analysis is also diachronic. Six historically distinct versions of the myth are examined (i.e., the biblical text and five midrashic texts). Initially each version was analyzed synchronically and then placed in the diachronic context of the other myths. It should be noted that the biblical text was examined first. All projections which emerged from the analysis of structure were made prior to analysis of the rabbinic texts. As stated, this diachronic depth provides a unique opportunity to test structuralist theory. It also presents an exceptional case for analyzing mechanisms of transformation of myth within a continuous mythological tradition (see p. 12 regarding the relationship of geography and diachrony).

The analysis also supports the need to recognize explicit and implicit myth. The majority of material in Genesis (except for a few brief texts, e.g., Gen. 32.33) is explicit myth, that is, pure narrative. Much of it seems to have been written with no clear moralistic or homiletical purpose. Similarly, many rabbinic texts are pure narrative (i.e., explicit myth). These texts were written against the previous versions of the myth (both rabbinic and biblical). Other rabbinic texts, however, are in the form of explanation (exegesis) rather than narrative. These explanations are seen as implicit myth (Lévi-Strauss 1981: 669). Such explanations, like those of informants, must be seen as part of the myth.

The rabbinic material also fits Lévi-Strauss's discussion of the nature of myth. He suggests that myths are always created in response to previous versions. This is the nature of the midrashic texts, which were written in a continuous process starting in (at least) the second century AD until today. Each version was both written against the biblical text and against the previous versions of the midrash. Although some midrashic texts have sermonic or clear moralistic purpose (it should be emphasized that most do not), this should not affect the underlying structure which is distinct from function or content (meaning is attached to structure [$s^{(2)}$] rather than structure created by meaning). Although Lévi-Strauss suggests that function can affect structure (e.g., 1976: 266), it does not necessarily do so. The analysis of the myths below (both diachronic and synchronic) suggests that (at least in this case) function has not obviated structure. The same patterns of transformation are found in the rabbinic texts regardless of function or style.

Several points should be noted concerning the status of the results of this research. In terms of both ethnography and mythological structure, this work makes no claim to analyze any period prior to the editorial present of the text (i.e., fifth century BC). It therefore does not address any questions concerning exogamy/endogamy in the patriarchal period nor during pre-exilic Israel. The work also does not claim to be an exhaustive analysis of all levels of the text; it is concerned only with the nature of the structures and their transformations found in the mythological texts. This narrow focus, however, is not meant to suggest that this is the only level of significant meaning in the texts.

Finally, the theoretical perspective applied here suggests that any examination or interpretation is reflexive. Lévi-Strauss writes that any analysis of myth is, at least in part, a new layer of the myth reflecting the person retelling the myth.[1] Thus, to some degree, this discussion is about modern American (Jewish) society as well as about biblical society. It is also reflexive in a second sense. To some extent I function as both anthropologist and informant. As part of Jewish culture (and occasionally functioning as a rabbi and teacher in the Jewish community) I am part of Jewish culture as it exists today. My explanation of the myth, as the explanation of any informant, will emphasize those elements of structure which are currently significant. Whether by coincidence or for this reason, several issues discussed are at the centre of Jewish dialogue and thought today. These elements include the problems of intermarriage, the relationship between the various branches of Judaism, which creates—at least in the mind of the Orthodox—a question of mediation (which is by definition rejected by the system). It also may include the way the Jewish community and Israel interact with the outside world. I trust that I have treated my own explanations and those of the diachronic informants as subjects for analysis rather than offering them as the analysis itself.

---

1.   See Lévi-Strauss's discussion of this type of reflexivity (1981: 628).

Chapter 1

MYTH AND THEORY

Structuralism provides an approach to understanding the manipulation of symbolic systems within culture.[1] It places mythological material in the context of symbolic systems as a whole. Each symbolic system, be it myth, ritual or social structure, is informed and organized by the underlying logic.[2] Each of these systems creates patterns of logic through which existence can be rationalized and accepted (Lévi-Strauss 1963: 216; see also Pace 1983: 156).

Cultural symbolic systems (e.g., myth, ritual, kinship systems and social structure) have a common underlying structure. This structure organizes the relationships which underlie these systems and organizes the articulation of the various systems. Using the analogy of structural linguistics,[3] underlying structure is compared with the rules or logic which organize phonemes, for example, into oppositions, and with grammar or syntax, which organizes the articulation of vocabulary, the meaning of which is structurally insignificant.

1.   Culture is defined as a basic pattern of thought around which the symbolic systems develop. In a sense the terms 'culture' and 'society' are used interchangeably. Society is taken as an aggregate of people whose lives are organized by culture, that is, this basic pattern of thought.
2.   The relationship of the various symbolic systems vis-à-vis society as a whole should be analyzed in light of the model suggested by Roy Wagner in *Invention of Culture*—as a pattern of interrelated metaphors. Other texts which serve as a foundation for this discussion are: Durkheim 1926; Firth 1973; Jacopin 1988; Lévi-Strauss 1963, 1966, 1969, 1988; Middleton 1967; Turner 1969.
3.   It should be emphasized that this is an analogy. It is not the direct application of structural linguistic methodologies to cultural structure. This mistake is made by Turner (1977) when he criticizes Lévi-Strauss for not sticking to the structural linguistic line.

1.1. *Signification*

Structural linguistics posits a system of meaning based on three elements: the signified, the signifier and the sign. Signifiers are arbitrary combinations of sounds taken from the repertoire of possible sounds. Signifieds are concepts, culturally determined elements of experience. The union of the signifier with the signified creates the sign. The essential point is that there is no necessary relationship between the signifier and the signified (Pace 1983: 159).[1] Structural linguists are concerned with the ways words (or sounds) can be organized, rather than with the surface level of vocabulary, that is, the meaning of particular combinations of words. In a sense, these structures, phonetic and syntactic, are analogous to structures (the syntax) of culture, which both allow symbols to be articulated meaningfully, as well as being the system by which 'logical' thought is created.[2]

It is in this sense that syntax or structure can be said to control what can be meaningfully expressed in a specific language; we see the world through the lenses of our language. To a degree, our thought processes are controlled by the logical possibilities available in a language; how (and which) things can be logically, grammatically and meaningfully equated. Equally, the underlying structure, through its creation of logical patterns, or through the manipulation of (and equally its manipulation by) symbolic systems controls what can be said in a myth (or other cultural construct). The symbols, the vocabulary, are given meaning through patterns of articulation with other symbols, which in turn are understood by being read through the framework of the underlying structure. Structures both create (and derive from) patterns of thought and the contents of those patterns. These structures derive from a process by which form is unconsciously imposed on content. In a sense the unconscious mind creates the structures which then act upon the mind to organize thought.

---

1.   It should be noted that there are two levels of arbitrariness: on the level of the signifier and the signified, and on that of the sign. The signifier itself chooses arbitrary sounds from the range of possible sounds; the signified is a culturally determined, and arbitrary division of the flux of nature. The relation of the two in creating the sign is also arbitrary as there is no natural link between the two (Sturrock 1979: 9). See also: Saussure 1959: 65-74; Sturrock 1979: 6-9.

2.   The term logic is used not to mean a particular mode of thinking, but rather to denote a mode of thinking particular to each culture. Logic then is a method of organizing thought in a culturally 'accepted' way.

1.2. *Metaphor and Metonymy*

Underlying structure, both in terms of language and culture, works on two related levels: the metaphoric and the metonymic.[1] On the one hand, the metaphoric is the level of categories and relationships based on similarity and class. It is at this level that the synchronic aspect is developed. Elements from any text that share a common attribute can be categorized with each other and with similar elements from unrelated texts—then the relationship between such categories can be analyzed. This aspect joins together all texts built on the structure.[2]

On the other hand, the metonymic reveals the diachronic development of the text. This level is concerned with the combination of elements and the association between them. The metonymic approach is concerned with order of development and presentation, and is therefore concerned with individual texts rather than diverse texts. This level manipulates and combines elements from the metaphoric level and thereby creates meaning. Any analysis of text requires both these levels.[3]

1.3. *Structure and Social Structure*

There is a fundamental relationship between the development of social structure, and the development of underlying structure. It may be impossible, however, to discover a causal relationship between the two (there is no doubt that $s^{(3)}$ responds to social structure, it is unclear whether $s^{(2)}$ is similarly affected). In some senses the underlying structure can be seen as an attempt to mediate the contradictions implicit in social structure. Underlying structure, mind, stands between nature and culture. On the other hand, social structure can be seen as an articulation or a reflection of the structural logic, validating the logic by its existence.

This work is concerned with both how communities manipulate their symbolic systems to create meaning and how an underlying mental structure uses these systems to create logic. With Lévi-Strauss I agree that an underlying mental structure is characteristic of all human society.[4] Underlying structures ($s^{(3)}$) are 'used' by culture (meaning is

---

1.   Turner also uses the terms paradigmatic and syntagmatic (1977: 121).

2.   One valid criticism of Lévi-Strauss's work suggests that he relies too heavily on the metaphoric (or paradigmatic) level at the expense of the metonymic (syntagmatic) (Turner 1977: 111).

3.   This is discussed in relation to specific texts in both Chapters 3 and 11.

4.   And therefore its presence should affect the symbolic systems of societies with both a consciousness of history, and those without such consciousness.

attached to structure) to give order to existence, to mediate existential
crisis, and to cloud the boundaries between existential opposites, for
example, life and death, human and non-human.

One level of difference between my work and that of Lévi-Strauss
relates to the distinction between 'hot' and 'cold' societies (also discussed
below regarding myth). Lévi-Strauss distinguishes between two types of
societies (1966: 233-34). 'Hot' societies are those which perceive themselves as dedicated to rapid change, and are conscious of change and
therefore history. 'Cold' societies are those which see themselves as
remaining static, and thus view themselves as unchanging. 'Cold'
societies lack a consciousness of history, since history would challenge
their perceptions of themselves. Lévi-Strauss suggests that 'hot' societies
are not amenable to structural analysis.[1] As suggested below, if perception of history (as related to understanding of self) is taken as part of the
myth, as part of the 'naturalization' process, then there should be no
qualitative distinction between the two. Indeed they should be viewed as
having two strategies for dealing with time, rather than being two distinct
types. Most (if not all) societies probably include elements of both 'hot'
and 'cold'.[2] David Pace suggests that Lévi-Strauss is suspicious of
modern society (which is roughly analogous to 'hot' society) and that
this may be a factor in his preference for applying his approach to 'cold'
societies (Pace 1983: 40-59).

Structuralist theory relies on a 'myth of societal development' to
explain the existence of these structures, and their relationship to social
structure.[3] Lévi-Strauss alludes to this myth in *Tristes tropiques* (taken
from Leach's adaptation):

Regardless of the form of the material, all symbolic systems are organized by such
underlying structure.

1.   Lévi-Strauss's discussion of literature in *The Naked Man* (1981) suggests
that underlying structure is present in creations of a 'hot' society.

2.   The notion of 'cold' society is also challenged by J. Hill (1988). He argues
that even the societies whose myth Lévi-Strauss studied cannot be considered 'cold'.
He suggests that the societies of South America all have consciousness of both myth
and history. The societies are characterized by a 'range of more-or-less dynamic
ways of interpreting historical processes of change' (Hill 1988: 5). He suggests
further, that no society has 'progressed beyond myth'; all are only relatively 'hot' or
'cold' (Hill 1988: 4-5). This point is also made by Turner (1988: 235-46).

3.   'Structuralist myth of societal development' is my term. It is likely, however,
that Lévi-Strauss would agree with this usage.

We cannot choose to be alone, it must be 'we' or 'nothing'.[1] 'But in choosing 'we' there is almost an infinite choice as to what kind of 'we' it shall be. Myth is part of the apparatus through which we make that choice clear to ourselves...the choice itself is free, not determined (Leach 1967: xix).

Underlying structure clouds the crisis created by this choice. Below, an expanded version of this 'myth' is given.

1.4. *Structuralist Myth of Societal Development*[2]

Due to the nature of human existence in hostile environments, groups and communities have greater survival potential than individuals. Over time these aggregates of individuals became communities and developed patterns of cohesion, that is, the beginnings of culture. Existence in society leads invariably to crisis, caused by perceived limitation of choice. When a specific society developed, certain choices were made—though they need not be perceived as choices. In each case the choice meant a limitation from what was perceived as naturally or logically possible. Certain patterns of organization develop which encourage or require particular patterns of behaviour, including various patterns of kinship, required or preferred patterns of marriage, or a concept of incest.

Where marriage was a basis for societal cohesion a variety of possibilities were available, including endogamy and exogamy. Choice among these alternatives meant a move away from perceived nature (i.e., possible marriage or sexual union with any person of the appropriate gender) creating a nature–culture opposition, that is, a limited number of acceptable possibilities (culture) as opposed to unlimited possibilities (nature). (It should be noted that this is only one of many possible areas of choice.)

As society continued to develop, the underlying contradiction remained, creating a point of crisis. In order to support its choices, in an

1. Echoing Tylor's famous dictum: Marry out or be killed out (1889: 267).

2. This 'myth' is both a product of Lévi-Strauss's thought and the approach to structuralism developed here. The myth seeks to remove one level of opposition found in Lévi-Strauss's work, that is, nature–culture. One of the primary motivating factors of structure is the clouding of the opposition—making nature of culture. The opposition itself is not philosophically necessary as the concept of nature or 'nature' is itself a cultural creation. See also Pace 1983: 152 for a similar formulation.

This 'myth' is accepted as an underlying theoretical model in the approach taken by this book. It should be emphasized that it is seen as a model, or a structure of organizing and understanding information, rather than as a description of actual historical processes.

unconscious process, society developed other phenomena which share the same logic as the contradiction. The existence of these examples of the logic in other spheres proves that society is correct. In effect, the existence of the same logic proves that the original choice was natural, because the logic is natural (i.e. it is pervasive).[1] The symbolic systems serve to cover up contradiction in order to validate society's choice as natural, and thereby obviate the nature–culture dichotomy.

1.5. *Nature and Culture*
This is not to suggest that the opposition itself is a central focus of the culture. In many cultures the two are perceived as being indistinguishable, which explains why possible disjunction of the two is problematic: it creates the possibility that they are not identical. Myths (as well as other manifestations of structure) work to prevent perception of this disjunction by making culture appear to be natural. In modern Western society, where these two realms are at the least philosophically distinct, it might be thought that structure is therefore unnecessary or serves a different purpose. It is likely, however, that this disjunction exists only on a philosophical or ideological level, and that many basic elements of culture are still perceived as natural, or rationalized as natural. Two examples of this might be our perception of incest as 'naturally' wrong, and our distinction between people on racist (i.e. 'biological' and therefore natural) lines.

The symbolic systems draw their power from the dialectic, from the points of crisis which need to be resolved. In order to exist in society, there must be a means of validating that existence, of proving that it is the 'natural' way to exist—myth, ritual and social structure provide this validation. As long as the underlying structure, the framework or logic of the system, is meaningful (i.e., the questions addressed are those which are necessary for the continued existence, functioning and cohesion of that society), and as long as the crises dealt with in the logic remain points of danger, power will be retained. Therefore, historical change only affects the power of the symbolic system when the cultural continuity is broken. Where this continuity is retained, even if its factuality is challenged, the power will remain. Thus far the nature of underlying structure has been discussed. The following section develops a working definition of myth based on the theory presented here.

1.   See also Pace 1983: 152: 'Each individual within a society follows a particular course of action because it is the "natural" thing to do'.

1.6. *Mythology*

Scholars have variously considered mythology as:[1] stories of heroes and the supernatural (Pitt-Rivers 1977),[2] perceptions of history (Beltz 1983), expressions of sacred tales (Durkheim 1926; Leach and Aycock 1983), primitive science (Frazer 1958), or as the symbolic statement of the underlying structure of society (Lévi-Strauss 1963). Each of these approaches has implications regarding the role of myth in society and its 'power' within that society. Any analytical approach to myth, especially in relation to myth written in a 'historical' manner, must deal with the dichotomy of myth–history. It also must explain how a myth exercises power over a community, the source of this power and the factors which allow the power to continue to exist.

The relation between myth and history is often ambiguous; history is generally the yardstick by which myth, if it is taken seriously, is judged. It is assumed that the myth 'lives or dies' depending on its assumed factuality. A 'broken myth' is one whose contents have been proven not to be historical.[3]

The question of power is another essential element in the understanding of myth. It is this power that transforms a story, or a historical event, into a myth. Myth is considered to exercise power over its cultural community, as evidenced by the categorization of myth based on the presence or absence of power, that is, the distinctions between 'live', 'broken' and 'dead'[4]. The distinction between these three terms is

1. This is not meant as an exhaustive list.

2. See also Oden (1979b) who, quoting Fontenrose, suggests that myths must be both 'traditional' and acts of the 'supernatural' (1979b: 353).

3. Lévi-Strauss suggests a different model for the death of myths. He argues that as myths go through a process of transformation (as they move geographically) the mythic material (the underlying structure) may deteriorate and thus the myth may 'die' (Lévi-Strauss 1976: 256-68). His discussion implies that this type of deterioration can occur when the myth passes through a succession of linguistic and cultural thresholds (Lévi-Strauss 1976: 263). He suggests three ways by which a myth dies. It can be transformed into a 'romantic formula' (Lévi-Strauss 1976: 265), into a simple (conscious) charter myth with a restricted purpose (Lévi-Strauss 1976: 266) or into legitimizing history (Lévi-Strauss 1976: 268). One point must be made about this final type of transformation. The structure is lost, not because the myth uses history, but rather because the structural elements are forced to conform with history.

4. This distinction views myth as embodying two essential factors: power, that is, the ability to mediate contradiction and crisis; and factuality, that is, if the myth is viewed as narrating actual events or fictitious events. A myth is considered 'alive' if it retains 'power' and is also considered (within the culture) to be factual. A broken

based on both the relation to empirical understanding and the power
retained by the myth. Structuralist analysis provides a framework to
understand these two vital elements of mythic systems. It also places the
symbolic systems into the context of societal requirements.

Structuralist theory differs in several important respects from other
theoretical approaches to myth. Non-structuralist methods of analysis
can be broadly categorized into two types: those which limit the definition of myth to a specific narrative element or source and those which
interpret all myth as dealing with one specific problem.

1.7. *Limited Definition Models*
The first type chooses one defining element which it assumes is characteristic of all myth, for example, the supernatural (Pitt-Rivers 1977; Frye
1963), accepting as myth only those 'texts' which describe the actions
of supernatural beings.[1] Texts which do not include interaction with the
supernatural are taken as in some sense more historical or factual.

Pitt-Rivers offers an expansion of this premise which we will examine
in detail because it relates directly to the biblical material examined in
this book. He suggests that within the field of myth, two poles should be
distinguished: pure myth at one end and at the other divine injunction,
that is, myth which conveys rules of law and behavior. Pure myth is that
of 'non-literate societies'. It is characterized by bearing no necessary

myth is one which retains power but is considered to be non-factual. Dead myths are
those which retain neither power nor factuality. See, for example, Gillman 1990: 54.
Although this distinction is of some methodological (or diagnostic) use, the element
of historicity or factuality is perhaps exaggerated—with little or no necessary
relevance to the role of mythology in culture. If myth is seen to mediate contradiction,
and cloud points of crisis, primarily on an unconscious level, then the factuality of the
myth would seem to be of secondary importance. The key issue here is the perception
or understanding of factuality—the importance of this element will depend on the
specific culture 'using' the myth. If the structures of the myth are still vital then it is
likely that, even if the myth is no longer considered to be historically factual, it is
likely that it will be reinterpreted in such a way to give it a new kind of factuality. To
some degree this has occurred among the modern wings of Judaism. Although it is
recognized that the events described in Genesis are not factual, they are considered to
be true in a more important sense, that is, spiritual truth.
    1.   This approach is also expressed in a slightly modified fashion by Middleton.
He suggests that myths generally describe situations totally different from current
social reality. People in myth live in patterns which are the inverse of normal human
(social) patterns and in that sense are more (or less) than human (Middleton 1967b:
52).

relation to cultural fact, and commonly includes the supernatural and fantastic social structures or events. Pitt-Rivers argues that this type of mythology should be the province of structuralist methodology.

Myth which moves towards the other pole, while lacking these fantastic elements, responds to and reflects actual cultural situations, and can be seen as 'historically accurate', at least in part. Pitt-Rivers agrees that 'pure myth' can and often does create images of culture precisely opposite to what exists, in order to serve the structural needs of the society. Nevertheless, he argues that as the other end of the spectrum is approached, this process stops, and is replaced by accurate description. Presumably these cultures no longer have structural conflicts needing resolution (Pitt-Rivers 1977: 140).

It is difficult to understand why this process of myth\thinking should not be present in texts of literate societies, as their symbolic systems (however factual) are also ordered by underlying structures. Nor is it clear why their historical sounding myths should be taken as being factual (Pitt-Rivers 1977: 140). Regardless of how factual a myth sounds, it must be assumed, in the absence of other evidence, that it may be subject to all the mechanisms affecting more 'fantastic' myths.[1]

Leach points out several failings of this approach regarding biblical texts. According to Leach, Pitt-Rivers assumes that Genesis 19 is a myth because it includes supernatural events, while Judges 19 which, both on the narrative level and structural level, resembles Genesis 19, is taken as in some sense historical because it lacks this supernatural element (1983: 11).[2] Clearly the supernatural element in these texts was not the

---

1.   Moye presents an interesting variation on this approach. He suggests that Genesis contains two types of material. The first half, Gen. 1–11, is myth in historical form. The second half, Gen. 12–50, is mythicized history (Moye 1990: 580). His approach has two implications: (1) that mythology does not have a diachronic level in respect to the progression of myths; (2) mythology can be distinguished from history by the presence or absence of fantastic elements.

2.   Gen. 19 (discussed in depth below M.I.10) describes events relating to Lot in Sodom. Two angels arrive in Sodom to inform Lot of the impending destruction of the city. The men of Sodom demand that the angels (whom they think are men) be given over to them. Lot refuses to do so, and offers his daughters in their stead (presumably to be raped). The story concludes with the men of Sodom being struck by blindness. In Judg. 19 a Levite brings his concubine to Gibeah where an old man gives him shelter for the night. As in the above story, the men of the town demand that he be given over to them. The old man offers his daughter in place of the Levite, but they refuse to accept her. Finally the concubine is given to them. The story concludes

operative force, as both texts appear substantially to deal with the same issues (and the second text may consciously allude to the first).[1]

A second problem with Pitt-Rivers's analysis lies in his view of the relationship of the texts (diachronically) to the development of Israelite culture. Pitt-Rivers implies that the diachronic development of the texts reflects actual changes in Israelite culture over time. Thus he states concerning Genesis 12, 20 and 26, 'the versions thus take us from incest to the preferred marriage of later times' (1977: 155).[2] It is probable that no historical progression of this kind can be deduced from the texts solely based on their current narrative order for several reasons.[3] The texts are fragmentary in nature and were created from diachronically distinct fragments. In addition, it is unlikely that the current narrative order bears any necessary correlation with actual diachronic development or that the editors were interested in preserving contents in actual historical order (or had enough knowledge to do so). This is not to suggest that myth cannot, by definition, include material which is historical in origin.[4]

not with divine punishment but with concerted action by the other tribes of Israel against Gibeah. Thus, Gen. 19 and Judg. 19 present stories which are similar on both the structural and narrative levels. In fact the story in Judges uses identical wording in many places with the text in Genesis: compare, for example, Gen. 19.2 and Judg. 19.20.

1. See Leach (1983: 11-12) for further discussion.

2. And likewise Pitt-Rivers takes the rape of Dinah (M.IV.1) and the resultant slaughter of the Shechemites as corresponding to an actual change in Israelite culture: from a pastoral form of economy to a sedentary form. Considering that the biblical text described is the product of at least two authors, and written at a time when the Israelites were living in a sedentary pattern, it is difficult to assume with Pitt-Rivers that such accurate historical information would be preserved. This is further emphasized by the fact that the myth can be seen as dealing with questions of endogamy—a crisis in Israelite myth which far outweighs incidental events. One could imagine that even if such an event had taken place, the myth included in the text need not reflect the actual outcome of the event. Mythologically speaking, the Israelites could not become one people with the Shechemites, thus the myth had to end as it did. The historical event, if such there was, could have ended in an almost infinite number of other ways.

3. It is probable that the current order bears no resemblance to the time of authorship or the initial editing of the fragments which make up our current biblical text. Two texts currently residing together may have been written hundreds of years apart.

4. Oden develops this point in reference to all aspects of 'empirical reality'. Regarding Near Eastern myths, he suggests that there is no necessary correspondence between the 'social setting' in the myth and actual social structures (Oden 1979a: 186). In examining the work of Jacobsen, he criticizes Jacobsen's reconstruction of Mesopotamian history in a manner similar to the questions raised here in respect to

Other similar approaches to myth stem (at least in part) from the view that monotheist religions (or at the very least, those of literate societies) are qualitatively different from polytheist religions.[1] They see polytheist texts as myth, while placing monotheist text (i.e., the majority of biblical text) on a higher plane by relating it in some way to factual history.[2]

The 'limited definition model' is narrow in a second respect, often imposing a view based on those cultures from which Western society developed (e.g., using Greek mythology as the pattern) upon all culture.

the work of Pitt-Rivers (Oden 1979a: 187-88). The possible discord between myth and reality is also highlighted by Lévi-Strauss (1969: 332).

1. One very weak, though telling, exponent of this approach is Walter Beltz in *God and the Gods: Myths of the Bible* (1983). Beltz argues that the biblical text as it now stands has been expurgated of its mythic elements. His primary aim is to recreate biblical myth by reintroducing the polytheistic element. For example, he states, 'the one God is only a sort of fascinating curtain behind which many Gods, once part of the lives of various tribes and peoples, play out their drama' (Beltz 1983: 28).

Beltz is able to demonstrate his point only at the expense of the texts he is trying to explicate. In his discussion of Gen. 20 he interprets the word אלהים as 'gods', even though the text clearly uses it to mean God. He is correct in stating that the word is in the plural, and thus may have polytheistic roots, yet in the biblical text it is used almost uniformly to mean God (in the singular). His argument also assumes that the characters in the text actually thought (in reality) in the same terms—thus the fact that the text uses the word אלהים (a word always used by one of the sources of Genesis) means that Abraham actually lived with 'many Gods' (Beltz 1983: 42). Beltz consistently confuses the world and words of the author with those of the character. Thus, based on this misinterpretation, he uses this passage to prove that monotheism was foreign to the 'popular piety of the ninth century' (Beltz 1983: 42). Elsewhere he mistranslates the text to support his arguments. Regarding Gen. 4.1 he mistranslates a punned etymology of Cain's name in order to suggest that Abel is God's child rather than Adam's (Beltz 1983: 56).

Beltz's work is insubstantial on two levels. On the one hand his limited definition of mythology forces him to disregard the actual text in favour of an unlikely recreated text, often based on error and wilful misinterpretation. On the other hand, his approach is flawed by his uncritical application of Robert Graves's methodology. Ignoring all modern theory and ethnography, Beltz finds in 'biblical mythology' numerous references to matriarchy, sacrifice of sacred kings and the like. He recreates ancient Israelite culture in the image of Graves's re-creation of ancient Greek culture.

2. This view is expressed in the work of Fohrer, who states, 'No Israelite myth is known to exist, either *in toto* or by allusion' (1986: 87). Fohrer argues that myth takes place in the world of the Gods and as such is an artifact of polytheism rather than monotheism (*ibid.*).

If the term myth is to be meaningful, it must be applicable to any society, not merely Western societies. Even if Western models are not chosen, this approach is limited in that it takes one element, which may be characteristic of one society's myths, and applies it to all cultures. Variations of this type of approach are found in the Myth-Ritual school (Gaster 1950; Hooke 1933),[1] and, in a subtle way, in those definitions which limit myth to 'sacred tales' (Durkheim 1926: 101).

Equally problematic are the approaches which see myth as the repository of history or cultural information. Although myth may contain historical material, this cannot be assumed *a priori*. Both structural and psychological analysis have shown that mythology often contains reversals, repetition or invention, serving and reflecting cultural needs rather than actual historical situations (Freud 1959). Sally Falk Moore in 'Descent and Symbolic Filiation' argues that depending on the needs of the system 'mythological symbolism may either repeat *or contrast* with reality' (my italics) (Moore 1967: 69). Myth sometimes describes situations or events which are precisely the opposite of actual historical situations or events.

Before any element of a myth is to be considered of 'historic' value its symbolic and structural role within the system must be examined. If it is shown that this element is an artifact of either of these systems its relevance in preserving historical or ritual information must be

---

1.   The supposed priority of ritual over myth has had pernicious effects in the analysis of biblical texts. Some scholars, for example, assume that certain texts in Genesis prove that child sacrifice was prevalent in proto-Israelite culture, and that these myths which once explained these practices are a remnant of that practice. Myths often express events which have no necessary relation to actual rituals, and symbolic sacrifice is seen to be an important element of the structural pattern of Israelite myth, without clear independent evidence to suggest widespread sacrifice (indicated by the fact that symbolic sacrifice can be discerned in almost every myth in Genesis). Hence, it is more logical to assume that this element was an artifact of the structure rather than a remnant of ritual. The apparent element of human/child sacrifice serves as a symbol for the transformation of the human condition, rather than necessarily being a remnant or rationalization of ritual.

In 'Myths and Rituals: A General Theory' (1979) Kluckholn argues convincingly for the interdependence of myth and ritual. Neither one has necessary priority. There is both myth independent of ritual and ritual independent of myth (1979: 71). He suggests that the apparent similarity of myth and ritual emerges from the fact that they both deal with similar issues and have the same ends (Kluckholn 1979: 74).

questioned. These elements may well reflect structural or symbolic need, rather than preserving archaic historical information.[1]

1.8. *Limited Explanation Models*
Theories using the 'limited explanation model' of analysis argue that all myths derive from a single aspect of human existence (or interpret all mythology as dealing with a single issue). A single point of reference is not necessarily problematic, but such interpretations often take one problem or explanation which is applicable to one culture and extend it to all culture: explanations based on fertility or seasonal ecology (Robertson Smith 1907); those which consider mythological thought (primitive thought) to be fundamentally different from 'rational' thought (modern thought), for example, based on emotion rather than reason (Cassirer 1955); and those based on various psychological theories (Spiro 1982; Jung and Kerenyi 1951).

Some scholars, for example, have viewed myth purely as explanation of natural cycles: the dry season, bringing apparent death of nature, is seen as causing an existential crisis which demands resolution (Robertson Smith 1907). Death and resurrection are immediately interpreted as the personification of these cycles. This approach is open to similar criticism as stated above. It takes an interpretation of Greek mythology and seeks to apply it indiscriminately. It also lacks an adequate explanation of the power which living myths are seen to have. One can envisage crises requiring more immediate resolution than the cycle of the seasons.

One theme which permeates many of these approaches, albeit often unstated, is the qualitative difference between 'primitive' or mythological thought and modern or rational thought.[2] This approach is clearly developed in the work of Cassirer who considers mythological thought and therefore primitive thought to be primarily based on emotional rather than rational processes.[3] Strenski suggests that Cassirer develops

1.   Graves and Beltz are two exponents of this approach (as was Frazer). See for example Beltz 1983; Frezer 1958.

2.   Although Lévi-Strauss argues strongly against this position (especially in respect to Levi-Bruhl), it can be argued that his distinction between 'hot' and 'cold' societies preserves this position—with only 'cold' societies having texts amenable to structural analysis.

3.   Cassirer posits that mythical thought is a necessary stage in the processual development of human consciousness. Myth is a framework of understanding, a synthetic whole, which was (and is) superseded by rational thought (Cassirer 1955: 60).

a set of oppositions which distinguish mythical thought from rational
thought: experience versus reflection, emotion versus reason, and
synthesis versus analysis (1987: 32).[1] Strenski suggests that Cassirer
considers mythical (or primitive) thought fallacious precisely because it is
based on emotion, and therefore out of hand rejects such beliefs. Thus,
for example, Cassirer draws an ethnocentric conclusion, judging the
validity of other cultural approaches to existence on the basis of his own
Western approach (Strenski 1987: 32).

It should be noted, however, that Cassirer does allow for the existence
of mythic thought in Western society. He identified many aspects of the
Nazi cult with myth, which suggests an explanation for his rejection of
such modes of thought (Strenski 1987: 14). This, however, strengthens
the ethnocentric aspects of his approach. He associates the worst
elements of his own culture with the mythological and preserves the
positive elements as rational. The two cannot exist together since the
mythological, by definition the irrational, annihilates the rational.

The psychological approach, because of its alleged universality—all
human psyches are similar or identical—partially evades the opposition
between primitive and modern thought.[2] It also begins to expand the

Cassirer expands his definition beyond consciousness and posits for mythical
thought a specific end; it attempts to create a sense of wholeness or unity which in
turn draws its power from the wells of emotion (Cassirer 1955: 87-89). Thus the
'logic' created by myth creates an emotional rather than rational coherence.

1.   The dialectical opposition of emotion over reason as a defining characteristic
of mythical thought is one of the primary weaknesses of Cassirer's approach.

Cassirer implies that cultures based on this type of thought are incapable of
rational thought. In a similar vein Cassirer considers ritual to be dialectically opposed
to reason—ritual (as in Freud) is merely the compulsive expression of the psychic
life. Far from manipulating symbols it disables reason. This rejection of ritual may be
due in part to the Hegelian opposition between sensory experience and intellection
(Cassirer 1946: 28).

Furthermore, he suggests that the two faculties, the emotional and the intellectual,
can be separated and distinguished as the motivating force behind one or another
culture (with Western culture being primarily defined by the intellect rather than
emotion).

2.   Jung, however, retains the distinction though it is not central to his approach.
He suggests that in the primitive mind the various aspects of the mind are not yet
differentiated. All functions remain rooted in the unconscious. Thus 'the primitive
does not think *consciously*, but rather…thoughts *appear*' (Jung and Kerenyi 1951:
100) (his italics). Thoughts are rooted in unconscious volition rather than conscious
volition. Jung posits further that due to the unformed state of 'the primitive's' psyche,

notion that all myths derive from one specific element to a more generally applicable approach—seeing myth as an expression of societal neurosis and crisis. It fails in that it seeks to apply universally those crises which are specific to the time and culture in which the approach developed (e.g., nineteenth-century Europe).[1]

The psychological approach is also problematic in its tendency to make an analogy with neurosis.[2] Myths are often interpreted as expressing individual crises as opposed to societal crises. Thus the Oedipus myth is seen as expressing a universal individual phenomenon, rather than as dealing with contradictions specific to the society that created it. Broader use of the psychological approach, for example, studies of the Oedipus complex in the Trobriands, tend to impose Western psychological models on non-Western cultures.[3]

Jung's approach to mythology compounds the problems already raised regarding Freudian theory.[4] These problems relate to his theories of 'primitive thought', the 'collective unconscious', and the associated analysis of meaning of symbols and myth. Jung makes a clear distinction between 'primitive thought' and modern thought. The primitive lives in a world dominated by the unconscious while the modern lives in one dominated by the conscious (Jung and Kerenyi 1951: 100-102). In the modern the unconscious is given free play only in dreams and the fantasies created by psychosis, while in the primitive these fantasies are the entire substance of his or her life. He suggests that 'myths are the

he does not know whether 'he dreamed something or whether he actually experienced it' (Jung and Kerenyi 1951: 101). Like the fantasies of the psychotic the primitive experiences his myths rather than creates them—'Myths are the mental life of the primitive tribe' (Jung and Kerenyi 1951: 102). Suffice it to say that ethnographic studies do not indicate this.

1.   See for example Dundes 1962. He applies Freudian theory to an American Indian myth.

2.   Stephen Jay Gould suggests that based on a model of psychological recapitulation Freud makes the following analogy: the primitive (being the actual ancestors of modern Western society), the savage (still living today), the child and the neurotic (1977: 158-60).

3.   See for example: Spiro 1982; Manisha 1975. This approach is also clearly presented on a broader theoretical basis in Spiro 1987: 98-102 and 242-47.

4.   Though, as Gould points out, although Jung accepts recapitulation, he does not consistently make the association between 'savage thought' and neurotic thought. He does, however, make the association between the child and the 'savage', with the child being the recapitulated eqivalent of the adult 'savage' (Gould 1977: 161-62).

original revelations of the pre-conscious psyche' (Jung and Kerenyi 1951: 101). Myth, the product of these primitive fantasies, is thus analogous to dreams and psychotic creations (Jung and Kerenyi 1951: 103).

This description of primitive thought corresponds little to ethnographic descriptions, which suggests that it differs from modern thought only in technology rather than quality. Witness, for example, the complex taxonomies described by Lévi-Strauss in *The Savage Mind*. Jung's definition of myth is limited in two other respects: it is centred on the individual, dealing solely with individual issues rather than societal issues; and it implies that myth (as a collective creation) exists only in primitive cultures and not in modern cultures.[1]

1.   Jung's concept of the 'collective unconscious' is also fraught with problems. Jung posits the existence of a universal 'collective unconscious' based on clinical work in Western Europe. He states that comparisons between the dreams and psychotic fantasies of his patients and mythology reveal sets of 'mythologems' common to both (Jung and Kerenyi 1951: 99). By mythologems Jung means mythological creatures (or narrative structures), for example, the cockatrice, or other mythological figures, or slaying a dragon. He states further that these mythologems are found in patients who lacked prior knowledge of the myths. He therefore concludes that these common elements must be present in the unconscious and inherited. Jung refers to these structures as the collective unconscious (Jung and Kerenyi 1951: 103).

The mythologems which comprise the content of the collective unconscious are referred to as 'archetypes'. The same archetypes are present in all human beings. They represent different aspects (or organs) of the unconscious, which he describes as analogous to physical organs of the body (Jung and Kerenyi 1951: 110). Whether in myths, dreams or psychotic visions, the archetypes are always represented by set groups of symbols or figures. He identifies several typical archetypal figures as 'the shadow, the wise old man, the child (including the child hero), the mother' (Jung and Kerenyi 1951: 219).

Symbolic expressions of archetypes are not limited to human beings or animals, they also include inanimate objects and geometric figures (Jung and Kerenyi 1951: 224). Where any of these figures (or their related manifestations) appear, regardless of the cultural context, they are interpreted in an identical fashion. Thus, for example, the child hero invariably represents the unconscious state struggling to find expression (Jung and Kerenyi 1951: 112).

The concept of the 'collective unconscious' is limited for two reasons. First, it is based solely on clinical material from one cultural context. Thus it is questionable whether the archetypes or their interpretations have application to any other culture. The differences in use of colour as a symbol in different cultures are sufficient to raise serious questions concerning the theory's application to more complex cross-cultural symbols. Secondly, the genetic aspect of the theory is problematic. The common mythologems are more likely to be created by the process of enculturation,

Clearly psychological analysis has much to offer the study of myth and symbols. Much less clear is the usefulness of applying (or imposing), *a priori,* Western psychological diagnoses and explanations of symbols upon societies whose social organization and world-view is very different.[1] Psychological theory should be used as a method of analysis, rather than as a universal framework exported to all societies to which they must be fitted.[2]

on the level of symbols and structure, rather than being a genetic endowment. If, however, Jung's approach is used within a single culture, based on clinical and ethnographic analysis of symbols within that culture, it may be useful in interpreting both individual and collective expressions. Its broader application, however, is problematic and seems to preserve the worst aspects of Western ethnocentric approaches to other cultures.

1.   Thus, for example, the psychological approach might view biblical circumcision as an expression of the castration complex. It might explain the existence of this myth (and related ritual) as reflection of individual fears. It probably would not, however, examine this element in the context of Israelite culture, or even in the context of the mythological system itself. This symbol (circumcision) is given meaning by its articulation with other cultural symbols, for example the covenant of the pieces, the death of Sarah, the Binding of Isaac, and should be examined in this cultural context rather than as merely the extension of an individual complex. The psychological approach has much to offer in regard to its understanding of symbols, this understanding, however, must be tempered by two methodological points: symbols are culture specific, and there should be a clear distinction between individual and cultural meaning (although the two may overlap). Rather than reflecting the fear of castration, this symbol, standing in relation to the parallel cancellation of female sexuality, that is, barrenness, works as part of a mechanism whereby the individual is removed from his specific, natural birth and parents, and symbolically made part of the broader cultural community.

2.   The work of Joseph Campbell begins to move in this direction. He provides a framework for understanding mythology, and a mechanism for broad characterization. His framework, however, has two main problems: (1) the imposition of Jungian archetypes as a means for interpretation; and (2) in order to be able to include myths of many societies, his framework is too broad to be useful.

Campbell's clearest presentation is found in *Myths, Dreams, and Religion* (1988: 138-75). He outlines 'four functions of traditional mythology': metaphysical, cosmological, sociological and most importantly psychological. I agree with Campbell that all four factors are present in the mythological text, I disagree with his emphasis on the psychological. His definition of the psychological describes this level as being universal—totally independent of sociological considerations. The psychological problems which he enumerates are sufficiently broad to include all human societies, but are equally too broad and vague to be of much interest.

His discussion of the hero myth, however, is very useful. It is interesting that some

The functionalist approach to myth, as developed by Malinowski, shares some of the problems mentioned above in that it limits myth to a single function. Essentially, Malinowski's approach posits that myth is a 'charter for social action'. Social action can mean custom, behavior, institution and so on (1954: 101; 1961: 328).[1] Malinowski's definition, however, is less limiting than those described above. It does not limit myth to legitimating a single area of social action, but rather offers it the full gamut of human affairs.

Malinowski's approach, as opposed to the psychological approaches, moves myth from the sphere of the individual to include that of the community. The definition also accounts for myth's power in the community by giving it the essential function of maintaining and supporting key elements of social structure. Further, Malinowski does not limit myth to 'primitive' societies—his definition is applicable to any culture. In several respects Malinowski's approach presages the structuralist approach described below.[2] Both argue that myth resolves societal crisis by legitimizing and supporting social structure. The primary difference is that of level. For Malinowski the legitimization is conscious and is found on the narrative level, while structuralists also find it on the level of logic or structure.[3] This type of legitimization is found at the level of opposition of mythemes, that is, $s^{(3)}$, and need not affect the other levels of underlying structure (though as Lévi-Strauss argues restricted legitimization can damage structural elements [1976: 266]).

In certain respects Eliade's approach provides a bridge between Malinowski's approach and that given below. Eliade describes myth as a source of ontology. He argues that the primary aim of myth is to reveal

---

of its key elements serve the same structural purposes in at least both Greek and Israelite myth. In both those systems the birth of the hero is surrounded by miraculous events. In Hebrew mythology these events serve to emphasize the divine origin of the hero (and by implication his people). It seems likely that the same structural purpose is served in Greek mythology.

1.   On occasion he does seem to imply that myths are tales of the gods, or men acting as gods (Malinowski 1961: 303).

2.   It should be noted from the outset, however, that a problem in his approach is his denial that myth had a 'symbolic character' as well as a functional character.

3.   The definition proposed by Neil Gillman shares the same distinction from the structuralist perspective. Like the structuralist approach Gillman sees myth as creating a framework for organizing and perceiving existence. He, however, places this structuring aspect on the surface of the myth, open to conscious manipulation (Gillman 1990: 84).

origins, and by doing so provides an ontological framework for organizing reality (1964: 37; 1971: 34-48). Where Malinowski is concerned with social action, Eliade is concerned with problems of existence (Strenski 1987: 74).[1] The structuralist approach offers a perspective which unites the two. It suggests that myths create (support) a logic which organizes both the material and the conceptual universe.

1.9. *Structuralist Model of Mythology*
To a great extent the structuralist approach synthesizes the two types of approaches discussed in §§1.7 and 1.8. It provides both a framework for understanding culture and a methodology for analyzing particular cultural systems. Myth is viewed as those 'texts' which create or support the framework of society (Lévi-Strauss 1963: 197).

Like the psychological approach, structuralist theory sees myth as dealing with crisis. It also views myth as a device for ordering cultural symbols and thereby creating a logical pattern. Through the imposition of this logic as natural, crisis is resolved. The structuralist approach,

---

1.   Blumenberg approaches the question of ontology from a different direction. He suggests that myth arises to resolve the ontological 'absolutism of reality', which refers to the perception of an uncontrolled, uncontrollable world in which humans are but a small unimportant part. This is best expressed by the words of A.E. Houseman: humans are 'alone and afraid in a world he has not made'. Myth and culture develop in response to this perception—myth gives order to chaos, personalizing it in order that it can be dealt with—it makes the uncanny familiar (Blumenberg 1985: 25, 35, 113).

Blumenberg suggests that myths are stories which are characterized by 'pregnance or significance', which enables them to retain meaning and power (1985: 69). The tales which embody this pregnance are of great antiquity, and have gone though a process of natural selection; and it is precisely this process which has endowed the texts with significance. Tales which have not emerged from such a process are considered created myths and have little or no value (1985: 152-54, 159). As in the structuralist approach, Blumenberg views modern uses of these texts as part of the myth, each generation works with the mythic substance which it inherits.

Blumenberg's approach is limited in several respects. He falls into the trap of qualitatively distinguishing between polytheism and monotheism. Polytheism is characterized by myth, while monotheism is characterized by dogma (1985: 122). On a content level he makes several assumptions which severely limit his conception of mythology. For example, he argues that myth is never localized in time or space, it is dialectically opposed to history with no view of the future; he argues that the distinction between the Old Testament and myth is its sense of being history (1985: 39, 75, 99, 125). On other occasions he implies that myths grow out of the passing of archaic rituals (as the non-sacrifice refers to the actual end of human sacrifice among the Israelites) (1985: 119).

however, does not identify a specific type of crisis. It observes that at the heart of any society there are contradictions which require resolution. The structuralist approach provides a method of analysis which reveals the crises, as well as the patterns of logic which seek to resolve them (Lévi-Strauss 1963: 216; 1981: 629).

Structuralism views myth as a collective 'text' of the society, which conveys a code that can be understood, both by members of the society and through structuralist analysis by the anthropologist. As stated in the paragraph above, the myth provides a means for expressing contradictions within a society, which are often revealed in the symbolic systems through oppositions. The conflicts, however, are not resolved, they 'merely shift the difficulty elsewhere' (Lévi-Strauss 1969: 5). The very shifting of the issue clouds it, thus hiding the contradiction.

The dichotomy underlying many of the contradictions dealt with in mythology is the conflict between nature and culture. In resolving this dichotomy, mythology, the creature and creation of culture, validates culture. Lévi-Strauss states, 'Although experience (nature) contradicts theory (culture) social life validates cosmology by its similarity of structure. Hence cosmology is true' (1963: 216). Because the logic of myth and the logic of culture are identical, they must also be natural.

The nature and structure of symbolic systems can be clearly discerned if we look at an example from the world of music? When one listens to a composition, it has both a synchronic and diachronic level. The progression of melody provides a diachronic time element; the melody, however, also establishes a common set of relations found throughout the piece of music. The need to view the piece as a whole, surveying its themes, variations and development in one breath, provides the synchronic element. The time element which is implicit in the narrative structure of mythology (as well as other symbolic systems) is only the most basic level. Like music, mythic time is 'reversible, non-reversible, synchronic and diachronic'; all the units within a myth are themes and variations and therefore interchangeable (Lévi-Strauss 1963: 211-12; 1969: 16-17). Just as in music, both the theme (diachronic) and the development of the variations (synchronic) are essential for interpretation. Both mythology and music are languages developed for and by culture.

The methodology used here views myths as being composed of 'gross constituent units'. These units are 'relations', that is, each is a 'function linked to a subject' (Lévi-Strauss 1963: 211) (the term mytheme is also used in reference to these relations). These relations can often be seen as having positive, negative or neutral value, which can be correlated with the value of other relations in logical patterns. To understand the meaning conveyed by the myth, these units must be examined in terms of 'bundles' of similar relations, and through the logic by which the bundles interact.

Each myth is broken down into its units, the units are then compared with the structurally equivalent units which are joined into a bundle of units. The bundles are composed of units which often 'appear diachronically at remote intervals'. Their combination is justified because of the nature of mythological time. The reorganized bundles have a time element which is both synchronic and diachronic (Lévi-Strauss 1963: 212). The message of the myths is revealed through analysis of the relationships and combinations of the bundles.

Although this approach can be applied to a single myth, the full significance can only be discovered through examination of a whole body of myth. This body of myth includes all synchronic variations of the myth, as well as translated or redacted texts.[1] Like the study of language, the grammar of mythology can only be understood through analysis of a large collection of texts. By examining the differences and transformations, and correlating these differences, the 'structural law' of the system can be understood (Lévi-Strauss 1963: 217).

Several approaches examined above suggest that one characteristic of myths is that they are traditional tales, for example, Blumenberg's suggestion that they are tales of great antiquity which achieve their significance through a process of 'Darwinism of words' (1985: 69). The structuralist position suggests that myths need not be traditional, rather they must fit the structural requirements of the culture.[2] Hymes presents an example in which a collector gathered both traditional material and material composed by his informant. Because they were structurally consistent, the collector could not distinguish between the modern and the traditional material (Hymes 1977: 224). This suggests that any material within the corpus, whether of traditional or modern composition,

---

1. As long as the redaction is done within a single society, the underlying structure (on a synchronic level) will transform in a consistent way—because it does not depend on any specific narrative element or order. If a myth from another community is taken into the mythic system, when it is recast its structure will likewise be recast.

2. Lévi-Strauss argues that while the structural elements are strengthened and emphasized through a process of transmission and generalization, the structure (certainly $s^{(2)}$) is found even in individual creations (1981: 626).

should be analyzed as part of and as transformations of the mythic structure (see also Lévi-Strauss 1981: 626).

The above theory implies the existence of myth, but does not define the parameters of myth. The definition of mythology used here is a synthesis of the work of Roy Wagner (1981) and structuralist theory. Mythology is defined as the logical framework or metaphor through which society views or creates its past, present and future—it is a creator of ontology (see Lévi-Strauss 1963: 209). A myth, then, is a text, historical or otherwise, which has been shaped by (and shapes) this logical framework.[1]

As stated above, the logical framework develops in order to resolve basic societal crises by showing that the logic which led to certain 'choices' is natural. This definition, though perhaps too broad to be easily workable, is an attempt to move away from 'myth as a fabulous impossible tale', 'myth as a sacred tale', as well as the other approaches discussed above.[2] These definitions often constrain myths to dealing with religious or theological questions, whereas they are seen here to deal with societal questions, both religious and secular. Furthermore, the boundary between the two, especially in biblical material, is often artificial and difficult to maintain.[3]

1.10. *Myth and History*
Several concepts transform the meaning of history regarding myth, in effect removing the opposition of myth and history. First, the 'historical' (i.e., the factual) elements within a body of myth are seen as only incidentally historical. The system contains events both historical and fictional based on the requirements of the underlying structure (the framework of the symbolic system). Those events which fit (or can be adapted to fit) the patterns of the structure become part of the mythology. Their factuality, or lack thereof, is incidental, and in no way affects the power of the myth, which is due to the crises which are

1. It should be noted that myth includes texts which are oral and written, narrative and non-narrative.
2. In an attempt to distance himself from other approaches, G.S. Kirk ends up by depriving the term of any meaning at all. At times he is forced to assert that myth is merely a story, while at others he sees it as a repository of unrelated functions; in fact he develops a phenomenology of myth which is sufficiently broad to include any text (1970: 28, 254), though even his category of 'traditional tale' is a limitation.
3. Myth should be seen as an expression of 'world-view'. Mythology both creates and reflects world-view. This approach is found in the work of Barr (1959).

clouded by the underlying structure. Similarly, actual historical events can be transformed to fit the needs of the structure.

Secondly, myth organizes history in another and perhaps more fundamental manner. Myth becomes a device for organizing (creating) history (i.e., as a subjective and coherent articulation of past and present events).[1] Events past, present and future are viewed through the framework which is found in the mythic system and become means for validating the system and being validated by it.[2] This type of reciprocal validation is central to the structuralist approach. Thus, for example, the exodus from Egypt can be seen as the archetypical event: all other events in Israelite/Jewish history are defined and validated by it—and by their perceived similarity to the archetypical event, equally validating and re-enforcing its centrality.[3]

Thirdly, there is a rabbinic concept 'that there is no earlier or later in the Torah' (*b. Pes.* 41b), in effect seeing the Torah as a synchronic document, with each element being both independent and dependent. This dechronologizing concept is also central to the structuralist approach. Lévi-Strauss argues that mythology and mythological time have no

---

1.   This aspect of the relationship between myth and history is discussed by Sahlins (1985) and Turner (1988). Turner sees myth and history as 'two sides of the same coin', both of which are 'complementary modes of...cultural structure' (1988: 237).

In his discussion of modes of historical consciousness Turner compares that of the ancient Greeks and Israelites. He concludes that there is no single mode of historical awareness, and that myth and history are 'harder to separate in practice than in theory' (Turner 1988: 249).

Moye discusses the relationship between myth and history. He discusses the ways by which myth is incorporated in and informs the idea of history (Moye 1990: 579). He also examines the duality of the term 'history', focusing on history as events, and history as narration of and model for events (Moye 1990: 577).

2.   This aspect of the relationship between myth and history is brought out clearly in several texts analyzed below.

3.   In a sense the State of Israel, as a symbol, has a similar function. In light of the ideology that it is the proper homeland and haven for all Jews, a reinterpretation of Jewish ontology and history has been consciously developed. Many Jewish 'histories' emphasize the aspect of persecution, the holocaust being part of a progression—the State of Israel is seen as the logical and natural outcome which resolves this unnatural process. In light of this view, all present Jewish existence outside the State of Israel is seen as anomalous and unnatural in the development of the Jewish people. And future Jewish existence is seen as residing totally within Israel's cultural and physical boundaries.

place in history and chronological time (1963: 211-12).

The events which occur in mythology cannot be viewed as having any set chronology. Mythological time is both reversible and non-reversible; the order in which the events occur has no effect on the message which the myth is developing. This approach has clear implications for those who rely on the Bible as a means for charting the development of Israelite culture. The order of events in mythology is incidental, and cannot be used to draw conclusions about actual chronology. This of course does not preclude the possibility that historical material may be employed, it merely emphasizes that the present order bears no necessary correlation with the order of occurrence or composition.

This synchronic element, however, is only one aspect of the myth. The basic oppositions or structures are revealed on this level, yet it is important to note that the very order of the texts or sequences of the narratives may be structured as well.[1] This is especially true in the biblical texts where time as well as narrative is structured.[2] Turner points out that important aspects of structure are revealed in the sequence of events within a narrative, and further that different stages of the narrative are often transformations of previous stages, so that the order of transformation is the key to the logical order created by the myth[3] (Turner 1977, 1985).

1.   Although Lévi-Strauss does not examine this type of diachronic development concerning structure, it is found in myths which are transformations of those studied by him. Stephen Hugh-Jones reports that the myths of the Barasana have a chronological order and progression (conversation with Stephen Hugh-Jones).

2.   Barthes suggests that 'myth transforms history into nature', as a general principle (1972: 129). (Although Barthes uses myth to mean ideology [and is therefore conscious], his principle can be extended in part to the meaning of myth used here.) I would suggest that it does this only in cultures which make use of history as part of their structure. This fits in with a general rule stated above (see §2.5). The object of myth is to make cultural creations appear as natural creations.

3.   Many of Turner's criticisms can be broadly applied to Lévi-Strauss's work. He suggests that Lévi-Strauss takes a methodology which was designed, in the first instance, for analyzing structures within a language, and applies it to structures between cultures (rather than within a single culture). For example, Lévi-Strauss looks at transformations between cultures (the basis of *Mythologiques*) rather than variations and transformations within a single culture (1977: 113). Turner's criticism, however, should not rule out cross-cultural comparison. Rather, it suggests that the myths and ethnography of a community should be analyzed in depth prior to analyzing its transformations in respect to other communities.

Fourthly, history (as both actual events and the selected presentation of events) can be a medium for mythology. Mythology uses history and the historical form as a further support for the logic it is attempting to develop. Mythology argues, in effect, that history (i.e., actual events) is governed by the same logic found in other spheres. The past becomes the stage for acting out the logic—validating both the logic and the actions. In effect the system suggests that since these events occurred (we exist as their outcome) and since the events reflect the same logic as the mythic system, therefore our existence and the events themselves prove that the logic is true.[1] In a sense the difference between history as history and history as myth is that myth is history that is used: history which is both paradigm and validator.

The concept or perception of history itself is part of the structure. Time can be understood (or created) in a number of different ways, including as a historical teleological consciousness, as the rotation of a wheel, as a spiral, or synchronically. Time is thus a medium of structure. The understanding of time will fit the structural requirements of the system, and thus is perceived as nature—what could appear more natural than time or history?

History is not the only field in which myth acts. It is also essential (especially in the material examined below) in creating a geography. Myth shapes one's view of geography and gives it meaning. As with history, the very existence of geographical points of reference provides complementary validation. Within the Hebrew texts sacred geography works on several levels. Each direction of the compass has specific mythological references, as do geographical locations. As a whole, the world is viewed as a series of concentric circles culminating in the Holy

Other criticisms reveal either wilful misunderstanding or an almost fundamentalist attitude towards Jacobson's approach. Turner chooses to ignore the fact that Lévi-Strauss transforms the usage of such terms as *parole* and *langue* to fit the needs of his approach, and therefore he misunderstands Lévi-Strauss's argument (1977: 120). In other places he criticizes Lévi-Strauss for changing the methodology, little realizing that structural linguistics can only be a metaphor, not a paradigm, for mythological structuralism (1977: 114).

It should be noted, however, that Turner's work is also flawed. While arguing against Lévi-Strauss's use of a single structure, his analyses are also limited to a single structure (which he suggests can be applied cross-culturally). Perhaps coincidentally, two myths, from entirely different cultures, are interpreted in exactly the same way (Turner 1977: 103-63; 1985: 49-106).

1.   For a similar approach see Dolgin and Magdoff 1977: 351.

of Holies. This aspect of myth and geography is discussed in detail below (Chapter 11).

In 'How Myths Die' Lévi-Strauss examines one aspect of the relationship between myth and history (1976: 256-68). He shows that when a myth is forced to fit into a historical framework, that is, to conform to actual events, it can lose its structural coherence—it can die. This is not to say, however, that actual events, if they are forced into a mythological framework, cannot become structured, that is, become myth. It also does not imply that myths written in a historical mode are necessarily dead. This is especially significant regarding the texts in Genesis. The text is written in a historical mode, yet it is unlikely that it has actually been forced to fit into an actual historical framework.

This point is supported by two facts. First, the myths were first written down more than a thousand years after the events they purport to describe (should those events have taken place). Secondly, the redaction process in the fifth century BC substantially recreated the myths by piecing together fragments of at least three earlier versions. Thus it is unlikely that the myths in Genesis were forced to fit a historical framework, it is more likely that the framework was created around the myths (and thus at this level should not be considered dead).

1.11. *Myth and the Bible*

Although several approaches examined suggest that biblical texts are not mythological (e.g., Pitt-Rivers and Fohrer regarding the 'historical' texts), the Bible is clearly myth under the definition suggested here.[1] For the Christian and Jewish worlds alike, the biblical text provides both a conscious and an unconscious framework for viewing reality. This framework emerges on several levels. It is a paradigm for time in that it creates a way of ordering and evaluating past, present and future events; it is a paradigm for space, creating a sacred geography pregnant with meaning; and finally it is a paradigm for text.

Structuralist interpretation has only been applied to biblical myth to a limited extent. Lévi-Strauss considered his approach inapplicable to

1.   As suggested above, the possible 'historicity' of the texts need not affect the mythical nature of the texts. Myth and history are not mutually exclusive, there is an interplay between them, and they can co-exist (Turner 1988: 237) History can, depending on its context, function as myth. And, in the interplay of the two, ideology need not determine structure. In the case of the biblical texts I will show that there is no structural difference between 'mythological' texts and 'historical' texts.

societies possessing a historical viewpoint.[1] Leach, however, challenges Lévi-Strauss on this point. He argues that biblical material provides an opportunity to analyze myth from a synchronic and diachronic point of view, detailing cross-cultural transformations as well as historical transformations (Leach and Aycock 1983: 1). The historic element of the biblical text also can be seen as an imposition of the myth on time, and thus the Israelites' very consciousness of history should be considered part of their mythic system.

Leach's analysis of biblical myth is limited on the synchronic level. This is due to limited coverage. He analyzes individual myths rather than the complete body of myth. Moreover, by excluding external texts he ignores the transformational aspect of diachronic development, thereby limiting his understanding of the basic grammar of biblical myth and its transformations. In order to understand the development of a mythological system in a (relatively) 'hot' society, both the synchronic aspects of the system and the diachronic developments of the system must be closely considered.

At this point it might be useful to discuss the criticisms of structural analysis developed by J.A. Emerton in 'Structuralist Analysis of Genesis XXXVIII' (1976). His analysis reveals problems in Leach's approach as well as several common misconceptions regarding the structuralist approach. The approach taken in this book is cognizant of the criticisms and challenges which he presents. In his article Emerton discusses Leach's analysis of five biblical texts which, according to Leach, relate to the legitimacy of Solomon (Emerton 1976: 79-98). Emerton raises six objections to Leach's analysis: (1) Leach 'probably exaggerates the influence of the outlook of Ezra and Nehemiah on the editing of the OT' (1976: 83); (2) it is unlikely that the 'ancient readers would see certain connections between different parts of the Old Testament' (1976: 84); (3) Leach does not consider the ages of the different strata within the text (1976: 86); (4) Leach bases certain conclusions on the 'anglicized forms of proper names' rather than their original forms (1976: 88); (5) Leach's arguments are based on assumptions which are not supported by the text (1976: 82); (6) Emerton questions various details and assumptions, for example, concern with the purity of Solomon's line.

---

1. In his more recent works, for example, *The Jealous Potter*, Lévi-Strauss implies that structuralist theory may be applicable to material from societies with a historical consciousness.

Moreover, Emerton questions whether the five texts deal with the same theme (1976: 80).

Several of Emerton's criticisms relate specifically to Leach's work, rather than to structuralist theory. The use of anglicized forms of names, instead of transliteration or the names in their original languages (i.e., Hebrew and Greek) is clearly problematic. Emerton usefully criticizes Leach's assumption that analogies or connections can be developed in respect to pairs of names which are similar only in English (though where there is similarity in the original forms such connections should be made). Certain details which Emerton discusses in relation to questioning the importance of the purity of Solomon's line are also justified.

Emerton's other criticisms, however, arise from a misunderstanding of structuralist theory. The first flaw in his argument is related to the question of the editorial present. Although editing or redaction may not affect the underlying structure, in the case of biblical material it is likely that significant cultural changes have taken place between the writing or origin of many of the myths and their redaction with the ensuing trans-formations in structure. Therefore, when edited texts are analyzed, the structure found must be assumed to be the product of the final stage of composition rather than that of earlier stages. The concept of editorial present is especially important regarding Genesis. Source criticism reveals that the texts in Genesis are composites, made up of pieces of earlier texts. The myths in Genesis have been created (or recreated) with perhaps only marginal similarity to the versions found in the sources from which they were taken. Thus the myths created by redaction should not be seen as a direct translation but rather as a new version told against the previous versions of the myth. The structures in the new version should be those of the editorial present rather than those of earlier versions of the myths.

This misunderstanding is revealed in criticisms (1) and (3). Leach assumes that the final redaction of the text occurred at the time of Ezra and Nehemiah and thus argues that the structures are tied to that cultural context. He is not arguing that Ezra and Nehemiah influenced the text, but rather that both the text and Ezra and Nehemiah arose from the same context, and thus deal in essence with the same issues.

Emerton argues that Leach ignores the different strata within the text. This criticism can be dealt with from two perspectives. If cultural continuity was maintained between the writing of the various texts, it can be assumed that the underlying structure (both $s^{(2)}$ and $s^{(3)}$) would be subject to few transformations. The texts can therefore properly be discussed together. If, on the other hand, we focus on the editorial present, then, even if there is no continuity, the underlying structure (especially $s^{(3)}$) will be transformed in the final version to reflect the community that created it. It is important to emphasize that the underlying structure is not an artifact embedded in the myth, revealing earlier needs of the culture. Rather, as the myth is used, re-told and edited, so the underlying structure is transformed in keeping with cultural change.

Emerton's second criticism arises from a misconception regarding the connections found within the text. He argues that it is unlikely that an ancient reader would see many of these connections. These connections, however, work in two ways. On the one hand, they arise unconsciously. The theoretical approach taken here suggests that myths of a single community deal substantially with the same issues and reflect similar structural patterns ($s^{(3)}$ $s^{(2)}$), at least on the level of structure. As a myth develops, elements will emerge which are similar or related to those of other myths. These relations or analogies can develop on a number of levels: identical events, similar names, or perhaps structural mirror images. These relations are not due primarily to conscious allusion, but to the fact that they arise from identical structures and serve identical functions. On the other hand, they do allow conscious connections to be made even if, as Emerton suggests, only occasionally. However, even with this proviso in mind, these allusions are available material for the modern scholar, whether structuralist or otherwise, for making connections and analogies between texts.

Although Emerton is correct in arguing that many of Leach's assumptions are not directly supported by the text, many of them are implied by the specific text or supported by reference to related texts. A case in point is Tamar (see M.IV.4). Leach assumes that Tamar is an Israelite, whereas Emerton argues that, at least in the original intention of the author, Tamar was probably Canaanite. Emerton bases this conclusion on the fact that 'most commentators believe that Tamar...was Canaanite' (Emerton 1976: 84), and on the fact that Judah was living in an area populated by Canaanites (as if this was a historical narrative). The text, however, does not support this conclusion. Regarding Judah's wife, the text specifically states that she was of Canaanite origin, while in Tamar's case, the text is silent. If it was not implying Israelite origin, it was at least creating ambiguity. The later texts cited by Emerton, rather than arguing against the main points of Leach's analysis, actually support it. They suggest that Tamar was either an Aramean or the daughter of Shem, both of which were mythologically acceptable marriages in Genesis.

Emerton's final criticism is equally problematic. Although he is correct in pointing out mistakes in detail and questioning the importance of the line of Solomon in the texts, his final point shows clear misunderstanding of the approach. Emerton questions the assumption that the five stories deal with the same issues. As stated above, structuralist theory suggests that all myths of a single community deal, at the level of underlying structure ($s^{(3)}$), with various aspects of a set of related crises or problems. The mythic system as a whole seeks to create a logic by which the crises are obviated. Thus, at least on the level of underlying structure, Leach is correct in taking the five myths together as part of a larger system.

The question of the legitimacy of Solomon, however, reveals the primary flaw in Leach's analysis. He ties the mythic structure to resolving a single (conscious) political question, rather than an (unconscious) cultural question. The structures in the myths he examines deal with the questions of endogamy and chosenness, with the genealogy of Solomon figuring as part of the structure rather than its goal.

This chapter has examined the meaning of myth from a variety of perspectives, concluding that a modified structuralist approach is the most comprehensive and useful type of definition. This is not to deny the value of the other approaches in examining different levels of the mythological texts. The texts work on several levels at once and are thus amenable to various kinds of interpretations. It is also seen that the biblical text is only the foundation for the complete structure of Hebrew mythology. A complete diachronic picture is necessary to move beyond the previous applications of this approach. In the analysis of texts which follows, the structuralist approach is the primary method applied. When appropriate to the argument, other levels are indicated, and the analysis focuses on both the synchronic and diachronic development of the text.

Chapter 2

ISRAELITE 'IDEALIZED' ETHNOGRAPHY

This section presents a summary of the ethnography of the Israelite community at the time of the editorial present of Genesis. It must be emphasized that neither the ethnography presented here nor the underlying structures presented in this and the following chapters refers to any period prior to the editorial present. For this reason much of the work of Pitt-Rivers (1977), for example, is not relevant to this thesis, as he is discussing the structures of previous periods in Israelite history.[1]

This ethnographic analysis is not exhaustive for two reasons: a complete study is outside the scope of this book; and, lacking actual ethnographic data, such an analysis might be impossible. Data on kinship appears in three different types of biblical material. It is found in narrative mythological texts, legal texts and genealogies. As discussed above (regarding the definition of mythology), it is dangerous to use mythological texts as equivalent to actual ethnography—the mythological texts may be subject to many types of transformation which

---

1. The difference between the research here and that of Pitt-Rivers lies primarily in regard to the status of Genesis as myth or history. Due to the nature of the textual material, and the lack of convincing archaeological evidence, it is probably impossible to determine the exact status of the material. This status, however, is an essential foundation of both his research and that undertaken here. If the material is considered to be primarily historical, then his type of analysis is appropriate as little myth would remain. If, however, it is primarily mythological then it cannot be used either for ethnographic or historical purposes. I believe that it is mythological due to the consistency of structure found throughout the texts.

Donaldson (1981), Oden (1983) and Steinberg (1991), like Pitt-Rivers, also treat the mythological texts as reflecting actual ethnography. In all three cases it is difficult to know to which period the authors are referring, that is, to the period of the patriarchs or some later date. Both Oden and Steinberg suggest that marriages, in the patriarchal line of descent, are characterized by a pattern of endogamy (Oden 1983: 195; Steinberg 1991: 51-52).

distort actual social structure (on the narrative level).[1] The legal texts
suffer from a slightly different problem. They reflect an idealized vision
of social structure rather than a picture of ethnographic reality. This
picture, however, does give indications of actual, post-exilic social
structure. The genealogies (especially the Table of Nations, Genesis 10),
while not accepted as depicting actual relations between nations, also
indicate aspects of the Israelite understanding of genealogical relationships
over time. The analysis here confines itself to using legal and
genealogical material.

2.1. *The Editorial Present*

The relative editorial present of Genesis (i.e., its final edited state, and the
suggested point of structuralist analysis) is in the fifth century BC.[2] Any
biblical texts which are contemporary or predate this are part of its
cultural context.[3] This context therefore includes all the laws found in
the first five books of the Torah, the editorial statements found in the
'historical' books and in Ezra and Nehemiah.

At the time of the editorial present, the Israelites lived mainly in the
area comprising the middle section of the modern state of Israel
(including the occupied territories), roughly a triangle with Lod, Jericho
and En-gedi being the three angles (see Figure 1). They did not fully

---

1.   An additional problem with Genesis is the complexity of its composition.
Genesis is composed of at least four sources. The earliest of the sources (J, E and N)
were written in the eighth century BC, while the latest (P) was possibly written during
or after the Babylonian exile in the sixth century. The text of Genesis as it exists
today, probably does not pre-date the fifth century BC.

2.   It is likely that the legal texts used here reflect a slightly longer period than the
editorial present. This is due to the fact that some of these texts, namely the
Deuteronomic texts (as well as J and E), were written prior to the exile and it is likely
that such texts would be subject to smaller transformation than the narrative texts
which were substantially recreated.

3.   Pitt-Rivers argues against this use of 'editorial present' which is found both
in the argument presented here, and in Leach's work. Pitt-Rivers sees no editorial
present, but rather a long term process of 'sifting and collating' (1977: 139). I accept
that the text was created by accumulation over time, yet its final form owes its existence
to a process of editing whereby fragments of texts were joined together. On a structural level I suggest that there must be a relative editorial present which reflects the
structures of the editorial process, rather than structures which might have existed
before.

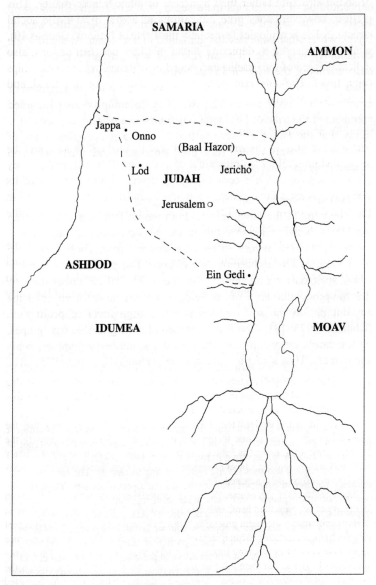

Figure 1. *Map of Judah under Persian Rule (Aharoni 1979: 416)*

occupy this territory, their settlements were centered around Jerusalem, the coastal plain and the Jordan Valley. After the fifth century the concentration of settlements increased in southern Judah (Blenkinsopp 1991: 43). The capital of Judah was Jerusalem. Some Israelites were in Egypt, while other Israelites also remained in Babylonia. At the time the community was under Persian rule and was primarily made up of descendants of the tribe of Judah.[1] Most of the members of the other tribes had been 'lost' with the destruction of the northern kingdom of Israel by the Assyrians in 722 BC. The community also included members of the tribe of Levi who functioned in a priestly capacity. It is likely that the Israelites were settled among other peoples, some of whom were closely related (i.e., the Samaritans) and others who had distinct languages and customs.[2]

2.2. *Israelite Economic Structure*
The economy of the Israelites was both pastoral and agricultural. The legal texts (both in relation to tithing and the sacrificial cult) suggest that the Israelites grew several different grains and fruit. These texts have been confirmed by archaeological evidence. The grain included barley, wheat, spelt, oats, rye and millet (Klausner 1975: 180). Klausner suggests that the production level of the fields was at the most fifteen times the amount put in the soil—which is not a high level of production (Klausner 1975: 181). The fruit consisted of pomegranates, figs, grapes, olives, carob, citrons, plums, cherries, dates, mulberries, apples, pears and quinces. They also grew almonds and walnuts (Klausner 1975: 181).

1.   The Persian political stucture in Judea and Samaria is unclear. At different parts of the post-exilic period Judea appears to have been under the governor of Samaria and later having its own governor (Ackroyd 1991: 20-23).

2.   The biblical text uses several words relating to identity. The term בני ישׂראל, meaning 'children of Israel' emphasizes the descent aspect of identity. The texts also use the term עם, 'people' and the similar term גוי, 'nation', is usually used in opposition to the other עמים or גוים, that is, 'peoples' and 'nations' respectively.

It is likely that the text creates opposition on two levels: on a general level between Israel and the nations, and on a more particular level between Israel and the inhabitants of the land at the time of the editorial present. At that time self definition may have been based on an opposition between those who returned from exile, which was equivalent with membership in the Temple community, and the inhabitants of the land who may or may not have had Israelite antecedents (Blenkinsopp 1991: 46).

Their herds probably consisted of sheep, goats and cattle (all of which were used in different sacrifices). The sheep were grown for both meat and wool (Klausner 1975: 185).

The majority of Israelites were involved in agriculture. With small-holding peasants being the major part of the population. The people lived in small towns which were surrounded by their fields (Klausner 1975: 189). Medium and large landowners also existed to a smaller extent. These landowners employed others to work their land in various capacities which included hired labourers, tenants, share croppers, Hebrew slaves and non-Israelite slaves. It is also likely that smallholding farmers supplemented their income by working the land of the larger farmers (Klausner 1975: 190).

The community also included a small number of craftsmen and artisans with, however, relatively few traders (Klausner 1975: 179, 205). Although the biblical text pays little attention to foreign merchants and trade, archaeological evidence suggests trade relations with much of the Mediterranean world (Hoglund 1991: 60). Hoglund also argues for the presence in the Judean community of a commercialized class, which gained the economic advantages associated with commercialization (1991: 62).

2.3. *Israelite Kinship*
The texts suggest that the Israelites were primarily patrilineal. All the biblical genealogies focus on descent from father to son. There are some indications in the text that the transformation from primarily patrilineal to primarily matrilineal descent had already commenced during this period. Thus, for example, Ezra 9 and 10 include commands for Israelite men to put away their foreign wives. Scholars suggest that this text indicates a matrilineal focus because it commands that only foreign wives be put away rather then foreign husbands (Hiat and Zlotowitz 1983: 41). This evidence, however, may not prove that the focus had moved. It only suggests that the Israelites were taking foreign wives (which was forbidden) and indicates nothing about the marriage patterns of Israelite women. It is likely that whereas Israelite men could exercise a great degree of control over their daughters' and sisters' marriages, that is exchanging them with other Israelites, they could not control the men to the same degree, especially because men could have as many children

as they wished. Thus it would be more likely for men than women to have foreign spouses.[1]

The structure of genealogies in Genesis suggests that the Israelite system may have had some elements characteristic of segmentary opposition. In

1.   This aspect of male control of women in marriage is also a key factor in the move from patrilineal to matrilineal descent. There are two main theories which attempt to account for the transformation. The first suggests that it relates to a problem in paternity. During the Persian and Second Temple period the number of rapes led to problems in status, as the father of a child might not be known, thus the transfer of inclusion in the people to the mother resolved this problem. This solution, however, is problematic on several levels. It is only a partial solution to paternity, as property and tribal membership still descended through the father. Thus a better solution to the paternity problem would have been to consider all children of a married woman to belong to her husband—with the children of unmarried women belonging to her family.

Others suggest that it was instituted to protect the purity of the priesthood and subsequently extended to the entire population (Hiat and Zlotowitz 1983: 41). Thus the analogy would require that the rules of marriage which applied to the priesthood be applied to the people in general. Just as a priest needed to have an Israelite mother and father (the father also had to be a priest) the analogy would require that all Israelites have an Israelite mother and father. The analogy suggests that it was not simply a transformation from matrilineal to patrilineal but rather transformation which emphasized the matrilineal line while retaining the patrilineal line.

The emphasis on the purity of the line alone, however, does not seem strong enough to explain such a significant cultural transformation within the entire people. Nor does it explain why matrilineal descent was emphasized at the expense of patrilineal descent. The logic of such an argument would require, as indicated, that both types of descent be equally emphasized.

It seems likely that the explanation lies between the two. After the return from the Babylonian exile Israelite men were marrying foreign women as well as exchanging their own (most likely among themselves). Thus in order to strengthen the pattern of endogamy (which is similar in function to preserving the purity of the priestly line) control of who the men were marrying was necessary rather than control of who the women were marrying. Thus the emphasis on matrilineal descent forced Israelite men to marry Israelite women in order for their children to remain inside the Israelite people thereby bringing in the paternity aspect of the argument. There was no need to emphasize the patrilineal line as men already controlled who the women could marry and thus it was clear that the legal husband/father would be an Israelite and actual paternity was not significant.

It is also likely that there was an economic aspect to this transformation, and to Ezra's demand for purity of descent. It appears that membership in the Temple community carried with it economic privileges—both in terms of financial support and land holding. Thus, there would be a strong incentive to limit those who would

Genesis 10 each group of brothers is opposed to each other, being considered a distinct people. On a broader level each segment of the Noahide genealogy is opposed to the others, based on their differing ancestors, that is, the three sons of Noah. Several narrative texts also support this characterization, see especially Judges 5 and 12.

Some scholars suggest that the Israelites ideally had three levels of segmentation.

1.   The שבט or 'tribe', a group of lineages claiming descent from a single ancestor (one of the 12 sons of Jacob). These 'tribes' correspond to the anthropologist's 'clan'.
2.   The משפחה or 'family', a group of families connected by patrilineal descent and geographic locality. This level probably corresponds to the level of lineage.
3.   The בית אב or 'father's house', an extended family consisting of a father and his sons (and their respective wives) (Gottwald 1979: 245-92; Rendtorff 1985: 80-81).

Ideally these levels were also territorial units. The tribe had a set portion of land which was subdivided among 'families/lineages' and further subdivided among the extended families.

During the period of the editorial and ethnographic present only the second two levels were significant, as there was effectively only one tribe remaining, that is, Judah. Thus the two remaining categories may represent higher orders of social organization than initially suggested. Thus the 'family' may represent a clan, a large unit united by connection with a fictitious ancestor. The 'father's house' would then represent a lineage, a corporate land-holding body descended from a common ancestor. The numerical make up suggested for the 'father's house' corresponds with this characterization. Estimates of numbers range from approximately 217 to 600. The land held by the 'father's house' was further subdivided among smaller family units (Blenkinsopp 1991: 49).

have access to these limited resources (Blenkinsopp 1991: 45-46). This point is also emphasized by Hoglund, who argues convincingly that the transformation in marriage patterns and self-definition was associated with the socioeconomic survival of the community (1991: 67-68).

It should be noted that, even with the emphasis on matrilineal descent, many aspects of patrilineality remained. Land and inheritance descended through the male line, membership in the priesthood or tribal status remained patrilineal, and genealogical descent continued to be reckoned through the male line.

Tribal membership and inheritance descended through the male line. The legal texts about inheritance suggest that each family (ideally) had a set portion of tribal land which was subdivided between the sons (or other inheritors) in each generation. The first born was given a double portion as his inheritance (see Deut. 21.15). One text, however, suggests that under specific circumstances a woman could inherit and continue her father's line, that is, when her father died leaving no male heir within the tribe (Num. 36). The text states that this is to preserve the father's name and keep the land (which would go to the daughters if no male heir was found) within its tribal portion.[1] It is possible, however, that a fictitious relationship was established with the men becoming in effect members of their wives' family and tribe, and thus inheriting on behalf of their wives.

The woman has little or no legal status in the biblical text. Prior to marriage she was her father's property, and after marriage she was that of her husband. If she was 'damaged' or killed, her father or husband had to be compensated. Whereas the husband could divorce his wife at any time, she had no independent right to divorce him. The situation of Israelite slaves (i.e., slaves who were Israelites) is analogous to that of women. They were considered the property of their master. The primary distinction was that they were entitled to their freedom after six years of slavery.

2.4. *Israelite Marriage: Exogamy or Endogamy?*
The text quoted above, from Numbers 36, also indicates that women could be given in marriage both within the same tribe or between tribes (though in the text's editorial present most Israelites were from the tribe of Judah). This raises the question of the characterization of Israelite marriage. If the Israelites were taken in isolation one can find neither a rule of 'tribal' exogamy nor endogamy.[2] At most, there is a clear

1.   Some narrative texts suggest that descent through the female line was also significant. Gen. 21 and 2 Sam. 13 suggest that if a brother and sister had different mothers they could marry (it is unclear whether they could marry if they shared the same mother but had different fathers). In the legal sections, however, it is clearly stated that such marriages were considered incest—whether of the same mother or the same father (Lev. 18).

2.   Some scholars (e.g., Mendenhall) suggest that the Israelites had tribal endogamy. They base this assertion on the preference found in narrative texts and the incest prohibitions. As observed by Pitt-Rivers this pattern of marriage is based on preference rather than a prescription and thus should not properly be called endogamy.

preference to marry as close to the nuclear family as permitted by the rules of incest. This preference, however, is found only in a few narrative texts in Genesis in which marriage is between parallel cousins. The preference is not specifically stated in any of the legal texts.[1] At this level of organization, in spite of the apparent preference to marry as close as possible, there appear to be no actual restrictions on choice. Thus it is likely that Pitt-Rivers is correct in stressing Israelite weighing of different marriage strategies, that is, alliance or strengthening the patrilineage (1977: 162).[2]

Within the Israelite community (or more specifically the tribes of Judah and Levi) there appears to be a structure of graded exclusiveness. The structure discussed below (as well as the related structures examined regarding Israelite geography, see §11.7) suggests that within the community the structure can be illustrated as a set of concentric circles culminating in the natal family. It should not be thought, however, that this pattern of concentric circles continued beyond the bounds of their self-defined community.

The question regarding the level of application of the pattern of graded holiness is clarified by the text's attitude toward the Samaritans (or if this usage is considered anachronistic, one could substitute those peoples of the land who were of Israelite origin, who the text places in structural opposition to the people who returned from exile [Blenkinsopp 1991: 45]). If the system was based on a pattern of graded holiness outside established boundaries of the people then the Samaritans would be relatively more positive than the other nations. This is based on both the genealogical and ideological proximity of the Samaritans.

The Samaritans were in part descended from 'Israelites' who had not been exiled to Babylon and thus were genealogically close to the people who returned. The religion of the Samaritan was also relatively similar, with the primary distinction being the location of the main temple. The

---

1. It is, however, supported by the findings of this volume which suggest that it is also developed on the structural level of the myth.

2. Pitt-Rivers asks whether the Israelites could be said to have a marriage system based on a principle (or requirement) of endogamy. He concludes that the marriage patterns of the Israelites should not be called endogamous. Rather, Pitt-Rivers suggests that the Israelites had a preference for 'keeping their daughters as close to the nuclear family as the prohibition of incest permits' (1977: 162); he calls this 'Mediterranean endogamy'. If this preference were the full extent of the Israelites' rules of marriage, one would have to agree with his conclusions. The preference, however, is only the most basic element of Israelite endogamy.

attitude of the text toward the Samaritans, far from being relatively
positive, is very negative (Torrey 1970: 212). Torrey suggests that one
of the major factors in the Chronicler's emphasis on creating and
preserving a pure Israelite line is a response to the Samaritan threat
(1970: 212). By emphasizing the rules against marrying out, the text
distinguishes between the pure line of Israelites, that is, those who
returned from Babylon (and at least in principle had not married out),
and the Samaritans and Northern Israelites who had intermarried
(Torrey 1970: 287).[1]

It is possible that the change from primarily patrilineal descent to
primarily matrilineal descent was also partly related to distinguishing the
Israelites (i.e., inhabitants of Judah and Benjamin) from the Samaritans.
If, as is likely, the Samaritans retained the previous definition of
'insideness' (patrilineal descent), then a redefinition to matrilineal descent
would eventually make a strong boundary between the two, with
Israelites being forbidden from marrying Samaritans because the
Samaritans, although patrilineally inside would be matrilineally outside
and therefore considered to be outside.[2] If the attitude toward the
Samaritans fits the pattern suggested by the research presented here, it
should be even more negative than the attitude toward the other nations.
Torrey's description of the motivation of the Chronicler supports this
characterization (1970: 208-12). Far from supporting a model of graded
holiness outside the self-defined boundaries, we find the opposite

---

1.   Torrey argues that the restoration or return from Babylon was an ideological
construct to distinguish the pure line of Israel from the Samaritans and other nations.
He argues that in actual fact the restoration was a minor affair of little influence or
significance (Torrey 1970: 208-13, 288-89).

2.   This pattern is repeating itself to some extent today, though in the opposite
direction. The traditional definition of descent is matrilineal. The progressive
movements have redefined their definition to include both matrilineal and patrilineal,
that is, a child whose father or mother (or both) is Jewish can be considered a Jew.
Eventually this change in rules of descent will preclude traditional Jews from
marrying Progressive Jews because the Progressive Jews will not be considered to be
inside by the traditional Jews. The pattern of graded holiness is also not found in this
modern situation. To a large extent the traditional community (especially in England)
is more willing to communicate with the non-Jewish world than it is with Progressive
Jews. Equally, in Israel non-Jewish religions are fully recognized and given legal
status, while the non-Orthodox communities are not recognized and have no legal
status.

pattern.[1] The closer (e.g., genealogically) a nation or group is to Israel the greater the ideological distance created in the texts.

The Israelites (as displayed in both the legal texts and the mythological texts) distinguished themselves from the surrounding peoples. By the time of the editorial present (fifth century BC), the Israelites considered themselves distinct from העמים the peoples or הגוים the nations grouped as a whole. This distinction is found throughout the biblical text (see the use of העמים in Exod. 19.5, Lev. 20.24, Deut. 7.6, 14.2; and regarding הגוים, in Deut. 9.4-5, 18.9, 1 Kgs 14.24). Thus, by the time of the editorial present the Israelites regarded the other peoples around as being different from themselves, outside the boundary of chosenness, and not differentially distinguished by circles of relative chosenness. A similar pattern is seen in the geography, mentioned above. Within 'Israel' the concentric circles move towards the centre, but the pattern of circles ends with the border of the land of Israel, the chosen land is opposed to the rest of the world.

It might be thought that the extensive Israelite incest prohibitions are themselves a mask for rules of exogamy, controlling marriage within the community. Careful consideration of these rules, however, does not confirm this suspicion. Israelite incest prohibitions are illustrated in Figure 2. The biblical text uses the same term for sexual relations between ego and any of these relatives, that is, 'uncovering the nakedness'. The text includes them all under the category of 'close relatives' with whom it is forbidden to marry. The text implies that sexual relations with all these relations are part of the same category, and are therefore considered incestuous. As indicated in Figure 2, ego is permitted to marry any of his cousins, thus no exogamous pattern is evident.

The biblical text is less forthcoming about actual kinship terminology (which would enable us to develop a clearer understanding of marriage patterns and their concept of incest). In most cases, both in the legal and narrative texts, each relation is described by specific terms. Thus the text uses descriptive terms like 'father's sister', or 'father's brother's wife'. No general terms or categories are used in the text. Nor are there clear cases where kinship terms like 'sister' are generalized to include cousins or other close relatives.[2]

---

1.   See, for example, Torrey's descriptions of the attitudes of the Judeans towards the Samaritans (1970: 325-26).

2.   The only case where this type of extension of kinship terminology may be found is discussed below in *Wife/Sister 2*.

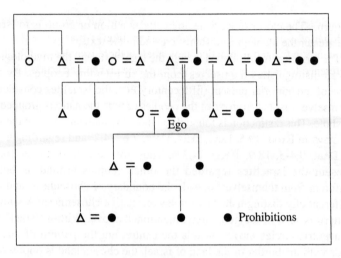

Figure 2. *Israelite Rules of Incest*

If the Israelites are examined in the context of the other peoples around
them, a pattern of endogamy emerges. The Israelites lived among many
different peoples and at times intermarried with them. The narrative
texts include several examples of such intermarriages. In most examples
of this type of intermarriage, however, the narrative also includes divine
retribution (see, e.g., Num. 25). Thus it is problematic how these texts
should be understood. They could be polemics against intermarriage
with details of the consequences should the laws be broken. Or they
could be descriptions of people who traditionally (or mythologically) had
married outside the usual pattern and were not meant to be followed in
practice.

The legal texts, however, are unambiguous. They forbid the Israelites
from exchanging women with the people among whom they lived. One
text contemporary with the editorial present, Ezra 9–10, includes a clear
prohibition on marrying out. It prohibits both taking the nations'
daughters and the giving of Israelite daughters to the nations in marriage
(Ezra 9.12).[1] In ch. 10 Ezra commands the Israelites to abandon their
foreign wives (10.11-44). Similar prohibitions were also found in texts
by the Deuteronomic author, written in the seventh century BC (see for
example 1 Kgs 11). Thus, at least ideologically, the Israelites must be

---

1.   A similar, though more limited, prohibition on both giving and taking
daughters is found in Deut. 7.3.

considered to have a rule against marrying out and therefore of endogamy. Although it is possible (even likely) that this rule was frequently infringed in practice, nevertheless there is a clear ideological preference for endogamy, supported by divine and human sanctions.

Chapter 3

ABRAHAM*

This chapter is the first of five analyzing in detail the structure of the myths in Genesis. Later chapters will pick up several of the themes raised here: the position of women in the structure, the use of mediators, and other methods of clouding the structure. The myths relating to Abraham are chosen for initial analysis, first, because they are among the most extensive in Genesis, and secondly, because they present the most comprehensive development of structure. This chapter discusses how the myths develop the three following oppositions: Israel–the nations, natural birth–divine birth, and wife–sister. It also shows how these oppositions support the logic of endogamy. Several theoretical points are also raised: the contextual nature of symbols; and the need, emphasized by T. Turner, for analysis of the narrative (diachronic) structure of myths as well as their overall synchronic structure.

The primary methodology (narrative) of this work is the presentation of the structuralist analysis in the main body of the text, and related analyses in footnotes. Where the other material bears directly upon the argument it will, however, be presented in the main body of the text. The myths concerning Abraham are divided into episodes or sections. Although these sections are summarized prior to the discussion, I suggest that frequent reference be made to the original biblical texts, either in Hebrew or in translation. I occasionally include a summary of the source-critical analysis when it has direct bearing on the overall discussion.

---

* In these texts two names are used for Abraham, Abram and Abraham. Abram is used prior to M.I.7, because it is in that text that God changes Abram's name to Abraham. Similarly, prior to M.I.7 Sarah is called Sarai. (In M.I.7 'M' means myth, 'I' refers to specific myth, i.e., Abraham, Isaac etc., '7' refers to the section of the myth.)

3.1. *Abram Leaves Haran*

This text introduces two levels of oppositions. On the one hand, Abram is opposed to his family on the horizontal level. He symbolically represents Israel (i.e., the people of) and his family represents the other nations. The text also works on the vertical level. It opposes Abram prior to symbolic 'divine birth' to Abraham after his 'divine birth'.[1] The text is the first of Abram's three symbolic 'divine births'.

> M.I.1. God commands Abram to leave his father's house. In return, God states that he will make of Abram a great nation. Abram leaves Haran with his wife Sarai and his nephew Lot (brother's son). Abram and his followers go to Canaan, where God tells Abram that he will give the land to Abram and his descendants. The direction of movement in the myth is south south west. (Gen. 12.1-9)

This episode contains several important relationships. The first opposition is that of Abram and his father (and his other biological relations). The myth creates both a geographic and qualitative distinction. The geographic movement is central to the development of this section. God tells Abram to leave his father's house, in return for which he will make Abram a great nation. The direction of this movement is significant. In the majority of myths prior to this in the biblical canon the movement is east. These movements are portrayed as ideologically negative, for example, Cain moves east of Eden. In this text the movement is west. Whereas prior texts dealt primarily with the ancestors of all humanity who moved eastward, Abram, and by implication his descendants, are distinguished by moving westward (see Gen. 12).

The qualitative aspect of the opposition is related to both the distinction between Abram and his family and to an opposition within Abram, that is, between Abram (a) as he was prior to the movement and Abram (b) as he becomes after the movement. Haran and its inhabitants, Abram (a) and his fathers and brothers, are portrayed as (logically) sterile in relation to Abram (b). This sterility is both on a physical and spiritual level. The main effect of the 'divine birth' in

---

1. 'Divine birth' is used here to mean a transformation whereby the individual is changed from being a product of natural (human) descent to one of divine descent. Although in many of the cases of 'divine birth' no actual birth takes place, the term birth is used because the texts often highlight the transformation with a denial of human or natural birth, they also often include elements associated with birth, that is, renaming and words meaning birth. These texts also often include rituals or events similar to rites of passage.

Abram is that he will become a great nation (abundant fruitfulness) and be blessed. The implication being that Abram (a) and his father's house did not possess these attributes.

The myth continues this opposition through the metaphor of birth. Abram's movement from the womb of his family should be taken as the first in a series of 'divine births'.[1] Two latter episodes of 'divine birth', M.I.5 and M.I.7, support the identification of this text as a transformation or birth myth. It should be noted that the theme of 'divine birth' is characteristic of almost every myth in Genesis. The text itself supports this identification. The introductory words לֶךְ לְךָ 'Go you forth' are also used in the text introducing Isaac's 'divine birth' (Gen. 22, see M.II.1 in Chapter 4), it is likely that there is both conscious allusion and structural relation between the two texts, suggesting that both deal with symbolic 'divine births'. This element is also emphasized by one of the words used to describe the place Abram is abandoning, מוֹלַדְתְּךָ translated as 'kindred', or 'birth place'. This word comes from the Hebrew root ילד, which is the basis of words meaning birth. The symbolic birth is associated with a complementary denial of natural birth—Abram denies his father, his natural progenitor, in favor of his divine progenitor.

Thus the text creates two levels of oppositions: Abram (a) : Abram (b) :: Abram's Family (Haran[2]) : Abram, which share the aspect of Sterility : Fruitfulness :: Spiritual Neutrality (–) : Positive Spirituality (Blessing) (+).[3] The text also develops the opposition of East : West :: Nations : Abram (b). Abram (b) (i.e., Israel) is qualitatively different, Israel moves west while the nations move east. The myth interestingly denies one type of fruitfulness in preference for a second kind. By definition Abram's father's house is fruitful (normal human fruitfulness), yet the myth chooses divine fruitfulness. The implication is that in comparison to

---

1.   This mytheme, as it develops throughout Genesis, brings together a set of symbols which relate to death and birth. Many of the texts include symbolic (or actual) deaths (see M.II.1 and M.V.2) or symbolic births suggested by a change in name (see M.I.7 and M.III.10). All of the 'divine birth' texts also include a denial of human fertility. The main goal of these texts is to emphasize divine fertility at the expense of human fertility. Taken as a whole (as opposed to individual expressions of the mytheme) the mytheme may be called 'symbolic divine birth'.

2.   For clarity 'Haran' is used for the name of the city and 'Harran' for Abram's brother.

3.   The symbols used in the text should be interpreted as follows: a single colon (:) = 'is to'; a double colon (::) = 'as'; X[(-)] inverted X.

divine fruitfulness, human fruitfulness is barren. This theme is developed more fully below.

It may be significant that v. 5 was not part of the original version of this myth (Fohrer 1986: 153). If the myth is emphasizing Abram's 'divine birth', then the strongest version would focus on Abram alone, rather than including Lot and Sarai—who for the time being are mediators—they remain tied to the place of Abram's origin, yet participate in the movement westward. Thus the original N text would not include mention of them, even if it knew of their existence, because it weakens the structural development. It is likely that they were added by P in order to keep this section consistent with the other narratively later texts that are included in the canon, that is, that Lot's presence, which is mentioned in narratively later texts, should be accounted for. Both problems created by the mediation of Lot and Sarai are resolved in opposite ways in the following sections.

3.2. *Wife/Sister 1*

The previous myth included two mediators, Lot and Sarai respectively.[1] Sarai, as Abram's wife, was especially problematic (because she suggested an inside/outside marriage).[2] This text is the first of two texts (*Wife/Sister 1* and *Wife/Sister 2*) that attempt to resolve this problem.

> M.I.2. Due to a famine in Canaan, Abram takes his family south to Egypt. Fearing that the Egyptians would kill him to take his wife, he asks her to say that she is his sister rather than his wife. Sarai is taken into Pharaoh's house to be his wife. God brings plagues upon Pharaoh for Sarai's sake. In order to end the plagues Pharaoh returns Sarai to Abram and commands Abram to leave Egypt. Abram returns to Canaan with great wealth. The direction of movement in this episode is south then north.[3] (Gen. 12.10–13.4)

1. In mythological texts mediators are figures which share attributes of both elements of the opposition and thus, by their similarity to both, cloud the opposition.

2. Steinberg suggests that inside marriages (in Genesis) had two basic requirements. First, they needed to be within the same patrilineage (in the case of Abram that of Terah). Secondly, the wife's mother also had to be inside (i.e., an acceptable partner) (Steinberg 1991: 51-52). This explains why Ishmael's daughters were outside (their mother was not an acceptable partner) even though their father belonged to Abram's patrilineage.

3. This section is composed entirely of texts taken from the N stratum. It is important to note that Fohrer distributes the three almost identical texts to the three different strata of Genesis. E is considered to be the author of Gen. 20 (1986: 161), J of Gen. 26 (1986: 147), and N of Gen. 12 (1986: 153). Although each author may

This episode resolves one of the central problems raised in the previous section—at least by P. Sarai is problematic in the text because she has not experienced the same process of transformation as Abram. In the previous text she mediates between the oppositions. She is of Haran and thus barren, while also moving west with Abram and therefore fruitful. The first opposition introduced by the text is that between wife and sister. Each of the two is associated with a qualifier: wife with danger and sister with safety. It is likely that this opposition relates to one that is implied in the first section, that is, of inside–outside.

In *Abram Leaves Haran* (M.I.1) this opposition is inverted. What was inside (father's house) becomes outside, while what was outside (Canaan) becomes inside. Abraham and his descendants are inside while Haran and the other nations are outside. Likewise, sister is relatively inside and can be thus considered qualitatively the same, while a wife is outside and therefore qualitatively different and more dangerous. This issue is examined below in relation to several individual texts, and in detail in Chapter 11.[1]

The second opposition is between Abram and the Egyptians, with Sarai as the lynch pin. In regard to Abram, Sarai signifies fruitfulness, at the very least future fruitfulness, whereas for the Egyptians she signifies plagues, that is, death and probably barrenness. This aspect of barrenness is suggested by the other similar text, Genesis 20 (M.I.12, *Wife/Sister 2*). Genesis 20 specifically states that the punishment for taking Sarah as a wife was barrenness: 'Because the Lord had closed all the wombs of the house of Abimelech, because of the matter of Abraham's wife'. Thus Sarai, the mediator, is the source of divine fertility, rather than natural fertility which is associated with barrenness.[2]

have had a slightly different version of the story, it is also possible that there was duplication of the same story even in the same text. Within the current text the three stories serve important mythical functions. For an in-depth discussion of these texts, see Biddle 1990: 599-611.

1.   This and related texts dealing with the danger posed by women is examined in detail in Kunin 1994a.

2.   Leach presents a similar argument in 'Genesis as Myth'. He suggests that Sarai's ultimate fruitfulness—through supernatural intervention—is evidence that the text condones the incestuous relationship between Abram and Sarai (Leach 1969: 21). I would go further and suggest that the text actively supports the relationship.

In 'Why Did Moses Have a Sister', however, Leach moves in a very different direction. He suggests an analogy between Abraham and Osiris, and explains the structure of the story as analogous to 'the stereotyped late form of the saga of Osiris'

Although this myth only poses the relationship of Abram and Sarai as brother and sister as a ploy, mythologically it is much stronger. Sarai's relationship as wife, representative of the outside, is problematic, so the text creates the possibility that she is sister, working on an essential building block of the system. This problem, however, is not fully resolved until Genesis 20, where Sarah is said indeed to be Abram's sister. The question of incest is not problematic because it resolves the question of inside/outside. (The question of incest is examined in more detailed fashion in Chapter 11).

The element of direction is also significant. The prevailing direction of this text is south, as is the direction of all similar texts. Movement south is opposed to movement north. Those texts which describe getting a wife are to the north, while the texts that make the relationship

(Leach and Aycock 1983: 39). He suggests that Abraham and the other patriarchs are equated with Pharaoh and therefore with Osiris. His primary support comes from Luke, a source diachronically, and probably culturally, distinct from the original Genesis text. The role of 'hero' in the Luke text, based on the model of Jesus, would embody aspects of 'God incarnate' not necessarily to be found in the earlier Israelite texts.

Leach is also mistaken in suggesting that Pharaoh and Abraham are interchangeable because they 'exchange' Sarah (Leach and Aycock 1983: 40). The outcome of this exchange highlights their difference rather than their similarity. Pharaoh's relationship with Sarah is barren, Abraham's is fruitful. It is also unclear, and theoretically inconsistent, to suggest that the Israelites would take a structural pattern from another society without materially transforming it to fit their own requirements. There is no reason, based on the rest of his discussion, to use cross-cultural evidence. His argument would be equally strong if it used only biblical texts.

Leach's argument, however, is intrinsically flawed for two reasons: he uses Christian material alongside Israelite texts as if they were from the same culture, and he uses evidence from the Dura Europa 'Synagogue', a site whose exact origins are unclear at best.

The goal of Leach's arguments is to make a structural association between Moses and Jesus. In order to develop this equivalence he needs to highlight points of structural similarity. Since Mary, Jesus's mother, and Mary, Jesus's symbolic sister, share a name they are structurally interchangeable (agreeing with the Osiris myth). Moses's sister therefore must also be his mother (irrespective of the lack of any structural evidence in Israelite myth). In association with Mary Magdalene (and relying on the external Egyptian myth of Osiris, Isis and Horus) he answers his own question (Why does Moses have a sister?) by asserting that Miriam is both sister and mother (Leach and Aycock 1983: 55). If, however, Miriam is placed in the context of biblical myth then the role of mother is structurally insignificant. I answer his initial question differently (an answer which he offers but does not properly develop): Moses has a sister because mytho-logic requires that his wife be his sister.

incestuous (making wife into sister) are always to the south.[1] One gets a wife from the outside, the northeast, and makes her into an acceptable wife, an insider, by taking her south.

The directional and locational elements of the text add one further support to this aspect of the logic. Egypt was the logical place for a wife to become a sister. Brother–sister marriage was common practice in Egypt, certainly in the royal house and possibly permeating other levels.[2] It is likely that this type of marriage served a similar structural role. If Pharaoh was considered a god, then in order to prevent dilution of the divine blood he needed to marry someone similarly divine. Likewise if Israel were qualitatively different from the nations, as a product of divine fruitfulness (see below), then logically it could only marry people who were equally distinct, that is, those of the same nation. The location for the transformation made the incestuous relationship more narratively acceptable, mirroring its mythological acceptance.

This text, and the analogous texts examined below (e.g., *Wife/Sister 2*), develops the central problem upon which the myth is working, the problem of endogamy. The narrative level of the myth creates a logical problem. Abram (inside) must get a wife from the outside. This, however, goes against the ideological preference for marrying within. The text resolves this contradiction by bringing Sarai within, thus removing the paradox, and thereby supporting the ideological preference for endogamy.

One further element raised in this section, and characteristic of the development of the myth, is the placement and effects of Abram's 'divine birth'. After the initial transformation (see M.I.1, *Abram Leaves Haran*), Sarai's status as mediator is resolved (or begins to be resolved) with the final resolution coming after the second transformation (see M.I.5, *The Covenant of the Pieces*). Lot's status is also resolved in the opposite direction, see below (M.I.3, *Division of the Land*). After the second transformation Abram has his first son—initial fruitfulness. And, after the third transformation (M.I.7, *The Covenant of Circumcision*), his son through divine fruitfulness is born. The third 'divine birth' mirrors

1.   See the discussion on incest above. Sister and half sister were both considered to be incestuous relations.

2.   Hopkins shows that brother–sister marriages were found in the Egyptian royal dynasties as far back as 2000 BC. They were also occasionally found outside the royal family (Hopkins 1982: 311). Hopkins states, in connection with Roman Egypt, that 'one-third and perhaps more, of all brothers with marriageable sisters married inside the family' (1982: 304).

both the first and the second, with more complete developments than either of the earlier sections. It mirrors the first in that it has a repetition of the above text (M.I.2). The resolution of Sarai's status is much clearer in the second version (M.I.12, *Wife/Sister* 2). It mirrors the second in the repetition of texts about the expulsion of Hagar (M.I.6, M.I.13), with the second developing the crises more clearly. The third 'divine birth' therefore heralds a recapitulation of Abraham's life, with the resolution of crisis being more complete.

3.3. *Division of the Land*

In the previous text, one of the two initial mediators was brought inside. In this text the problem of the second mediator is resolved. Lot moves in the opposite direction from Sarai; Sarai is being made inside while Lot is made outside. It should be noted, however, that all symbols (Lot included) retain flexibility and can be used in different contexts to fill opposing structural roles.

> M.I.3. There is a conflict between Lot's shepherds and Abram's. To end the conflict, Abram offers Lot half the land. Lot chooses the eastern half, comprising the plains of the Jordan and Sodom and Gomorrah. The text alludes in two places to the future destruction of Sodom and Gomorrah, as well as to the wickedness of their inhabitants. After the separation God promises Abram that his descendants shall have all the land (symbolized by the four directions), and that they shall be very great in number. Abram moves in a westward direction, while Lot moves in an eastward direction.[1]
> (Gen. 13.5-18)

This text can be seen as a structural inversion of the previous text. Whereas Sarai was made inside, Lot is made outside. This resolves the crisis developed in episode M.I.1. A clear opposition is developed between Lot and Abram, emphasized by the narrative conflict between their herdsmen. The conflict is resolved by the two moving in opposite directions, Abram to the west, Lot to the east. The structural significance of these two directions has already been mentioned. Lot moves in the direction of all negative movement, while Abram moves in the direction of positive movement. This can be seen in the equation Abram : Lot :: West : East.

---

1. This text, like the above text (M.I.2), derives primarily from the N stratum. Fohrer suggests that vv. 4-5, 7-11a, 12b-18 are from this source. The remaining verses are identified as coming from the P strata. Of the verses he attributes to P, only 11b is structurally significant. This verse emphasizes the move east, while the previous and following verses name Lot's destinations rather than the direction.

The opposition is further developed on the narrative level through Lot's choice. Abram offers Lot either half (a qualitatively positive action), while Lot chooses what is apparently the best, ignoring the respect he owes to his uncle (a qualitatively negative action). The values of the land are also reversed: the rift valley, which appears positive is negative (–), while Canaan, which appears relatively negative, is positive (+).

The text also develops an opposition between two life styles, the nomadic life style of Abram and the city life chosen by Lot. Throughout the texts in Genesis, from the city founded by Cain (or his son) onward, city life is described as corrupt and corrupting. This opposition is one reason for Fohrer's attribution of this text to the N source (1986: 153). I am not suggesting that the Israelites were nomadic at the time the text was written, or indeed that they ever were nomadic, rather that they retained or developed an ideological preference for the nomadic way of life and associated it with God's choice of Israel.

It is likely that Lot is structurally distinct from the other nations, and that some of his mediating characteristics remain even after the immediate crisis is resolved. Some of these make him similar to Abram. Like Abram, he is the father of nations. And, at least in one text (M.I.10), he fills Abram's structural role, developing the logic of inside/outside.

Abram's 'divine births' are placed at structurally significant points in the narrative. Only after the two main problems developed in the first section of the myth have been completely resolved can Abram have his second 'divine birth', the subject of section M.I.5. *Wife/Sister 1* begins to resolve the problem posed by Sarai and *Division of the Land* resolves that of Lot.

3.4. *The War of Nine Kings*

This text emphasizes the distinction between Abram (Israel) and the nations of the world. The nine kings, which represent all the nations of the world, are symbolically defeated by Abram (he defeats the winners in the war between the kings and is therefore greater than all the kings). The text implies that Israel is greater than all the nations, and also reintroduces Lot in a mediating role.

> M.I.4. Four kings make war upon a coalition of five kings including those of Sodom and Gomorrah. The four kings are victorious and Lot is taken captive. Abram pursues the four kings and rescues Lot. On his return he is blessed by Melchizedek, called a priest of the Most High. Abram takes nothing of the spoils. Abram moves in a northward direction (as does Lot). (Gen. 14)

This text differs from both texts that precede it, and from the texts that follow it, on both the thematic and narrative levels. Structurally, it both further develops the opposition between Lot and Abram and likewise introduces a further distinction between Abram (Israel) and the nations.

The nine different kingdoms involved in the conflict are structurally significant. The four kings who attack the coalition of five kings are all from the far east. Shinar is possibly Babylonia (or Sumer) (BDB, 1042), Ellasar is located near Ur in Mesopotamia (BDB, 48), Elam is located in the lower Tigris valley (BDB, 743), and Goiim is probably also in Babylonia (BDB, 157). The five kings who are attacked, on the other hand, are all located in the far west (though all are located to the east of Canaan). All five kingdoms—Sodom, Gomorrah, Admah, Zeboiim, and Zoar—are located in the Jordan valley.

It is likely that the two groups of kingdoms, from the far east and the far west, are meant to represent all the kingdoms of the earth. This identification is supported by the names of two of the kingdoms selected for mention in the myth. The consonants of Goiim also can mean 'nations' and those of Admah also can mean 'earth' (or 'world'). Thus Abram's defeat of the four kings represents the qualitative difference between Abram and the nations—Abram : Victory (Blessing) :: Nations : Defeat (Curse). By refusing to take any of the spoil, Abram refuses to align himself with any of the kings.

The position of Lot is again made ambiguous, perhaps in preparation for his structural role in M.I.10 (*The Destruction of Sodom*). He again becomes a mediator between Abram and the nations. Like Abram, he is mentioned separately from the other nations involved in the myth. Like the five kings, however, he is captured. Thus he shares characteristics of both sides. His structural position is transformed in this text: in the beginning he is distinct from the nations, while at the end he is identified more closely with them.

The final element of the text is also structurally significant. Melchizedek is described as a 'Priest of the Most High', that is, of the God of Abram. His name means 'King of Righteousness'. The location of his kingdom is also significant—he is said to be king of Salem, identified as Jerusalem. Structurally he fills the same role as Abram. Abram represents Israel, whose capital was Jerusalem, and whose centre was the Temple in Jerusalem. Melchizedek, king of Salem, is structurally equivalent to Israel and therefore Abraham. Melchizedek also fills a role given to Abram, to be a blessing and to bless the nations of the earth. The blessing itself distinguishes between Israel and the other nations. Jerusalem, the source of blessings, blesses Israel. The other nations are not blessed and only can partake of the material spoil. The nations' reward is therefore a short-term sterile blessing, while Abram's blessing is long term and fruitful, as emphasized in the following section where God again promises Abram abundant blessing and descendants.

3.5. *The Covenant of the Pieces*

The Covenant of the Pieces describes a ritual through which Abram's relationship with God is transformed. The ritual reifies and concretizes the relationship. It is suggested that the text describes a symbolic birth. It is the second of three texts about 'divine birth', preparing Abram to bear the divine seed, to be the conduit of divine fruitfulness.

> M.I.5. After these things God appears to Abram in a vision. Abram asks God if he will be childless and if Eliezer his servant will be his inheritor. God tells Abram that he will have children and that their descendants shall number as the stars of the heavens. God makes a Covenant with Abram symbolized by cutting in half a heifer, a goat, a ram, a turtledove, and a pigeon. These are made into a bloody path. During the night an eagle alights on the carcasses but Abram drives it away. God predicts that Abram's descendants will be slaves for four hundred years and that they will come forth with great wealth and return to Canaan. A burning torch is passed through the pieces. (Gen. 15)

This text contains several important developments in structure. The first is an emphasis on Abram's current barren state, which is developed in two ways. Eliezer is opposed to Abram's future seed, and should be seen as structurally equivalent to Ishmael, Abram's first son. This covenant is structurally related to the second covenant, which is also a symbolic 'divine birth'. In this covenant Abram implies that he expects his line to be carried on by Eliezer, who is subsequently rejected by God. In the second covenant Abram asks if his seed will be carried on by Ishmael, who is similarly rejected. Ishmael and Eliezer are thus structurally equivalent and Eliezer can be treated as a son. (This element is also developed below in regard to M.I.7 *The Covenant of Circumcision*.) With this equivalence in mind, the following equation is possible: Eliezer ('son' born prior to 'divine birth') : Sons born after final 'divine birth' :: Rejection : Chosenness or Blessing. The text rejects Eliezer because he is born (in this case adopted) prior to Abram's divine transformation.

The element of barrenness also works in a second way, parallel to the barrenness of Sarai in later texts, and to the barrenness of most female figures in the biblical canon. Barrenness should be seen as the denial of human sexuality, in this case the denial of Abram's sexuality. The text develops a structural pattern whereby human sexuality is denied while divine sexuality is fruitful, creating the following equation: Human Sexuality (natural fruitfulness) = Barrenness, while Divine Sexuality (chosen line) = Fruitfulness. This creates the apparent paradox of Abram's barrenness being more fruitful than the nations' fecundity.

The element of symbolic 'divine birth' or transformation is found throughout this section. The first half emphasizes the aspect of birth focusing on the divine promise of the birth of an heir. The second half is even clearer. Abram is asked to make a bloody pathway consisting of progressively smaller animals. If this text is analyzed with the structurally equivalent second covenant, where Abram's name is changed to Abraham, the passage through the bloody path can be interpreted as a symbolic birth or new beginning. The eagle or bird of prey introduces the opposition of divine versus natural. In order to protect the divine nature of his transformation, Abram drives away a creature attempting to fulfil its natural function.

As stated, the text develops the opposition of divine versus natural birth. Natural birth, on the one hand, is sterile, it has no future and cannot carry on the line. Divine birth, on the other hand, leads to abundant fruitfulness which is emphasized in the repetition of the promise that Abram's descendants will be as numerous as the stars of the heavens. It also has a future, indicated by the prophecy given Abram after the covenant of the pieces.

Another element emphasized by the text is Abram's westward movement. Instead of stating that Abram came from Haran which was a southwest movement, the text emphasizes movement from Ur, a clearly westward movement. This is characteristic of several texts in which God states that he took Abram out of Ur in order to give him the land of Canaan.

3.6. *The Expulsion of Hagar 1*
Through the transformation of Abram in *The Covenant of Pieces* the distinction of inside/outside is strengthened. The text raises a mythological question: can inside join outside and be (acceptably) fruitful? Initially, the answer appears to be 'yes'. With the conclusion of this text, the answer is resoundingly 'no', both the baby and its mother are expelled from the family and line of descent.

M.I.6. Sarai, seeing that she is barren, gives her Egyptian handmaid to Abram to bear children for her. Hagar becomes pregnant causing Sarai to become jealous. Abram gives Sarai permission to do as she will with Hagar. Sarai's harshness with her makes Hagar flee into the desert. She is met by an angel who tells her to return to Sarai and comforts her with the prediction that she will bear a son. The text also gives a poem describing (predicting the future of) Ishmael and his descendants.

He will be a wild ass of a man;
His hand against every man,
and every man's hand against him;
and he shall dwell in the presence of all his brothers.
Hagar returns to Abram and bears a son whom she names Ishmael.
(Gen. 16)

This text expands several of the oppositions developed in the previous texts. It also emphasizes the importance of the narrative order in regard to the development of the structure. The initial opposition is between Sarai and Hagar. Sarai is barren, and her barrenness is emphasized by the text, while Hagar is fruitful. The difference is focused on through the identification of Hagar as an Egyptian. Sarai, without indication of national origin, is within, while Hagar, the Egyptian, is without. Thus the initial equation is: Sarai : Hagar :: Inside : Outside :: Barrenness : Fruitfulness.

Sarai's barrenness works on two related levels. On the one hand, it is the denial of her role as a natural mother. This is part of a wider theme throughout the texts which attempts to remove the natural parents from Israel's line of descent. Her very barrenness denies the possibility that she could be a mother. This corresponds to Abram's sterility found in M.I.5 above, as well as the elements denying Abram's role as father, that is, circumcision (M.I.9), and the symbolic slaughter of his son in M.II.1. On the other hand, the barrenness also develops the corresponding aspect of divine fruitfulness. Sarai cannot conceive naturally, she can only bear a child through the agency of God. On a higher level, it emphasizes the difference in origin between Israel and the other nations (embodied by Ishmael): Israel is of divine origin while the other nations are of natural origin.

There is, however, a negative aspect to Sarai, namely her jealousy. The text portrays her reaction to the pregnancy of Hagar as inappropriate in two ways. Hagar is saved by a divine messenger receiving a blessing/ prophecy, and she returns to Abram at the end of the narrative. It is likely that this negative aspect of Sarai is due to the fact that she retains ambiguous elements. Although she has been made inside (see *Wife/Sister 1* above), her transition is not complete and she thus retains negative characteristics from the outside. In fact she retains these characteristics until M.I.7 (*The Covenant of Circumcision*) when she is transformed into Sarah. In almost every text in Genesis the woman retains a slightly negative aspect. This is due to the fact that even in an endogamous (patrilineal and patrilocal) society, women are outside relative to their husband's family (see the discussion in 11.2).

Abram's role in this structure is ambiguous. He is both the source of natural fruitfulness, as in this text, and the conduit of divine fruitfulness—indicated both by the birth of Ishmael and the statement in the covenants that he will be the source of blessing for the nations of the earth. Ishmael reflects this ambiguity.

The very ambiguity of Abram's role, however, helps to emphasize the importance of his final 'divine birth' (see below, M.I.7). Whereas prior to his final 'divine birth' he is the source of natural fruitfulness, after his new beginning he is the source of divine fruitfulness. This leads to an opposition between Ishmael (natural) and Isaac (divine) that is carried through the rest of the text.

It is likely that the text also emphasizes the importance of both the father and the mother in the endogamous equation. Both must be inside for divine fruitfulness: both are equally essential. Inside plus outside, Abram plus Hagar, can never make inside. This element also may be seen in the explanation of Abram and Sarai's relationship. Abram and Sarai share the same father but have different mothers, justifying their marriage (see text M.I.12 *Wife/Sister 2*). This implies that true relationship required identity both in the father's and mother's line.

This text also illustrates the importance of diachronic development within the narrative itself, and the importance of the order of texts for the creation of the structural logic. The six texts correspond closely with each other, and their placement is essential to the structure. They can be divided into three pairs: M.I.2 with M.I.12 (*Wife/Sister 1* and *2*), M.I.6 with M.I.13 (*Expulsion of Hagar 1* and *2*), and M.I.5 with M.I.7 (*The Covenant of the Pieces* and *The Covenant of Circumcision*). The final pair are the two covenants between Abram and God. The other two pairs have M.I.7 as their center. Before the final covenant (M.I.7), in M.I.2 Sarai is partially made inside, though the text implies that Abram is lying about their kin relationship. After M.I.7, M.I.12 makes it clear that he was not lying and the relationship actually existed. In M.I.6

Abram participates in natural fecundity, while in M.I.13 he is the source of divine fruitfulness. M.I.6 and M.I.13 are opposed to each other, one being natural and the other divine; the transformation centers on M.I.7, where Abram is transformed to Abraham. He is transformed and thus can participate in divine birth. The two texts also oppose the role of Sarai. In the first, when she is relatively outside, her actions are portrayed as negative. In the second she is opposed to Hagar, whose actions there are portrayed as negative with Sarai, Sarah now being completely inside and therefore positive. The narrative uses the change in Abram as a focus to develop the oppositions (on a broad level) between pairs of related texts, using their apparent similarity to highlight the differences.

3.7. The Covenant of Circumcision

The Covenant of Circumcision is the third 'divine birth' text. It contains structural elements that join it with the other two. This text is the most explicit. It contains a symbolic sacrifice, circumcision (which also may be a symbolic castration). The element of 'new beginning' is also emphasized through the change in Abram's name to Abraham.

> M.I.7. When Abram is 99 years old God again appears to him. God makes a covenant with Abram, promising that he will multiply Abram's seed. As a sign of the covenant God changes Abram's name to Abraham. In return, God commands that Abraham and his descendants should be circumcised (on the eighth day after birth). Any descendant of Abraham's not circumcised breaks this covenant. God also changes Sarai's name to Sarah and promises that she will bear a son. Abraham does not believe that Sarah, who is 90 years old, can bear a child and therefore asks God if Ishmael could be chosen to carry on Abraham's line. God tells Abraham that although he has blessed Ishmael and that Ishmael will be the father of twelve princes, God's covenant will be established through Isaac, whom Sarah will bear. The text concludes with Abraham circumcising himself as well as every male in his household. (Gen. 17)

There are several significant elements in this text. The new beginning in this text is perhaps clearer than in the two previous 'divine birth' texts. It heralds the 'divine birth' by changing Abram's name to Abraham, an addition of one letter in the Hebrew. Sarai is also complementarily transformed to Sarah, with the addition of the same letter.

The text emphasizes the ages of both Abraham and Sarah, 99 and 90 respectively. This emphasizes the impossibility of people of that age naturally having children. It thus emphasizes the divine aspect of the birth of Isaac. This element is further stressed in this text and in M.I.8, where both Abram and Sarah laugh at the possibility of their having children.

The element of circumcision is also significant. If taken in the context of the previous texts, it is related to the following set of symbols: barrenness (in Sarah), sterility (in Abram), and those elements that deny human (natural) birth in favour of divine birth. It is thus possible that circumcision might be seen as a symbolic form of castration, the ultimate denial of human fruitfulness. Indeed, only after Abraham is circumcised and human fruitfulness denied can divine fruitfulness come to the fore in Isaac's birth.

Ishmael is implicitly opposed to Isaac, whose birth is predicted later in the myth. Ishmael is doubly the product of human fruitfulness, that is, of the pre-covenant Abram and the Egyptian Hagar. Isaac, however, is the product of divine fruitfulness since both his parents have been symbolically transformed. Ishmael is also paired with Eliezer, who was similarly rejected as inheritor of the covenant in M.I.5 (*The Covenant of the Pieces*). Ishmael, however, retains one aspect of ambiguity: like his father he is said to be the father of nations, with the twelve Ishmaelite princes descended from him.[1]

3.8. *Abraham and the Three Men*
The promise of a son, of acceptable seed, is the culmination of the previous texts. In those texts Abraham and Sarah were symbolically transformed, and thus became acceptable conduits of divine fruitfulness. Both were, however, denied their natural roles as parents, emphasizing the opposition between divine and natural fruitfulness.

> M.I.8. While Abraham is sitting in his tent he sees three men approaching. Abraham invites them to sit and be refreshed, washing their feet and slaughtering a lamb for them to eat. They tell Abraham that within a year Sarah will bear a son. Sarah hears this prophecy from the tent door and she laughs to herself, thinking that both Abraham and she are too old to have children. God reproves Sarah for laughing, stating that nothing is too hard for God. (Gen. 18.1-15)

---

1.   The number twelve is characteristic of genealogies in Genesis. It usually indicates the end of a line of descent explaining the origin of a nation. Both Israel and Edom similarly are composed of twelve segments (see the discussion of genealogies in Chapter 8 below.)

One key element developed in this text is the emphasis on Abraham's behavior towards his guests. This behavior is mirrored by Lot, with a few significant exceptions, in M.I.10 (*The Destruction of Sodom*). Abraham, upon seeing the men, offers them a place to rest and washes their feet. Then he runs, gives them bread and kills a kid to make a meal for them. The text stresses Abraham's actions by describing each one in detail, for example, he fetched a kid 'tender and good'. The text uses more than the usual number of adjectives for every aspect of the feast. This description creates a subtle opposition to Lot, a dweller in the city, and a clear opposition to the other inhabitants of Sodom. In Genesis 19 Lot, like Abraham, bows to the ground, offers the men a place to stay and to wash their feet, and a feast. There is, however, no elaboration of detail in the Lot narrative, nor is there the sense that Lot rushed to do any of these things as Abraham had done. The opposition with the people of Sodom is more obvious: instead of tending to the needs of travellers they wish to take advantage of them.

The main element of this text, however, is the annunciation of the birth of a son. This follows the pattern of other similar texts throughout the Bible (Old Testament as well as New Testament). In all the cases of this type of annunciation, the son grows up to be a great leader of the people, often having almost supernatural powers, for example, Samson and Jesus. This element also highlights the divine aspect in the birth, emphasizing God's direct involvement in a birth which was unlikely due to Sarah's age and her previous barren state.

The unlikely, even unnatural, aspect of the birth is further emphasized by both the text and Sarah's actions. The text stresses that it was no longer possible for Sarah to have children naturally. It states, 'Sarah and Abraham were old, advanced in years, and it had ceased to be with Sarah after the way of women' (Gen. 18.11). Sarah had reached menopause. Secondly, upon hearing the prophecy, she laughs to herself and asks, 'can I being old have the pleasure, and my husband is also old' (Gen. 18.12). This mirrors Abraham's words in the previous section, where he questions the possibility of Sarah having a child. This text adds Abraham to the unlikely outcome. It is unlikely or impossible that either Abraham or Sarah should have a child naturally. Thus the divine element of Isaac's birth is emphasized. This text is one of several that deny both Abraham's and Sarah's role as parents.

3.9. *Abraham Challenges God's Justice*

After Sarah's pregnancy, and the promise of a chosen line, the text emphasizes the opposition between that line and the other nations of the world. It develops the opposition in two ways. Abraham's righteousness is emphasized through his argument with God. The wickedness of the nations is emphasized by the absence of even ten righteous men.

> M.I.9. The three men who visited Abraham move on to Sodom accompanied by Abraham. God tells Abraham that he is about to destroy Sodom and Gomorrah because of their wickedness. Abraham challenges God's justice, asking if God will destroy the righteous along with the wicked. After this bargaining, God agrees not to destroy the cities if he can find ten righteous men. (Gen. 18.16-33)

This text forms part of the Lot saga, and is primarily concerned with the distinction between city and nomadic life. Abraham is established as the ideal positive type. God feels that he must inform Abraham of his upcoming actions. The text ascribes this to the fact that Abraham will become a great nation and the fact that, through Abraham's descendants, the nations of the earth will be blessed. Thus it ties Abraham, as an ideal type, to his descendants—Israel—who also are this ideal type.

The text establishes the opposition between Abraham and the people of Sodom (and the other cities of the Jordan rift) in two ways. On the one hand, God's intentions towards Abraham and the cities are opposite. He intends to make Abraham a great nation because Abraham will be a blessing, while intending to destroy the cities because they are sinful. On the other hand, Abraham's positive aspect is emphasized through his arguing with God to save the cities for the sake of justice. The opposition is further strengthened when it is found that the cities lack even ten righteous men and they are destroyed. The opposition developed in this text is between Abraham (nomadic life) and the people of Sodom (city life). On a broader level the city dwellers can be taken as symbolizing the other nations, who are portrayed as sinful in relation to Israel.[1]

---

1. It is important to note, that although the Israelites may not have been nomadic at the time of this text's composition, and indeed may never have been nomadic, this text clearly preserves the ideological comparison of nomadic life (+) and city life (–). Fohrer believes that the N text, the primary source for this myth, was composed by a reactionary group who wished to return to (or preserve) the nomadic way of life (Fohrer 1986: 153).

3.10. *The Destruction of Sodom*
The Destruction of Sodom continues the process begun in the previous text. In this case, however, it is Lot rather than Abraham who represents Israel. This emphasizes the structural flexibility of symbols. In the texts examined here, Lot fills three structural functions: negative, mediator, positive.

> M.I.10. (A) Two of the men, now identified as angels, approach Sodom in the evening. Lot sees them, and invites them to stay in his house. He convinces them to stay with him and provides a feast and unleavened bread. All of the men of Sodom gather outside Lot's house and demand that the two men be given to them (the implication being that they will be sodomized). Lot refuses and offers his daughters in place of the angels. When the men of Sodom attempt to attack Lot's house the angels smite them with blindness. The angels inform Lot that God is going to destroy Sodom and so Lot and his family should leave. (B) Although Lot is tempted to stay, the angels bring him, his wife, and his daughters out of the city. As they escape, the angels tell them not to look back lest they be destroyed along with the cities. Lot is afraid to escape to the mountain, and asks the angels if he can go instead to the city of Zoar. The angels tell him that he can. Lot's wife, however, looks back upon Sodom and is transformed into a pillar of salt. The narrative concludes by telling us that Abraham sees the destruction of Sodom and Gomorrah. Lot's movements in this text are to the south.[1] (Gen. 19.1-28)

The symbolic system encompassed in the figure of Lot is interesting from several perspectives. Most importantly, it reveals the flexibility of symbols within the system. In certain texts, M.I.1 (*Abram Leaves Haran*) and M.I.4 (*War of the Nine Kings*), Lot plays the role of mediator. In other texts, for example, M.I.3 (*Division of the Land*), he is developed in opposition to Abraham (Abram). While in the third group of texts, M.I.10 and M.I.11 (*The Destruction of Sodom* and *Lot and his Daughters*), he is structurally equivalent (or almost equivalent) to Abraham.

The structural progression can be illustrated as follows: the equation in text M.I.1 is Abram(+) → Sarai–Lot(+/–) → Haran = (the nations)(–); in text M.I.2 (by implication, as Lot is never mentioned and his structural position remains unresolved) it is Abram–Sarai(+) → Lot(+/–) → Egypt =

---

1. This text is composed of material from both N and J (Fohrer 1986: 147), but it seems likely that much is from N. The text betrays a strong bias against city life, not only concerning Sodom and Gomorrah, but also in regard to Zoar. Although Lot is structurally the positive center of the text, he is still criticized for choosing city life in favour of nomadic life (which was Abraham's choice).

(the nations)(–); in text M.I.3 it is Abram(+) → Lot = (the nations)(–); in text M.I.4 it is Abram(+) → Lot(+ becoming –) → the nations (–); in text M.I.10 A it is Abram = Lot(+) → Sodom = (the nations); M.I.10 B is the same as equation M.I.2; and M.I.11 is the same as M.I.10 A. It is apparent that there is no logical development in the use of the symbol. Rather, it is used differently in each text depending on the structural requirements of that text.

Although, in the overall progression of texts, Lot is outside the line of chosen descent, within the context of this text (M.I.10) Lot is used mythologically in the same way that Abraham is used in the other texts. Lot, in this text, is opposed to the people of the city, and in text M.I.11 and following is used to deal with the problem of marrying out (and incest).

Thus a theoretical distinction must be made. There are certain elements that carry over in narrative progression, for example, the repetition of texts around a central focus examined above, and thus must be examined as a set of transformations. Other elements, rather than being part of a development of structure, are complete and independent, and therefore must be analyzed metaphorically instead of metonymically. Lot must be examined, in this text, as a member of a category (Abraham, Isaac, Jacob, Lot, etc.), rather than in relation to his development in previous texts.

Section M.I.10 associates Lot with Abraham in several respects. They both offer the angels hospitality and prepare a meal. Lot is clearly opposed to the people of the city. Rather than being hospitable, they demand that the angels (who they think are men) be turned over to them to be sodomized (the inversion of hospitality). Further emphasizing Lot's difference from the people, he offers to give his daughters in place of his guests. In response, the men of Sodom threaten Lot's life as well. Interestingly, the people of Sodom are blinded by the angels, a punishment often associated with sexual perversion.

At this point in the text the association with Abraham is weakened. Instead of leaving the city immediately, Lot hesitates and is dragged from the city by the angels. With the broader development in mind, the text seeks to create an implicit opposition with Abraham, who never lived in the city. Lot's connection with the city is further strengthened by the fate of his wife who, upon looking back to the city, is turned into a pillar of salt.[1] The text concludes with a similar element. Rather than

---

1. In regard to Lot's wife, I disagree in part with Aycock's analysis. He suggests that the wife mediates between the 'two men' and Lot's daughters. She is an

going to the mountain (a positive direction) Lot chooses to go to another city, further implicating himself in the sin of the cities. The opposition to Abraham, now possible with the destruction of the other pair (Sodom and Gomorrah) in opposition to Lot, is emphasized through mention of Abraham's witnessing the destruction.

3.11. *Lot and his Daughters*
Lot and his Daughters develops the same oppositions as M.I.10. Lot continues to be structurally equivalent to Abraham. The major theme of the myth is the incest between Lot and his daughters. The incest is prepared for by the removal of Lot's wife, who mediates between Lot and Sodom.

> M.I.11. Lot leaves Zoar and dwells in the mountain. His two daughters, seeing that they have no husbands, make him drunk and have sex with him. Both daughters bear sons. The eldest daughter calls her son Moav, while the younger daughter calls her son Ben-ammi. The text informs us that Moav is the ancestor of the Moabites and Ben-ammi that of the Ammonites. (Gen. 19.29-38)

This text continues the narrative from the previous two sections. Instead of distinguishing Lot from Abraham, this text continues to equate Lot with him. Lot serves to continue the development of the structural resolution of marrying out. Other similar texts (i.e., the wife/sister texts M.I.2, M.I.12) resolve the problem of 'wife' through brother–sister incest. This text resolves it through father–daughter incest. The problematic wife is removed and the daughters take her place.

Lot's wife should be understood as a mediator between two aspects of Lot himself. As a daughter of the city she represents the city and as a pillar of salt she represents nature. Initially she ties Lot to the city, yet,

intimate part of the household like his daughters, yet, like the two men, she is not named (Leach and Aycock 1983: 116). The two men, however, are identified (although not to Lot) throughout the texts as angels. The previous myth, *Abraham Argues with God*, concludes by stating that two angels went to Sodom. It is more likely that the wife mediates between the people of Sodom and Lot and his daughters. Both the people of Sodom and the daughter's initiate (or wish to) sexual intercourse. The mother shares with the people 'outside' origin and with the daughters, is at least partially 'inside'. With the removal of the mother the daughters are completely distinguished (made inside) from the people of the city. The transformation of the mother is exactly centred between the cities (outside) and the mountains (inside). With her transformation into a pillar of salt the following equation is developed: wife = salt = dead sea = infertility; allowing the equation of the daughters with fertility.

with her transformation, she allows him to move to the wilderness. Lot's tie to the city needed to be removed before he could become 'Abraham' and be fruitful. Likewise the wife (outside) needed to be transformed and removed to allow Lot and his daughters (inside) to be fruitful. Structurally, the wife (outside) becomes the daughters (inside). Like the case of Abram in M.I.1, normal values of inside and outside are inverted. Culture, the city, is outside while nature, the cave and pillar of salt, are inside.[1]

It is likely, however, that father–daughter incest was less mythologically acceptable than brother–sister incest. Thus Lot, rather than Abraham, is used in this text. Although it helps to create the structural logic by emphasizing the need for inside–inside relationships, the text is peripheralized because its main character is separate from the main line of descent and because the product of the incest, the Ammonites and the Moabites, were enemies of Israel. (See Chapter 8 where this element is developed regarding Israelite genealogies.)

3.12. *Wife/Sister 2*
Wife/Sister 2 is the final preparation for the birth of Isaac. Like *Wife/Sister 1*, this text resolves the ambiguous position of Sarah. She is completely transformed from wife (outside) to sister (inside).

> M.I.12. Abraham moves south to Gerar. Abraham tells Abimelech that Sarah is his sister rather than his wife; Abimelech takes her as a wife. God appears to Abimelech in a dream, telling him that Sarah is Abraham's wife. Abimelech returns Sarah to Abraham, asking Abraham why he had lied. Abraham answers that he was afraid he would be killed for his wife, and further, that she is indeed his sister, having the same father but a different mother. Abimelech gives Abraham great wealth. Abraham prays to God, and Abimelech and his people are healed; the text states that God had closed the wombs of the house of Abimelech.[2] (Gen. 20)

1. Throughout the biblical texts there is a constant opposition of city (settled life) with wilderness (nomadic life). Although the majority of Israelites lived in cities and therefore in actuality the city was inside (one lived in it), ideologically the city was outside. Thus the city (which was walled and safe) was ideologically dangerous, while the wilderness (dangerous and wild) was ideologically safe.

2. Fohrer attributes this entire section to E (1986: 161). It is already mentioned (see M.I.2) that he distinguishes between the three similar texts, assigning them to three different sources. It should be clear from the arguments presented above that it is equally possible that at least the two discussed in this chapter, M.I.2 and M.I.12, come from the same source, fitting into a pattern of doubled texts. In all the cases

The placement of this text immediately after the previous text is
significant. Both texts serve identical purposes, to make the wife (outside)
inside. As stated, the type of incest developed in this text is likely to have
been mythologically more acceptable than that developed in M.I.11. It
will have also been noted that this text is almost identical in structure to
M.I.3. This text, however, goes beyond the (narratively) earlier version.
Whereas the earlier text implied that Abram was lying, this text concludes
that Abraham was telling the truth. Sarah was indeed his sister—they
shared a common father but a different mother. Thus, where the earlier
text made Sarai relatively inside, this one completes the process.[1]

   This text also emphasizes the barrenness of natural fruitfulness. When
Sarah is taken into Abimelech's house all the women are struck barren,
yet when she is returned to Abraham she bears a son (in the following
text). In regard to Abraham Sarah signifies fruitfulness, while regarding
the Philistines she symbolizes barrenness.

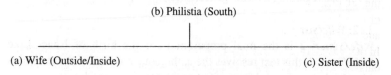

Figure 3. *Wife/Sister 2*

discussed, the second text of each pair contains new information which builds on the
previous text. The final redactor, at the very least, is creating a structure whereby the
latter half of Abraham's life recapitulates and finalizes the events which occurred in
the earlier parts.

   1. In 'Structure, Contradiction, and 'Resolution' in Mythology' (1981) Wander
applies the findings of Murphy and Kasdan (1959) to biblical myth. He convincingly
argues that the marriages of the patriarchs can be understood as FBD (father's
brother's daughter) marriages (consistent with the endogamous societies analyzed by
Murphy and Kasdan). In several respects, however, he misunderstands the biblical
text. In regard to Gen. 20.12, 'She is the daughter of my father but not the daughter
of my mother', he suggests that this merely means that Sarah is related to Abraham's
father's line but not his mother's (Wander 1981: 84). There seems, however, little
reason not to take the plain meaning of the text, that is, that she actually is his half-
sister. Nor does his argument explain the presence of no less than three texts in which
the patriarch claims his wife as a sister. In his later discussion of the incest of Lot and
his daughters, he concludes, 'By reducing FBD marriage to father–daughter incest, this
variant demonstrates just how close endogamous marriage is to incest while serving
yet to distinguish the two' (Wander 1981: 90). By the same structural logic brother–
sister incest would serve equally well, and equally emphasize the FBD relationship.

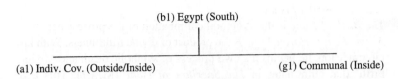

(b1) Egypt (South)

(a1) Indiv. Cov. (Outside/Inside)   (g1) Communal (Inside)

Figure 4. *Israel in Egypt*

a = a1   b = b1   (d = d1   e = e1   f = f1)   c = g1

a, a1, wife from north; b, b1, brought south; c, g1, brought completely inside; (d, d1, enslaved; e, e1, king punished; f, f1, emerge with wealth)
( ) = elements not diagrammed in Figures 3 and 4

Figure 5. *Structural Comparison of Wife/Sister 2 and Israel in Egypt*

The structures of *Wife/Sister 2* (and *Wife/Sister 1*) are mirrored on the broader level of Israelite myth (see Figures 3-5). The entire episode of Israel going down to Egypt, described in the last chapters of Genesis and concluded in Exodus, contains most of the same structural elements. In that case, however, the roles are reversed. Israel is outside (or relative outside) while God is inside—Israel is equivalent to the wife, God equivalent to the husband. The structural elements of the cases in Genesis are as follows: (a) the wife is brought from the north, (b) after a famine she is taken to the south (Egypt), (c) she is claimed as a sister (brought inside), (d) taken as a wife by the local king, (e) the king's people are punished, (f) Abraham emerges with great wealth. The structural elements of the Israel in Egypt myth are as follows: (a1) God brings Israel (Jacob and his family) from the north, (b1) after a famine God brings Israel into Egypt, (d1) Israel is enslaved by Pharaoh, (e1) the Egyptians are plagued, (f1) Israel emerges with great wealth, (g1) Israel makes covenant with God on mount Sinai. The only element not present in the second myth is (c). Yet if the function of the second myth and of the group of myths as a whole is examined it is clear that (c) is implicit in the second myth.

The role of this group of myths is to complete the process of making outside into inside. Thus, in the second myth, God completes the process of making Israel his people, represented by the covenant at Sinai. The myth clarifies what was implicit in Genesis. An individual covenant between Abraham and God becomes a permanent communal covenant in the same process that made Sarai, and later Rebekah, inside and thus fit to carry on the seed. Israel becomes God's eternal bride with the covenant on Mount Sinai.

3.13. *The Birth of Isaac*

The Birth of Isaac is the structural culmination of the process begun in *Abram Leaves Haran*. Isaac is the product of divine fruitfulness. With his circumcision, he begins his own process of symbolic death and 'divine birth' that culminates in *The Sacrifice of Isaac* (M.II.1). This text reintroduces Hagar and Ishmael, to emphasize the distinction between natural and divine fruitfulness, and between Israel (Isaac) and the nations (Ishmael). As in the previous case (*The Expulsion of Hagar 1*) both Ishmael and Hagar are rejected.

> M.I.13 (a) The Lord remembered his promise to Sarah, she bore a son who is named Isaac. Isaac was circumcised on the eighth day after his birth. When Isaac was born, Abraham was one hundred years old. The etymology for the name Isaac, given in the text, is that Isaac caused Sarah to laugh (see M.I.8 above).
>
> (b) *Expulsion of Hagar 2*
> Sarah sees the son of Hagar 'making sport' (perhaps of Isaac), and asks Abraham to cast out Hagar. Abraham is grieved at the loss of his son. God tells Abraham to follow the word of Sarah. He tells Abraham that the chosen line of descent will be through Isaac, yet Ishmael also shall be a nation. Hagar departs and goes to the wilderness of Beer Sheba. When the water runs out she fears Ishmael will die and calls upon the Lord. God tells her that Ishmael will be a great nation, and provides a well for them. The text concludes stating that Ishmael thrived in the desert and that he was given a wife from Egypt. (Gen. 21.1-21)

In the first half (a) there are several elements emphasizing the unlikely (unnatural) aspect of Isaac's birth. The first verse stresses God's part in the birth, stating that God 'visited' Sarah, and using the Hebrew root פקד. This root can mean 'visit', as well as 'visit upon' (i.e., 'cause to occur'). Thus this brings God in as a participant in the birth. Isaac's name also works to develop this structure. The name itself, meaning 'laughed', reminds us of Abraham's and Sarah's disbelief at the possibility of their having a son. This is strengthened by the last verse of part (a), v. 6, which provides the etymology of the name and adds that Sarah considered the birth to be, if not impossible, at least unlikely. The final element in this pattern is the statement of Abraham's age, one hundred years old, which would naturally preclude him from fathering a child.

The P stratum also brings in the element of circumcision. Circumcision functions on two related levels. Firstly, it may be seen as a denial of the male role in conception and as the male counterpart of barrenness. Both elements, in the male and female lines respectively, emphasize the divine aspect of the line of descent rather than the human element. Secondly, it should be seen as a symbolic sacrifice. Through circumcision the boy as a child of particular parents is symbolically sacrificed and transformed into a cultural entity of divine descent.

The second half of the text opposes Sarah and Hagar, as well as Isaac and Ishmael. The text negatively opposes Ishmael with Isaac by having Ishmael mock Isaac. Hagar is likewise negatively opposed to Sarah by the emphasis on her role as bondwoman. These oppositions are further developed through the creation of geographic distance; at Sarah's request Hagar and Ishmael are sent away from Abraham's household.

There is, however, an ambiguous note in the opposition of Isaac and Ishmael. In v. 12 God tells Abraham to heed the voice of Sarah, and that, although Isaac will carry on Abraham's line, Ishmael also will become a nation. This ambiguity about Ishmael stems from his mother being a concubine (see Chapter 8). His apparent genealogical closeness was removed through being only half inside,[1] a feature that opposes him to Edom, which was completely inside, as well as to Ammon and Moav who, due to their parents' incest, were also mythologically inside. The verse does, however, preserve a distinction between Isaac and Ishmael. Isaac remains in the line of descent as bearer of Abraham's seed, while Ishmael is a separate father of a nation. (See the distinction in terms in vv. 12 and 13.)

The text develops the opposition between Isaac and Ishmael on a second level. Hagar takes Ishmael to a well. This refers to a type-scene well known in biblical literature. Throughout the biblical text there was a convention that a well was a place of marriage (Alter 1981: 51). Thus, this text inverts the typical situation; here the well is tied to being cast out. Ishmael is therefore cast in a negative role. The usual equation developed is: hero (Israel) (+) + well (marriage), whereas in this text it is: hero (not-Israel) (x) + well (cast out). Since both the hero and the outcome are inverted then the value positive or negative also must be inverted therefore: $x = (-)$.[2]

There remains, however, an ambiguity, in that the text states that God

1. In this paragraph, inside and outside refers to the status of the parents rather than the mythological status of the nations, all of which were outside. Thus, completely inside means that both parents were inside at the time of birth, for example, Isaac and Rebekah the parents of Esau (Edom).
2. In this equation x = an unknown value. In this case the qualitative value is negative.

was with him as he grew up. Yet even that does not move his ideological value to positive. The negative element remains in the statement that he became an archer or hunter, an occupation ascribed to two negative figures, Esau and Nimrod. The text concludes with a final negative element firmly tying Ishmael to the outside, that is, Ishmael's marriage to an Egyptian.

There is, however, a second opposition developed in this text, between Abraham and Sarah. Abraham is saddened by the expulsion of his son and only expels him at God's assurance that God will be with Ishmael. This text puts Sarah into a negative light. It is possible that this opposition relates to the ambiguous position of the wife. Even within an endogamous system the wife must still be brought in from the relatively outside. Sarah remains ideologically unclear and consequently retains negative elements. This negative aspect of wife has been noted in several texts. In the two wife/sister texts examined above, wife was relatively dangerous compared to sister. Likewise Sarai as wife was negative in the initial expulsion of Hagar.[1]

3.14. *The Fight for the Well*
This text develops two types of oppositions. Abraham is opposed to the Philistines (the nations) who unjustly deprive him of his property. Perhaps more significantly, they deprive Abraham of a symbol of natural fruitfulness, leaving him with divine fruitfulness.

> M.I.14. Abraham makes a covenant with Abimelech, king of the Philistines. Their relationship, however, is marred by Abimelech's servants taking a well from Abraham, presumably Beer Sheba. The text concludes with Abraham giving Abimelech oxen, sheep and seven lambs. The seven lambs represent Abraham's right to the well which he had dug. The etymology of the name is attributed to this act (or to the oath that was taken, as the Hebrew word for oath is composed of the same letters). The word for seven in Hebrew being שבע (pronounced 'sheva'), the well was named Beer Sheba (in Hebrew pronounced 'Beer Sheva') (Gen. 21.22-34).

This text does not appear to develop any of the oppositions discussed above.[2] It distinguishes between Israel and the nations in that Abraham is pictured as magnanimous while Abimelech and the Philistines are portrayed as offending against the covenant between them. The only

1. The relationship between wife/women and danger is also examined by Aycock (1992: 481).
2. See M.II.5 where a similar text is discussed more fully.

other important element is that it establishes Israel's claim to the land.

It is possible that the well is symbolically connected to natural fruitfulness. Wells are often connected in the biblical text with marriage (see M.I.13 and M.II.2) and therefore natural fruitfulness. They are also logically the source of water for irrigation and therefore are necessary for the earth to bear life. Abraham's gift to Abimelech also emphasizes this connection. By seizing the well, the nations claim natural fruitfulness for their own.

3.15. *The Cave of Machpelah*

This is the first of two texts about Abraham which appear after M.II.1, *The Sacrifice of Isaac*. This text addresses the question of whether Sarah (and Abraham) can 'live' among the nations after they are dead. The text implicitly answers in the negative, the land must be Abraham's not the nations.

> M.I.15 After Sarah's death Abraham went to the city of the Hittites (Hebron) to get a cave in which to bury Sarah. He bargains with one of the Hittites (Canaanites), Ephron, who offers the cave as a gift to Abraham. The text concludes with Abraham buying the cave. The last verse (23.20) states that the cave and the field where it was located, passed from the possession of the Hittites to that of Abraham (Gen. 23).

This text can be understood in two opposing ways. On the one hand it can be seen as viewing relations with the local populations positively (rather than in the hostile manner found in other texts). On the other hand, it can be seen to fit into the pattern of opposition highlighted in the other Abraham texts. Abraham takes possession of the land by purchasing it and thus separates his portion from that of the local population, establishing his right to the land in perpetuity.

Abraham chooses not to accept the cave as a gift. On the narrative level, although Ephron (and the Hittites) may not have intended to give Abraham the field and cave, the offer is made. The offer is similar to that made by Shechem and Hamor in M.IV.1 (*The Rape of Dinah*) suggesting that Abraham can become (at least after death) part of their community. By emphasizing that Abraham bought the cave and further emphasizing the shift in possession (not from Ephron who owned it, but from the Hittites, suggesting that it was no longer part of their portion of land) the text rejects the possibility of living with Ephron and the Hittites, and thereby the possible identification of Abraham with the Canaanites. Sarah (and ultimately Abraham, Isaac and Jacob) cannot be buried among the Canaanites, rather they must be buried on their own land.

3.16. *Abraham and Keturah*
Like the previous text, this text appears (narratively) after M.II.1, *The Sacrifice of Isaac*. *Abraham and Keturah* emphasizes the transformation that has taken place. Abraham, no longer the bearer of the divine seed, marries a woman from the outside and has structurally outside children. These are placed in opposition to Isaac's children who are (at least for the time being) structurally inside.

> M.I.16 Abraham takes a third wife named Keturah. She bears him six sons and the text also lists ten grandchildren. The text states that Abraham gave all he had to Isaac, but to the sons of the concubines (Hagar and Keturah) he gave gifts. The sons of the concubines are then sent east. The text concludes with the death and burial of Abraham. (Gen. 25.1-18)

In this text Abraham as a progenitor becomes again, as he was prior to his third 'divine birth', the source of natural fertility. Keturah's children are clearly distinguished from the divine line of descent. This transformation in Abraham mirrors the opposite transformation in Isaac, who is transformed (M.II.1) and becomes the source of divine fruitfulness. It is clearly incompatible with the logic developed in the myth that there should be two simultaneous sources of divine fruitfulness. This would create the possibility of two divine lines of descent, and therefore defeat the logic of endogamy. Thus with his 'divine birth' Isaac replaces Abraham as the source of divine blessing.

Although the text initially calls Keturah the wife of Abraham, in v. 6 she is called a concubine. Like the child of Abraham's first concubine, the descendants of Keturah are ambiguous. This is discussed below regarding the genealogical material (Chapter 8). In a purely endogamous system it is logical that both the male and the female line should be essential for descent. Both must be inside (i.e., both from acceptable lines of descent). Thus it is internally consistent that those nations which are descended from a wife, rather than a concubine, should be mythologically more problematic. This element also explains Abraham's relationship with his sister. In effect she was not truly his sister because they shared only one parent in common.

As mentioned, v. 6 distinguished between the descendants of wife and those of concubine; between those who are inside and those outside. Isaac is given all that Abraham possessed (especially his blessing and role as carrier of the divine seed), while the sons of Hagar and Keturah are only given gifts. The opposition between the two is further developed by their relative movements. Isaac moves west, a positive direction, while the sons of the concubines are sent east, a negative direction.

3.16. *Synthesis*
The mythological texts about Abraham develop three interrelated oppositions. The primary opposition is between Israel and the nations, with Abraham representing Israel. This opposition is found in almost every text. It ties in with a genealogical paradox discussed below. If all the nations are descended from a single family, how can one nation be ideologically distinct from the rest? The development of this opposition resolves the paradox by creating logical distance between Israel and the other nations.

The second opposition also relates to this question and creates a logical distinction between Israel and the nations. Throughout the texts two types of fruitfulness are compared: divine and natural. Israel is the product of divine fruitfulness, while the nations are of natural fruitfulness. The text develops a logic in which natural fruitfulness is relatively barren in comparison to divine fruitfulness, and therefore implies that the nations are barren and thus distinct from Israel which is fruitful.

This opposition is also developed in a second way. As the text progresses Israel becomes genealogically distinct from the nations. This distinctness is due to the distinction in origin. The line of Israel is the product of God, while the nations are the product of nature. Thus there is a logical distinction between the two that overrides the original genealogical similarity. This opposition is supported by the texts which emphasize God's role in the birth of Israel as opposed to the human role. This is seen most clearly in regard to the birth of Isaac. Sarah's role is denied first by her barrenness and later by the natural impossibility of her bearing a child at so advanced an age. Likewise, Abraham's role is denied first by his circumcision (symbolic castration) and later by the related natural impossibility. Thus God becomes the ancestor of Israel rather than its actual human progenitors.

The distinction between natural and divine birth is also highlighted by the element of divine transformation. All of the ancestors of Israel go through a process whereby their natural birth is denied; they are symbolically sacrificed or killed, and then have a new beginning. This process of 'divine birth' removes them from the natural line of descent and emphasizes the element of divine descent. The process of 'divine birth' is also a process of transition between heros. After the 'divine birth' of Isaac, Abraham no longer carries the line of descent; the system, after all, is based on a single line, it would be logically impossible for both Abraham and Isaac to carry God's blessing and seed. Thus after Isaac's 'divine birth' M.II.2, Abraham's children would be outside rather than inside (see the discussion of M.I.15).

The third opposition is between the wife and sister, respectively outside and inside. The need to marry creates a logical problem: outside must be brought inside. The wife is always outside the husband's family and is therefore dangerous. The text develops a logic whereby the wife is brought inside. Rather than remaining wife she is transformed into sister and therefore made safe. Even with this transformation, however, the wife retains an aspect of danger and is often ambiguous or the source of trouble.

All of the oppositions center around the problem of inside/outside. They either work to develop strong logical boundaries or to obviate the problem when the two domains overlap. As is discussed below, all three oppositions relate to the logical problem of endogamy, with endogamy being the logical outcome of the structure. If the structure is attempting to create a clear pattern by which Israel is distinct from the other nations, then exogamy would blur or remove this distinction. Israelite endogamy, however, relies on this distinction to give it logical power. The first two oppositions create a logic whereby endogamy becomes the natural answer. If Israel alone among the nations is descended from God, then it is naturally impossible to marry into other nations. The third opposition resolves both a mythical question and a systemic question. Abraham (and his son and grandson) need to find wives from the outside; the text resolves this narrative requirement by showing that although the wives seemed from the outside, they were in fact inside. On a systemic level, the myth recognizes that even if wives are taken from inside, they are still ambiguous and dangerous to the husband's family because they are relatively outside.

Two important theoretical elements have also been highlighted in these texts. The differing uses of Lot by the text emphasize that symbols need not have fixed meanings. In different contexts symbols will have different context-related meanings, the meaning of the symbol being related to the structural needs of the particular text, rather than to the symbol itself. Thus in certain texts Lot is logically opposed to Abraham, while in others he is logically equivalent. This highlights the importance of understanding symbols contextually rather than through fixed interpretations.

The texts also highlight the importance of narrative development. Throughout the discussion of these texts, reference was made to the development of logical structures. Structures developed in one episode are often counterpoised to those developed in the previous or following text. It is also seen that the myth itself has a broader logical structure that organizes the relations of the different parts, and that knowledge of this broader structure is essential to the understanding of the logical structure as a whole. This supports T. Turner's reformulation of structuralist principles, by which both the metaphoric and metonymic are considered significant.

Chapter 4

ISAAC

This chapter examines in detail the myths about Isaac. Isaac mediates between Abraham, who initiates the relationship with God but comes from the outside, and Jacob who is the father of the people. Jacob is Israel and is inside from his very birth. This mediatory aspect of Isaac is reflected in his minor (and repetitive) role, even in the texts in which he is the primary figure. The majority of the narratively earlier texts about Isaac either include Abraham as a main character, for example, M.II.1, *The Sacrifice of Isaac*, or are almost direct repetitions of myths about Abraham, for example, *Wife/Sister 3*. In the rest of the texts Jacob is the primary actor with Isaac playing a supporting role. The texts examined also have several points of theoretical interest. In the discussion of M.II.1, *The Sacrifice of Isaac*, the process of inversion is analyzed, as well as the role of mediators in the text.

4.1. *The Sacrifice of Isaac*

The Sacrifice of Isaac sets the tone for all the texts about Isaac. Isaac is a passive (sacrificed) rather than an active figure. This text is, however, one of the clearest sacrifice and 'divine birth' texts (albeit symbolic) examined.

> M.II.1. God commands Abraham to take Isaac to a place that he will indicate and offer him up as a sacrifice. Abraham takes Isaac and two young men. After the third day, they arrive at Mount Moriah. Abraham and Isaac walk to the top of the mountain while the two young men wait at the bottom. Abraham builds an altar and places Isaac on top of it. Just as he is about to sacrifice Isaac, a voice comes from heaven telling him not to kill the lad. Abraham sees a ram caught in a thicket and sacrifices the ram in place of Isaac. God calls out a second time and tells Abraham that, because he did not withhold his son, God will multiply his descendants, and Abraham (and his descendants) shall be a blessing. Abraham then returns to his young men and they go to Beer Sheba. Upon Abraham's return Sarah dies (Gen. 22.1–23.2).

The initial opposition developed in the text is between Isaac and Ishmael. Ishmael, however, is not mentioned by name in ch. 22, and thus the opposition is implicit rather than explicit. In v. 2 God tells Abraham, 'take now thy son, thy only son Isaac, whom you love'. The text is clearly comparing Isaac to Abraham's other son, Ishmael, since the terms are used to single out Isaac. Rather than using a single term to describe Isaac, the text uses three. Each of these establishes Isaac as ideologically positive and, by implication, Ishmael as ideologically negative. He is the opposite of the terms used to describe Isaac.

This opposition ties into the one discussed in Chapter 3 (Abraham) regarding the distinction between Israel and the nations (i.e., that the nations are ideologically negative in respect to Israel). By characterizing Ishmael as structurally opposite to Isaac, the myth creates ideological distance between the two, overriding the genealogical closeness. A similar process is examined below regarding the genealogies in Genesis, where ideological distance is used in place of genealogical distance.

The text goes a step further, describing Isaac as Abraham's only son. Although this is false on a narrative level, it is an essential point on the mythological or structural level. It is the logical outcome of the opposition already established. The initial opposition created ideological distance between Isaac and Ishmael. This statement creates the logical possibility of genealogical distance as well, thereby strengthening the logical opposition of the two.

Although Ishmael is not mentioned by name in this text, there is a clear pattern of opposition developed in the narratively earlier sections of the myth. Ishmael is born prior to Genesis 17 (M.I.7, *The Covenant of Circumcision*) in which Abram is transformed into Abraham. Isaac is born after Genesis 17. The texts after Genesis 17 recapitulate the earlier events of Abraham's life. The recapitulated events are presented as the completion of the previous events, and as ideologically positive in relation to them.

There is also a clear ideological distinction between the respective mothers of Ishmael and Isaac. Whereas Hagar is identified as an Egyptian concubine, and therefore structurally outside, Sarah, at the very least, comes from Abram's family in Haran, and is therefore relatively inside. This ambiguous status of Sarah, however, is clarified in Genesis 20 (*Wife/Sister 2*) where the text states that Sarah is Abraham's sister, and therefore structurally inside.

The opposition is also developed regarding God's rejection of Ishmael and acceptance or choice of Isaac. God's rejection of Ishmael as the bearer of his blessing in Genesis 17 is identical with that of Eliezer in Genesis 15 (M.I.5, *The Covenant of the Pieces*), making Ishmael and Eliezer structurally equivalent. This equivalence is seen below in the discussion of Genesis 22 in the wider context of Hebrew mythology. Isaac, however, is specifically chosen to be Abraham's inheritor. And finally, upon Isaac's birth, geographic distance is created between the two with the expulsion of Hagar from Abraham's household. Thus in Genesis 22 and the preceding chapters there is a clear pattern of opposition between Isaac and Ishmael.

The second opposition developed in the text is between Abraham and Isaac. This opposition centers on the sacrifice (or attempted sacrifice). Abraham is opposed to Isaac through being the principal actor in the sacrifice. In effect Abraham symbolically reverses his role as parent, killing rather than creating a child. This opposition is weakened through the imposition of the ram, which prevents the sacrifice from occurring. The text, however, does not completely remove the possibility of Isaac's death. In v. 6 the text describes Abraham and Isaac's ascent up the mountain, stating that they went יחדו, 'together'. However, when the text describes Abraham's descent from the mountain, Abraham goes alone and Isaac is never mentioned. The text forces the careful reader to ask, 'where is Isaac?'

The sacrifice is seen as a structural element for several reasons. It is central to the text, being the primary focus of all action. Although the actual human sacrifice does not occur, a sacrifice is completed. The ram is sacrificed specifically in Isaac's place and the ram is thus structurally equivalent to Isaac. Finally, if the text is compared to the other structurally equivalent texts (see below) then it is seen that the fact of sacrifice, rather than the prohibition, is structurally significant.

The opposition between Abraham and Isaac, like that between Isaac and Ishmael, has its roots in earlier texts. This opposition, however, is of a different kind. The myth does not create ideological distance between Abraham and Isaac, rather it serves to remove Abraham from his parental role, allowing the possibility that Isaac was of divine origin.

Throughout the texts leading up to Genesis 22 there is a continual process whereby Abraham's role or possibility of being a parent is denied. In ch. 17 (M.I.7, *The Covenant of Circumcision*) Abraham is symbolically castrated through the covenant of circumcision. Circumcision may be taken as a symbol for castration because it is part of a structural set denying human fertility. It is parallel to barrenness in women (see M.I.6). Throughout Genesis the structure creates a paradox: natural, uncircumcised, uncastrated is barren, while divine, castrated, barrenness and circumcised is fruitful. Abraham himself articulates the unlikelihood of his having additional children in Gen. 17.17. In several places his advanced age is mentioned, further emphasizing the fact that the birth of a child was naturally unlikely. A similar pattern is developed regarding Sarah. Throughout the text her barrenness is emphasized, and, as in the case of Abraham, she denies the possibility of bearing a child at the age of 90 years. The final denial of Sarah's role in Isaac's birth comes after the sacrifice of Isaac. Prior to Isaac's symbolic 'divine birth' Sarah dies, emphasizing that she had no part in the transformation which can be seen as a symbolic 'divine birth' (as Isaac is symbolically sacrificed).

The death of Isaac (or the symbolic death of Isaac) is necessary in order to enable him to be symbolically transformed. The element of transformation or birth (the reverse of the sacrifice) is the structural center of the text; and, with the progressive denial of his physical parent, his spiritual parent comes to the fore. In Gen. 21.1 the text suggests that God played an important role in Isaac's birth: 'the Lord did to Sarah as he had spoken'. This creates the possibility that God was the parent rather than Abraham.

This denial of human parenthood is tied directly to the question of sacrifice. The sacrifice (or abortive sacrifice) removes Isaac from the line of human descent. His parents have been symbolically removed, and thus his 'divine birth' can be solely through divine agency rather than human agency.[1] Thus the opposition between Abraham and Isaac is really the opposition of two types of birth, that is, Human Birth–Divine Birth. This opposition can then be tied to the initial opposition, that is, Isaac–Ishmael—Isaac : Ishmael :: Divine Birth : Human Birth. As in the initial opposition the ideological value of Ishmael and human birth relative to Isaac and divine birth is (–).

The opposition can then be taken to a higher level. In Genesis heroes tend to have a corporate rather than purely individual identity. This

---

1. Isaac's sacrifice must be understood in the context of the structurally similar texts, that is, *The Murder of Joseph* and *The Murder of Abel* as well as the 'divine birth' texts M.I.5 and M.I.7. Although Isaac is not killed in the text and therefore also not reborn, he is structurally and symbolically killed, and structurally and symbolically 'divinely born'. This is emphasized by the role of the ram who replaces Isaac as the sacrifice.

phenomenon is best illustrated in the use of the name Israel for Jacob, and the names of the twelve tribes for his sons.[1] Thus Isaac structurally stands for Israel (the people of) and Ishmael for the Ishmaelites (and most likely the other nations). Thus the final equation is as follows: Isaac : Ishmael :: Divine : Human :: Israel : The Nations.

There is a second opposition that finds its center in the sacrifice: between Isaac prior to the sacrifice (a), and Isaac after the sacrifice (b). The text, however, imposes a mediator between this pair. In this case the ram is the mediator between Isaac (a) and Isaac (b). The ram is inverted in relation to Isaac. Prior to the sacrifice Isaac is a product of natural birth, and after the sacrifice of divine birth. The ram mirrors these elements. It is initially given by God (divine birth) but in its essence it is natural.[2] Thus the ram, in mediating between the two, is the logical replacement for Isaac in the sacrifice.

The opposition between the two aspects of Isaac is tied to a transference of blessing from Abraham to Isaac, passing of the divine seed from one to the other. Earlier in the text, Genesis 12, 15 and 17 (M.I.1, M.I.5 and M.I.7), Abraham went through a similar process of transformation. His relationship with his father's house was denied and he was symbolically transformed in *The Covenant of Pieces*. It is also possible that circumcision was also symbolic sacrifice supported by Abram's change of name to Abraham (see M.I.7, *The Covenant of Circumcision*). And, after the final 'divine birth' in Genesis 17 (M.I.7), the divine seed becomes fruitful and Isaac is born. With the symbolic sacrifice of Isaac (a), Isaac (b) is symbolically reborn and becomes the bearer of the divine seed and blessing in the place of Abraham.

It would be structurally illogical for both Abraham and Isaac to be carriers of the seed simultaneously, because the system is based on a single line of descent. The transfer of blessing is highlighted in Genesis 25, where Abraham, as in Genesis 17 before his final 'divine birth', has children with a concubine. These children are structurally opposed to Isaac. The opposition of Abraham's second set of children with Isaac is

---

1. The table of nations discussed below in regard to Israelite genealogies is also a good example of this phenomenon. In that text the nations are described in genealogical terms with each 'brother' or 'cousin' standing for a different nation or group of nations.

2. The text implies that the ram miraculously appears to be sacrificed. Earlier in the text Isaac asks, 'where is the animal for sacrifice?' Abraham replies that God will provide a sacrifice.

highlighted further on in Genesis 25 by a list of descendants of Ishmael, structurally equating the two groups. The opposition is completed in v. 23 where the birth of Isaac's sons is described.

Ideological distance was created between Isaac and Ishmael to overcome genealogical closeness.[1] The equation presented above adds a second level of distance. It suggests that Israel is of divine origin, rather than human origin, and therefore creates both genealogical and ideological distance. These two levels of distance are necessary to overcome a paradox created by Israelite ideology.

The text creates a paradox based on two mutually exclusive structures. On the one hand, if one God created the world, and people are descended from a single couple, then all nations are related and are, therefore, if not the same, at least similar. On the other hand, the text develops the ideology of endogamy that suggests that people are naturally distinct from one another, supporting the requirement to marry within. This paradox is reflected in the two types of genealogies found in Genesis: linear genealogies detailing the origins of Israel, and segmentary genealogies outlining the origins of the nations. The segmentary genealogies are tied to the ideology of single origin, while linear genealogies are tied to that of endogamy (see the discussion in Chapter 8).

The paradox is resolved initially by the imposition of ideological distance and then by the denial of genealogical relation by bringing in the element of divine descent regarding Israel. Genealogical closeness is dangerous, because it challenges the ideology of difference that is the basis of endogamy. If a nation is described as your brothers, then in effect they are almost you (at least relative to those nations genealogically more distant). Mechanisms must be developed to overcome, or cloud, the similarity.

Thus, although Genesis 22 does not include an actual sacrifice, by making the sacrifice the center of the text it creates the structural possibility that the sacrifice actually occurred, and by creating this possibility serves the structural needs of the system by developing an avenue of genealogical distance which overcomes the apparent similarity. This text leaves two ambiguous elements. The ambiguous nature of the sacrifice has already been mentioned. The second is found in the two unnamed young men whom Abraham takes with him to mount Moriah.

---

1. The pattern of using ideological distance indirectly related to genealogical closeness is found in regard to the genealogies of Israel and the nations in Genesis. See discussion in Chapter 8.

Both ambiguities are clarified when Genesis 22 is examined regarding the structures found in Genesis as a whole.

Genesis 22 is part of a broader structural set found throughout the book of Genesis. The same structural patterns of oppositions are found in the murder of Abel and the birth of Seth in Genesis 4, the myths about Abraham centering on his 'divine birth', that is, in Genesis 12, 15 and, with special emphasis, in Genesis 17 , the myths about Jacob with their center in Genesis 32, where Jacob wrestles with an angel and is transformed into Israel, and the myths about Joseph with their center in Genesis 37 (*The Murder of Joseph*). They are also partially found in Genesis 3, 6 and 48 (regarding Adam and Eve, Noah, and Ephraim and Manasseh respectively). They are also found in texts relating to Moses, and in the New Testament in myths about the birth, death and rebirth of Jesus.

In each of these texts the central opposition is the denial of human, natural birth in favor of divine birth. In several of the texts the sacrifice/ murder is actually carried out (e.g., Cain and Abel, Jesus). In other texts the sacrifice and associated birth are symbolic. This overall structural pattern resolves one of the initial questions, was Isaac sacrificed? Structurally, the answer is yes.

4.2. *Comparison of Genesis 22 with Genesis 37*

It is through comparison with an inverted version of the myth that the second ambiguous element of Genesis 22 can be clarified. The basic structural elements of Genesis 22 can be diagrammed as follows. On the horizontal are three points: A the father, B the son (as well as b being the ram) and C the two young men (*x* the unknown radical). The text also has a vertical axis, representing the direction of movement, in this case (+) an upward movement (Figure 6). The upward movement is illustrated in two ways: the mountain where the sacrifice is to occur; and the word for sacrifice itself להעלות, 'to raise up'. In Genesis 22 A (the father) raises (+ movement) B (the son) leaving C (the two young men) behind, b (the ram) is killed in the place of B (Figure 7).

Genesis 37 (M.IV.2 *Joseph and his Brothers*) is an inverted version of Genesis 22. In Genesis 37 Joseph is sent to the fields by his father, who remains behind. When he arrives, his brothers place him in a pit and discuss whether to kill him. Eventually he is removed from the pit and sold to the Ishmaelites or Midianites. Both the Midianites and the Ishmaelites should be regarded as mediators between the Israelites and the Egyptians. Whereas the Egyptians are completely outside in regard to Israel—they became genealogically distinct from the line that led to Israel in Genesis 11—the Midianites or the Ishmaelites are half inside and half outside. They are both descended from Abraham (albeit the Ishmaelites prior to his final 'divine birth' and the Midianites after he passed the divine seed to Isaac) and an outside mother. The brothers kill a goat and use its blood to prove that Joseph was dead. The structural elements of the text can be diagrammed as follows. On the horizontal axis are three points: A1 father, B1 the son (with b1 being the goat) and C1 the other sons of Jacob (Figure 8). The vertical axis in Genesis 37 is (–) because it involves a downward movement. In Genesis 37 C1 (the sons) lower (– movement) B1 (Joseph) leaving A1 (the father) behind, b1 (goat) is killed in the place of B1 (illustrated in Figure 9). In Genesis 37 the positions of the radicals are reversed from the positions found in Genesis 22, and the movement in the text is reversed.

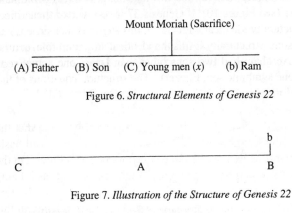

Mount Moriah (Sacrifice)

(A) Father   (B) Son   (C) Young men (*x*)   (b) Ram

Figure 6. *Structural Elements of Genesis 22*

b

C   A   B

Figure 7. *Illustration of the Structure of Genesis 22*

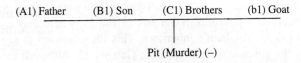

(A1) Father   (B1) Son   (C1) Brothers   (b1) Goat

Pit (Murder) (–)

Figure 8. *Structural Elements of Genesis 37*

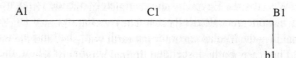

Figure 9. *Illustration of the Structure of Genesis 37*

The inversion is clearest in reference to the structural positions of A and C in Genesis 22 and A1 and C1 in Genesis 37, and on the y axis, the directional element in the text. The four radicals, the father's, the slave's and the brother's roles in the two texts are exactly inverted. In Genesis 22 the father sacrifices the son, while the young men remain behind, while in Genesis 37 the father remains behind while the young men kill their brother. The y axis is also inverted, Genesis 22 moving in an upward direction, and Genesis 37 downward.

Thus the relationship between the two texts is: A = C1, B = B1, C = A1, and b = b1 (see Figure 10). If Genesis 37 is re-inverted then C can be seen as structurally identical with $C1^{(-)}$, this suggests that since C1 is Jacob's other sons, structurally C fills the identical structural role, that is, that of sons (Abraham had two sons other than Isaac, one actual son, Ishmael, and one symbolic son, Eliezer).[1] The structural equations of the texts are therefore: $A : B :: A1^{(-)} : B1^{(-)}$ and $B : C :: B1^{(-)} : C1^{(-)}$.

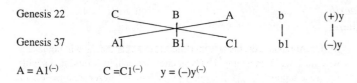

Figure 10. *Comparison of the Structures of Genesis 22 and Genesis 37*

Eliezer is mythologically equated with Ishmael (as a son) due to their structurally equivalent positions in Genesis 15 and 17, where they are rejected by God as Abraham's inheritors. This identification is also supported by the absence of Ishmael from Genesis 22. Although that text implicitly opposes Isaac and Ishmael, the opposition is weakened by the absence of Ishmael himself. If the young men are structurally equivalent to Abraham's sons, the structural logic of the text becomes much stronger.

1.   It is not suggested that the two young men were actually or necessarily Abraham's other sons, rather it is suggested that they fill the same structural position.

The two directional elements of the texts are also significant. Both the mountain and the pit are liminal spaces. They are the points where opposing domains meet. The mountain joins earth with sky, and the pit joins the world with the underworld. The liminal aspects of the movement enhance its danger and equally they strengthen the symbolic equation with death. The upward movement is more explicitly tied to death, 'to raise up' being the word used for sacrifice. The downward movement is tied to the Israelite conception of death, which involved going down to Sheol, a cave where the bones of the dead were gathered. Thus the two directions become structurally equivalent in Genesis 22 and 37.[1]

The final section of the text is the genealogy of Abraham's brother Nahor. This text centers on Rebekah, Isaac's future wife. The genealogy prepares the reader, and in structural terms justifies the upcoming marriage of Isaac. By showing the genealogical relationship of the two it suggests that Rebekah is structurally inside, and therefore an appropriate marriage partner.

4.3. *The Wooing of Rebekah*
With his 'divine birth' in the previous text, Isaac took on the mantle of the divine seed. He was symbolically prepared to continue the line of descent. *The Wooing of Rebekah* is the logical conclusion of the *Sacrifice of Isaac*. The significant element in this text is the role of Eliezer, who mediates between inside and outside.

> M.II.2. Abraham asks his servant (Eliezer) to swear that he will not take a wife for Isaac from among the Canaanites. Instead, he should find a wife for Isaac among Abraham's relatives in Haran. Eliezer then travels to Haran. When he arrives he waits at the city's well and asks God for a sign to indicate which girl is destined to be Isaac's wife.[2] Rebekah arrives and fulfils the dictates of the sign. Eliezer then asks Rebekah who she is. When he finds out that she is related to Abraham (brother's son's daughter) he thanks God. Eliezer asks Rebekah's family if he can bring her to Canaan to be Isaac's wife, and they agree. Rebekah travels to Canaan and marries Isaac. The text concludes by stating that his marriage consoled Isaac for the loss of his mother (Gen. 24).

1. The structural significance of the type of death and its relation to the vertical and horizontal levels of opposition is discussed in Kunin 1994: 69.
2. The importance of the well as a symbol of a proper marriage is discussed above in regard to text M.I.13. For a similar text, see M.III.5, *Jacob Marries Rachel and Leah*.

The initial section of the text emphasizes the element of endogamy. Isaac's wife must come from Abraham's family back in Haran rather than from the Canaanites. This element is further emphasized in the following chapter (Gen. 25), which lists both Abraham's children from his third wife, Keturah, as well as Ishmael's wives and children. Isaac and his descendants are logically opposed to the children of Keturah and those of Ishmael. As mentioned above, after M.II.1 (*The Sacrifice of Isaac*), Abraham has passed on the divine seed to Isaac. His children born after M.II.1 are equivalent to those born prior to M.1.7 (i.e., Ishmael) and are structurally outside. This is emphasized through Keturah (presumably a Canaanite) who is also structurally outside. Likewise Ishmael is logically opposed to Isaac and his descendants through his marriage. He marries an Egyptian woman, logically outside, thus emphasizing his distinction to Isaac who must marry inside. This myth explicitly develops the equation Israel : Nations :: Endogamy : Exogamy :: Divine Seed : Natural Seed, with the product of endogamy carrying both the divine seed and the blessing.

Eliezer acts as a mediator in this text. He is both inside and outside. The text introduces Eliezer using three terms: his servant, the elder of his house, ruler over all his possessions (Gen. 24.2), thus making him structurally inside—possibly equivalent to Abraham. He does, however, retain the outside elements developed in the previous texts (see M.I.5 and M.II.1). This is emphasized throughout the text by his own words. He always describes God as 'the God of Abraham my master', rather than 'my God'.

Eliezer mediates between two worlds: Canaan, which is inside and that of Haran which is outside. The danger of Haran is stressed through Abraham's making Eliezer promise that Isaac should not return to Haran. Eliezer, who includes elements of both, is the logical person to go to Haran and bring back a wife for Isaac. By mediating the gap, Eliezer is able to begin transforming Rebekah from outside to inside. This transformation, however, is not completed until M.II.4 (*Wife/Sister 3*).

Although Rebekah's family is inside relative to the other nations, they are still outside in regard to Israel. The text develops this aspect in two ways. The first is through the behavior of Laban, Rebekah's brother. The text implies that Laban fulfilled his obligations as a host only after seeing the gold and gifts which Eliezer had given Rebekah, subtly opposing his greed to the behavior of Abraham described in earlier texts. This element is also found in v. 55 where Rebekah's family attempts to delay Eliezer's return to Canaan.[1]

It is likely that the ambiguity of the wife's family works on two related levels. First, in the myths in Genesis the wife's family is, by definition, outside of the chosen line of descent. In a sense the parallel-cousin marriage described is making the best of a bad situation. Marriage to a sister would be ideal (totally inside) but, since this is impossible, marriage to a cousin is the next best thing. Mythologically, the wife is later transformed into the object of preference, that is, sister. On a sociological level, even in a community following a rule of endogamy, the wife is from outside the immediate family and is thus an object of suspicion. This latent hostility may also be projected onto her family.

4.4. *Two Nations at War*
Like the opposition between Ishmael and Isaac developed in the texts about Abraham (and implicitly in *The Sacrifice of Isaac*) *Two Nations at War* continues the pattern. The opposition between Jacob and Esau, however, is more significant. Jacob (as seen below in M.III.10, M.III.12) is directly associated with Israel (his name is changed to Israel) and Esau is associated with Edom, Israel's greatest enemy.

> M.II.3. Isaac entreated the Lord because Rebekah was barren. The Lord hearkened to Isaac's prayer and Rebekah conceived twins. The twins struggled within her and she despaired and sought advice from God. The Lord told her that the two fetuses in her womb represent two nations. And that the elder nation shall serve the younger. When the babies are born the first born is called Esau because he was ruddy (and hairy). The second is called Jacob because he held onto his brother's heel. The word יעקב (the Hebrew name for Jacob) meaning one who takes by the heel. Upon growing up Esau becomes a hunter, while Jacob becomes a quiet man (Gen. 25.19-26).

This text contains several important elements. The initial point of interest is Rebekah's barrenness. Her condition is identical to Sarah's as described in the previous chapter (M.I.5 and M.I.7), and like Sarah, Rebekah requires special intervention by God to bear children. Hence, barrenness in the matriarchs, that is, Sarah (M.I.5) and Rachel (M.III.6), as well as many other key feminine figures in the text, is part of a broader process of denial of human participation in birth in favor of divine participation.[2] Birth of the Israelites requires divine intervention

---

1.   This myth is retold in expanded form in text M.III.3, *The Wives of Jacob*.
2.   Wander incorrectly suggests that barrenness is a denial of only the female

and thus establishes the logic that the origins of Israel are different from those of the other nations.

This text emphasizes the distinction between divine fruitfulness and natural or human fruitfulness in a second respect. Rather than bearing a single child, Rebekah bears twins after God's intervention.[1] This highlights the paradox illustrated in the following equation: Human Fertility : Human Barrenness :: Parent of One (normal birth) : Parent of Many. Although divine fruitfulness is based on human infertility, it is much more fruitful than natural human fertility. This is further emphasized by the explanation of the struggle in Rebekah's womb. Not only is she the mother of twins, she is also the mother of nations.

The text also emphasizes the element of chosenness regarding Israel, as opposed to the other nations who are part of the natural order in which elder is greater.[2] Israel is specifically taken out of the natural order. Israel is descended from people chosen by God rather than by nature. This element is found throughout the text: Seth is Adam's third born, Shem is Noah's third son, Isaac is Abraham's second son, Joseph is Jacob's eleventh son, Ephraim is Joseph's second son, and Moses is also a second son. This aspect of chosen descent is part of the logic by which Israel is distinguished from the nations: Israel : Nations :: Chosen Order : Natural Order :: Divine : Natural.

The text also begins the process of opposing Esau to Jacob. Their struggle begins in the womb and the prophecy suggests that it will be ongoing. Their appearances and names are also opposed. Esau is so red

---

line. In his argument emphasizing FBD marriage he attempts to show that the female line is denied in order to strengthen the ideology of descent in the male line (1981: 81-82). Although he is correct that the female role is consistently denied, he ignores the fact that the male line is also denied in several ways, including a direct statement in which Sarah emphasizes the unlikely nature of Abraham bearing a son. When Wander deals with this section he ignores this statement (1981: 92).

1.   Wander suggests that the two children (who are logically opposed) reflect a duality in Rebekah herself. Rebekah is a mediator (my terminology) between inside and outside, the two aspects are divided between her sons: Jacob is inside and Esau is outside (1981: 86).

2.   This is based on the concept of primogeniture. This concept is taken for granted throughout the text (even though it is consistently overturned): Cain's murder of Abel may be tied to Cain's understanding of his rights as eldest son; Isaac planned to give Esau his blessing; Reuben sleeps with his father's concubines, a sign that he expected to inherit his father's position; and Joseph expected Manasseh to receive the blessing from Jacob (see also the discussion of primogeniture in 2.3).

(an abnormal condition) that his name is derived from the color. The name also implicitly ties Esau to Israel's greatest enemies, the Edomites (whose name comes from the Hebrew word meaning red). Later in the text Esau is said to be the ancestor of the Edomites. Esau is hairy while Jacob is smooth.[1] Jacob's name is taken from his actions, holding on to his brother's foot; his name also can mean supplanter, prophesying that he will be chosen to carry on the line, as opposed to Esau, the elder, who would normally inherit the birthright and blessing. The description of the two as boys also adds to the opposition. On the one hand, Esau is described as a hunter. This occupation is mythologically negative since both Nimrod and Ishmael (who are ideologically negative or, at the very least, ideologically opposed to Israel) were also described as hunters. Jacob, on the other hand, is described in terms neither positive nor negative.[2]

4.5. *Wife/Sister 3*

Like the two previous wife/sister texts, this text examines the problematic position of wife in the Israelite system. The wife represents the outside and is therefore dangerous. Like the previous texts, this text resolves the crisis by symbolically making the wife into sister.

> M.II.4. Due to famine in the land of Canaan, Isaac and his family go south to the land of the Philistines. Fearing that the people of the land would kill him to take possession of his wife, he asks her to say that she is his sister. After Isaac has been in the land a short while, Abimelech, king of the Philistines, sees Isaac sporting with Rebekah and concludes that Rebekah is Isaac's wife rather than sister. Abimelech confronts Isaac, who admits that she is his wife. He stays among the Philistines and becomes even more wealthy. The Philistines envy Isaac and stop up the wells which Abraham had dug. Abimelech, fearing Isaac's strength, asks him to leave. Isaac moves north to Gerar (Gen. 26.1-17).

Of the three wife/sister texts examined (M.I.2, M.I.12 and M.II.4), this text is the most abbreviated. It occurs in the same location (Gerar) and

---

1. Hallpike suggests that hairiness in biblical texts is associated with being outside of society (1979: 104). This fits in with my argument that Esau = hairy is outside while Jacob = smooth is inside. All the biblical texts which he mentions develop this opposition of inside–outside. I suggest, however, that this opposition can equally be associated with sexual license (in agreement with Leach 1958). If inside = endogamy, that is, in Israelite terms sexual control, then outside = exogamy, that is, sexual license. Thus hairiness = outside = sexual license.

2. It is likely that Jacob's ambiguous nature before his 'divine birth' is meant to emphasize the transformation which occurs in that myth when he becomes Israel.

with the same king (Abimelech) as did M.I.12. In this text Rebekah is not taken as a wife by the king and therefore there is no immediate punishment. Indeed, after seeing her 'sport' with Isaac, he prohibits any man from touching her. Even in this shortened form, however, the structural purpose is still served. Mythologically, the connection between wife and danger is made, as well as the associated correlation of sister with safety. The logic is weaker than M.I.12 because the text has clearly stated Rebekah's actual relation to Isaac, yet the mythological possibility that they are brother and sister is created and Rebekah is thereby brought within.

This text is a necessary preparation for M.III.1 in which Rebekah, now inside, perceives the will of God. Rebekah, rather than Isaac, understands that God has chosen Jacob over Esau. In line with this understanding, Rebekah forces Isaac to accept God's choice. It is seen, however, that Rebekah's actions are also part of a broader structure in which the wife, as representative from the outside, is a source of danger and potential conflict within the family structure (see the discussion regarding M.III.1, *Theft of the Blessing*).

Wife/Sister 3 has many of the structural elements found in the exodus from Egypt. This structural connection was also observed above regarding *Wife/Sister 2*. There is one additional element in this text. Whereas in the previous two texts Abraham left Egypt and Gerar respectively after Sarah was discovered to be his wife, in *Wife/Sister 3* Isaac remains and grows increasingly wealthy until the Philistines fear him. A similar pattern is perceived regarding Israel's stay in Egypt. This adds further support to the argument that the two groups of texts (i.e., the wife/sister texts and the exodus texts) serve similar purposes. The wife/sister texts make Sarah and Rebekah suitable wives for Abraham and Isaac, and the exodus makes Israel a suitable wife for God.

In *Wife/Sister 2* the punishment for taking Sarah as wife was barrenness. This punishment was directly related to the transformation in Sarah's mythological role, that is, with the change in her name she became the source of divine fruitfulness. This element seems to be lacking in *Wife/Sister 3*, though it may be present in a transformed form. The text concludes with the stopping up of the wells dug by Abraham. Thus they actually destroy the fruitfulness of the land, representing natural fruitfulness. If the symbolic tie of wells to marriage is added to the equation, then stopping up of wells should be seen as metaphorically stopping up wombs, that is, barrenness, in both cases caused by the actions of the Philistines: in *Wife/Sister 2* by the actions of the king and in *Wife/Sister 3* by actions of the people.

4.6. *War of the Wells*
This text examines two related oppositions. On the one hand, it examines the relationship between divine and natural fertility. On the other hand, it further develops the opposition between Isaac and his neighbours, and thereby the opposition between Israel and the nations.

> M.II.5. Isaac unstopped the wells that the Philistines had stopped. As he unstopped these wells, his herdsmen fought with the people of Gerar who claimed the wells for themselves. Isaac then returned to Beer Sheba where God appeared to him and told him not to fear. The Philistines approach Isaac and, seeing that God was with him, ask to make a covenant with him. They make a covenant at Beer Sheba. The text concludes with a brief statement that Esau married two Canaanite women and that his parents were very upset by this (Gen. 26.18-35).

The initial section of this text is almost identical to M.I.14. It is likely that digging wells was tantamount to a claim on the land, thereby explaining the conflict over the possession of the wells. It is also possible that there is a second structural element. We have seen above (M.I.13) that the well was symbolically (or narratively) tied to the concept of marriage. Thus digging wells may be connected to marriage with the land. A further step is also possible. The land was intimately connected with God's promise to Abraham and his descendants, in effect a bride price. Thus the claim on the land enacted in the digging of wells is also a claim on God, in distinction to the Philistines who lacked such a claim.

The text concludes with a further statement opposing Jacob and Esau. It states that Esau married two Canaanite women. This makes Esau and his descendants both ideologically and genealogically more distinct from Israel. This text should be seen as preparation for Jacob's return to Haran to find a wife (M.III.4).

4.7. *Synthesis*
The texts about Isaac are part of a broader pattern whose beginnings were traced in the previous chapter, which attempts to create a logical distinction between Israel and the nations. This opposition is developed on the genealogical and ideological levels, creating genealogical distance through death and resurrection, and ideological distance through rejection. The opposition of natural and divine is also developed through the concept of choice. Throughout Genesis there is a pattern in which

natural choice is opposed to divine choice. In almost every case individuals who would normally carry on the line of descent, who by birth were the natural leaders, are set aside in favor of divine choice.

This characteristic pattern is seen in the choice of Isaac over Ishmael, of Jacob over Esau, of Joseph over his brothers, of Judah over Reuben, and possibly of Shem over his brothers. The age of Shem given in the text suggests that he was not the eldest son.[1] The pattern is also found in the 'historical books' regarding Samuel and David, both of whom conform to most of the structural elements described above. The element of divine choice is found on a tribal level with Saul. Saul (the first king) is said to come from the tribe of Benjamin, the smallest and youngest tribe. This opposition is mirrored in the broader concept of chosenness. Chosenness should not be seen as a separate ideology from endogamy, but rather as the theological expression of endogamy.

All of the oppositions that were developed in the texts about Isaac are part of the overall structure of Genesis and Hebrew mythology. They are further developed in the texts about Jacob and Joseph. Isaac is a transitional figure mediating between Abraham (outside to inside) and Jacob (inside). With the birth of Esau, the process of segmentation is concluded. Esau's (the Edomites) is the last nation descended from the main line, while in respect to Jacob, all his children are included within Israel. Genesis itself works to resolve the paradox alluded to above. It uses both mythological text and genealogical material to create ideological and genealogical distance, thereby resolving the paradox in favour of endogamy, which is the cultural choice.

The mythological texts about Isaac, concluding with the birth of Jacob and Esau, prepare for an important transformation. There is a diachronic progression in the text in which, in each generation, the main (divine) line is distinguished from the off-shoots (natural). With the birth of Jacob, this process is complete. All Jacob's children and descendants are inside and part of the chosen line of descent. This process of transformation is

1.   The question regarding Shem's genealogical position is based on Noah's age when his first child was born. The text states that Noah was five hundred years old when he began to have children (Gen. 5.32), and that the flood occurred in the six hundredth year of his life. Therefore at the end of the flood his oldest son would have been one hundred years old, and thus could not have been Shem—who would only have been ninety-eight. Therefore his oldest son must have been either Yaphet or Ham. One other indication in Genesis itself that this may be the case is found in Gen. 10. Here, in the table of nations, the descendants of Shem rather than being enumerated first are listed after those of Yaphet and Ham.

tied to Isaac's role as a mediator. Abraham had two (three) wives, one within and one (two) without. Likewise, each wife produced a son, one within and one without. Isaac, like Jacob, has a wife who is within, yet like Abraham he produces one child within and one without. And finally, all Jacob's wives are within (even the origin of the concubines is not mentioned) and all his children are within.

Chapter 5

JACOB

The previous two chapters introduced the structures of Israelite mythology. The chapter about Abraham examined texts that included most of the essential structures and illustrated many of the processes through which they developed. The Isaac myth presented in Chapter 4, rather than substantially developing or introducing new structures, served as a mediator between Abraham and Jacob. The key area of transformation between Abraham and Jacob is the movement from outside to inside. Abraham is the father of nations (inside and outside), while Jacob is the father of the nation. This chapter examines the process through which Jacob is transformed into Israel and the divine line passes to all the sons rather than one chosen son.

Two paradoxical structures are developed in the Jacob texts. On the one hand, all Jacob's children are inside as the ancestors of tribes of Israel, and the primary opposition is therefore between the tribes and the nations. On the other hand, the structure of opposition between brothers persists, and is most clearly developed in the following chapter ('Joseph and his Brothers').

Of the structures of transformation investigated in the previous chapters, several are also present in the texts examined here. These structures include inversion in *Jacob and the Ladder*, and mediation and clouding in *Jacob Steals the Blessing*. An additional element is present in this text, that is, doubling of structure. This transformation is found throughout the Joseph story and is introduced in *The Covenant at Bet El*.

5.1. *Esau Sells his Birthright*

The conflict between Jacob and Esau, the opposition between Israel and Edom, is the central focus of the first few texts of the Jacob myth. The texts, besides developing the broader opposition, examine a narrative question: how does the younger son inherit in place of the elder? This text offers one possibility. The elder son sells his position to the younger.

> M.III.1. Esau became a hunter and Jacob stayed by the tents of his parents (perhaps as a shepherd). Isaac loved Esau because Esau was a hunter and brought him game from the field. Rebekah loved Jacob. One day Jacob was making some pottage when Esau returned from hunting. Esau was starving and begged Jacob to give him some pottage. Jacob said, sell me your birthright for the pottage. Esau agreed to this bargain, and sold Jacob his birthright (Gen. 25.25-34).

The text begins with an interesting inversion. The father loves the rejected son while the mother, who is from the outside, loves the chosen son. This inversion of expected affections in the family is probably tied to the theme of divine chosenness rather than human choice or expectation. The text sets up the situation in which not only is the eldest son, by definition, the possessor of the birthright,[1] he is also the father's favourite and has every expectation of receiving the blessing. As part of the general structure of denial of natural patterns and human expectations, it is the second son who supersedes his brother and becomes God's chosen. In later texts this inversion is emphasized by Isaac's blindness. His physical condition also can be taken as symptomatic of spiritual blindness. He is blind to God's choice.[2]

The narrative level of the text recognizes this inversion. In order to counterbalance the association between Isaac and Esau, and Rebekah and Jacob (each an inside outside pair) it makes a narrative association between Rebekah and Esau. Both Rebekah and Esau use almost identical words: Rebekah when complaining about the struggle inside her (25.22) and Esau in despising his birthright (25.32). Thus the use of common words unites Rebekah and Esau, both of whom are outside, and makes the implicit association between Isaac and Jacob, both of whom are inside.

This myth compares Jacob and Esau, with Esau being consistently ideologically negative. As stated in Chapter 4, Esau is described as a hunter or an archer, symbolically tying him to Nimrod and Ishmael, both of whom were ideologically negative. In this text the opposition is also on a second level. Esau is the hunter connected with the field, and possibly nature and natural processes, while Jacob stays at home and

---

1. The word for birthright in the text comes from the word meaning eldest son.

2. Compare Isaac's blindness with Jacob's in *Jacob Blesses Ephraim and Manasseh*. In that text, although he is blind, Jacob crosses his hand to give Ephraim (the younger son) the primary blessing.

cooks and is closely tied with the normative cultural form (pastoral nomadism).

Jacob's pottage is not a 'natural' product. It is more likely that he is cooking a domesticated lamb, that is, a product of culture. This identification of the pottage as a product of culture is supported by comparison with a variation of the text in Genesis 27. In that text Jacob, with Rebekah as a mediator, cooks for Isaac a pottage of goat (cultural/ domesticated), in opposition to the pottage of game that Esau is to prepare. As in this text, it is the pottage prepared by Jacob that obtains the blessing.

Although it is not suggested that a nature–culture opposition is characteristic of all mythological systems or cultures, it is hard to escape the opposition in this text. Esau is symbolically tied to nature, the hunt and game, while Jacob is symbolically related to the tent, cooking and domesticated animals. In the conclusion of this and related myths Jacob, culture, is chosen over Esau, nature.

Esau is opposed to Jacob in a second respect, which is also introduced in the previous chapter. This opposition works on two related levels. On the one hand, Esau is described in the text as a stupid man. Rather than identify the pottage by name he says, 'give me some of the red red stuff'. His limited intelligence is also emphasized by his short-term approach to life. He sees only his immediate need instead of the long-term benefits of keeping his rights as eldest son.

Jacob, on the other hand, is by implication and description the opposite of Esau. He takes advantage of Esau's needs to gain important long-term ends. The text concludes with a blanket condemnation of Esau stating, 'thus Esau despised his birthright'. Thus, throughout this text, Esau is portrayed as ideologically negative. Jacob, however, is not completely positive. In all the narratively early texts about him, he gains his ends by trickery. This ideological ambiguity is only transformed in M.III.10, *Jacob Wrestles with the Angel*, when Jacob is transformed into Israel.

On a second level, the words 'red red stuff' emphasize a more significant opposition between Jacob and Esau. Esau's words are used to explain a second etymology of his name. In M.II.3, *Two Nations at War*, Esau was called אדמוני ('admoni' meaning 'red') because he was ruddy. In this text the name is tied to his use of the word 'red'. 'Give me some of the red red stuff, for I am faint; therefore was his name called Edom (red)' (Gen. 25.30). In both cases the emphasis is on Esau's tie to the nation of Edom. This identification of Esau with the Edomites, more than any other element in the texts, emphasizes his opposition to Jacob. Historically Edom was Israel's greatest enemy.

The text progressively deepens the opposition between Jacob and Esau. This opposition develops from a struggle in the womb, to Jacob and Esau finally meeting as leaders of opposing peoples, and agreeing to go their separate ways. As discussed below regarding the genealogies in Genesis, the ideological opposition is necessary to create distance to overcome mythological genealogical closeness. Esau is Edom, precisely because Edom and Israel were ideologically diametrically opposed.

5.2. *The Wives of Esau*
The Wives of Esau offers a justification for Esau's rejection. He marries outside, and is therefore rejected. The text prepares the ground for the following text (M.III.3) that is possibly negative in respect to Jacob. Through rejecting Esau, it makes Jacob's questionable acts acceptable.

> M.III.2. When Esau was forty years old he married two Canaanite women. His parents were not happy with his action (Gen. 26.34-35).

It is Esau, the beloved son, who marries out and causes his parents grief, not Jacob. The text clearly indicates that in spite of Isaac's preferences, Jacob is the son meant to carry on the chosen line rather than Esau.

This opposition is further emphasized at the end of the next text M.III.3. Here Rebekah tells Isaac that Jacob should not take a wife from the daughters of Het (as Esau had done) and Isaac charges Jacob not to take a wife from among the Canaanites, but to return to Paddan-aram (another name for Haran) and take a wife from Rebekah's family. The importance of 'not marrying the daughters of Canaan' as a structural element is further emphasized at the end of the second text. It states that Esau, seeing that Isaac blessed Jacob and commanded him not to marry a Canaanite, went and married a daughter of Ishmael (Abraham's son). Although this lessens Esau's ideological opposition, it does strengthen the emphasis on endogamy. Ishmael's daughters, however, like the Canaanites remain outside and are thus structurally unacceptable. This text emphasizes the ideological imperative of endogamy as well as creating further ideological distance between Jacob and Esau, and Israel and Edom.

5.3. *Jacob Steals the Blessing*
This text completes the process that began in M.III.1. In that text Jacob bought the rights of the first-born, in this text he steals the blessing.

Rebekah functions as a mediator, removing some of the blame from Jacob.

> M.III.3. (a) Isaac is old and blind. He realizes that his death is approaching, so he calls Esau, his first-born son, to him. He asks Esau to go out and hunt and bring him some venison to eat, after which he promises to bless Esau. Rebekah hears this discussion and reports it to Jacob. She tells Jacob to get two goats from the flock, out of which she will cook food for Isaac (in order to trick Isaac into blessing Jacob rather than Esau). Jacob reminds his mother that Esau is a hairy man while he is smooth, and that perhaps Isaac will feel his arm to see who is speaking to him. Rebekah dresses Jacob in Esau's garments and places the skin of kids on Jacob's arms. Then Jacob approaches Isaac, gives Isaac the food and asks for the blessing. Isaac hears the difference between Jacob's and Esau's voices but is finally convinced when he feels Jacob's arms. Isaac eats the food and blesses Jacob. After Isaac finishes blessing Jacob, Esau returns from his hunt and brings a dish of food into Isaac's tent. Isaac realizes that he has been tricked, but only one son can receive the blessing. Isaac does, however, bless Esau, prophesying that Esau will serve Jacob and that he will live by the sword. Esau hated Jacob and promised himself that, after their father's death, he would kill Jacob. Rebekah tells Jacob to leave Canaan and go for safety to her brother's house in Haran.
>
> (b) Rebekah tells Isaac that she does not want Jacob to marry a Canaanite woman (as Esau had done). Isaac calls Jacob and tells him to go to Paddan-aram, to the house of Betuel (MB), and to take a wife from Betuel's family. Isaac commands Jacob not to marry a Canaanite and blesses him a second time. Then Jacob goes to Paddan-aram. Esau hears his father's command to Jacob not to marry a Canaanite woman. He therefore takes a wife from the daughters of Ishmael (Gen. 27.1–28.9).

The opposition between Jacob and Esau introduced in the preceding texts, implicit in the text describing their struggle in the womb, continues in this myth. In M.III.1 the text introduced a pattern of opposition based on appearance. Esau was ruddy while Jacob presumably had normal coloring. This type of opposition is carried into this text. Esau is described as hairy while Jacob was smooth. This pattern also applies to personality and occupation. Esau is a hunter while Jacob is a shepherd.

These oppositions function on a variety of levels. The primary level of the physical characteristics is discussed below in regard to the semantic associations of the words שֵׂעָר and אָדוֹם ('hairy' and 'red' respectively). These characteristics, however, also work on a simpler level. On the one hand, they create a clear opposition between Jacob and Esau, who, as twins, should be identical and therefore structurally interchangeable. By developing these opposite physical characteristics, their identity as twins is overcome. On the other hand Esau's characteristics are, in certain respects, similar to animal characteristics, that is, he is exceptionally hairy. This association is emphasized both by a semantic association (the word שער 'hairy' also means goat) and a narrative element, Jacob uses kid skins to convince Isaac that he is Esau. There is a clear association of Esau with nature (and thereby natural birth) and, by implication since he is Esau's opposite, a connection of Jacob with the divine.

In using divine as the opposite of 'nature' or, as discussed above, 'natural birth', there is also an association of divine with culture. The opposition suggested here is that the myth creates a dichotomy in which the other nations and their cultures are associated with nature and natural birth, while Israel and its culture is associated with culture and divine. Israelite myth, as a handmaiden of Israelite culture, validates Israelite culture as divine.

This type of dichotomy is also developed regarding the respective professions of Jacob and Esau. Jacob is a shepherd fitting the ideal cultural model (at least regarding the ideological preference for the nomadic way of life). While Esau is tied directly to the natural world as a hunter. This opposition is further developed in the respective foods prepared by Jacob (Rebekah) and Esau. It has been noted above (regarding M.III.1) that Esau prepares a natural product, venison, and Jacob prepares a cultural product, domesticated lamb.

It was discussed regarding the birth of Jacob and Esau that the physical aspect of 'ruddiness' was symbolically and etymologically tied to the Edomites, Esau's descendants and the principal enemies of Israel throughout their history. It is probably not too far-fetched to suggest that the term (and characteristic) was used precisely to make this connection.

Another similar connection is developed in this myth. Esau is described as a hairy man. The word for hairy in Hebrew is שער, This word is virtually identical (and in sound precisely identical) to an alternative name of the Edomites based on a mountain in their territory, Mount Seir. This characteristic, like ruddiness, makes a linguistic connection between Esau and the Edomites. Both examples emphasize the structural opposition between Jacob and Esau. Esau, from the moment of his birth, is identified and condemned with his descendants, the Edomites, as the enemies of Israel.

The second opposition central to this text is between Isaac and Rebekah. This opposition emphasizes in part the unlikely (unnatural) aspect of

Jacob receiving the blessing, and thereby emphasizes the element of divine choice. It also works on a second level—a level that is found throughout the Jacob texts—the ambiguous nature of the women. The role of Rebekah is ambiguous if not negative (or at least dangerous). She, rather than Jacob, develops the plans through which Isaac is tricked and the blame for the fraud rests on her shoulders rather than Jacob's. This is emphasized in vv. 12-14 where Jacob fears that, if Isaac finds out, he will curse him. Rebekah states that the curse (i.e., the blame) will be upon her.

Rebekah acts as a mediator in the text, being both inside and outside. She has become a sister (*Wife/Sister 3*) but still represents an external force; the stigma for the fraud is removed from the chosen line of descent and placed on the representative of the outside. Some of the blame must be shifted from Jacob as he must be mythologically acceptable as the bearer of the divine blessing.

In almost all biblical texts about women, they are ambiguous or dangerous. This was already observed in regard to Sarah (and Rebekah) in the wife/sister texts. It is also seen regarding Eve (M.V.2), and later regarding Tamar (*Judah and Tamar*, M.IV.4) and Dinah (*The Rape of Dinah*, M.IV.1). The woman is a representative of the outside, with her relations and alliances in the family. Mythologically she is dangerous because she challenges endogamy which would prefer to be purely incestuous. Sociologically, the wife is at best a necessary intruder from the outside, possibly retaining ties with families competing for the same resources. This aspect of the ambiguity is developed below regarding Rachel's family—especially her father—who are consistently portrayed in very negative terms.

The first half of the text creates a structurally problematic situation. Although it supports the structural element of chosenness through inverting the natural (perceived as natural) pattern of descent, Jacob still has received the blessing under false pretences and therefore the blessing and divine seed may not have been truly passed to him. This problem is resolved in the beginning of the second half, where Isaac again blesses Jacob, but this time knowingly. This part of the text does not seem to know (to take into account) the previous story. Thus, part (b) confirms the blessing and the divine descent that were ambiguously presented in part (a).

Part (b) also emphasizes the importance of endogamy as a structural element. Rebekah introduces the text by complaining about the daughters of Het (who were Esau's wives). The text emphasizes that such women were not appropriate wives for Jacob and, by implication, for Israel. The proper source of wives is introduced, namely Abraham's (and Rebekah's) family in Paddan-aram (Haran). This point is further emphasized in the conclusion of the text, where even Esau attempts to follow the rules of endogamy. Esau as symbol is transformed in the text. In part (a) he is used in opposition to Jacob/Israel while in part (b) he is used positively to support the logic of endogamy.

5.4. *Jacob and the Ladder*
Symbolic 'divine births' are found throughout Genesis. *Jacob and the Ladder* is the first of three 'divine birth' texts in the Jacob myth. This text begins the 'divine birth' of Jacob and prepares for Jacob's marriage in the following texts.

> M.III.4. Jacob went from Beer Sheba towards Haran. He arrived at an unnamed place and spent the night there. He used a stone as a pillow and slept. During the night he dreamed. In his dream he saw a ladder between earth and heaven, with angels ascending and descending. The Lord stood beside him and blessed him. When Jacob awoke he declared that God is present in that place. He used the stone to build a pillar and called the name of the place Beth El (House of God). He then swore that, if God would aid him in his journey, he would serve God (Gen. 28.10-22).

It is likely that this myth is a highly clouded sacrifice and birth text. Several elements are missing. Jacob is the only human participant and therefore there is no one to kill or sacrifice him, and no actual sacrifice or murder takes place. However, it does have several elements that support this identification. The text is both narratively and thematically parallel to M.III.10, *Jacob Wrestles with an Angel* and M.III.12, *The Covenant at Beth El*. The first two texts are in complementary places regarding Jacob's stay in Haran. M.III.4, *Jacob and the Ladder*, occurs just prior to Jacob's arrival in Haran and M.III.10, *Jacob Wrestles with an Angel*, occurs just after his departure. Both texts occur when Jacob is alone in a liminal space. In M.III.4 the ladder ties heaven and earth and in M.III.10 Jacob is in the fork of a river—that is, neither fully water or land.

The third text, M.III.12, *The Covenant at Beth El*, directly corresponds to the second. Each text gives a different reason for the change in Jacob's name to Israel. The third text also structurally corresponds to the first text. Both are said to occur in the same location, have substantially similar blessings, and Jacob builds a pillar in both. As discussed below regarding the specific texts (M.III.10 and M.III.12), the second two texts center on Jacob's symbolic 'divine birth', emphasized by his being given a new name. The second text, M.III.10, *Jacob Wrestles with an Angel*, also includes the element of sacrifice, graphically depicted in the night of wrestling. Thus if the current text is structurally equivalent to these texts, it is likely that it too deals with sacrifice and 'divine birth'.

Other elements within the text that support this identification include the stone which Jacob uses as a pillow (possibly a symbolic altar), and the presence of the ladder in the text provides a visual metaphor for Jacob's (possible) ascent to heaven and therefore his symbolic death. The angels ascending and descending also should be seen as mediators for Jacob. By having the angels ascend (sacrifice) and descend in Jacob's stead the possibility of Jacob actually ascending in the structure of the myth is completely clouded.

This text is also an inversion of M.I.1, *Abraham Leaves Haran*. In that text Abraham leaves his father's house (Haran) for Canaan and is blessed by God. In this and the previous text Jacob leaves his father's house (Canaan), travels to Haran, and he is blessed by his father. Both texts center on the aspect of symbolic birth. The difference in source of blessing is significant. Whereas Nahor (Abram's father) was outside, and thus could not be the source of blessing, Isaac is inside and thus can be. Jacob must, however, leave his father's house to be transformed, because divine birth is antithetical to human birth.

5.5. *Jacob Marries Rachel and Leah*

Jacob Marries Rachel and Leah contains several interesting elements. It emphasizes the ambiguous role of affinal kin. In this text and the following texts, Laban (who represents the affinal kin) is consistently negative. The text also functions in a similar way to the wife/sister texts, making Rachel sister instead of wife.

> M.III.5. (a) Jacob continued his journey and arrived at a well, which he is told is at Haran. Rachel (MBD) then arrived at the well. Jacob rolled away the stone covering the well and watered the flock of Laban (MB). Jacob then identified himself to Rachel and to Rachel's family. (b) Jacob then agreed to serve Laban for seven years in exchange for Rachel as his bride. After the seven years Laban gave Jacob Leah, his elder daughter, as a bride rather than Rachel. After Jacob complains, Laban agrees also to give Jacob Rachel as his wife in exchange for another seven years of service. Jacob loved Rachel more than Leah (Gen. 29.1-30).

This text is a typical well text, a mythological motif that is discussed above (M.II.2). There is, however, one difference. In this text the well is covered by a stone that the local shepherds apparently cannot move. This obstacle is removed by Jacob in order to feed Laban's sheep. The connection between well as a symbol of natural and divine fertility has already been developed. This myth further expands that theme. Jacob, representing divine fertility, is able to move the rock and release the fertility of the well, whereas the shepherds, representing natural fertility, are unable to do so. Thus this emphasizes the equation Natural Fertility : Divine Fertility :: Barrenness : Fertility. Natural fertility is barren while divine fertility is fruitful. The text also develops the other level of the opposition, that is, between Israel and the nations. The shepherds, the men of the land, represent the nations while Jacob represents Israel. Thus Israel : Nations :: Fruitfulness : Barrenness.

The second half of the myth (b) is structurally equivalent to the wife/ sister texts discussed in the previous two chapters. Like the previous three myths (*Wife/Sister 1*, *Wife/Sister 2* and *Wife/Sister 3*), this myth seeks to resolve two related problems: the danger and ambiguity of the wife, and the problem of outside–inside. The dangerous position of the wife (and the associated negative view of her family) is given human form in this text by the figure of Laban, Jacob's father-in-law. Throughout the text he is consistently portrayed as a negative character. He cheats Jacob, forcing him to work a second seven years for Rachel, attempts to withhold Jacob's wages, and in the first text which mentioned him (M.II.2, *The Wooing of Rebekah*) implies that he is greedy. In the subsequent texts Laban pursues after Jacob to prevent him from returning to Canaan with his family and wages (see M.III.6 below). Thus Laban personifies the structural and sociological problem inherent in the myth and system: the need to take a wife from outside the immediate family. In the earlier three wife/sister texts the danger was portrayed as coming from a totally external source (with a king— possibly a symbolic father—mediating, clouding the crisis by removing the actual father and family). In this text the crisis is placed directly into the wife's family of origin.

This myth uses a different method than the wife/sister texts for bringing the wife inside, that is, making her a sister. Jacob is initially forced to marry the unwanted sister, Leah. By becoming his wife, due to the structure developed in the earlier (wife/sister) texts, she is already mythologically almost his sister. When he eventually marries Rachel, rather than marrying someone from the outside, he actually marries his symbolic sister, because she is his sister's sister.

5.6. *Jacob's First Eight Children*

Although, all Jacob's children are structurally inside, the process of opposition of brothers (and wives) continues. The primary mytheme apparent in this text is Rachel's barrenness. This mytheme is found consistently throughout the biblical text and usually highlights the chosen line.

> M.III.6. The Lord saw that Leah was hated so he opened her womb, while Rachel was barren. Leah then had four sons: Reuben, Simeon, Levi and Judah. Seeing that she did not get pregnant, Rachel gave her handmaiden (Bilhah) to Jacob to bear children for her. Bilhah had two sons Dan and Naphtali. These sons were named by Rachel and claimed as her own. Leah then gave her handmaiden (Zilpah) to Jacob. She bore him Gad and Asher who were named and claimed by Leah (Gen. 29.31-35; 30.1-13).

The children of Jacob are structurally distinct from either the children of Abraham or Isaac. Whereas Abraham and Isaac each had one son inside and one outside. All Jacob's children were inside. As the myth progresses narratively, there appears to be a process of removing the metaphorical dross until the pure product remains.

Although on the surface the pattern of one barren mother and one fertile mother appears to be identical to that described regarding Sarah and Hagar, there are significant differences. These differences are focused on in the first words of the section. The fruitful wife, rather than representing natural fruitfulness, is also remembered by God. The text states that 'her womb was opened by God'. Leah's children, like the future children of the barren wife, are products of divine fruitfulness.

The myth does, however, work on both levels. On the one hand, Leah's children must be of divine descent because they represent tribes of Israel. On the other hand, the myth, perhaps paradoxically, develops the previous structure. The wife, through whom the chosen line will continue, is barren in order to emphasize that God is necessary for divine fruitfulness—as in the texts about Abraham denying the human element of fertility in favor of the divine. Joseph, Rachel's eldest son, as first among equals with his brothers, carries on the chosen line.

The role of God is also emphasized regarding the birth of both Leah's children and the children of the handmaids. The text gives an etymology of each name that focuses, in many cases, on God's role in the birth.

The name Reuben, for example, is explained as deriving from ראה יהוה
בעניי, meaning 'God saw my affliction'. Thus God is the active partner in
the birth of the sons from all four mothers, be they actual wives or
concubines.

The role of the handmaids in this text is also clearly distinguished from
that of Hagar and Keturah described above in Chapter 3. In that myth
the concubines' children were outside and separate from the chosen line,
while in this myth and the following myths the children of the
handmaids are inside and represent tribes of Israel. In Genesis 16 Hagar
is described as an Egyptian, making her outside. In this chapter the
origin of the handmaids is never mentioned, creating the mythological
possibility that they were, like Rachel and Leah, inside.[1]

There is also a difference between how Sarah received the birth of
Ishmael and how Leah and Rachel received the birth of their handmaids'
children. Although Sarah, like Rachel and Leah, gave Hagar to Abram
to bear sons for her, she did not accept Ishmael as her son. In this myth,
however, Rachel and Leah accept and claim their handmaids' sons as
their own, thereby bringing them inside. This is further emphasized by
the naming of the boys. In each case it is either Rachel or Leah who
names the baby and, as if it was their own, the name given represents
how the 'mother' felt upon the birth. In the myths describing the birth
of Ishmael, he is named by either his actual mother or Abram, his father.

5.7. *Reuben and the Mandrakes*

Reuben and the Mandrakes is probably an incest text. In the context of
the other incest text in which Reuben plays a part (*Reuben Sleeps with
his Father's Concubine*), it is negative rather than positive. This
ambiguous or negative quality is due to Reuben's structural position. As
first-born, he is structurally rejected.

> M.III.7. One day Reuben went out to the field and found some mandrakes
> which he brought to his mother. Rachel asked for some of the mandrakes,
> and in exchange agrees that Jacob should lie with Leah that night. Leah

---

1. This possibility is further developed in the post-biblical and midrashic
expansions of the text. In the *Testament of Naptali*, a second-century BC text from the
Pseudepigrapha, Bilhah and Zilpah are said to be the daughters of Rotheus who was
from Abraham's family and thus inside. This tradition has its roots in a time close to
the canonization of the biblical text and is also found in a Qumran 4 fragment. (I am
indebted to M. Jacoby for bringing this text to my attention, Jacoby 1994: 6-8).

bears two more sons and a daughter: Issachar, Zebulun and Dinah. Finally God remembered Rachel and she bore a son that she named Joseph (Gen. 30.14-24).

At first glance, the initial section of this text is structurally ambiguous. It is unclear what role the mandrakes play, or why Reuben is the one to find them. The structural role is somewhat clarified by comparison with a structurally similar text discussed below, M.IV.2, *Reuben and his Father's Concubines*. In that text Reuben, seeking to take the privileges of his father (as first-born), sleeps with his father's concubines. *Reuben and his Father's Concubines* fits structurally in the context of M.I.11, *Lot and his Daughters*, as well as the wife/sister texts. In order to emphasize the structural premise of endogamy (in this case), symbolic incest is emphasized in the text. In M.IV.2 and in *Lot and his Daughters*, however, the type of incest illustrated (i.e., father–daughter or mother–son—between generations rather than across generations) appears culturally problematic. Thus in one case it is condemned and in the other it is applied outside of the main Israelite line.[1] Condemnation aside, the texts still function to focus on the mythological preference for incest.

Thus *Reuben and the Mandrakes* may be a subtle reference to this type of incest, structurally parallel to *Reuben and his Father's Concubines*. Mandrakes were a plant that resemble the male sexual organ, thus a son giving them to his mother may represent incest between the two. Due to the apparent problematic nature of this type of incest (though it was mythologically and structurally acceptable) the events are hinted at rather than graphically portrayed.

The mandrakes also function on a second level. They, as a product of nature, represent natural fruitfulness, and as such Rachel requests some of them to make her fruitful. Rather than make Rachel fruitful, God remembers Leah (who lacks mandrakes) and she has three more children. This text works on the opposition of natural fruitfulness, represented by the mandrakes and Rachel being barren, and divine fruitfulness, represented by Leah who has no mandrakes (and has symbolically made herself barren by giving away a source of fruitfulness), being fruitful. The text concludes with a further emphasis on divine fertility by attributing Rachel's ultimate pregnancy to God's agency: 'God

---

1.   There is, however, one case of intra-generational incest which is not seen as negative, that is, that of Judah and Tamar. In that case the incest should be seen as redressing an imbalance created by Judah's marriage to a Canaanite women. This is discussed in detail in regard to M.IV.4, *Judah and Tamar*.

remembered Rachel, God harkened to her, and opened her womb', stressing God's role through the use of three different terms.

5.8. *Jacob Returns to Canaan 1*

Jacob Returns to Canaan 1 continues to focus on the same elements as the previous text. The antagonism towards affinal kin is strongly emphasized. The element of danger is also found. This mytheme is found in the final part of the text, in which Rachel steals her father's household gods.

> M.III.8. (a) After the birth of Joseph, Jacob decided that it was time to return to Canaan. Jacob asked Laban to give him his wives and children and wages for his work. Jacob offered to take as his wages all the speckled and streaked goats and the dark sheep. Laban agreed to this, yet before giving the herds to Jacob, he removed all the types specified by Jacob and gave them to his sons. After receiving the herds Jacob used sympathetic magic and selective breeding techniques to increase the number and the strength of the streaked and spotted goats and the dark sheep that remained in the herd.
>
> (b) Jacob heard that the sons of Laban accused him of taking all their father's property. He then saw a vision of God, commanding him to return to Canaan. He called his wives and explained to them why he wanted to leave their father's house. Furthermore, Jacob attributed the increase in his flocks to divine intervention. Rachel and Leah agree that they should leave. Prior to their departure Rachel steals her father's teraphim (household gods) (Gen. 30.25-43; 31.1-21).

This text focuses on the opposition between Jacob and Laban. Laban, the father of Jacob's wives, attempts to cheat Jacob of his wages and, in turn, is tricked into giving Jacob the best of his flocks. This opposition works on two related levels which have been alluded to above: the problem of endogamy, and the structural conflict between in-laws. Laban, as an ideologically negative figure, mediates between his daughters and Jacob. Since Rachel and Leah have been made inside, they are not structurally suitable to express the danger they represent in the system. Laban, who is their father, stands one step further outside and therefore is a more appropriate carrier of the hostility. Through his negative characteristics, actions and portrayal, Laban represents the danger of marrying out, and thereby emphasizes the importance of endogamy.

It is also likely that Laban exemplifies a sociological hostility, even within the group, expressed towards the wife's family. Her family, although inside and acceptable to provide brides, is still relatively outside the husband's family and therefore dangerous. This internal hostility is best understood when compared to the Israelite understanding of space. The world is understood as a set of concentric circles, with each smaller circle being progressively holier until the center is reached culminating in the Holy of Holies in the Temple. Likewise, people form such circles, with each family being its own center. Thus tribal endogamy unites the disparate families who must go beyond their boundaries because of the laws of incest. Incest, however, is structural and mythological preference. It should be noted, however, that this image of concentric circles ends at Israel's borders on both the geographic and kinship levels.

The text includes two versions of Jacob's breeding programme, one in part (a) and the second in part (b). Both of these presentations include a magical or divine element in the programme. In the second version, which is reported as a dream, the divine element is the primary aspect (thus better developing the structural opposition).[1] Both cases work on the opposition of divine and natural fruitfulness. Laban, by removing the spotted and streaked animals, expects that, through natural fruitfulness Jacob will end up with very few animals. Through divine (or magical) intervention, however, Jacob gains the majority of animals supporting the structural logic in which divine fruitfulness is more fruitful than natural fruitfulness.

The text concludes with Rachel stealing her father's household gods. Like the initial opposition discussed, that is, between Jacob and Laban, this element of the text is linked to the structural danger presented by the wife to the family (as an intruder from the outside). The act itself brings physical danger to the family in the form of pursuit by Laban (see *Jacob Returns to Canaan 2*). It also emphasizes that the wife brings external (and possibly negative) elements into the family structure that can lead to its destruction. This text is part of a broader structure in which women are consistently portrayed as dangerous or negative. An exemplar of this structure is the story of the apple in the garden of Eden, where all men's troubles are attributed to Eve.

5.9. *Jacob Returns to Canaan 2*
This text continues developing the same structures as *Jacob Returns to Canaan 1*. The central point of the text is Rachel's theft of her father's gods. As in the wife/sister texts, the wife creates a situation whereby the chosen line is endangered.

---

1. It is possible, however, that Jacob is lying about the dream. This is the only dream in Genesis which is not independently reported by the narrator.

M.III.9. After several days Laban returned to his home and found that
Jacob has fled. Laban gathered his men and pursued after Jacob and after
seven days caught up with him. That night God spoke to Laban and
commanded him not to harm Jacob. Laban then approached Jacob asking
why he had fled secretly and finally accusing him, 'why did you steal my
gods?' Jacob responds that he left because he was afraid and that Laban
can search all of his goods. Rachel hides the household gods from her
father by sitting on them, telling Laban that she is menstruating. Jacob then
accuses Laban of having dealt falsely with him over the twenty years of
their association. Finally they agree to make a covenant. Laban asked
Jacob to swear that he will take no wives other than his daughters. The
heap of stones they set up serves as a boundary between the land of the
Arameans (Laban's people) and Israel. The next morning Laban returned
to his home (Gen. 31.22-54; 32.1-3).

This text continues the primary opposition developed in the previous
text. Throughout the myth Laban is opposed to Jacob. And equally,
Rachel is highlighted as a potential source of danger. The text also
creates an opposition between the God of Israel and the Teraphim. After
accusing Laban of having dealt falsely with him, Jacob attributes all his
good fortune to the God of his fathers. Indeed, in the previous section,
the increase in his flocks is directly tied to divine action. This is opposed
to the impotence of the Teraphim. Not only were they impotent to
prevent the growth of Jacob's flocks, but they were also stolen and
hidden by Rachel under the pretext of menstruation—ritual uncleanliness.
Thus the text develops five levels of opposition. Jacob : Laban :: Family :
In-laws (affines) :: Israel : Nations :: God : Teraphim :: Clean : Unclean.
Based on this equation Laban, affinal kin, nations and the Teraphim are
all equally negative and impotent.

5.10. *Jacob Wrestles with an Angel*
Jacob Wrestles with an Angel is the second of three 'divine birth' texts.
On the narrative level (and on the structural level) this text prepares for
Jacob's meeting with Esau. Jacob is no longer the same man who fled
from Esau. He becomes the transformed bearer of the divine seed. This
text also introduces an important transformation in structure. Jacob is
transformed into Israel, a transformation of both himself and his sons.
They are all inside as tribes of Israel.

M.III.10. (a) After the departure of Laban, Jacob sent messengers to his
brother Esau. The messengers were to tell Esau that Jacob was returning.
The messengers returned and told Jacob that Esau was coming to meet

him with four hundred men. Jacob was greatly afraid at this news. He divided his camp in half in the hope that Esau would only smite half. Jacob then called upon the Lord to remind him of his promise. He then sent ahead gifts of animals of the flock to Esau.

(b) Jacob then arose and sent his family across the river and waited. He wrestled with a man all the night until sunrise. The man touched Jacob's thigh and it was strained, and the man asked that Jacob release him. Jacob refused unless the man would bless him. The man asked him his name and then renamed him Israel, giving the etymology of Israel as 'one who struggles with God'. When Jacob asked the man his name, he replied, 'why do you ask my name?' The man then blessed Jacob. Jacob named the place Penuel (the face of God). The text concludes by associating the prohibition from eating the sinew of the thigh to this myth (Gen. 32.4-33).

The first half of this text develops the opposition between Jacob and Esau which culminates in the next myth, *Jacob and Esau*. The text builds suspense by emphasizing the likelihood of revenge in Esau's approach with four hundred men. It is possible that the structural opposition between the two is also indicated in the division of his camp. The two camps representing Israel and the nations respectively.

The second half of the text (b) is structurally more straightforward. It is one of three myths of 'divine birth' included in the Jacob saga. The first, *Jacob and the Ladder* (M.III.4), was discussed above and the third, *The Covenant at Bet El*, is discussed below (M.III.12). M.III.4 and M.III.10 frame the events in Haran and thus are structurally equivalent (at least regarding narrative structure).

This equivalence is strengthened when all three texts are analyzed together. The key elements of the first text are the stone (implicit altar for sacrifice), the ladder, the blessing and the name of the place (Bet El). Of these elements three (five) are shared with the third text: (the symbolic sacrifice and birth), the location, the blessing, and building a memorial pillar. The second text includes elements of both the first and third. With the first text it shares two inverted elements (and a third uninverted element): Jacob approaches Esau (as opposed to running away); Jacob is returning from Haran to Canaan (as opposed to going to Haran from Canaan); (the symbolic sacrifice and 'divine birth'). It shares one mythologically central element with the third myth: the symbolic 'divine birth', through which Jacob becomes Israel. When all three texts are taken together, each progressively strengthens the structural equivalence, adding elements missing in the others, with the second text bridging the gap between the other two.

The structure of symbolic sacrifice and 'divine birth' is most clearly presented in this version of the myth. The element of sacrifice is emphasized in the wrestling and in the name of the place, Penuel (Face of the Lord). Jacob states, 'For I have seen God face to face, and my soul was delivered' (Gen. 32.31). This statement implies that the usual result of seeing God's face is death. The verb that is translated as 'delivered' (נצל) is strange in this context, usually meaning saved or rescued. It suggests that, upon seeing God's face, he indeed died and his soul was rescued.

The identity of the 'man' or angel is also ambiguous. Throughout the text he is identified as חאיש, 'the man'. He is identified as an angel (God or a god) only by implication. The man fills three structural roles: father, brother and God. These structural identifications are based on structural comparison with M.II.1, *The Sacrifice of Isaac*, and M.IV.3, *Joseph and his Brothers*. In the former the father sacrifices, and in the latter it is the brothers. The role of parent or brother in the sacrifice is structurally important because it emphasizes the opposition of divine and human birth, as well as that between Israel and the nations (see *The Sacrifice of Isaac*, M.II.1).

The identification with the structural role of brother is supported by Esau's prominent role in the surrounding texts and by this text's preparation for the reconciliation and final separation of Jacob and Esau. The identification of the man with the role of brother is supported in another respect. The wrestling is structurally equivalent to the fighting between Jacob and Esau in Rebekah's womb. This equivalence is also further evidence that this text is a symbolic birth.

The identification with the role of father is suggested by an element in the structurally equivalent text M.III.12, in which Rebekah's nurse (Jacob's mother) dies. It is likely that, structurally, this refers to Rebekah, that is, Jacob's mother, rather than a nurse who was never previously mentioned. Thus, upon Jacob's 'divine birth' (symbolized by a new name), his mother is symbolically removed, thereby denying human fertility in favor of divine fertility. This denial would be strengthened by a parallel denial of the father.[1]

The third structural role filled by the wrestler is that of God. In the other 'divine birth' texts discussed above, the final element of the myths was the symbolic transformation or birth. In each of those cases the text

---

1. These two identifications, however, are not developed in the text. It is likely that one or the other will be found in rabbinic expansions of the myth.

implies that God is the agent of the transformation or symbolic birth. The element of 'divine birth' is present in the conclusion of this myth, symbolized by the change in name. As the 'man' is the agent of 'divine birth', he fills the structural role of God.

The final element is the damage to Jacob's inner thigh. It is probable that this refers not to the thigh but to the male reproductive organ. In M.II.2, *The Wooing of Rebekah*, Abraham asked Eliezer to swear an oath by placing his hand under Abraham's thigh, in effect swearing on Abraham's future generations. The damage to Jacob's thigh can thus be understood as a euphemism for symbolic castration analogous to circumcision. Indeed, this text is structurally equivalent to M.I.7, *The Covenant of Circumcision*. Both texts include changes in names (symbolic birth) as well as symbolic castration. In each case the text seeks to emphasize the aspect of divine birth at the expense of natural birth.

Perhaps coincidentally the two texts also conclude with ritual actions and their explanations. Thus, in *The Covenant of Circumcision*, the text gives the rules concerning circumcision, and in *Jacob Wrestles with an Angel* the text explains the prohibition against eating the sinew of the thigh in animals. This connection of ritual with myth works on several levels. It emphasizes the complementary role of ritual with myth. Ritual uses symbols in a similar way to myth with the same structural ends. Ritual and myth also mutually validate each other. Thus, by its existence and performance, the ritual proves (in its cultural context) that the myth actually occurred, because we are still performing the act that it established. Equally, the myth justifies and validates the performance of the ritual.

5.11. *Jacob and Esau*

The opposition between Jacob and Esau characterizes much of the Jacob myth. This text offers the possibility of ending the opposition, but rejects it at the conclusion of the text. Jacob goes one way and Esau the other.

> M.III.11. The next morning Jacob saw Esau approaching. He approached Esau at the front of his family and bowed down before him. Esau welcomed Jacob with open arms. Although Esau invites Jacob to journey with him, Jacob begs to follow behind (because the children and animals will slow Jacob down). Esau continued his journey to Seir, and Jacob journeyed to Sukkoth and then on to Shechem in the land of Canaan (Gen. 33).

This text is structurally similar to M.IV.1, *The Rape of Dinah*. M.IV.1 deals with the crisis of similarity. It poses the possibility of the people of

Shechem becoming part of Israel, concludes that the similarity is not authentic and creates ideological distance with the destruction of Shechem. Similarly, this text offers the possibility of a complete reconciliation and unification with Edom.

The text opens with the reconciliation of Jacob and Esau that is necessary to prepare for the separation. Prior to this point in the myth, the fault (or negative element) in the relationship lies with Jacob. He caused the split through questionable action. With his 'divine birth' in the previous text, this ambiguity is removed and Jacob becomes ideologically positive. This transformation is reflected in his positive reception by Esau. Thus this text (and the previous text) allow Jacob and Esau to part on Jacob's terms rather than Esau's. The text raises the possibility of similarity and, by their separation, responds that the similarity is more apparent than real. The text itself makes the analogy with M.IV.1, *The Rape of Dinah*, by mentioning Shechem and Hamor in its concluding verses.

5.12. *The Covenant at Bet El*

The Covenant at Bet El is the final 'divine birth' text. It offers an alternative version of Jacob's transformation into Israel and symbolically removes Jacob's parents with the death of Deborah, Rebekah's nurse. The text also prepares for the transition to Joseph. Rachel, Joseph's mother, dies in childbirth thereby denying her role as mother. Benjamin (the child born in this text) is structurally equivalent to Joseph.

> M.III.12. God commanded Jacob to go to Bet El and make an altar to God. Jacob told his household to put away all strange gods, and Jacob hid them under the Terebinth in Shechem. Deborah, Rebekah's nurse, died at Bet El. God appeared to Jacob and again changed his name to Israel. God blessed Jacob, and Jacob built a pillar in the place where God spoke to him. He called the name of the place Bet El (House of God). On their return journey from Bet El, Rachel went into labor. She died upon the birth of a son whom she called Ben-oni (son of my sorrow) but Jacob called him Benjamin (Gen. 35.1-20).

This text is the third that deals with Jacob's 'divine birth', symbolized by his being given a new name, Israel. As discussed above (M.III.10, *Jacob Wrestles with an Angel*) all three of these texts are structurally equivalent. The third, however, includes several significant additions. At the beginning of the myth Deborah, Rebekah's nurse, dies and at the end Rachel dies in childbirth. I have suggested that Deborah structurally represents Rebekah, Jacob's mother. This association is likely for three reasons. First, Deborah is not mentioned in any other text and thus it is difficult to understand the text's concern with her. Secondly, a nurse (possibly wet-nurse) shares many elements with the mother and takes on elements of the mother's role, and should be seen as structurally equivalent.[1] Thirdly, if the text is compared to other structurally similar texts, for example, *The Sacrifice of Isaac*, the mother is often symbolically removed to emphasize divine fruitfulness. Similarly, Isaac is removed at the conclusion of this text. Gen. 35.29 describes the death of Isaac.[2]

Rachel's role as mother is denied upon the birth of Benjamin. Although the myth includes all Israel's sons as part of Israel, Rachel's two sons still function mythologically as if they were the sole bearers of the divine seed. They are children of the favored wife (as in the case of Isaac). Their mother (like Sarah and Rebekah and many other women in the text) was barren and required specific divine intervention to have children. In addition, their mother symbolically dies to emphasize their divine origin.

Benjamin should be seen as a doubled form of Joseph (rather than as a significant figure in his own right). Throughout the Joseph texts there is a consistent double structure, reflected in all the events. Benjamin fits in with this general pattern (see Chapter 6). Thus his birth comes after two significant events. He is born after his father's final 'divine birth' and symbolic castration, and his mother is immediately removed. Thus his birth fits the general structural pattern in which the bearer of the chosen line is born after his father's 'divine birth'. Both parents are then removed through death or symbolic castration.

1.   This is supported by the mythological role of Moses' mother. After Moses was found by Pharaoh's daughter and became her 'son', his actual mother acted as his wet nurse.

2.   This association is also found in the structural transformations of this text. In midrashic texts ranging from *Genesis Rabbah* to *Midrash HaGadol* Deborah's death is associated with Rebekah's. The texts, based on a Greek etymology for the word אלון, suggest that Jacob was weeping for both Deborah and Rebekah his mother. The texts offer interesting reasons for not mentioning Rebekah directly. *Genesis Rabbah* suggests that she is not mentioned lest she be cursed for having born Esau—that is having a child who is outside and ideologically negative. A related explanation is found in *Tanhuma Buber* (Ki Tetze 4) and *Midrash HaGadol* 597. For an interesting discussion of these texts see Jacoby 1994.

5.13. *Synthesis*

The texts discussed in this chapter deal with similar oppositions to those developed in the Abraham and Isaac chapters.[1] These oppositions center around the distinction between Israel and the nations, between natural birth and divine birth, and regarding the ambiguous position of the wife as mediator, between inside and outside. The structural problem of the wife is, perhaps, the one most completely developed in this myth. The ambiguities and dangers presented by the women are introduced in *Jacob Steals Esau's Birthright*, and are developed and emphasized in

1.   Prewitt observes that the texts about Abraham contain similar oppositions to those of Jacob. Based on such similarities he concludes that the structure is based on a 'simple alternating patten' on lines suggested by Leach in *Rethinking Anthropology* (Prewitt 1990: 11). He suggests that Abraham should be paired with Jacob, and Isaac should be paired with Terah. The pairing of Abraham with Jacob is clear enough: both serve identical structural purposes. The pairing of Isaac with Terah, however, is structurally unlikely. Isaac was inside while Terah was outside. Prewitt bases this division on two elements: the Terahite genealogy, and the geographical movement of Terah and Isaac respectively.

Prewitt's concept of a Terahite genealogy is based on a misunderstanding of the genealogical structure of Genesis (on the narrative level). Prewitt makes a connection between Adam, Noah and Terah, assuming that each is the head of a genealogical table. This argument is not supported by the text. The genealogies begin with the sons of these figures, Seth, Shem and Abram. (See, for example, Gen. 10 where the Shemite, Hamite and Yaphet genealogies are given, not Noah's.) Each new genealogy begins with three sons rather than their father. This pattern continues in Exodus, where Moses, Aaron and Miriam begin a new line of descent, with the divine seed being carried by the descendants of Aaron—the priests are called the descendants of Aaron, not Amram, his father. Thus it is structurally incorrect to base Abraham's genealogy on Terah. Terah is outside Abraham's genealogy and would not logically be paired with Isaac.

His second criterion is based on the movement patterns of the four figures. He shows that Abraham and Jacob moved between Aramea and Egypt, while Isaac and Terah were relatively immobile (Prewitt 1990: 11). Such an argument could equally pair Isaac and Joseph, both of whom were also relatively immobile. On other levels (e.g., symbolic 'divine birth') Isaac and Joseph share many more similarities than Isaac and Terah; Joseph is inside while Terah is not. These objections aside, it is structurally unlikely for this type of 'moiety' system to be developed in Israelite culture— the structure is working to create unity inside in order to logically oppose it to the outside. A moiety concept would weaken this opposition. (In *Rethinking Anthropology* Leach applies this system to a specific case, that is, a myth in which alternating generations are allied. It is unlikely that he would have argued for general extension of this pattern to societies which do not exhibit such solidarity [Leach 1961: 131]).

the texts dealing with Jacob's relations with Laban. I suggest that this opposition is tied to the problem of endogamy, as well as the mythological preference for incest challenged by the need to choose a wife from another family.

In the Jacob texts a process found in the earlier chapters of Genesis comes to an end. In the earlier myths development can be characterized by a segmentary genealogy. A primary line of descent develops, beginning with Seth, and in each generation segments break off, detailing the origin of the other nations. This process continued through Abraham and Isaac. In each case there was a chosen and a non-chosen line. This process was highlighted by a structure in which the non-chosen line or brother was used to emphasize the divine nature of the chosen line. With Jacob, the segmentary process ceases. All Jacob's children are inside, and are opposed to all other nations. This transformation is necessary to transform the divine line from an individual to a people.

The mythological structure of opposition, however, persists throughout the entire Bible and is illustrated in the Joseph texts in the next chapter, 'Joseph and his Brothers'. The persistence of this structure reveals an important theoretical aspect of structure in general. As suggested by T. Turner, structure within text does include various types of progressive transformations that are organized at the same level as the narrative structure. There are, however, structures that are not dependent on the narrative level and that characterize the system as a whole. These structures may, as in the case presented here, conflict with the lower level structure, but this in no sense weakens their power.

Chapter 6

JOSEPH AND HIS BROTHERS

The story of Joseph is the primary myth examined in this chapter. This myth is characterized by a doubling of structure at every level. Most, if not all, elements of the myth are doubled: Joseph dreams two dreams, as do pharaoh and his servants, and Joseph himself is doubled in the form of Benjamin. This double structure is one of several patterns found in the biblical text which serve to cloud or obscure the underlying structure.

The Joseph story contains most of the oppositions already highlighted in the narratively earlier texts. The text is introduced by an opposition between Joseph (the youngest son) and his brothers. This opposition is part of the broader opposition between Israel and the nations. The text develops the opposition between generations, which is tied to the denial of human fertility. It also contains symbolic death and birth which are the center of the two above oppositions.

There is, however, a significant transformation which is mentioned in Chapter 5: all Jacob's children including Joseph's brothers are inside. It is suggested that this is due to two phenomena. Although narratively the process of segmentation is complete, on a synchronic level segmentation is a structural principle of Israelite myth and thus will be found, albeit in clouded form, even where it is narratively no longer necessary. It is also possible that segmentation and opposition of inside to outside were cultural structures, even within Israel, as the logical outcome of endogamy.

This chapter also includes several independent texts relating to Jacob's other children. Three of these texts explore varying aspects of the position of women: *The Rape of Dinah*, *Joseph and Potiphar's Wife* and *Judah and Tamar*. These texts raise the possibility of the wife or sister being outside but conclude that such a position would be structurally untenable and dangerous. Other texts, including *Reuben Sleeps with his Father's Concubine*, examine the role of incest in the structure.

6.1. The Rape of Dinah

The initial text analyzed in this chapter examines the possibility of exogamy.

> M.IV.1. Dinah, daughter of Jacob, went out to see the daughters of the land. Shechem son of Hamor rapes her, but he subsequently falls in love with her and asks his father to get Dinah as his wife. Hamor goes to Jacob and asks that Dinah be made his son's wife. He states that the two groups of Jacob and Hamor respectively should exchange women. The sons of Jacob reply that they cannot give their sister to an uncircumcised man, stating that they will give their sister to Shechem only on the condition that all of Hamor's men be circumcised. Hamor convinces his people; every male of the city is circumcised. After the third day when all the men are still in pain, Shimon and Levi (Dinah's brothers) slaughter them. The other sons despoil all the wealth of the city. The myth concludes with Jacob criticizing his sons' actions, yet they are given the last words: 'Shall our sister be treated as a prostitute?' (Gen. 34)

This text is one of three related texts that examine the position of women in the structure of Israelite myth. Each one of the texts examines a different aspect of the question and arrives at structurally consistent answers. These texts include *The Rape of Dinah* (M.IV.1), *Judah and Tamar* (M.IV.4) and *Joseph and Potiphar's Wife* (M.IV.5). *The Rape of Dinah* raises two primary questions. First, is it proper for Israel to give its daughters to other peoples? Secondly, can Israel join with other nations to become one nation?

In a sense the two questions are actually one. Shechem and Dinah both represent corporate entities rather than individuals. Shechem is clearly corporate being the name of a city in Canaan, while it is likely that Dinah serves as a feminine representation of Israel (feminine because of the needs of the narrative). Thus the possible union with Shechem is also the possible union of Israel with a non-Israelite nation or the nations.

The negative aspect of Shechem, and thereby the nations, is emphasized in both the actions of Shechem and his father. The rape itself is a strongly negative action. The text emphasizes the severity of the act and uses three terms to describe the rape: 'He took her, he lay with her, and he humbled (afflicted) her' (Gen. 34.2).[1] The negative element at the beginning of the text accentuates the opposition between Israel (Dinah) and the nations (Shechem) and provides the necessary answer to

---

1.	Note that three terms (describing one action) are used in several places in Genesis; see M.I.1 and M.II.1.

Shechem's offer of marriage and unification.

After the rape the text introduces an offer of marriage. Shechem, through his father Hamor, asks for Dinah's hand in marriage. Hamor suggests that Jacob give his daughters to the people of Hamor and that similarly Hamor will give his people's daughters to Jacob. He suggests further that the people will dwell together. Essentially Hamor's suggestion is that the two peoples become one. This element is clarified later in the text when Hamor addresses his people and states explicitly, 'Only on this condition will the men agree to dwell with us and *agree to be one people*' (Gen. 34.22). Thus the text introduces the possibility of amalgamation of peoples, as well as the question of exogamy.

The text appears to raise a resolution to the opposition that was created in earlier texts in Genesis between Israel and the nations. The sons of Jacob state that they will agree only if the men of Shechem be circumcised. Circumcision is posited as the primary division between the two poles in the opposition.[1] There are several clues, however, even at the beginning of the text, which indicate that circumcision would not remove the boundaries. Jacob's sons speak with 'guile', thus their offer of marriage (or even the possibility of marriage) was never serious (Gen. 34.13).

The final blow to this type of resolution occurs at the conclusion of the text. The peoples are not amalgamated; Jacob's sons destroy Hamor and all his people. The text supports this action by giving Shimon and Levi the last word: 'Shall our sister be treated like a prostitute?'

The text includes a second element which emphasizes the distinction between Israel and the nations and which dictates that the structural difference between the two lies beyond circumcision. Shechem's father was named Hamor. His name means 'donkey' in Hebrew. Thus Hamor's people are symbolically descended from an ass and are thus qualitatively distinct from Israel who are descended from God. A similar analogy of the nations is seen below in the discussion of *Genesis Rabbah* on *The Sacrifice of Isaac* where Ishmael and Eliezer are said to be similar to an ass.

The text answers the question of exogamy on two levels. On the level of the individual, the text concludes that Israel should not exchange its daughters with its neighbors. On a national level, the structure

---

1. This is essentially the second of Prewitt's three stages of Israelite development. This text, however, explicitly refutes the possibility of circumcision as a sole identifying characteristic. This is discussed in connection with M.IV.1.

emphasizes the distinction between Israel and the nations and the impossibility of Israel merging with other nations. The two levels together suggest that, if Israel exchanges women, it will become indistinct from the nations and essentially one of them.

The text also examines a second question regarding the role or position of women in Israelite society. In the texts examined above, for example, *Wife/Sister 1* and *Wife/Sister 2*, it is shown that women are dangerous. In those texts the danger was focused on the position of wife as representative of the relative 'outside'. This text reveals that the position of sister and daughter is also structurally dangerous. The sister must be given away in marriage and thus breaks the cohesion of the family and creates an opening to the outside.

This ambiguous or dangerous element is emphasized in the first verse of the text: 'And Dinah, the daughter of Leah, who was born to Jacob, went out to see the daughters of the land' (Gen. 34.1). The text implies that Dinah improperly joined the Canaanite women and thus created the situation of danger. Her action should be seen as analogous to that of Judah in the beginning of *Judah and Tamar* where he went among the Canaanites and improperly married a Canaanite women. The analogy between the two texts is emphasized by the Hebrew text. The root ראה 'see' is used in both texts. Judah is compared both with Dinah who went to see and was seen, and to Hamor who saw her and took her. Although the same Hebrew root is not used with respect to Potiphar's wife, the action of seeing is also emphasized. She lifts up her eyes upon Joseph (Gen. 39.7). It is possible that the action of seeing is used here to indicate lust.[1]

In *The Elusive Covenant* Prewitt suggests that three stages of ideal social or tribal organization may be identified within Genesis. The second of these stages (which occur diachronically in both narrative and presumably history) is a system in which marriage exchange is based on circumcision. Israel would only exchange women with groups that were

1. This suggestion is supported by the wife/sister texts in which the danger posed by Sarah and Rebekah is tied to being seen—and lusted after. Although the same root is also used in regard to Jacob and Rachel, the context and results are slightly different. In the case of all three of the texts examined in this chapter the action of seeing is followed by a direct sexual response. Dinah is raped by Hamor, Judah takes and sleeps with his wife, and Potiphar's wife orders Joseph to sleep with her. In the Jacob and Rachel text the seeing comes only after Rachel is clearly identified as an acceptable wife. And, although the seeing leads to desire, Jacob negotiates properly with Laban for Rachel rather than improperly acting on his desire.

circumcised, that is, the Ishmaelites and the Edomites (Prewitt 1990: 30). A surface reading of *The Rape of Dinah* appears to support this argument though, as discussed above, the text concludes that circumcision is not a sufficient criterion for marriage. It is unlikely that this text reflects a transition in cultural norms, that is, from a system based on circumcision to one based on other criteria.

First, it is theoretically unlikely that previous systems would be reflected in underlying structure (which reflects current cultural structures rather than artifacts). Secondly, throughout the text, from the moment it is suggested, it is clear that circumcision would be rejected as a criterion for exchange. The very offer to become one people is diametrically opposed to the underlying structure found throughout the text.

There are several other problems with Prewitt's analysis. Although the Ishmaelites and the Edomites circumcise their children, it is unlikely that the text included them in the covenant of circumcision. The promises given in that covenant apply particularly to Israel the chosen line rather than the rejected lines. Prewitt is also unable to produce any textual evidence that the Edomites or Ishmaelites even mythologically exchanged women with Israel. The only marriage mentioned between any of these groups is between Esau and one of Ishmael's daughters, and there is no evidence in the text that such a marriage would have been acceptable for an Israelite.

The weakest part of his argument concerns the workings of underlying structure. He posits three layers, the last of which is the accepted form of endogamy. It is theoretically inconsistent that the other layers should be preserved in a text which even he agrees is substantially edited. Like Pitt-Rivers (discussed above, 2.7) he assumes that narratively earlier texts actually describe historically earlier periods (Prewitt 1990: 30). His misinterpretation lies in mistaking narrative and surface structure for underlying structure.

6.2. *Reuben Sleeps with his Father's Concubine*
One element central to this part of Genesis is the rejection of the first-born in favor of a younger brother. This text serves two functions: it explains the rejection of Reuben and is part of the broader structural preference for incest.

> M.IV.2. Israel journeyed and set up his tent at Migdal Eder. It came to pass that while Israel dwelt in that land, Reuben went and lay with Bilhah the concubine of his father, and Israel heard of it (Gen. 35.21-22).

This text is parallel to *Reuben and the Mandrakes* (M.III.7), in that it also fits the context of the incest texts, that is, *Lot and his Daughters* and the wife/sister texts. The type of incest described in this text, in effect incest between mother and son, appears to be more problematic than that described in the narratively earlier text. Reuben is condemned for his incest, both by implication in this text, and again in Jacob's blessings in Genesis 49. The condemnation, however, is not necessarily tied to the incest, but is associated with trespass on his father's rights. In the blessing Reuben is criticized, not for incest, but for 'going into his father's bed', that is, assuming the rights of inheritor before his father's death (Gen. 49.4).

The situation of *Reuben Sleeps with his Father's Concubine* is analogous to sections in 2 Samuel (16.22) and 1 Kgs 2.13-25. In 2 Samuel, Absalom rebels against his father, David. As a sign of his taking on the mantle of kingship, Absalom sleeps with his father's concubines. The text implies that this would have been correct had his father been dead, that is, that the concubines would have been part of his inheritance. In the text from 1 Kings, Adonijah asks his brother Solomon, who has just been made king, for Abishag one of David's concubines. Solomon has Adonijah put to death because this request challenges Solomon's right to rule: she belongs to him. Thus Reuben's crime is not incest but trespass. The crime is exacerbated because Joseph, rather than Reuben, is Jacob's primary beneficiary, and Joseph receives the primary blessing. On a structural level this text continues to develop the mythological preference for incest.

6.3. *The Murder of Joseph*

The myth of Joseph is the central focus of the last quarter of Genesis. The other myths included in this section, for example, *Judah and Tamar*, highlight related questions. Although the myth of Joseph (M.IV.3 through M.IV.10) is divided into sections for ease of analysis, it should be understood as a synchronic whole. It is a more unified novella than those discussed above and is substantially the product of the same authors or schools.

> M.IV.3. (a) Joseph was seventeen years old, his father's favourite son. Jacob gave him a coat of many colours.[1] His brothers hated him. Joseph dreamed two dreams in which his parents and brothers symbolically

---

1.   'Coat of many colours' is the usual translation of כתנת פסים. There are, however, several other explanations of the word פסים. BDB translates it as a tunic

bowed to him (as sheaves of wheat and heavenly bodies). His brothers interpret the dream to mean that he will rule over them. (b) Joseph is sent by his father to his brothers who are keeping the flocks. As he approaches them, they plan to murder him by casting him into a pit and blaming his death on a wild beast. Reuben convinces them not to kill him, and plans to restore him to their father. When he arrives they remove his coat and place him into a pit 'in which there was no water'. They see a caravan of Ishmaelites and Judah suggests that they sell him as a slave. A group of Midianites pass and remove Joseph from the pit and sell him to the Ishmaelites for twenty shekels. Reuben returns and sees that Joseph is gone. He rents his clothes and wonders what he will tell Jacob. The brothers take Joseph's coat, dip it in a goat's blood and send it to their father. Jacob rends his clothes and mourns the death of Joseph. Joseph is sold by the Midianites to Potiphar, Captain of Pharaoh's guard (Gen. 37).

The key to understanding the underlying structure of the myth of Joseph is doubling: the mechanism of clouding employed by the myth. At every level elements of the story are doubled. On the narrative level the dreams come in pairs. Likewise, Joseph's movements are doubled. In Canaan he first goes to Shechem and then to Dotan. His overall movement is also doubled: he goes down into the pit and down to Egypt (and in Egypt he is placed in a pit by his symbolic father).

The double structure is also found in Jacob's sons and wives. Jacob has two wives and two concubines. Jacob's sons also come in doubled sets. Leah initially had four sons who can be divided into two sets of two. Reuben (first-born) is often paired in the narrative with Judah (fourth son).[1] Historically Judah replaces Reuben as the pre-eminent tribe. Shimon and Levi (second and third sons) are also paired in the narrative (see *The Rape of Dinah*, M.IV.1, where Shimon and Levi are the primary actors in the slaughter of Shechem). All the other sons are

which reached the palms and soles, taking כפ to mean flat of hand and feet (BDB, 821). Gesenius suggests that this type of cloak was worn by women and men of noble rank (1846: 683).

1. Reuben and Judah function as a doubled pair in this text. Initially it is Reuben who prevents his brothers from killing Joseph. Later on in the text Judah suggests that Joseph should not be killed. This doubled pair is also found in other texts which are part of the Joseph novella. Later in the narrative both Reuben and Judah offer themselves as surety for the safety of Benjamin. In that text, however, Judah is singled out by having his offer accepted. It is likely that there were two different traditions, one based on Reuben and one on Judah. The author of the myth, however, in preserving both traditions, fits the two into a doubled structure that is consistent throughout the story.

born in paired sets. Dan and Naphtali (fifth and sixth) are born to Bilhah. Gad and Asher (seventh and eighth) are born to Zilpah. Issachar and Zebulun (ninth and tenth) are born to Leah. Finally, Joseph and Benjamin (eleventh and twelfth) to Rachel (see Figure 11). The doubling process continues with the sons of Joseph, Ephraim and Manasseh, who are later adopted by Jacob in Joseph's place.

Leah (W)	Rachel (W)	Bilhah (C)	Zilpah (C)
(A) Reuben			
(B) Shimon			
(B1) Levi			
(A1) Judah			
		(C) Dan	
		(C1) Naphtali	
			(D) Gad
			(D1) Asher
(E) Issachar			
(E1) Zebulun			
	(F) Joseph		
	(F1) Benjamin		

$A = A1, B = B1, C = C1, D = D1, E = E1, F = F1; (C + C1) = (D + D1)$
W = Wife C = Concubine

Figure 11. *The Sons of Jacob*

This type of double structure must be kept in mind when interpreting any element of the narrative. It is especially important in understanding the structural relationship between Joseph and Benjamin. Prewitt ignores this implication. He suggests that Benjamin is the chosen son in the text rather than Joseph (Prewitt 1990: 20). Furthermore, Benjamin is the younger of the two, linking this text with previous texts where the younger son is chosen. He points out further that Benjamin is the only of Jacob's sons to be born in Canaan, and the only son born after Jacob's transformation to Israel (Prewitt 1990: 44). On its own this last element would be compelling, but in the light of the doubling of structural elements it must be re-examined. If Benjamin is merely a doubled Joseph, then anything which is mentioned concerning him structurally refers to Joseph. Structurally they are one rather than two.

The text itself does not support Benjamin as the bearer of the chosen line. The text examined here, which occurs after Benjamin is born, refers to Joseph as Jacob's favorite, the son of his old age. Benjamin is never mentioned. Joseph's position as chosen son is also given divine sanction.

He is given dreams which predict his future eminence, and throughout his journeys God caused him to prosper in whatever he did. At the conclusion of the myth Joseph is blessed twice, once with and once without his brothers. The blessing of Joseph is one of two substantially longer blessings—of Joseph and Judah—while Benjamin receives one of the shortest. Joseph is also given a double inheritance, being the father of two tribes. Like Jacob, it is Joseph's bones that are brought back to Canaan not Benjamin's. Once the doubling of structure is recognized, it is apparent that Joseph, as bearer of the chosen seed, does fit the structural pattern of 'choosing the younger son', because structurally he is the younger son. This text suggests a general rule similar to that stated above regarding inversion (M.II.1). Where a text is doubled, all structurally significant elements will be doubled, and proper analysis of the text should regard each doubled pair as a single unit (see the discussion in §11.6).

Prewitt, like Leach (see the discussion of 'The Legitimacy of Solomon' in §2.11) sees structure as a device for legitimizing a particular dynasty or political system. He suggests that the texts were written to support Saul's (Benjamin) line rather than David's (Judah) (Prewitt 1990: 18). He argues that Benjamin is equivalent to Isaac, being the chosen son and therefore the chosen tribe, while Judah is rejected because of his misalliance with Tamar (see below, *Judah and Tamar*, M.IV.3). His analysis ignores the actual structurally insignificant position of Benjamin, as well as the place of *Judah and Tamar* in the broader structures of biblical myth (i.e., the incest texts).[1] The essential criticism, however, is that structure legitimizes essential cultural foundations, not particular political dynasties or situations.[2]

The main opposition developed in the text is between Joseph and his brothers. This opposition is analogous to that found regarding Isaac and Ishmael, and Jacob and Esau. Although on a narrative level all the

---

1. He also ignores the fact that Judah's blessing clearly indicates divine sanction for Judah's rule over the other tribes: 'The sceptre shall not depart from Judah, nor the rulers staff from between his feet' (Gen. 49.10). Benjamin's blessing, however, is ambiguous at the very least: 'Benjamin is a devouring wolf; in the morning he eats his prey, and in the evening he divides his spoil' (Gen. 49.27).

2. This problem relates to a distinction between the structuralist approach and that of Malinowski (see §2.8). Structuralist theory suggests that underlying structure is unrelated to particular political events or manipulation, because if structure was subject to them it would not remain constant (as it is observed to do), but would change every time the myth was used.

brothers are 'inside', that is, they are all part of Israel, on a structural level the myth continues to develop the opposition of chosen versus non-chosen. Thus structurally, although not narratively, the brothers are outside in relation to Joseph. This opposition is developed on several levels in the text. On the one hand, it is given human sanction through Jacob's relationship with Joseph. Joseph is Jacob's favorite son, and the son of his favorite wife. The opposition is reflected on the material level through the 'coat of many colours'. Throughout the myth of Joseph, coats and clothing play a significant role: his father gives him a coat; his brothers take it from him; Judah loses his rope (belt) and signet; Potiphar's wife takes Joseph's robe; Pharaoh gives Joseph a robe and signet. On the other hand, the other brothers are described as analogous to Ishmael. Like Ishmael they are described as the sons of the concubines; Leah's name is never mentioned (even though she was the senior wife).

The opposition is also reflected on a divine level in both of Joseph's dreams. Spiritual justification is found both in the dreams and in his having them. The first dream indicates his precedence over his brothers, and the second the fact that he bears the divine seed in place of his father (his father and mother symbolically bow down to him).

Joseph also fits into the related structural pattern of chosenness. Like the previous figures in Genesis—Seth, Shem, Isaac and Jacob—Joseph is the younger son. This element is further emphasized in his case by also being a son of the junior mother. This pattern of inheritance by the younger son is sometimes taken to indicate a cultural pattern of ultimogeniture (Prewitt 1990: 44). Unwitting evidence in the text suggests that this is an incorrect analysis. In every text where the elder son comes from a mother who is inside, that is, Esau and Reuben, the text implied that he would, under normal circumstances, expect to inherit. Thus Esau expects the blessing and Reuben takes his father's concubines as his right. The normal pattern developed in the text appears to be primogeniture rather than ultimogeniture. The significance of chosenness is the overturning of expected and 'natural' patterns. The text implies that God sets aside natural law to choose Israel and distinguish it from the nations.

The relation of this text to *The Sacrifice of Isaac* has already been developed above (see M.II.1). There are, however, several other points of structural interest. The roles of the fathers and brothers are reversed in the two texts. In this text the father remains behind while the brothers commit the 'murder'. Jacob's role, however, is also doubled (fitting the double structure of the text). After sending Joseph to Shechem, Joseph meets a man there who sends him on to Dotan. Thus Joseph is sent to his brothers twice. The unnamed man also may be structurally equivalent to God in *The Sacrifice of Isaac*, sending Joseph on to his death.

The element of sacrifice/murder is present throughout the second half of the text. The brothers plot to kill Joseph and finally place him in a hole representing descent to Sheol (Hell). This descent is further emphasized through Joseph's being sold to Egypt, a journey always described as a descent. The brothers' role in the 'murder' represents a further strengthening of the opposition between them and Joseph. Similarly, by giving Joseph into their hands Jacob participates in the murder.

The opposition between Joseph and his brothers, however, is mediated in several ways. This mediation exists because of the dual nature of the myth. On a synchronic level, the brothers represent the outside, non-chosen line: they need no mediation because it would weaken the opposition. On the diachronic level (based on narrative development), however, they are inside and thus need mediation to weaken the opposition. The mediation works in three ways. First, when the brothers are introduced in v. 2 the text mentions Bilhah and Zilpah and does not mention Leah. Thus, the sons of the concubines mediate between Joseph, his brothers (sons of Leah), and the outside. The sons of Leah are structurally inside (their mother was inside), while the other sons included an ambiguous element being children of concubines, and thus were relatively outside. Secondly, two of Joseph's brothers attempt to save him, thus reducing their culpability in the murder. Reuben, Leah's first-born, convinces his brothers to place Joseph in the pit, planning to return and save him. Judah, the tribe of the Davidic dynasty, convinces the brothers to sell him rather than kill him.

On the other hand, the text never describes the brothers as actually selling Joseph. The text includes several different alternatives for the sale. Gen. 37.28 states that Midianite merchants took Joseph from the pit and sold him to the Ishmaelites. Gen. 37.36 states that he was sold into Egypt by the Midianites. Finally, Genesis 39 states that he was brought down by Ishmaelites. Thus a mediator is placed between two elements: the brothers and the sale, and Israel and Egypt. On the first level, the Midianites remove some of the culpability for the sale of Joseph. On the second level, the Midianites and Ishmaelites stand between two opposites. Israel is completely inside and Egypt completely outside, with no possible direct communication between the two. The Ishmaelites and

Midianites, however, structurally contain elements of inside and outside. They are both descendants from Abraham, yet they are born either before or after the chosen line. Thus, by including elements of both sides, they bridge the gap and are a perfect conduit to bring Joseph to Egypt.

The pit is also significant on several levels. I have already mentioned the aspect of descent as a symbol of death, it is also a symbol of fertility and life (or birth and transformation). The pit is described in the text as a 'hole with no water in it'; it can thus be understood as an empty well (Gen. 37.24). A well in the biblical text was a center of natural fertility;[1] a source of water for plants, animals and human beings. It also symbolized marriage. The empty pit is the opposite of the well. It is the source of death, but emergence from it is also the source of divine birth and divine fertility. This is similar to the mountain of sacrifice, which through death (or symbolic death) brings life and divine fruitfulness. The pit fits into the paradox cited above: natural fruitfulness (the well) is barren, while divine barrenness (the empty pit) is fruitful. This fits into the general equation of Genesis : Barrenness : Fruitfulness :: Well : Pit :: Israel : Nations.

The myth concludes by tying Joseph's death (and transformation) to Jacob's death. Jacob states, 'I will go down to the grave mourning for my son' (Gen. 37.35). This statement employs the same image for death used regarding Joseph, that is, 'going down', strengthening the analogy of the pit with the grave. It fits into the broader structural pattern of removal of parents by death to emphasize the spiritual aspect of 'divine birth', as seen above in myths about Isaac (*The Sacrifice of Isaac*, M.II.1) and Jacob (*The Covenant at Bet El*, M.III.12). This element, with the other oppositions highlighted above, is further developed as the myth of Joseph progresses.

6.4. *Judah and Tamar*
Judah and Tamar intrudes on the flow of the Joseph narrative. It does, however, deal with a question that is raised again in *Joseph and Potiphar's Wife* (M.IV.4), that is, the permissibility of marrying (having sex with) a woman who is structurally outside. Both texts conclude with a similar answer: such relations are forbidden and structurally dangerous.

> M.IV.4. Judah leaves his brothers and marries a Canaanite woman. She
> bears three sons: Er, Onan and Shelah respectively. Judah takes a wife for
> Er named Tamar. Er is killed by God before bearing any children. Judah

---

1. See also the discussion of wells in regard to M.II.4.

tells Onan to go into his brother's wife to 'raise up seed' for his brother.
Onan, not wanting to engender children for his brother, spills his seed
before going into Tamar. God kills him for this. Judah tells Tamar to wait
until Shelah has reached adulthood. Meanwhile, Judah's wife dies and he
goes up to Timnah to shear the sheep. Tamar also goes there dressed as a
temple prostitute because she saw that Judah had not given her Shelah.
Judah takes her for a prostitute and goes into her. He gives her his signet
and cord as a pledge for payment. After three months, Judah hears that
Tamar, his daughter-in-law, has become pregnant. He orders that she be
brought forward to be killed. She sends him his signet, stating that it
belongs to the father. Judah recognizes the signet and declares that she is
righteous because he had not given her Shelah. Tamar bears twins. Upon
the birth, one child puts out its hand and the midwife marks it with a red
thread. The baby then pulls its hand back and the other baby is born first.
The baby with the thread was called Zerah and the first born was called
Peretz (Gen. 38).

The myth of *Judah and Tamar* should be divided into two related
sections. The first section deals with Judah's marriage to a Canaanite
woman and the subsequent death of their children. The second half
examines Judah's relations with Tamar and the subsequent birth of her
children. In certain respects the two halves are mirror images, with the
second half resolving the questions raised in the first.

The primary question examined by the myth is the permissibility of
exogamy. There are several elements of the first half which prefigure
the outcome of the text. The text begins with the statement that Judah
left his brothers and 'saw' a certain Canaanite woman. This introduction
is reminiscent of that to *The Rape of Dinah*. In that text Dinah goes out
from her family to see the daughters of the land and is, in turn, seen by
Shechem. In a similar fashion, Joseph's troubles in Potiphar's house
begin after Potiphar's wife has seen him. All three texts deal with two
related elements: endogamy and the danger posed by women. All three
'relationships' end in danger or tragedy. The danger is further highlighted by the national origin of Judah's wife, a Canaanite. Narratively
earlier in the myth, Abraham asks Eliezer to swear not to give Isaac a
Canaanite wife, and later Isaac and Rebekah were angry with Esau for
marrying a Canaanite woman.

As the first half progresses, the structural opposition to exogamy is
developed. Judah's first-born son is killed (by God) for being wicked,
though the exact nature of his sin is not presented. It is with Onan,
Judah's second son, that the text emphasizes the opposition. The myth
implies that Onan is forced to marry his brother's widow due to the

levirate. Not wishing to carry on his brother's line, he 'spills his seed'. God punishes him for this sin by killing him. Onan is a structural inversion of Judah. Whereas Onan refuses to use his seed properly and is killed, Judah has used his seed improperly in marrying a Canaanite woman and is structurally condemned.[1]

The second half of the text works on two related levels: resolving the question posed by the first half and creating an incestuous relation between Judah and Tamar (son's wife was forbidden by the Israelites as an incestuous relation). The first half of the text raised the possibility of exogamy. It concluded, however, that exogamy was forbidden, expressing this prohibition through the death of Judah's sons and his wife. In the second half, Judah is tricked into having sex with his daughter-in-law, and engenders twins.

Unlike Judah's first wife, Tamar's origins are not mentioned by the text. This suggests that the text is trying to intimate that she is Israelite rather than Canaanite.[2] In most cases Genesis describes the origins of women if they marry into the Israelite line. By not stating Tamar's origins, the text includes an ambiguity which creates the possibility that she was an acceptable wife.[3] This is also supported by her structural role in the text.[4] Thus Judah's 'second marriage', initiated by his relationship

1.   Using an essentially functionalist argument, Mars suggests that Onan's crime was effectively murder. In refusing to perpetuate his brother's seed, he murdered his brother's line (1984: 436). The primary flaw in Mars's argument is one which he alludes to himself. Although the levirate was legally allowable and morally correct in Israelite law, one could legally refuse to do it, and thus not perpetuating his brother's seed can not be exactly analogous to murder. There is, however, a serious problem in detail. He suggests that by having children through Judah, Tamar perpetuated Er's name (Mars 1984: 438). In fact, Tamar's children are never called Er's children and are structurally distinct from Er and his children.

Mars also compares the myths of Judah and Joseph, suggesting that Judah's impropriety was rewarded while Joseph's restraint was punished (1984: 438). Although this is essentially correct it misses one step. Judah was rewarded not because his actions were immoral but because Tamar (as opposed to his original wife) was an acceptable mother for his children. Potiphar's wife is structurally analogous to Judah's first wife (outside) rather than Tamar (inside).

3.   Vawter also suggests that Tamar may have 'been' of Hebrew origin (1977: 393).

4.   Carmichael agrees with this characterization of Tamar as 'Israelite' (1982: 402). He suggests further that Judah's sons died precisely because they were only 'half-Israelites' which would be a forbidden mixture with an Israelite woman (Carmichael 1982: 402). Carmichael also includes an interesting argument about the

with Tamar, was a structurally acceptable marriage unlike his first. Although Judah's first wife did bear three children, her fertility is compared unfavorably with Tamar's. Tamar bore twins, the ancestors of the tribe of Judah, while Judah's sons by his first wife died childless, with Onan's act being the opposite of fertility. Thus this level of the myth fits into the equation presented above: Outside (Marriage) : Inside (Marriage) :: Sterile : Fruitful. This fits into a general structural rule that endogamy is fruitful while exogamy is barren.

The second half of the text is also part of the broader structural pattern of incest. Tamar is 'inside', both as a possible daughter of Israel and as Judah's daughter-in-law. In effect, she is almost his daughter. All the elements highlighted in the other 'incest' myths are also present in this text. Three elements are present: (1) the opposition of natural fertility (outside) to divine fertility (inside) which has already been discussed; (2) the transformation of relatively outside to inside; (3) danger. The second element is the key element of the text. By becoming his daughter prior to becoming his 'wife', Tamar is brought structurally inside and becomes the appropriate conduit for the divine seed. Tamar is also structurally appropriate because of her genealogical position. She, as wife of his sons, is one generation down, just as the wives of Isaac and Jacob are also one generation down. As in previous cases of incest (the wife/sister texts), incest is structurally positive as the logical conclusion of the structure of endogamy.[1]

The element of danger is developed in two ways. Judah's first son dies upon marrying Tamar, and Onan dies rather than fathering children with Tamar. The danger is also expressed in Tamar's disguise as a prostitute. Although the outcome was structurally acceptable, the pretence suggests uncontrolled sexuality and therefore danger. It is also linked with the rape of Dinah, which concludes with the words 'shall our sister be treated as a prostitute?' Thus Tamar acts inappropriately (though mythologically necessarily) in the way that Dinah was treated (mythologically unnecessary and negative).

The text also includes a direct structural equation of Judah and Joseph. Tamar, like Joseph's brothers, takes part of Judah's clothing. Judah, like Joseph, bears two 'acceptable' sons, one of whom is the bearer of the

relationship between 'forbidden mixtures' and endogamy. He suggests, for example, that the prohibition on ploughing with an ox and ass is a metaphor relating to sexual intercourse between an Israelite and a Canaanite, with the ox standing for Israel and the ass for the Canaanites (1982: 403).

divine seed. This element is emphasized in later Jewish folklore which says there are two messiahs, one descended from Joseph and another from Judah.[1] Judah is also genealogically equivalent to Joseph. He is the youngest of Leah's first four sons. This is part of a general pattern that begins with the sons of Jacob. No longer is there a single chosen line; now all the brothers equally (with some more equal than others) pass on the divine seed (twelve equals one).

The text also includes a structural equivalence between Peretz and Zerah, and Jacob and Esau. Obviously, both are sets of twins. It is developed on several more fundamental levels. Like Jacob and Esau, the 'younger son' supplants the elder. In this case, the 'first-born' is replaced even before his birth. Zerah is associated with Esau in two other respects. For identification, a red thread is placed on his wrist, red being a direct allusion (although a different word is used) to Edom, that is, Esau (see M.II.3). The name Zerah is also the name of one of Esau's sons. Peretz, like Jacob, is the chosen son and the ancestor of the chosen line, the line of Judah and the Davidic dynasty.

6.5. *Joseph and Potiphar's Wife*

Joseph and Potiphar's Wife is the third text in this section to examine the role of women and the problem of endogamy. Like *Judah and Tamar* it poses the possibility of sexual relations (in effect marriage) with a woman who is structurally outside. The strongest element developed in the text is the structural danger posed by women (both inside and outside). Danger is developed in both her uncontrolled passion for Joseph and her unjust treatment of him. The text, however, also fits into the structure of the 'incest' texts.

> M.IV.5. Joseph was bought by Potiphar, Captain of Pharaoh's guard. Joseph prospered in Potiphar's house and his master appointed him overseer of all that he owned. His master's wife desired him and asked him to sleep with her. Joseph refused, yet she kept entreating him day after day. One day she caught him by his cloak and he fled, leaving behind his cloak. She called the servants of the house and accused Joseph of attempting to rape her, using the cloak as proof. When Potiphar returned she laid the accusation before him and he sent Joseph into Pharaoh's prison. Even in prison Joseph prospered. The keeper of the prison gave Joseph charge of all the prisoners and the prison. The Lord made Joseph prosper in all he did (Gen. 39).

1. See for example *b. Suk.* 52a.

The primary element examined in this text is the question of endogamy. Is it appropriate for Joseph (Israel) to have (sexual) relations with other peoples? Unlike the previous two texts (*The Rape of Dinah* and *Judah and Tamar*) this text is not ambiguous. Joseph never engages in sexual relations with his master's wife, and thus the logical possibility of exogamy is never raised. On the narrative level such relations are presented as even more negative in two related ways. Joseph would be taking unfair advantage of his fortunate position as steward of his master's house if he also took his master's wife. On a legal level, Joseph would be committing adultery if he slept with her, a crime punishable by death in biblical law. Thus this text, unlike the previous two, presents an immediate rejection of exogamy on both the structural and narrative levels.

The aspect of danger is characteristic of the texts dealing with women. In the wife/sister texts the wife is equated with death, being a possible source of conflict between peoples. In *The Rape of Dinah*, Dinah goes out into the land, making herself available, and is thus the cause of strife. She creates the possibility of joining two peoples (a structurally unaccept-able solution), and ultimately leads to the destruction of Shechem. In *Judah and Tamar* the danger is subtle, embodied by Tamar's disguise. Her pretence as a prostitute suggests uncontrolled sexuality (i.e., uncontrolled fertility) which is structurally antithetical to endogamy and controlled sexuality. It is this final element that is embodied in Potiphar's wife. She represents uncontrolled sexuality which leads inexorably to death. Her actions lead to Joseph's second symbolic death. He is again placed in a pit.[1]

In keeping with the double structure found throughout the myth, Joseph has two symbolic deaths. These events include the same key elements, with some transformations. In the first death, the brothers take Joseph's coat and throw him into the pit. In this text Potiphar's wife (structurally equivalent to the brothers) takes Joseph's clothing, and Potiphar (structurally equivalent to Jacob) throws Joseph into prison. In *The Murder of Joseph*, Joseph's brothers symbolically represent the outside (analogous to Ishmael and Esau). By symbolically murdering him they strengthen the opposition between inside (Joseph) and outside (themselves). In *Joseph and Potiphar's Wife*, Potiphar's wife represents the outside and, by her unjust accusation against Joseph, strengthens the opposition. Potiphar is a structural inversion of Jacob (analogous to

---

1. In Gen. 41 the word בור 'pit' is used for the prison in which Joseph was kept.

Abraham in *The Sacrifice of Isaac*). He functions within the opposition of father to son, in which the father is denied and replaced by God.

Potiphar fits the structural role of father in several ways, including as master to servant and as being a generation above Joseph. Structurally, Potiphar is equated with Jacob (and Abraham) by symbolically killing Joseph in order that he be transformed. Potiphar also contains a final element which ties him to the structural opposition of father–son; he is a eunuch.[1] Thus, by equating Potiphar with 'father', and thereby with Jacob, this supports the denial of human fertility.

The text, however, works on a second level, as one of the 'incest' texts. If Potiphar fills the structural role of father and is thereby equivalent to Jacob, then Potiphar's wife is structurally equivalent to Joseph's mother or, at the very least, to one of Jacob's wives. Thus the possibility that Joseph might sleep with his symbolic 'mother' is part of the broader extension of endogamy.[2]

6.6. *Joseph in Prison*

The remaining texts in this chapter continue the story of Joseph's rise to power and his reunion with his brothers and father. Many of these texts do not introduce new structural elements. In a sense, the myth of Joseph (including M.IV.3, M.IV.5 and M.IV.6–M.IV.10) is analogous to a 'novella' in which a short story is expanded and dramatized without the addition of new elements. Thus the structures in the novella are analogous to the structures of a single text, rather than a group of texts. Therefore the discussion of the remaining texts will highlight the structural elements, rather than presenting a detailed analysis of each text.

> M.IV.6. Two of the prisoners incarcerated with Joseph were Pharaoh's chief butler and chief baker. One night each of them had a dream. Joseph interpreted the dreams to mean that the butler would be returned to his post in three days, and that the baker would be executed in three days. The

---

1. The word סריס can be translated as either 'eunuch' or 'servant'.
2. Although the symbolic 'incestuous' (i.e., symbolic mother–son) relationship is not consummated in this text, it is possible that it is continued in Gen. 41.50. In that text Joseph marries the 'Daughter of Potiphara'. Although the name is different from Potiphar, and may be a different person, the similarity in form raises possibilities of at least assimilation of the two (equally Potiphara could be the feminine form of Potiphar, perhaps Potiphar's wife). If the similarity is taken in conjunction with the structural roles suggested by this myth, then the daughter of Potiphara fills the structural role of Joseph's sister, again an incestuous relationship in Israelite law.

butler promised to mention Joseph to Pharaoh. Joseph's predictions
turned out to be true. The butler was returned to his post and the baker was
hanged (Gen. 40).

As mentioned above, the primary aspect of the prison is as a second
symbolic death. Although the word בור, 'pit', is only used once in relation
to the prison, it makes a direct allusion to the pit in the first part of the
Joseph myth, that is, *The Murder of Joseph*, M.IV.3. In both of those
cases descent into the pit represents a symbolic death. The element of
divine transformation (or divine support) is also present. In Potiphar's
house, the extension of the first pit (going to Egypt was also a descent),
God helps Joseph in all he does. Likewise, God is with Joseph in prison.
In each case God replaces Joseph's father—Jacob in the original pit and
Potiphar in the prison. Joseph's ability to interpret dreams is also a clear
indication of divine favor.

Several of the elements already mentioned fit into the double
structure of the Joseph myth. The pits and symbolic deaths are doubled.
This is clarified by Joseph's good fortune in each case. God is with
Joseph and his masters (Potiphar and the warden of the prison give over
all they have into Joseph's hands). This element may be doubled in
another respect. In the next section Pharaoh gives over control of Egypt
into Joseph's hand, symbolized by a change in raiment (see Gen. 41.42).
This may be related to Jacob's gift of the 'coat of many colours', further
explaining his brothers jealousy of him. The dreams of the butler and the
baker are also part of the general pattern of double structure.

6.7. *Pharaoh's Dreams*
These elements are further developed in *Pharaoh's Dreams*. The double
structure of the text is maintained (Pharaoh dreams the dream twice).
The text is also a reversal of the 'murder' texts and is the basis for
Joseph's transformation.

M.IV.7. Two years after Joseph interpreted the dreams of the butler and
the baker Pharaoh dreamed two dreams. The two dreams were almost
identical. One had cows and the second ears of grain. Each dream began
with seven well-favoured cows and ears of wheat respectively, and concluded with seven ill-favoured cows and ears of wheat eating the healthy
ones. None of the magicians or wise men of Egypt could interpret
Pharaoh's dreams. The butler, remembering Joseph, tells Pharaoh that
Joseph can interpret dreams. Joseph interprets Pharaoh's dreams to be
one message. Egypt will have seven years of plenty followed by seven
years of famine. Joseph suggests that Pharaoh appoint a man to gather the

produce of the seven years of plenty in order to prepare for the years of famine. Pharaoh appoints Joseph as Viceroy over Egypt to fulfil this task. He gives Joseph his signet, vestments and a gold chain. Joseph is given a new name by Pharaoh—Zephenathpaneah. Joseph marries Asnath, daughter of Potiphara, and has two sons, Menasseh and Ephraim (Gen. 41).

This text is an inversion of the previous 'murder' texts in which part of Joseph's clothing is taken from him and he is placed in a pit. Here Joseph is given new raiment and removed from the pit. Just as the two narratively earlier texts relate to death, this text is a symbolic birth (birth is the inversion of death). This interpretation is also supported on the narrative level; Joseph is given a new name. Thus this text is structurally equivalent to *The Covenant of Circumcision* and *The Covenant at Beth El*.

The name given to Joseph is also significant. Zephenathpaneah is translated in BDB as 'The God Speaks and he Lives', emphasizing the divine aspect of his birth/transformation. There are, however, certain ambiguous elements in the text. Pharaoh, rather than God or a man of God, gives Joseph his new name. This may be resolved in two ways. On the one hand, Pharaoh is acting for God in raising Joseph to a position of prominence. In a narratively later section of the myth, Joseph claims that God brought him to Egypt to enable Jacob and his family to find a refuge there. On the other hand, in Egypt Pharaoh was considered a god and thus could fill that structural role in this text.

The second ambiguous element is Joseph's wife. According to the pattern of inside/outside she should not be structurally acceptable, and similarly her sons (like the first three sons of Judah) should be rejected. Asnath is identified as the daughter of Potiphara, thus possibly related to Potiphar and his wife. If that text (*Joseph and Potiphar's Wife*) functions in part as an incest text, then it is likely that Joseph's wife is structurally and symbolically equivalent to Joseph's sister (daughter of characters fitting the structural role of father and mother). Thus, by making her inside she becomes acceptable as his wife after his transformation, while she was not acceptable prior to his transformation.[1]

6.8. *Joseph Sells Corn to the World*
Joseph Sells Corn to the World begins the process through which Jacob and his family go down to Egypt. Links with the wife/sister texts have

1. It is likely, however, that in the rabbinic expansions of this text, Asnath will be made fully inside, removing all possible ambiguities.

already been shown in regard to *Joseph and Potiphar's Wife*. This text introduces elements of the broader structural pattern, which continues through the book of Exodus.

> M.IV.8. (a) The famine spread throughout Egypt and all the world. Jacob saw that there was wheat in Egypt and sent all his sons, except Benjamin, down to Egypt to buy wheat. Joseph recognized his brothers but they did not recognize him. He accused them of being spies, telling them he would not let them go unless their youngest brother was brought down to him (to prove that their story was true). He imprisoned them for three days and finally allowed one brother to remain imprisoned while the others return to Canaan to get Benjamin. The brothers discussed this proposition, and tied it directly to their treatment of Joseph, expressing their guilt. He took Shimon as his prisoner and sent the brothers back to Canaan placing their money in the bags of grain. When they returned to Canaan and reported to their father, he refused to allow Benjamin to be brought down to Egypt (Gen. 42).
>
> (b) The famine continued in Canaan and Jacob was forced to send his sons back to Egypt. Judah offers to stand as surety for Benjamin, and Jacob finally agrees that he can go. The brothers were brought before Joseph, who returned Shimon to them. He gave them sacks of grain. He also commanded his steward to place in Benjamin's bag a goblet that he used for divining. After the brothers began their journey to Canaan, Joseph sent men to stop and accuse them of stealing the goblet. Joseph's officer tells the brothers that he will only detain the thief, the rest are free to go. When the goblet is found in Benjamin's bag all the brothers return with him to Joseph. Judah asks Joseph to let Benjamin go, stating that if Benjamin does not return their father will die of grief. He asks that he be allowed to remain in Benjamin's place. Joseph breaks down and reveals to his brothers who he is, telling them not to fear because it was God who brought him to Egypt so that he could save his family. Joseph tells his brothers to return to Canaan and bring Jacob down to Egypt. Pharaoh also welcomes Joseph's brothers and offers them land in Egypt. The brothers return and Jacob agrees to come down to Egypt. Jacob brings all his people to Egypt (and the text lists all his sons and grandsons). They are given the land of Goshen to dwell in because it is the best land in Egypt for sheep. It was also separate from the rest of Egypt because the Egyptians were said to abhor shepherds (Gen. 44.1–47.27).

It was suggested in *Wife/Sister 2* that the structural pattern of the wife/sister texts was also found on a broader mythological plane: the descent of Jacob and his family into Egypt and their eventual exodus as a people covenanted to God (see M.I.12). This text develops two structural elements found in the wife/sister texts: famine in Canaan and subsequent descent into Egypt. The element of danger that was characteristic of the wife/sister texts is also present in Joseph's treatment of his brothers and culminates in the enslavement. The pattern serves a similar mythological function on each level. At the level of the individual, the wife of the patriarch (i.e., of Abraham or Isaac) was brought inside. At the national level, God is equivalent to the patriarch and Israel to his wife. Through descent to Egypt and the covenant at Sinai, Israel becomes a proper (and eternal) wife for God.[1]

Benjamin is structurally a double for Joseph and he shares many characteristics with Joseph. Both are sons of Rachel and favored by their father. He is symbolically Joseph reborn, that is, the 'divine' replacement for Joseph. More importantly, however, he is part of the broader pattern of double structure, repeating (at least in part) the actions of Joseph himself. Thus the structure requires that Benjamin be brought down to Egypt.

The differences between events concerning Benjamin and Joseph are significant. Whereas Joseph's symbolic murder is carried out—Joseph is placed in the pit and sold—the brothers refuse to give up Benjamin. The texts about Benjamin are, in several respects, inversions of those concerning Joseph. Benjamin is accused of stealing and the brothers protect him. Joseph is robbed (of his coat) and sold by his brothers. This weakens the structural association and the impact of the original murder. It is likely that this weakening reflects the paradoxical nature of the brothers' role. On the one hand, they fit into the broader structure of 'inside/outside', while on the other, at least on a narrative level, they and their descendants are structurally inside.

It is significant that Judah rather than Reuben is accepted as surety for Benjamin. Throughout the text there is a movement in quality between Reuben and Judah. In the first text, *The Murder of Joseph*, Reuben is initially positive (+) and the brothers negative (–). As the narrative progresses, Judah is introduced as an ambiguous figure (–/+). In this final text Judah is singled out from his brothers as a positive figure (+). This transformation no doubt reflects political developments, that is, the political pre-eminence of the tribe of Judah. It is also structurally consistent. Judah is the youngest of Leah's first set of children, thus his pre-eminence fits in with the pattern of choosing the youngest (emphasizing divine rather than human or natural and expected choice).

1.	The imagery of Israel as God's wife (with Sinai as the point of marriage) is found throughout the Prophets. See, for example, Hos. 2.17.

6.9. *The Death of Jacob*

Jacob dies prior to the conclusion of the myth of Joseph. The central element of this text is the replacement of Jacob by Joseph, in the form of Ephraim and Manasseh. The text concludes with Jacob blessing all his sons, emphasizing that all the sons and their descendants are part of Israel.

> M.IV.9. As his death approaches, Jacob requests that he not be buried in Egypt but rather that his sons bring him back to Canaan. Joseph then brought his sons before Jacob to be blessed. Jacob takes Joseph's sons as his own. He states that any further children that Joseph may have will be called after their elder brothers (i.e., shall be members of their tribes). Joseph placed Manasseh near Jacob's right hand and Ephraim near his left, in order that Manasseh (the elder) would receive the first-born's blessing. Yet Jacob crossed his hands and placed his right hand on Ephraim's head and his left on Manasseh's. Jacob then blesses Joseph's sons (and the text says Joseph as well). Joseph tried to have his father bless Manasseh with his right hand, but Jacob answers that he knew what he was doing. Jacob tells Joseph that Ephraim shall be greater than Manasseh, and further that God will be with Joseph, emphasizing that he has given Joseph a portion above his brothers. Jacob called his sons together and blessed each one. The blessings often use animal metaphors and describe the nature of the son or the tribe that will descend from him. Jacob then reminds his sons of their promise to bury him in the cave of Machpelah in Canaan (Gen. 47.28–49.33).

The text is introduced by Jacob's request that his bones be brought back to the land of Canaan and placed with those of Abraham and Isaac. This request relates to an opposition between Canaan and Egypt. Canaan is a fitting place for 'chosen' bones to reside while Egypt is not. This opposition conforms to an understanding of geography that is characterized by similar oppositions to those found between peoples. Just as there are chosen people and peoples, so there are chosen places. This opposition is emphasized by the following text where Joseph, the chosen son of Jacob, makes a similar request.

The second significant element in the text is the adoption of Ephraim and Manasseh. Prewitt suggests that the adoption of Joseph's sons represents a replacement of Joseph, and that the sons are blessed in Joseph's place and further that Joseph is structurally opposed to Israel as a secular leader (1990: 19).[1] He incorrectly diminishes the primacy of

---

1. A similar point is made by Steiner (1985: 21-25). He suggests that, because of his enslavement, Joseph was no longer part of Jacob's family (1985: 22). There

Joseph because of his emphasis on the importance of Benjamin. In the
text both Joseph and his sons are blessed (see Gen. 48.15)[1]. Far from
replacing a marginalized Joseph, his father gives him a double blessing,
two tribal portions in the place of one. The double inheritance is tied to
his position as Jacob's chosen son.

Prewitt also argues that Joseph is marginalized by the exclusion of any
other sons which he might have (1990: 19). This is based on a misunderstanding of the text (Gen. 48.6), since the position of these children
would be directly analogous to any children Joseph's brothers might
have. Joseph's children would be part of either the tribe of Ephraim or
Manasseh (the two tribes of Joseph). Similarly any children Judah might
have would be part of the tribe of Judah. Thus the adoption of Ephraim
and Manasseh, and the position of any future sons, far from proving that
Joseph was marginalized, emphasizes instead his role as bearer of the
divine seed.

The adoption also fits into the broader pattern of chosenness. Joseph
expects that his oldest son Manasseh will receive the fuller blessing. He
places Manasseh at his father's right hand. Yet Jacob crosses his hands
and gives the fuller blessing to Ephraim. The divine element of this
choice is emphasized by Jacob's blindness: it is God who directs his
movements. Thus corresponding to the general pattern it is the younger
son who is chosen, contrary to all expectations.

The adoption of Ephraim and Manasseh also should be seen in the
framework of the myths dealing with 'divine birth'. In that context they

---

are, however, several flaws in his arguments. He bases his suggestion on ethnographic
evidence from societies which are in no way similar to the Israelites who wrote the
text (Northwest American Indians) (1985: 23). He also ignores the fact that, in other
biblical texts slavery does not affect the family status of an individual. He also raises
questions about the form of Joseph's oath, that is, placing his hand on Jacob's thigh.
He suggests that this cannot be on the genitals for two reasons: it conflicts with
current Arab custom, and would be forbidden by Israelite family purity (1985: 22).
The first reason has no standing on its own because Israelite customs would not
necessarily conform to modern Arab customs. His second reason is also intrinsically
flawed. He bases his argument on Gen. 9.21-25, and Lev. 18.6-18. These texts,
however, clearly refer to incestuous (or sexual) relations, not merely touching, and
thus do not support his contention. In the two cases where this type of oath is used
(Gen. 24.2; 47.29) the text is concerned with descendants, thus the genitals of the
patriarch, who symbolizes the family, would be a logical place for such an oath.

1.   In fact Joseph is blessed both in ch. 48 and in ch. 49, where his blessing is the
longest.

should be seen as Joseph symbolically reborn, the double birth fitting into the double structure of the text as a whole. The element of symbolic birth is structurally tied to Jacob's death, the center of the entire text (and the pretext for all the action). Thus upon Joseph's symbolic rebirth Jacob dies, removing his parental role.

The text concludes with Jacob blessing all his sons. The blessings are significant in revealing the structural relations of the tribes. Figure 12 places the tribes in order of length and quality of blessing. Figure 12 suggests that Judah and Joseph are singled out from the other brothers. Both are analogous genealogically, Joseph being the youngest son (disregarding Benjamin), and Judah being the youngest of Leah's first set of sons. Reuben and Simeon/Levi are given negative blessings emphasizing their replacement by Judah. As opposed to Prewitt's suggestion, the length of Benjamin's blessing—one verse—argues against giving him prominence.

Leah	Rachel	Zilpah	Bilhah
Judah (+) [5]	Joseph (+) [5]		
			Dan (+) [3]
Shim./Levi (−) [3]			
Reub. (−) [2]			
Zeb. (+) [1]		Gad (+) [1]	
Iss. (+) [1]	Ben. (+) [1]	Asher (+) [1]	Naph. (+) [1]
( ) = quality	[ ] = number of verses		

Figure 12. *Jacob's Blessings*

6.10. *The Death of Joseph*

The final text of this chapter focuses on the death of Joseph. The text highlights Joseph's structural prominence by treating him similarly to Jacob; he too is to be buried in Canaan.

M.IV.10. Joseph and his brothers brought Jacob to Canaan and buried him there. Upon their return the brothers fear that Joseph will take his revenge on them. They tell Joseph that, before he died, their father commanded him to forgive his brothers. Joseph tells them not to worry. Before his death Joseph asks his brothers to bring his bones out of Egypt when God brings them forth. Joseph died and was embalmed in Egypt (Gen. 50).

This text reintroduces the opposition between Joseph and his brothers. The opposition is offered as a possibility (the brother's fear that he will take revenge), but is rejected by Joseph. Genesis concludes with unity rather than division. Joseph is, however, distinguished from his brothers. Like his father before him, he too asks that his bones be carried back to Canaan. As in previous texts in the Joseph novella, the text contains the paradox of structurally continuing the opposition of chosen to non-chosen (i.e., Israel and the nations) while, on a narrative level, referring to people who are equally chosen.

6.11. *Synthesis*

The central focus of this chapter is the Joseph novella. As a single myth, it contains all of the structural elements examined in the previous chapters. The text examined the question of endogamy, that is of inside/outside (in regard to Potiphar's wife), as well as the denial of human fertility in favor of divine fruitfulness (Potiphar as eunuch). The text includes symbolic death and birth, emphasized by a clear opposition between Joseph and his brothers. This is part of the broader structure of segmentation, by which a single line is qualitatively distinguished from the other lines. This structural pattern, however, was mediated in a number of ways: the ambiguous role of the Midianites, Reuben's attempt to save Joseph, and Judah's defence of Benjamin at the conclusion of the text. The mediation served to weaken the opposition in order to tie into the narrative requirement of bringing all of Jacob's sons inside.

The paradoxical element which is found throughout the Joseph myth reveals an essential theoretical point. On the synchronic level, all myths deal with the same structural problems. Thus, on that level, the Joseph myth is structurally identical with the *Sacrifice of Isaac* (especially in regard to the rejection of Ishmael and Eliezer) and the myths relating to the rejection of Esau. Like Ishmael and Esau, on the synchronic level Joseph's brothers are equated with the nations (structurally outside), and the myth serves to emphasize the opposition between the two. This opposition is also connected to the principle of endogamy, whereby the structure of inside/outside can be carried to the lowest level of social structure.

On the diachronic level, however, the structural relations are transformed according to narrative requirements. Thus, with respect to the biblical narrative, the story requires that the brothers be brought inside because they are the ancestors of the tribes of Israel. Thus the mediators are brought in to weaken the opposition developed on the synchronic level. The doubling of the myth as a whole is part of this mediation process. The diachronic level of the myth does not replace the synchronic, it merely transforms the oppositions to enable them to serve both structural requirements.

The second element of theoretical importance emerging from the Joseph novella is the process of doubling. Doubling, like inversion, is one of the mechanisms through which the structure of the myth is clouded (or in part transformed; the very clouding weakens the structural oppositions). In this text every element of structural importance is inverted. This suggests a similar rule to that stated above: where elements in a text are doubled, all elements will be doubled in a similar way. The rule can be extended to a general structural principle: where structural elements are transformed, all elements will be transformed in a consistent way (see M.IV.3, The *Murder of Joseph*, and §11.5).

This chapter also examined three texts that dealt with the role of women. All three texts posed a challenge to the principle of endogamy (two dealing with a woman from the outside, and one a man). Each of the texts concluded with an affirmation of endogamy. In the case of the *Rape of Dinah*, in which the principle was openly challenged (we shall become one people), Shechem and his people were killed. In *Judah and Tamar* Judah's 'outside' children die (one through a sexual crime emphasizing Judah's sexual crime). The text concludes with Judah finding an acceptable wife—with inside fertility being emphasized by the birth of twins. In *Joseph and Potiphar's Wife* Joseph's actions (rejecting her) reaffirms the principle.

Aside from a rejection of exogamy, all three texts also developed the ambiguous nature of women in Israelite structure. In all three cases the women were structurally dangerous. This danger is tied to an inherent problem in Israelite endogamy: the system moves in two directions. On the one hand, it moves inward: the principle of inside–outside opposition is carried down to the family. On the other hand, due to extensive rules of incest, it moves outward: the family must look beyond its boundaries to find women. The system requires that wives from outside the family be brought inside, thus creating a crisis of logic and structural danger. This element is examined in the following chapter in regard to Adam and Eve and will be discussed in some detail in the broader discussion of Hebrew myth in Chapter 11.

Chapter 7

CREATION

This chapter examines the first eleven chapters of Genesis. This section of Genesis is discussed after the narratively later sections because we find in it oppositions which are based on a similar structure ($s^{(2)}$) to those in the other chapters of Genesis, yet which do not (at least explicitly) deal with the same issues. Thus, for example, in M.V.1, *The Creation of the World*, a similar form of opposition is developed in respect to the natural world and to time.[1] In M.V.6, *The Flood*, the same form of opposition discussed in the earlier chapters is extended to the animal world (i.e., dialectical oppositions with impermeable boundaries). Both texts function to reveal that the oppositions existing in humanity exist also in other spheres and thus are based on natural rather than cultural logic.

Some of the texts examined in this chapter deal with the same oppositions as the previous chapters. Thus *The Murder of Abel* (M.V.3) examines the opposition between brothers and that between Israel and the nations. *Lamech* (M.V.4) presents the opposition between generations. *The Sons of God and the Daughters of Men* introduces the divine element. *Noah and his Sons* (M.V.7) examines the question of incest. All of these oppositions are presented in a fashion consistent with those in the previous sections.

---

1. It might be thought that this chapter, dealing with material narratively earlier in the text, should have been placed before the previous five chapters. It is placed here for two reasons. On the one hand, it introduces oppositions at a global level rather than at the particularist level. Although these may not be extensions of the particularist oppositions, they are not directly related to social organization and thus are considered secondary oppositions rather than primary oppositions. On the other hand, with Gen. 11 there is a shift in focus in the narrative. The texts coming after this shift do not rely on the diachronically earlier texts for their structural message—there is no diachronic development of structure between the two parts. And finally, since structuralist theory suggests that diachronic order is irrelevant to structure, this section is examined last.

7.1. *The Creation of the World*

This text describes the creation of the world by God. It introduces into the order and form of creation the same type of logical structure that was found in the opposition between Israel and the nations. Dichotomous oppositions are offered as the basic structure of the universe.

> M.V.1. In the beginning (i.e., the first day of creation) God created heaven and earth, and distinguished between light and darkness, calling the darkness night and the light day. On the second day God placed a firmament in the midst of the waters, distinguishing between the water above the firmament and that below. On the third day God gave the water boundaries and created dry land. He also created grasses and fruit trees. On the fourth day God made the lights of the heavens, to distinguish between the night and the day. He created the two greater lights (the sun and the moon). The sun to rule the day and the moon to rule the night. He also created the stars. On the fifth day God created the beasts of the sea and the birds of the air. God commanded them to be fruitful and multiply. On the sixth day God created the beasts of the field. Finally God created man in 'his image'. God gave man dominion over the rest of creation, and commanded man to be fruitful and multiply. When God completed creation he rested on the seventh day, and blessed the seventh day (Gen. 1.1–2.4).

This entire section is composed of oppositions.[1] Each day of creation is characterized by an opposition and there are two further oppositions superimposed on the entire text. There is an opposition between humanity and the rest of creation. Humankind is given dominion over creation and, after humankind's creation, God calls creation 'very good'

---

1. In 'Lévi-Strauss in the Garden of Eden', Leach suggests that this myth is characterized by opposition and mediation (1970: 55). Leach is correct that the myth develops binary oppositions. These oppositions, however, are not mediated. Carroll convincingly shows that most of the mediators suggested by Leach are not supported by textual evidence (1985: 127-30). Many of the mediators he describes do not fit his definition of mediators. Sky shares no attributes with either firmament or sea, rather it is empty space. By suggesting that the oppositions developed in Gen. 1 require mediation, Leach misunderstands the structural role of the text. The text serves to create oppositions rather than to cloud them. Mediators work on two levels. Within a specific myth they either cloud oppositions which are problematic, or they bridge gaps to help the narrative develop. On the broader level, the myth itself mediates and clouds crisis and opposition. In societies in which exchange is positive, and therefore boundaries are permeable, oppositions will be mediated by positive mediators emphasizing that the boundaries do not really exist. In societies, like Israel, where exchange is ideologically forbidden, opposition will be emphasized and therefore mediators of the sort used by Leach in regard to this text will either be absent or be negative.

while he calls the other days only 'good'. There is also a distinction between the seventh day—the Shabbat—and the rest of the days of the week; it alone is blessed.

In the previous texts discussed, the structure functioned to create a logical distinction between Israel and the nations. Humanity could be divided into two distinct types, Israel being qualitatively different from the rest. This text argues that the same logic of a similar form is also present in all aspects of the world. Creation, which seems unified, can actually be divided into oppositions: day and night, fish and birds, and so on. This is because the same logic present in social organization was also present in creation. The logic is proved by the text to be natural and therefore unassailable. This logic is also projected onto time. The week is divided into the six working days and the Sabbath. The seventh day is qualitatively distinguished from the other day: it alone is blessed. The seventh day is also alone in being given a name, שבת coming from the root meaning 'rest'. The other days are called by number.

The oppositions found in each day of creation do not appear to be qualitative: fish and birds seem to be qualitatively equivalent. The element of qualitative distinction is found in the two overall oppositions. Humanity is qualitatively distinguished from the world, being given dominion over it, and Shabbat is qualitatively separated from the other days. This text thus develops the following equations: The World : Humankind :: Weekdays : Shabbat.

7.2. Adam and Eve
Genesis offers two versions of the creation story. The first myth centers around the logical oppositions implicit in creation. The second myth focuses on the creation of humanity, and its expulsion from the garden.

> M.V.2. Before creating any plants, God took dust and formed it into man and breathed into him the breath of life. God then planted a garden in Eden and placed man there to tend it. In the center of the garden God planted two trees: the tree of life, and the tree of the knowledge of good and evil. God commanded man not to eat of the tree of the knowledge of good and evil lest he dies. God formed all of the animals and gave them to man to name. He took one of Adam's[1] ribs and made Eve. The serpent convinced Eve to take a piece of fruit from the tree of knowledge. She in turn gave it to Adam and they both ate of it. After eating, they realized they were naked

---

1.   The word אדם means 'man' in Hebrew. Thus Adam is generic man and, like those figures after him, is corporate rather than individual.

and made coverings from fig leaves. When God found out what they had done he cast them from the garden and cursed them. The myth suggests that the reason for their exile from the garden was to prevent them from eating from the tree of life (Gen. 2.5–3.24).

The first half of this text follows the pattern of incest texts described above (see, e.g., *Wife/Sister 1*). God provides two sets of partners for Adam: the animals and Eve. In v. 18 God creates the animals to be a helper/mate for Adam. In v. 21 Eve is created because no appropriate helper/mate was found among the animals. The primary difference between Eve and the animals is that the animals were independent creations, while Eve was created from Adam. Thus the animals were structurally outside (a different species), while Eve was structurally inside (part of Adam).[1]

The second element linking this text with the other incest texts is danger. Although the serpent mediates the danger posed by the woman, it is ultimately Eve (woman) that brings death to humankind. The element of danger is tied to the ambiguous position of the women in the Israelite system. No matter how close she is, the woman is always relatively outside.

The element of opposition within creation is also present in this version of creation.[2] Essentially, the knowledge given by the tree of knowledge is that of oppositions. The text also presents the opposition of divine to human. Humanity is characterized by ignorance and death, while divine is knowledgeable and immortal. There is an inversion of the human condition in the myth. Prior to their expulsion from the garden, humans were ignorant but had eternal life. After the expulsion they had knowledge but were mortal. Their state on expulsion is the normal human state. It is likely that there is also an opposition between human and animal. One distinction, unacceptability as a mate, is already mentioned. A second distinction lies in humankind's role in naming the animals, an ability not shared with the animal world.

The myth also contains the element of symbolic or divine birth. This

1. Diachronic development of the text clarifies this element through introduction of an independently created spouse, Lillith, for Adam as well as Eve.
2. Stordalen suggests that there is a structural opposition on another level in this text, arguing that the terms שׂיח and עשׂב are structurally opposed. He suggests that שׂיח refers to uncultivated plants (nature) while עשׂב refers to cultivated plants (culture). Stordalen further proposes the following equation (my formulation) שׂיח : עשׂב :: Nature : Culture :: Curse : Blessing :: Inside : Outside (1992: 19).

element is doubled. Adam and Eve are of autochthonous origin: they are created by God from dust. The text emphasizes the distinction between their birth and natural birth by denying human sexuality. Neither Adam nor Eve realized that they were naked, they were not aware of their sexuality. The element of transformation (symbolic birth) is also emphasized by their expulsion from the garden. Only upon expulsion are they truly human, sexually aware and subject to death. Like newborn babies, Adam and Eve are clothed by God (their parent).

The expulsion of Adam and Eve from the garden was in an easterly direction (Gen. 3.24). Throughout Genesis east is presented as negative movement, reflecting movement towards a more negative qualitative state. In M.V.3, *The Murder of Abel*, Cain moves east after the murder of Abel. The builders of the Tower of Babel also move east. Finally, Lot takes the east bank of the Jordan, leaving Abraham the west. Apart from Egypt, the primary centers of civilization were to the east of Canaan.

7.3. *The Murder of Abel*

M.V.2 introduced two oppositions: between divine and natural birth; and between inside and outside in respect to the wife. The *Murder of Abel* introduces the opposition between brothers. This opposition is developed in two ways: through the murder of Abel, and through the introduction of genealogical material (creating two opposing genealogical lines, one descended from Cain and the other from Seth).

> M.V.3. After leaving the garden Adam and Eve had two sons: Cain and Abel. Abel was a shepherd and Cain was a farmer. After some time, both Cain and Abel decided to make an offering to God. Cain brought an offering from the fruit of the earth, and Abel from the first-born of the flock. God accepted Abel's offering, but did not accept Cain's. Soon after these events, Cain rose up and murdered Abel his brother. God accuses Cain of Abel's murder and curses him. He, however, places a sign upon Cain's head in order that no one should kill him. Cain went and settled in the land of Nod where he had a son. The text then gives the genealogy of Cain. It attributes to Cain and his descendants the foundation of civilization: Cain builds a city; Tuval was the father of those who live in tents; Yuval was the inventor of music; and Tuval Cain was the father of the smiths. The text concludes with the birth of Adam and Eve's third son Seth (who was given in the place of Abel). It also mentions Seth's son Enosh, who was the first person to call on the name of God (Gen. 4.1-22, 25–26).

The primary opposition in the first half of the text centers on the murder of Abel. This text is part of the same structural complex as *The Sacrifice of Isaac* and *The Murder of Joseph*.[1] In this text, however, unlike the other versions, the murder is actually carried out. The murder is introduced by an opposition between Cain and Abel. It is likely that their respective occupations were qualitatively weighted. Although, at the time the texts were written the Israelites were settled, there seems a bias throughout the text in favor of shepherds. Thus Abel was in the preferable occupation. This preference is made apparent in God's acceptance of Abel's sacrifice rather than Cain's.

The element of divine choice (as in the Joseph story) is the motivating factor in the murder: Cain kills because he was rejected. Like Ishmael in the *Sacrifice of Isaac* and Reuben in *the Murder of Joseph* respectively, Cain was the first-born. Thus Cain has every expectation that his offering will be given preference. Rejection of his sacrifice is rejection of his position as first-born. It has been noted on several occasions that there is a structural pattern throughout the text in which a younger son is always chosen over the first-born. Like the structural element of death and symbolic birth, this element serves to emphasize the divine aspect of descent, rather than the human.

The murder itself removes Abel from the line of human descent. Yet, rather than being reborn (resurrected), Abel is replaced. Seth mediates between human descent and divine birth. The text clearly indicates that

---

1. Although on the narrative level Cain murders Abel, on a structural level it can be understood as a sacrifice. This is supported by the structurally similar myths, for example, *The Sacrifice of Isaac*. It is also supported by the internal structure of the text described by Carroll (1985: 127-35). He suggests an internal structure in which Cain's murder of Abel is structurally equivalent to Abel's sacrifice of an animal earlier in the text (1985: 128). The second half of his argument, however, has several problems. He suggests that Cain is the founder of culture (as qualitatively positive) and further that the text logically supports exogamy (1985: 130). He consistently ignores the negative elements in the text relating to Cain and his descendants (and that Israel is descended not from Cain, who practised exogamy, but from Seth). He equally misunderstands the role of incest in Genesis by only focusing on two ambiguous (or negative) cases of incest (i.e., Lot and his daughters and Ham and Noah). He ignores all the positive cases, as well as all the texts emphasizing endogamy (1985: 133-34). In his discussion of Jacob and Esau he argues that the quarrel between Jacob and Esau is a 'devaluation of close kin' (i.e., against endogamy) (1985: 134). He misses the fact that Esau represents Edom, that is, a separate nation, and thus the quarrel supports endogamy rather than exogamy.

Seth is a replacement for Abel; he is Abel reborn. Upon his birth, Eve says that Seth was given to her in place of Abel. Thus Abel is structurally equivalent to pre-sacrifice Isaac, and Seth is equivalent to post-sacrifice Isaac. Like the other texts which deal with symbolic birth, this text is a rejection of human descent in favor of divine descent.[1]

The opposition between Abel and Cain is developed in four ways in the text.[2] First, a distinction based on occupation, as discussed. Secondly, the murder itself. Thirdly, Cain goes to a different land and marries there (outside). Cain's movement is negative by definition. He moves east, a direction which is always ideologically negative. Fourthly, by opposing the genealogies of Cain and Seth (Abel) respectively. Cain's descendants

1.   Aycock completely misinterprets this text (a fact pointed out by Leach in Leach and Aycock 1983: 4-5). He suggests that Cain and Jesus are structurally analogous (1983: 120). Leach suggests that Jesus is structurally equivalent to Abel rather than Cain. Both Jesus and Abel were sacrificed (Cain is the killer rather than the killed). All elements related to Jesus and Cain are inverted. Cain kills, Jesus is killed; Cain founds a sinful mortal city, Jesus a divine city; Cain is marked as a killer, Jesus is marked as killed. Their respective stigmas are significant. Jesus is marked as a sacrifice, while Cain's stigma prevents him from being eligible to be sacrificed. Thus the two are structural opposites rather than equivalents.

Leach, however, is incorrect in emphasizing Cain's role in creating civilization as a positive act (Leach and Aycock 1983: 19). The text does not consider Cain's act to be positive. His city is built east of Eden, a consistently negative direction. And cities are often, in the biblical texts, seen to be wicked places. The creations of Cain's line are also structurally opposed to those of Seth's line; material as opposed to spiritual. Leach also incorrectly continues Aycock's line of argument in suggesting that Cain replaces Abel. Structurally Cain is opposed to Abel, who is replaced by Seth, a fact mentioned by Leach himself earlier in his discussion (Leach and Aycock 1983: 4).

2.   Schapera misses the reason for Cain's escape of death as punishment for murdering Abel (Schapera 1985: 26-41). Cain and his descendants must survive (mythologically) to be structurally opposed to Seth and his descendants. If Cain had been properly punished then the text would not have fitted the structural requirements. This raises questions about his arguments as a whole. He suggests that Cain was not punished because he was a brother, and therefore could not be killed by members of his own family (Schapera 1985: 28). He uses several other biblical texts to back up his contention. In the other texts that he cites the murderers are all men of power, who would be able to escape punishment because of their power rather than because of their family relations. In all of the cases (except Solomon) the murderers were eventually punished (by God or man) (Schapera 1985: 29). In Solomon's case he had a legal right to kill his brother because his brother attempted take their father's concubine, symbolically announcing that he was the one fit to be king. Thus both the interpretation of the original text and of the subsequent texts are open to challenge.

are listed and tied to the creation of city life. The qualitatively negative aspect of his line is emphasized through a short text interposed between the 'Cainite' genealogy and the 'Sethite' genealogy. This text, which is examined below, *Lamech*, centers on the murder of Cain by his descendant five generations removed. Thus it is likely that Cain's line and the civilization it created was perceived as ideologically negative. It is significant that urbanization is said to have its origins in the east, emphasizing its negative status. This is opposed to the qualitatively positive aspects of Seth and his genealogy.

Seth and his descendants have three positive elements distinguishing them from Cain and his descendants. Seth is the replacement for the chosen son Abel. Seth remains in the land outside Eden and presumably takes an acceptable wife (inside). Furthermore, Seth's son Enosh is credited with being the first to call upon the name of God. This text is part of the equation: Cain : Seth (Abel) :: Urbanization (Godless) : Religion. This distinction is further emphasized in the longer Sethite genealogy (Gen. 5.22) where Seth's descendant Hanoch is said to 'walk with God'.

7.4. *Lamech*

The myth of Lamech is found in a fragment in Genesis 4. Lamech is Cain's descendant five generations removed. It is likely that the primary narrative function of the myth is to emphasize the negative elements of Cain and his descendants.

> M.V.4. Lamech married two women, Adah and Zillah. Adah bore him two sons and Zillah one. Each one of the sons initiated an element of civilization. Lamech recited the following to his wives (in the form of a poem). 'Adah and Zillah hear my voice, the wives of Lamech pay attention to what I say. Because I have killed a man for wounding me and a young man for wounding me. Cain will be avenged sevenfold, and Lamech seven and seventy' (Gen. 4.23-24).[1]

This fragment is ambiguous. It is unclear whom Lamech killed or why his punishment should be so heavy. The text offers two possibilities, either a boy or a man. It is possible that it fits into the context of the *Sacrifice of Isaac*. Thus Lamech's victim could have been his son, thus indicating the reason for his remorse and the use of the word ילד, 'boy'. A second equally likely explanation is that Lamech murdered Cain,

1. Fohrer assigns this text to N (1986: 160).

hence the mention of Cain in the next verse. The murder of Cain would be an inversion of the usual pattern. Such an inversion would fit with the qualitatively negative understanding of Cain and his descendants. The primary narrative function of the fragment is to emphasize the depravity of Cain's line in opposition to that of Seth (Abel).

7.5. *The Sons of God and the Daughters of Men*

Like the text about Lamech, this text is also a small fragment. On the narrative level the text explains the shortening of the human life span. In the texts prior to this myth humans live an average of nine hundred years, in the texts after it the average life span is four hundred years. The text also explains in part the presence of giants on the earth.

> M.V.5. After human beings spread in the earth, the 'sons of God' saw the 'daughters of men' and took wives from among them. God decided to cut man's life span to one hundred and twenty years. The giants were in the land in those days. The offspring of the sons of God were the mighty men of old (Gen. 6.1-4).

This text works on two structural levels: introducing the divine element into humanity and illustrating the result of inappropriate unions. One of the primary structural elements discussed above was the denial of human fertility in favor of divine fertility. This text explicitly introduces the divine seed into humanity. The last verse of the text suggests that the fruit of this union was ideologically positive, men of renown. On this level they are logically opposed to the נפלים the 'giants'. In the context of the general structural pattern, the giants fill the same structural role as the nations (lacking the divine seed) and the men of renown as Israel (products of the divine seed).

A second possible reading of the text suggests that the giants were the products of the union. Thus a union between two types produced negative rather than positive results. The rejection of this union suggested by God's action (i.e., taking the divine element out of humanity) is a rejection of exogamy. This interpretation is supported in the verses following this text where God sees the wickedness of humanity and decides to destroy all living creatures.

7.6. *The Flood*

The flood myth is to a great extent a second (or third) creation story. The world is destroyed and humankind and animals are reborn out of a floating womb. Like the original story, humanity is again descended

from a single pair, Noah and his wife. Like Adam, Noah too has three
sons, one of whom—Shem—is the ancestor of the chosen line.

M.V.6. God saw that wickedness had spread over the earth and he
repented that he had created humankind. God descended to destroy all life
from the earth with the exception of Noah, because Noah found favor in
his eyes. God told Noah of his plans (to flood the earth) and commanded
Noah to build an ark. God made a covenant with Noah. He told Noah to
bring his family into the ark and to take with him two of every living
creature (one male and one female).[1] It rained for forty days and nights.
All life, except for that in the ark, perished. God remembered Noah and
dried up the flood. Exactly five months after the beginning of the flood (the
flood began on the 17th day of the second month and ended on the 17th
day of the seventh month) the ark rested on Ararat. Noah sent out birds
(first a raven and then a dove) to discover if the land had dried up. It was
only on the 27th of the second month—exactly a year and ten days after
the beginning of the flood—that Noah and his family were able to leave the
ark. God commanded Noah, his family and all the animals to leave the ark,
and to be fruitful and multiply. Noah built an altar and sacrificed upon it
one of each of the pure animals. God promised that he would not 'curse
the ground' for humankind's sake because humankind's inclination is to
evil. God blessed Noah and his sons and gave them all the animals of the
earth to be their food. Humankind was forbidden to eat of animals that
were still alive and prohibited from killing each other. God established
a covenant with all that went from the ark, promising never to destroy
all life from the earth. God made the rainbow, a sign of this covenant
(Gen. 6.5–9.19).

The initial opposition presented in this text is between Noah and the
people around him. Noah is characterized as a righteous man while the
other people are wicked. Noah's righteousness is comparative. He is a
righteous man compared to other people.[2] Thus his righteousness
emphasizes his opposition to other people and their wickedness. This
myth is part of the broader pattern opposing Israel and the nations.
Noah is structurally equivalent to Israel. He is the descendant of the
chosen line, that is, from Seth, and he is qualitatively distinguished from
his fellows. Noah is righteous and chosen by God. The people who are

---

1. The text then continues with an alternative version. God tells Noah to take
seven pairs of pure animals yet only two pairs of impure animals. (There is a similar
distinction between Noah and the other people: God saves him because he was
righteous.) The text then carries on according to the original version.

2. Gen. 9.6 states, 'Noah was a righteous man in his generation', that is, Noah
was righteous in comparison with his generation.

destroyed are structurally equivalent to the nations. This text develops
the equation: Noah : People :: Salvation : Destruction :: Israel : Nations.

The destruction of people other than Noah is narratively significant,
but structurally insignificant. Even though the people are destroyed and
therefore not the ancestors of later peoples, the opposition is still
mythologically developed. The other people remain logically associated
with the nations, and with the destruction of the other people, the
nations are also destroyed.

The *Flood* also works on a second level as a myth of transformation
or symbolic birth. The text is one of re-creation. The world is destroyed
and re-created through the inhabitants of the ark. Although the J text
mentions seven pairs of pure animals, in most of the text each animal
(humans included) comes in a pair. Noah and his wife are structurally
and narratively equivalent to Adam and Eve. The ark is a symbolic
womb through which Noah and his family are reborn. As in the other
texts of transformation, this 'divine birth' is through God rather than
humankind. This aspect of transformation is similar to the second level
of opposition between Israel and the nations. Israel, like Noah, is of
divine descent (and fruitful) while the nations, like the people, are of
human origin and barren (symbolically emphasized by their destruction).

The J text develops a similar opposition among the animals. J divides
the animals into two types: pure and impure. The opposition is highlighted
by the differing number of animals to be taken onto the ark: fourteen
(seven pairs) pure animals as opposed to two impure animals. The pure
animals are also qualitatively distinguished from the impure animals. At
the conclusion of the text Noah sacrifices only the pure animals, not the
impure, implying that only the pure animals are fit for offering to God.
This division is similar in structure to that between Israel and the nations.
The opposition between different categories of animals is elaborated in
later books of the Bible. All animals are divided into two classes: kosher
and non-kosher. Kosher, or pure, animals can be eaten or sacrificed by
Israel, and non-kosher (impure) animals may not be eaten or sacrificed
by Israel (the food of Israel is from the same animals as God's food).
Thus the opposition in animals works on two levels: developing a similar
structure in the natural world and dividing the human world into those
who eat and sacrifice pure animals and those who do not.

The opposition between types of animals is part of a generalization
process. In order to naturalize (make cultural patterns appear to be
natural patterns, see 2.5) the logic, it is perceived in all spheres. In this

text it is developed in the animal world. In *The Creation of the World* the logic was developed in respect to time, and in *The Tower of Babel* (M.V.9) it encompasses languages. Other biblical texts develop similar oppositions in regard to geography, and within Israel itself between the Israelites and the priesthood. By presenting the logic in these other areas the following argument is developed: since everything in our experience of the natural world is divided into oppositions, with one side qualitatively distinct from the other, then it is logical and natural that a similar pattern should be present in human beings as well.

7.7. *The Sin of Ham*

The text that concludes the Noah narrative develops two related themes. It suggests that the wickedness of the people around Noah still exists among his sons (a possibility suggested by God in the conclusion of the previous section). The text also develops oppositions between Shem and Ham and on the intergenerational level between Shem and Noah. It is possible that the text was once an 'incest' type of myth. Apparently, however, due to the nature of the incest, it was transformed, making the incest negative rather than positive.

> M.V.8. Noah became a man of the earth and planted a vineyard. He drank from the wine and became drunk. He was uncovered in his tent. Ham, the father of Canaan saw the nakedness of his father, and he told his two brothers who were outside. Shem and Yaphet took a garment and placed it on their shoulders and went in backward and covered the nakedness of their father, and they faced the other direction and did not see their father's nakedness. Noah awoke from his stupor, and knew what his younger son had done to him. He said, 'Canaan is cursed. He will be a servant of servants to his brothers. Blessed be the Lord, God of Shem; and Canaan shall be their servant. God will enlarge Yaphet, and he shall dwell in the tents of Shem. And Canaan shall be their servant.'(Gen. 9.20-28)[1]

The previous text (*The Flood*) created a structural imbalance (on the diachronic level). It suggests that all the people other than Noah (i.e., the nations) have been destroyed and only the chosen line remains. This possibility is the exact opposite of the structural role of the myth; M.V.6 introduces an argument against this type of conclusion. God tells Noah that wickedness (the nations) has not been wiped out because 'man is wicked from his youth'. This, however, does not serve to create an

---

1. This is a translation of the text rather than a summary. Fohrer suggests that it is from the N stratum (1986: 161).

opposition between the chosen line and the other lines. That structural problem is resolved in this text. Ham, Noah's youngest son becomes the embodiment of wickedness and is cursed and logically opposed to both his brothers.

Ham's crime is not explicitly described in the text. The text merely states that 'he saw his father's nakedness'. If, however, the Hebrew expression used here is compared to similar usage in other sections of the Torah it appears to have sexual and incestuous overtones.[1] In other cases where the term ערוה, 'nakedness', is used, it refers to an incestuous sexual relationship (either heterosexual or homosexual). Ham's crime appears to be sexual relations with his sleeping father and is thus similar to that of Sodom and Gomorrah (M.I.10) and possibly of the other people before the flood. Ham is thus structurally equivalent to the other people and logically opposed to Noah and Shem.

It is interesting that throughout the text Ham is associated with his son Canaan; being identified as Ham the father of Canaan. It is Canaan, not Ham, who is cursed by Noah. Of all the peoples with whom the Israelites dealt, the Canaanites were potentially the most structurally problematic. The Israelite settlement was among the Canaanites. In addition the 'historical' texts suggest that Canaanite cities existed well into the time of David. Thus, the Canaanites were the closest population to the Israelites, and if the Israelites were to intermarry, the Canaanites were the most likely partners. Canaan is associated with Ham's sin and, through the curse, is ideologically distanced from Israel. Similarly Canaan is genealogically distanced from Israel.[2]

---

1.   See, for example, Lev. 18.6-23.

2.   The structurally problematic nature of the Canaanites would be even stronger if the conclusions of some recent studies are correct. These studies suggest that the Israelites were not primarily invaders from outside Canaan, but were Canaanite peasants (among others) rebelling against the 'feudal' political system (Mendenhall 1970: 100-20; Bright 1972: 133-37; Gottwald 1979: 210-19, 489-92). If this theory is correct, it would explain several aspects of the Israelite ideological attitude toward the Canaanites. It is suggested that one of the goals of both the mythological texts and the genealogical texts is to create ideological distance between Israel and her neighbours. Thus the Canaanites are genealogically distant from Israel in order to create distance between the Israelites who, in reality, are too close. Unlike the other nations which are said to be genealogically close, whose closeness is resolved by ideological distance, the Canaanites were too close, and ideological distance was not sufficient. Ideological distance is created both by the curse and the innumerable texts which emphasize the ideological distance between Israelites and the Canaanites.

Shem is also distinguished from Yaphet and Noah. In the blessing Noah calls God the 'God of Shem', rather than 'my God'. This emphasizes the distinction between Shem and Yaphet. It also emphasizes that the divine seed and divine relationship had passed from Noah to Shem. Noah is also implicitly criticized. It was his drunkenness which led Ham into sin. The distinction between Shem and Yaphet is not entirely clear. In Noah's curse/blessing he states, 'he shall dwell in the tents of Shem'. This phrase can be understood to apply to Yaphet or God. Structurally it is likely that it refers to God rather than Yaphet, emphasizing rather than minimizing the distinction between Shem and all his brothers.

Through Ham's sin this myth is tied to the incest texts in the rest of Genesis. This myth, however, is inverted. It is homosexual rather than heterosexual incest and is thus barren rather than fruitful. Whereas the other cases of incest brought the two partners inside relative to each other, this incest marginalized Ham and his descendants. It is likely that Canaan is symbolically the barren fruit of this relationship, explaining the emphasis on Canaan rather than Ham throughout the text.

7.8. *The Tower of Babel*

The Tower of Babel is the final text examined in this chapter. It is also the final myth prior to the birth of Abram and, effectively, the birth of Israel. After *The Tower of Babel* the text as a whole changes focus. It moves from a global view to a particularist view, focusing primarily on Abram and his descendants. As with myths found earlier in Genesis this myth extends the structural logic, suggesting that like the elements of the natural world languages are divided into opposing types: the mixed up languages of the peoples versus the holy language of Israel.

M.V.9. All the earth had one language and one speech. And it came to pass in their journeying east that they found a plain in the land of Shinar and settled there. Each man said to his neighbor, 'let us make bricks and burn them, and they had bricks in the place of stone and cement for mortar'. They said, 'let us build a city and a tower, with its head in the heavens and make for ourselves a name'. God came down to see the city and the tower that the sons of man had built. And God said, 'behold they are become one people, and they all have one language. This is what they have begun to do, and now they will be able to do anything they want. Come, let us go down and mix up their language in order that a man not be able to understand his neighbor. God spread them over the face of the world, and they stopped building the city. Because of this the name was called Babel, because God confused the languages there.[1] From there God scattered them over the face of the earth. (Gen. 11.1-9)[2]

This text creates an opposition in relation to languages. Boundaries are created between nations by the creation of mutually exclusive languages. The opposition also relies on a primary question. Were the ancestors of Israel, the line of Shem, included in this event, did they participate, and was their language also mixed up with the rest? Although the myth implies that all humanity participated, there are several indications that the line of Shem (structurally equivalent to Israel) was excluded. The text opens with an eastward movement. In other texts in Genesis the chosen line never moves east, the direction suggests that they did not take part. In the text immediately following this, the line of Shem is given, suggesting that they were not part of the events. Thus the language spoken by the descendants of Shem would not have been confused like the languages of the other peoples.

7.9. *Synthesis*

The texts in this chapter employed several of the clouding methods examined in the previous chapters. In *Adam and Eve* the serpent mediates between humankind and the sin, while Eve mediates between Adam and the sin. In *The Murder of Abel* Seth mediates between Abel prior to his murder and reborn Abel. Seth, as a gift of God, replaces Abel without necessitating an actual resurrection. Benjamin is a similar, although redundant, replacement in the myth of Joseph. In all the cases of mediation found in the first ten chapters of Genesis, the mediator typically shares elements of the two opposing elements, and by its similarity to each clouds the distinction or transformation.

The second mechanism of clouding (or transformation) found in these texts is inversion, seen primarily in regard to the *Sin of Ham*. As in the other cases of inversion documented above, all elements are equally inverted: Homosexual : Heterosexual Incest; Curse : Blessing; Barrenness : Fruitfulness; Youngest Son Rejected : Elder (possibly first-born) Chosen. Throughout the early chapters of the book of Genesis, two levels of oppositions are developed. These myths, like the myths found in the remaining chapters of Genesis, distinguish between Israel and the nations through the opposition of brothers and peoples. This type of opposition

1.   The word Babel is similar in sound to the verbal root meaning 'confuse'.
2.   This is a literal translation. Fohrer assigns this text to N (1986: 161).

is found in regard to the following individuals: Cain, Abel and Seth; Noah and the people; and Shem, Ham and Yaphet. Similarly, the element of sacrifice/murder and divine birth (transformation) is present in two of the above texts: Cain, Abel and Seth; and Noah and the people. The incest pattern of text is also found in regard to Ham and Noah, albeit in an inverted form.

The second level is the development of a similar pattern of structural logic in another sphere. In *The Creation of the World* the opposition is presented in respect to time, distinguishing between the Sabbath and the six days of the week. This text also includes an implicit opposition between humanity and the animal world (animals and nature are 'good' while humankind is 'very good'). In *The Flood* it is extended to types of animals and in *The Tower of Babel* to languages. This is part of the naturalization process by which the structural logic ($s^{(2)}$) is employed as the organizing principle for all categories of existence. In later texts in the Bible the logic is extended to other cultural spheres. On the geographic level it is extended to concentric and opposed sacred space, and on the microsociological level to distinguishing between the people and the priests, and ultimately the priests and the High Priest.

Chapter 8

THE STRUCTURE OF GENEALOGIES IN GENESIS

8.1. *Genealogical Fluidity*
Any discussion of biblical genealogies must take into account genealogical fluidity. Ethnographic evidence suggests that oral genealogies are subject to transformation at several levels.[1] Several formal mechanisms of fluidity are distinguished, many of which relate to the role of genealogies in society: the expression or justification of social reality. Genealogies reflect relationships within society.[2] When these change, the genealogy is often changed to reflect the new reality (Vansina 1985: 24). They also reflect significant relationships; significant ancestors' names are remembered.

Anthropologists have observed various kinds of genealogical fluidity.[3] The first kind is fluidity resulting from conscious deliberations. Richards describes a process by which various royal genealogies are examined to determine which is the accepted form (1960: 180-88). In the culture described by Richards, the Bemba, this examination is done in secret by a specific group of officials. In other societies the process is public.[4]

1. Wilson comprehensively discusses the question of genealogical fluidity in both oral and written genealogies (1977: 27-36).
2. This fact is observed by Goody and Watt, who make the analogy between biblical genealogies and those of the Tiv and Bedouin (1975: 30). They also highlight the fact that the biblical genealogies refer to nations rather than individuals. They state, in regard to the twelve tribes, the genealogies 'regulate social relations' (Goody and Watt 1975: 31). They do not, however, extend their argument to the other nations found in the genealogies.
3. Goody and Watt divide genealogical fluidity into three types: that arising from birth and death, that tied to rearrangement of 'constituent units' including migration and fission, and that resulting from 'changes in the social system'. The second two processes reflect the essential role of the genealogy as a charter for social relationships (Goody and Watt 1975: 32).
4. Among the Tiv the genealogies are discussed in public, with the assembly

Fortes describes a similar process among the matrilineal Ashanti. Genealogies were used for determining inheritance and succession to office. Each candidate had to produce a pedigree tracing his descent from a past office holder. The pedigree had to be accepted by the lineage assembly. It was at that time that the genealogies were carefully examined and corrected (Fortes 1969: 167). The main function of this process was to prevent groups grafted on to the lineage from taking office (Fortes 1969: 168). This case is of interest from two perspectives: its correcting of and determining the acceptable form of the genealogy, and the grafting of unrelated groups onto lineages and their genealogies.

The second kind is a fluidity that results from changes of the position of names within a genealogy. This may be due to the fact that the exact positions of the names are not significant. Such a process is described by Evans–Pritchard with regard to Nuer genealogies. Only those names that are significant to the lineage structure, and whose genealogical positions is a point of reference within that structure, must be retained in a set order. The inclusion and order of other names is functionally unimportant (1940: 199). Because many segmentary genealogies reflect hierarchical relationships, position within the genealogy can be significant. Thus common ancestors of the segments and their genealogical positions are significant, while the order of those in-between is functionally insignificant and therefore subject to change.

There is another aspect of this kind of fluidity: change in position due to change in status. If the genealogies reflect actual political relationships then, when those relationships change, so too should the genealogies. This is described by Cunnison in regard to the Baggara Arabs (1966: 106) and Laura Bohannan in respect to the Tiv (1952: 309).[1] Another

coming to a 'practical compromise', establishing the correct genealogy (Bohannan 1952: 179). The genealogy chosen for practical, legal considerations is seen as the best expression of Tiv reality. Bohannan states, 'The current state of affairs was taken as proof of the past state of affairs' (1952: 309). Current considerations transform the past and the genealogies which express the past. This type of fluidity is, for the most part, not done cynically or for purely political reasons. Richards emphasizes that it is usually due to 'conflicting facts or ill-remembered ones, rather than consciously imagined ones' (1960: 178).

1. Bohannan suggests that the Tiv feel that size and order of segmentary groups ought to correspond to genealogical position, and find it difficult 'to accept a genealogy that does not make them correspond' (Bohannan 1952: 309). She emphasizes that, at least among the Tiv, genealogies change as social structure changes. Genealogies are primarily charters for current social relationships (Bohannan 1952: 310).

reason for this kind of fluidity is change in social relationships, such as changes in alliances within the lineage (Vansina 1985: 182).

The third kind of fluidity is reflected in the disappearance of names from the genealogy. This may be due to 'structural amnesia', citing only those names which are structurally relevant (Barnes 1947: 52). The P genealogies which list only the relevant progenitor may be an example of this process. Evans–Pritchard described the process of disappearance of names, 'telescoping', through which names that are no longer significant disappear. These names tend to come from the middle sections of the genealogy because they do not represent founders of lines, so their presence in the genealogy in unnecessary (Evans–Pritchard 1940: 199).[1]

The fourth kind of fluidity results from the addition of children's names to the genealogy and the addition of new individuals or segments of formerly unrelated individuals. The position in which the segment or individual is placed reflects position within the lineage (Evans–Pritchard 1940: 220-28). Fortes describes this process among the Ashanti (1969: 168). It is also described by Cunnison among the Baggara Arabs (1966: 82). Among the Bedouin of Cyrenaica, new groups could be grafted onto existing structures. They were usually grafted onto the area of ambiguity in between the static and dynamic levels of the genealogy (Peters 1960: 38).

This process may be seen in the position of the tribes of Ephraim and Manasseh. Although the other tribes were genealogically Jacob's children, Ephraim and Manasseh were his grandchildren. Their inferior genealogical position may reflect later inclusion into the twelve tribes or a change in status of Ephraim and Manasseh (perhaps connected with the revolt of Jereboam).

---

1.   Peters describes a process in which names disappear because of repetition of names or titles (1960: 33). Among the Bedouin of Cyrenaica genealogical change was restricted to the lowest level. Peters suggests that this type of restricted fluidity was essential to their social structure. He found that between the tertiary level and the secondary level was an ambiguous area, separating the area of known kinship ties from that of fixed relationships. The tertiary level expressed actual descent, while in the levels above the names and relationships were static. Thus in the context of these higher levels all the actual kinship groups (the tertiary groups) maintained the same relationship to the founding ancestor (Peters 1960: 38). Peters suggests two other mechanisms of fluidity: death of a line and lack of inheritance (1960: 34).

8.2. *Fluidity in Written Genealogies*

Wilson points out similar processes in written Mesopotamian genealogies.[1] Telescoping takes place in the genealogy of Esarhaddon, where 62 names of Assyrian kings are omitted in order to tie Esarhaddon with the founder of the dynasty (1977: 65). In an example from the Sumerian King List, there is a change in attribution of paternity and generation. The King List states that Su-Sin was the son of Amar-Suen, the king who preceded him; other texts say he was the son of Sulgi, Amar-Suen's predecessor. Thus in the Sumerian King List, where the concern was sequence of kingship, genealogical order was changed to reflect order of reign (Wilson 1977: 75-76). Wilson also points out that the lists of antediluvian kings varied in order and number (1977: 80). Thus it appears that at least some of the processes of fluidity found in oral genealogies are also present in written genealogies.

This discussion of genealogies raises several implications in regard to biblical material. The proposition that biblical genealogies reflect historic relationships or migrations must be reconsidered in light of the fact that genealogies can be, and often are, manipulated (consciously or unconsciously) to reflect current sociological reality. This sociological reality may be a charter for political relationships, justifying existing social configurations. Genealogies may, however, be closely tied to 'mythological reality', creating a world-view based on mythological needs and structure rather than actual political relationships. Both of these approaches are examined below in relation to biblical genealogies.[2] Genealogical fluidity also may explain some of the repetition of names within the biblical genealogy, based on changed perception of that nation. Aram may be an example of this. In Genesis 10 Aram is a son of Shem, whereas in Genesis 22 Aram is son of Kemuel. Any explanation of

1. Goody and Watt observe the same phenomena in written genealogies of the Tiv. They describe a case in which the colonial administrators recorded the genealogies of the Tiv (so that they would be readily available in case of dispute). Forty years later, although still using the same genealogies, many of the Tiv considered the genealogies to be incorrect while the administrators considered them statements of fact. Goody and Watt suggest that this disagreement occurred because neither side realized that genealogies are subject to constant adjustment (1975: 32).

2. The relationship between myth and genealogy may be even closer. Goody and Watt observe that, at least in respect to the Tiv and Gonja, genealogy serves the same functional purpose as myth (i.e., as a charter for social relations) (1975: 33). Their observation is supported by the material studied here.

biblical genealogies must take all forms of genealogical fluidity into account.

The evidence suggests that genealogical texts cannot *a priori* be taken as expressing actual historical events or relationships. It is far more likely that they are related to current realities at the time the texts were redacted. Because of the composite nature of the biblical text, it is likely that evidence of such fluidity will be retained by the text, for example, in regard to the genealogical position of Aram. Analysis of the genealogical material in Genesis 10 indicates that these genealogies do not represent actual (or demonstrable) kinship ties or descent. Rather, they are a projection of either ideological or perceived relationship. It is likely that this type of genealogy would be more amenable to fluidity at all levels than a genealogy expressing actual relationships.

8.3. *Genealogies: Form and Content*

Two primary kinds of genealogies are found in Genesis: segmentary genealogies and linear genealogies (or pedigrees). Segmentary genealogies are those that trace all lines of descent from a given ancestor. This type of genealogy is characteristic of societies whose social structure is based on lineages. Description of Israelite social structure in Exodus and Numbers suggests that it was based on a segmentary lineage structure.[1] Genealogies in Genesis 10 are modeled on this structure. Linear genealogies or pedigrees express a single line of descent, tracing only significant ancestors. Both of these forms are found in both J and P materials. Gen. 4.17-22 is an example of the linear form of J, while Gen. 10.8-19 is an example of the segmentary form. Gen. 5.1-28 and 10.1-8 represent P's linear and segmentary forms respectively.

The genealogies describing the origins of nations are all segmentary, with the exception of the genealogy found in Gen. 4.17-22, considered by some scholars to be the tribal genealogy of the Kenites. Taking Cain as the eponymous ancestor of that tribe, Johnson states,

> It is possible also to consider this distinctive genealogy of Gen. 4.17-22 as a tribal genealogy, i.e., a glorification of the tribe by the tracing of its origins to a primeval father from whom…sprang all civilization (1969: 7).

Johnson posits that the Kenite genealogy was an independent source of Kenite origin which was incorporated into the text. He argues that two

---

1.   Gottwald's comprehensive analysis of early Israelite social structure supports this characterization (1979: 338).

biblical texts prove that Cain is the Kenites' eponymous ancestor (Num. 24.21-22 and Judg. 4.11) because both texts use the name Cain as parallel to Kenite.

Regardless of its origins it is difficult to see the Kenite genealogy in its present form as depicting the origins of the Kenites. Even if the Kenites saw a figure named Cain as their eponymous hero (and occasional Israelite texts reflect this), there is no evidence that the Kenites connected themselves with the 'primeval father', the Cain of the creation texts. Nor is there evidence that the Israelite narratives relating to Cain were shared with the Kenites. The current placement of the Kenite genealogy is within an Israelite text, as organized by the underlying structure of that society. It is impossible to know where the Kenites, if this is indeed their genealogy, would place themselves in relation to other nations and the primeval figures.

The Kenite genealogy is distinguished both by form and location from the texts concerning the origin of nations. As mentioned above, the Kenite genealogy is linear rather than segmentary; all other lineages dealing with the nations are segmentary. Prior to Noah (tenth generation) no other eponymous ancestors are mentioned. It also should be noted that two other texts describe Kenite origins (1 Chron. 2.55 and Exod. 2.18). In one case they are seen as a clan of Midianites and in the second as related to the Rechebites. Thus it is unlikely that the Kenite genealogy in Genesis serves an eponymous function. The text does, however, describe the origins of civilization. Cain (or Hanoch) is the founder of the first city. It is possible that this genealogy concerning the origins of civilization was set in opposition to the 'Sethite' genealogy, in which we find the origins of the worship of YHWH (Gen. 4.26).[1]

The linear genealogies, regardless of source, share a similar form. After lists of 7 (in J) or 10 (in P) lineal descendants the genealogy segments into three lines.[2] Interestingly, the genealogy in Gen. 4.17-22

---

1.   Although some scholars suggest that the Cainite and Sethite genealogies arise from the same source and are not independent genealogies, Bryan argues convincingly that the two genealogies are distinctive, independent genealogies (1987: 180-88).

2.   In this light it is interesting that Wilson considers the three sons of Noah to be an addition to the original text. He argues that their inclusion serves no function within the genealogy, and that it in fact 'runs counter to the genealogy's function', namely as a list of first-born sons (1977: 160). While it is apparent that an important aspect of this type of genealogy is to trace the line of descent between the important figures, Wilson appears to be ignoring the force of formal structure. Aside from function, structural rules (on the textual level) would play an important role in shaping

has seven linear descendants from Cain to the sons of Lamech. This number corresponds to the seven *apkallu*, 'the seven wise ones', who, in Sumerian mythology, teach humanity the art of civilization (Westermann 1984: 324). Westermann suggests further that this role is given to the line of Cain to clarify that civilization was the 'common patrimony of humankind'. The number ten in the 'Sethite' genealogy corresponds to the number of antediluvian kings (or heroes) in the Mesopotamian tradition, the last of whom was the hero of the flood (Wilson 1977: 166).[1]

The segmentary lineages are not as formally structured as the linear genealogies. It is possible that the original documents had a clear literary structure but, due to the fragmentary nature of their presentation, this structure is no longer discernable. It should be noted that by literary structure I am not referring to the terms used within the specific genealogies, nor those used to introduce the genealogies. In the P genealogies, for example, there is a distinguishable pattern at that level. There is no consistent pattern, however, in numbers and generations. The only clear patterning is in the last generation of the genealogy. Each of the main lines ends in six or twelve.[2] In Edom's case this is found only in the second Edomite genealogy, and requires moving the children

the genealogy. Thus in this text it appears that a triad of sons was used to conclude each section of the genealogy, and indeed this is found in every linear genealogy in Genesis. It is possible that Miriam is included in Exodus to fill out the triad of Moses and Aaron. Thus it is likely that the sons of Noah were part of the original text.

Wilson's emphasis on 'first born sons' may also lead to misinterpretation. He suggests, for example, that in P's genealogy (Gen. 5.3) 'Seth is clearly the first born son of Adam', while in J (Gen. 4.1) Seth is Adam's third son (1977: 163). This interpretation seems to ignore the primary function of the P linear genealogies, namely to trace the ancestors of the Israelites, not necessarily the first-born sons. My contention is supported by a second example of apparent fluidity between two different texts attributed to P (Gen. 10.22 and 11.10 respectively). In Gen. 10.22, part of a segmentary genealogy, Arpachshad is designated as Shem's third son, while in Gen. 11.10 he is the only son mentioned. As in Gen. 5.3 Arpachshad is the only son mentioned (as if he were the first born) because it is through him that the line of descent was traced. Wilson is thus misinterpreting the nature of linear genealogies. These genealogies do not, necessarily, list first-born sons, rather they list ancestors significant to the line of descent.

1.   In some Mesopotamian traditions the names of the *Apkallus* and the kings associated with them were similar. An analogous process of correlation may explain the similarities of names in the Kenite and Sethite genealogies (Finkelstein 1963: 50).

2.   Aram, Gen. 22.20-24; Ishmael, Gen. 25.12-16; Esau, Gen. 36.20; Keturah, Gen. 25.1-5; Israel, Gen. 46.8-27.

of Oholibamah from the first descending generation from Esau to the second, and excluding Amalek, who was a concubine's son (Johnson 1969: 24).[1]

Most of the genealogical references in this section come from 'secondary' genealogies, genealogical information that has no necessary independent existence outside of the narrative text. For the purposes of this analysis there is no material difference between that which is found in 'primary' genealogies (independent of the narrative text) or secondary genealogies. The current placement of nations is considered to be shaped by the same underlying logic.

It might be argued that secondary genealogies are not fluid since they originate in narrative texts which predicated certain relationships. The genealogies of the nations closest to Israel are derived from the narrative texts. This contention, however, far from weakening the theoretical approach, strengthens it. If the genealogical relationships were imposed by the narrative, by the myth, then we return to the question of why, in the narrative or mythological material, this genealogical relation, rather than any other, was developed? I suggest that the same logic working within the narrative works in the genealogy. It is also likely that specific names or relations within myth are equally fluid as genealogical material.

Many of the genealogies in Genesis chart the relationship between nations rather than individuals. This is especially true of Genesis 10, The Table of Nations. Thus it is necessary to chart Israel's relations with these nations. Our primary interest is the relationship between Israel's ideological relations and the relationships found in the genealogies. A variety of different criteria are used in the survey of ideological relations in this thesis. Included are explicit descriptions of wars or treaties as well as the respective lengths of those descriptions. This second criterion is applied only in cases where there is a clear distinction in length of description.[2]

---

1.   The exclusion of Amalek on the grounds of his mother is discussed below. It is supported by the fact that the Amalekites were considered a separate people from the other sons and grandsons of Esau.

2.   One example of this kind of differentiation is in the notices of wars with the Philistines in 2 Kings and 2 Chronicles which are single verses, as opposed to wars with other peoples which are often given ten or more verses. I consider wars with the Philistines in these cases to be less ideologically significant than the other wars described.

8.4. *The Edomites*

The Edomites are the closest nation genealogically to the Israelites. Esau, the eponymous ancestor of the Edomites, was the brother of Jacob and therefore father's brother (FB) to the Israelites.[1] Scholars differ about the actual relationship between the Edomites and the Israelites. Noth suggests that the Edomites, like the Israelites, were part of the Aramaic settlement of the region in the first millennium BC (Noth 1966: 227).[2] Bartlett, on the other hand, argues that, rather than being an Aramaic tribe, Edom had links with the Arabian world (Bartlett 1973: 231). The Edomites settled in the highlands, between the southern tip of the Dead Sea and the gulf of Aqabah (Bright 1972: 120). They were, however, primarily nomadic into the thirteenth century BC (Bartlett 1973: 232). The Edomites appear to have developed a centralized monarchy earlier than Israel, though this is based primarily on biblical sources (Bartlett 1973: 232).

The explicit attitude of the text seems to have undergone a shift from slightly negative to strongly hostile. The hostility between Israel and Edom is developed in several ways in Genesis. Jacob and Esau struggle in Rebekah's womb (Gen. 25). In Gen. 25.23 a prophecy predicts hostility between the descendants of Jacob and Esau. Esau is also explicitly criticized for marrying two Canaanite women (Gen. 26.34-35), as opposed to Jacob who returns to Haran to get a wife (Gen. 36.1-43).

In Exod. 15.15 the princes of Edom are included among those who are dismayed at the approach of Israel to Canaan. This text implies that these nations have reason to fear the coming of Israel, and thus should be considered ideologically negative.[3] Num. 20.14-21 portrays the Edomites as refusing to allow the Israelites to go through their land on the way to Canaan. In the prophecy of Balaam 'Edom becomes a conquered land; a conquered land is Seir' (Num. 24.18). All the above texts describe a hostile ideological position in relation to Edom.

1. Or, if Jacob is seen as structurally equivalent to Israel, then the genealogical relation is brother.

2. It should be noted that this concept of an Aramaic settlement, and therefore the associated relationships described, is ultimately derived from biblical texts which may not owe their origin to actual 'historical' sources. See, for example, the discussion in Gottwald, who suggests that the Israelites were of Canaanite origin (1979: 210-19).

3. Ideologically negative is used here to mean that the nation or people is depicted in a negative manner in the text. The word 'ideological' is used to emphasize that this depiction may not be directly related to actual relations between Israel and that nation.

In Deuteronomy, however, we find a slightly less hostile position. It states, 'You are about to pass through the territory of your kinsmen, the sons of Esau...take care not to provoke them. For I will give you none of their land' (Deut. 2.1-7). This text presents Edom in a relatively positive light, in clear distinction to the Canaanite tribes which Israel was commanded to destroy.[1] This apparent change is discussed below. it should suffice to suggest here that, at the time Deuteronomy was written, the Canaanites were no longer a political force. The other nations mentioned remained powerful, and therefore could not have been destroyed by the Israelite invasion. The prohibition was a retrospective description of current political reality. Deut. 23.8 is similarly positive in respect to the Edomites.

The Edomites are mentioned as enemies of Israel once in Judges (3.7-11). Judg. 11.17 retells the events of Num. 20.14-21. In 1 Sam. 14.47 Edom is listed among the enemies of Israel defeated by Saul.[2] Edom is also listed among those nations defeated and subjugated by David in 2 Sam. 8.14. In that text the statement on Edom is elaborated in greater detail than those regarding other nations.

In 1 Kings there is a strong condemnation of Solomon's foreign wives, including those from Edom. The text includes a clear prohibition against marriage to Edomite women.[3] In 1 Kgs 11.14-22 Hadad the Edomite is described as an enemy of Solomon. In Psalm 83 Edom is listed as one of the enemies of Israel.[4]

In the relations between Israel and Edom described in the 'historical' books, war is the basic state of affairs.[5] Edom is only mentioned once as having an alliance with Judah and Israel against Moav (2 Kgs 3.4). The ideological relations can be characterized as hostile and negative. In Figure 11, which lists the ideological relations between Israel and the nations, the Israelites and Edomites are at war more frequently then the

---

1. The Israelites received a similar prohibition against attacking either the Moabites or the Ammonites.
2. The other nations mentioned are the Philistines, Moav, Ammon and the Kings of Zova. BDB suggests that this last nation was an Aramean kingdom (BDB, 884).
3. The other nations mentioned in that text are Moabites, Sidonians and Hittites.
4. The other nations listed are Ishmael, Moav, the Hagarites (probably parallel to the Ishmaelites), Gebal, Ammon, Amalek, the Philistines, the Tyrians and Assur. Midian is mentioned as a past enemy.
5. Texts describing wars with Edom: 1 Kgs 11.14-25; 2 Kgs 8.20-22; 14.7; 16.6; 1 Chron. 18.12-13; 2 Chron. 20.1-30; 21.8-10; 25.11-14; 26.7; 28.17.

mean. Approximately 12 percent of Israel's wars were with Edom (Judges through 2 Chronicles).

It has been noted above that the ideological relationship described in Deuteronomy ranges from ambiguous to positive. Two statements were cited in which Edom was described as Israel's brother. These statements highlight the genealogical position of Edom, literally as Israel's brother. This close relationship creates many ambiguities, relating to two opposite trends. On the one hand, closeness suggests similarity and thus brotherhood, while on the other, chosenness suggests difference. Thus Edom, which was as close as genealogically possible, is both a brother, but is also too close (i.e., is almost the same). Thus it is expected that the majority of the texts will emphasize hostility in order to obviate the similarity.

8.5. *Amalek*

Amalek, being Esau's grandson (possibly considered FBS in regard to the children of Jacob), is mentioned infrequently in the text. Ideologically, however, Amalek is perhaps the most strongly negative. He is separated from the rest of the Edomites by having a different mother, a concubine (Gen. 36.12).[1] The Amalekites appear to have been a purely nomadic people who dwelt in the Sinai desert (Noth 1966: 82).

In Exodus Amalek is the first to attack the Israelites on their journey to Canaan. The section describing these events concludes, 'YHWH is at war with Amalek from age to age' (Exod. 17.8-16). In Num. 13.29 the Amalekites are listed by the spies as one of the powerful nations inhabiting the land. In Balaam's prophecy it is stated that Amalek's 'posterity shall perish forever' (Num. 24.20). Deuteronomy commands the Israelites to remember what Amalek did to them, and to blot Amalek out from the earth (Deut. 25.13-19). The subsequent books continue this extremely negative attitude towards Amalek.

Amalek is mentioned three times in Judges as participating in wars against Israel (3.13; 6.1-6; 6.33). In 1 Samuel Amalek is mentioned three times. 1 Sam. 14.48 lists Amalek as one of the nations defeated by Saul. Chapter 15 describes a holy war against the Amalekites. It is during this war that Saul is rejected by God for failing to destroy the Amalekites completely (vv. 1-35). Chapter 30 describes a raid by the Amalekites on

1. The role of mother in biblical genealogies, especially of concubines, is discussed below. In the case of Amalek this fact seems to serve to distinguish them as a separate nation from the Edomites, while keeping them genealogically close to Israel.

the cities controlled by David, followed by David's revenge. In 2 Sam. 8.12 and 1 Chron. 18.11 Amalek is mentioned as one of the nations subdued by David. Amalek is mentioned in Psalm 83 as an enemy of Israel (83.7). Although the number of wars with Amalek falls below the mean, less than six percent of the total number, ideological relations with Amalek are in general strongly negative. This attitude is carried over into the book of Esther where Haman is said to be an Amalekite.

8.6. *Ishmael*

Ishmael (FFFB in regard to the descendants of Jacob, FFB in relation to Jacob) is one of the most ambiguous of the nations closely related to Israel. The Ishmaelites were a nomadic people who lived in northwestern Arabia and the Sinai Desert (Noth 1966). It is perhaps important that Ishmael had a different mother than the Israelite line: Hagar rather than Sarah.[1] The text introduces a negative note by identifying his mother as an Egyptian (Gen. 16.1). The blessing pronounced upon the birth of Ishmael is ambiguous. It begins with an assurance that God will make Ishmael's descendants numerous, but it continues, 'A wild-ass of a man he will be, against every man, and every man against him, setting himself to defy all his brothers' (Gen. 16.11-13), indicating hostility between Israel and the Ishmaelites.

In Judges (6.3) there is a possible mention of Ishmael, if the identification of Ishmael with the בני קדם, the 'Sons of the East', is correct.[2] Ishmael is also mentioned twice in 2 Chronicles where the term ערבים (Arabians) is used—21.16 and 26.7. Ishmael is also listed among the ten enemies of Israel in Ps. 83.6.

It is difficult to characterize ideological attitudes towards Ishmael. Although we find no positive statements we also find no strongly

---

1. The importance of the mother in determining descent is usually ignored in relation to the figures in Genesis. Several aspects, however, suggest that the mother may have played an important role in determining descent. The distinction between the Amalekites and the Edomites—possibly due to Amalek being descended from a concubine—has already been mentioned. The distinction between the descendants of Hagar and Keturah, and Sarah is also suggestive. The importance of the mother in descent is also found in the three wife/sister myths (See above). These texts suggest that even if Sarah had been Abraham's sister, provided they had different mothers then they could be married. This suggests that the mother was at least as important as the father in determining descent.

2. This identification is supported by Gen. 25.15 where Kedem is listed as one of Ishmael's sons.

negative statements. Because all statements outside of Genesis involve hostile encounters, Ishmael will be considered slightly negative.

8.7. Midian

Midian (FFS), like Ishmael, is also ideologically ambiguous. Similarly, Midian (and the other tribes descended from Keturah) have a different mother than the main line of descent. Of the Keturite tribes, Midian appears to be the only ideologically significant group. The Midianites were pastoral nomads, relying primarily on camels. They lived on the east side of the gulf of Aqabah. Midian is mentioned in Exodus as the place of origin of both Moses' father-in-law, Jethro, and his wife. The positive attitude toward Jethro suggests a positive attitude toward Midian.

In Numbers, however, we find a slightly different picture. In cooperation with Moav, Midian hires Balaam to curse Israel (Num. 22.4, 7). Numbers 25 presents an even more hostile picture of Midian. The text blames the Midianites for leading the children of Israel into sin, and concludes with the command 'Harry the Midianites and strike them down for they harassed you with their guile in Peor' (Num. 25.1-18). Numbers 31 describes a holy war against Midian. This war, however, can be distinguished in intensity from the holy war against the Amalekites. In the war against Midian described in Numbers, the taking of prisoners and booty was permitted. In the war against the Amalekites, however, everything had to be destroyed. In Judges (6.8) Gideon defeats the Midianites following their enslavement of the Israelites. The only other significant text which mentions Midian, Psalm 83, lists it as a past enemy. This text suggests that, at the time of its composition, the Midianites were no longer active enemies of Israel. Internal evidence suggests that the psalm was written at the beginning of the Assyrian incursions against Israel.[1]

There is a clear transformation in the texts relating to Midian. In Exodus Midian is viewed positively, while in the other texts it is strongly negative. Interestingly, however, Midian does not appear to have been ideologically significant after the book of Judges.

8.8. Aram

The ideological position of Aram (FFFSS) also goes through a clear transformation that is mirrored in the genealogy.[2] In Gen. 10.22 Aram is

---

1. This is suggested by the verse 'Assyria is also joined with them' (Ps. 83.9).
2. It is possible that Aram can be viewed as FFFB as the sons of Nahor are considered the 12 Aramean tribes.

said to be a son of Shem, whereas in Gen. 25.1-6 he is a grandson of Nahor. Some scholars attribute this contradiction to different authors, P and J respectively (Speiser 1964: 64, 167). Others attribute them to the same author (or school), stating that the duplications reveal 'the fact that several attempts at a genealogical classification of the same tribes were made in the earliest sources' (Johnson 1969: 5). It is possible, on the other hand, that the change in classification mirrored a change in ideological relations between the Israelites and Aram.

The term Aram refers both to a group of culturally related peoples, and a city in Syria. The Aramean people mentioned in biblical texts dwelt in what today is Syria and northern Jordan. In 1 Samuel the Aramean Kingdom of Zoba, in southern Syria, is in conflict with Saul and David. Other Aramean kingdoms were Aram beth-Rehob, possibly in Lebanon, extending into the Syrian desert (Wiseman 1973: 140), and the extensive kingdom of Aram-Damascus in Syria.

In Genesis the overall trend is positive. The patriarchs have close ties with Aram, and send their sons back to Haran, to the Arameans, for wives. Yet it is possible that some negative relations are revealed in relation to Laban, called the Aramean (Gen. 28.5), as seen in Jacob's (Israel's) relations with Laban (Gen. 29–31). It should be noted that in Num. 23.7 there is an ambiguous to negative statement. This text refers to the origins of Balaam in Aram.

There are few texts which mention relations with Aram (either positive or negative) until 2 Samuel. In Judges Aram is mentioned twice. Judg. 3.10-11 describes the enslavement of Israel by the king of Aram-Naharaim. In a second text, Judg. 10.6, the children of Israel are condemned for following the god's of Aram. In 1 Samuel Zoba is listed among the enemies of Saul. In 2 Samuel a war against Zoba is described (8.3). In 2 Samuel (8.5) the Arameans are included among the nations subdued by David. In 10.6-19 they assist the Ammonites in a war against Israel.

The Arameans are mentioned five times in 1 Kings (once in alliance with Judah against Israel): 11.23; 15.16-23; 20.1-21; 20.26-43; 22.1-38. Aram is mentioned seven times in 2 Kings (twice in alliance with Israel against Judah): 6.8-21; 6.24–7.20; 12.18-20; 13.3-8; 13.22-25; 15.37; 16.5-20. The Aramean participation in the Ammonite campaign of David is mentioned in 1 Chronicles 19, as is the alliance with Judah against Israel in 2 Chronicles 15. Two other wars mentioned in Kings are also detailed in 2 Chronicles: chs. 18 and 20.

The Arameans are mentioned a total of 21 times, nearly twenty percent of the total. Although the initial picture of the Arameans is positive, by Numbers all save one reference are hostile. It is perhaps significant to the genealogical position of Aram that, over the course of Israelite ideological history, their ideological position changed. It is likely that the change in genealogical position reflects changes in ideological position.

8.9. *Moav*

The Moabites were part of the Aramean settlement of the region at the end of the Bronze Age (Wiseman 1973: 230). They controlled the area between the Dead Sea and the Syro-Arabian Desert (Noth 1966: 80). The Moabites probably adopted Canaanite dialects (Noth 1966: 227), and developed centralized monarchy prior to the Israelites (Noth 1966: 80).

With Moav as with Edom, there is a clear difference in portrayal in Deut. 2.8-13 and the majority of other texts. This may be due to the reasons mentioned above. The general picture of Moav is, however, strongly negative. Gen. 19.30-38, describing the origins of the Moabites and the Ammonites, can be understood in two ways. Incest is not an ideological problem in Genesis, witness Abraham and Sarah, and Adam and Eve. It is an element in the underlying structure of the system. The system is trying to make a clear distinction between Israel and the other nations, thus marrying as closely as possible preserves the distinction, whereas marrying out dilutes the distinction. Thus incest becomes 'mythologically' acceptable (or necessary). If this is the case, then Lot being seduced by his daughters can be understood as working within the system, making the daughters' behavior 'mythologically' acceptable at least on the level of the underlying structure this myth (see M.I.11).

The incest in Gen. 19.30-38 is, however, different from that found in the other texts, being father–daughter rather than brother–sister incest. This type of incest may have been less ideologically acceptable than brother–sister. Thus it is possible that, while the myth developed as part of the Israelite system, with the same underlying logic, its narrative level, however, was not ideologically acceptable. On the narrative level it therefore became an attack on the origins of the Moabites and the Ammonites, suggesting that they originated from sexual depravity.

The text itself, however, makes no judgment on the deeds of the daughters. It gives them a positive justification since they believed that their father was the last man on earth. They were acting to preserve the human race in what they thought was the only way possible. It should be noted that cross-generation marriage, and therefore father–daughter marriage by implication, may not have been as 'mythologically' problematic as suggested. Indeed, Nahor, Isaac and Jacob married across generations.

Moav is included among the nations dismayed at the coming of Israel in Exod. 15.15, 'The princes of Moav fall to trembling'. It is the king of Moav who calls upon Balaam to curse the Israelites, and is cursed in their place (Num. 24.17). Balaam's curse predicts the destruction of Moav by the Israelites.

The theme of sexual depravity is seen again in Num. 25.1-3, 'The people gave themselves over to debauchery with the daughters of Moav'. In Deut. 23.4 a clear distinction is made between the Moabites and the Ammonites vis-à-vis the other nations: 'Neither a Moabite nor an Ammonite should be allowed to come into the community of the Lord'. Interestingly, when Ezra restates this commandment, Egypt is added.[1] The list given in 1 Kings is also more inclusive, adding Edom and Sidom.

It is possible that this added distinction of Moav and Ammon was due to the circumstances of the origin. Due to the nature of the incest, an analogy may have been made with the legal status of a ממזר, a child of a forbidden sexual union who was also legally forbidden from joining in the community (or marrying a member of the community).

In Judg. 3.12-30 there is one mention of Moav. This text alludes to the debauchery of Moav by describing the king of Moav as extremely fat. Moav is listed in 1 Sam. 14.47 as one of the peoples defeated by Saul, Moav is mentioned in 2 Sam. 8.2 as one of the nations subdued by David. In 1 Kings there is a strong condemnation of Solomon's foreign wives, and Moav is included in this group. The text states, 'From those people...You are not to go to them nor they to you...' (1 Kgs 1–9). Moav is mentioned three times in 2 Kings: in rebellion against Israel (1.1), in a campaign against Israel (3.4-27), and as part of wide-spread attacks on Israel (24.2-3). The conquest of Moav by David is also mentioned in 1 Chronicles. Moav is included in Psalm 83 among the ten enemies of Israel (v. 6). In all the texts relating to Moav (save Deut. 2), Moav is ideologically strongly negative.

---

1. The text of Ezra reads, 'The people of Israel...have not separated themselves from the peoples of the land, doing their abominations, even of the Canaanites, the Hittites, the Perezites, the Jebusites, the Ammonites, the Moabites, the Egyptians, and the Ammorites. For they have taken of their daughters for their sons; so that the holy seed have joined themselves with the peoples of the land' (Ezra 9.1-2).

8.10. *Ammon*

Like the Moabites, the Ammonites were part of the Aramean settlement, though somewhat later than either Moav or Israel. They settled near the headwaters of the Jabbok with their capital, Rabbah, at the site of the Jordanian city of Ammon (Bright 1972: 120). The Ammonites were the second tribe descended from a daughter of Lot. Moreover, Israel is prohibited from provoking the Ammonites (Deut. 2.19) as it was from provoking the Edomites. The Ammonites are also included, with the Moabites, are prohibited from joining the Israelite community (Deut. 23.4).

The Ammonites are mentioned three times in Judges; in 3.13 participating with the Moabites and the Amalekites, and again in 10.6-18. In Judg. 11.4-15, the Israelites call upon Jephthah to lead them against the Ammonites. In 1 Kgs 11.1-12, the text describes an Ammonite attack on Jabesh-Gilead. The text concludes with the defeat of the Ammonites by Saul. In 1 Sam. 14.47 the Ammonites are listed among the enemies of Saul. In 2 Kings they are listed among the nations subdued by David (8.12). The text then includes two campaigns by David against the Ammonites (chs. 10 and 11). David's subjugation of Ammon is also mentioned in 1 Chron. 8.11. Ammon is included in Ps. 83.7. In all the texts relating to Ammon (save perhaps Deut. 2.19), Ammon is ideologically strongly negative.

Figure 13 summarizes the ideological history of these six nations. Edom's, Moav's and Ammon's interactions with Israel are at, or just under, the mean. Aram and Amalek, however, have different patterns. In the case of Aram, more than 80 percent of its interactions with Israel occurred in 1 Kings and the later 'historical' texts. This major shift may reflect a change in relations between Israel and Aram. It is already suggested that the genealogies may reflect this change in relations. The Amalekites, on the other hand, have few interactions; only six percent of the whole. All of these occur either prior to, or in the time of, David. Yet interestingly they are perhaps the most strongly ideologically negative, as well as being genealogically very close.

It is clear from the texts examined above that all of the nations genealogically close to Israel are also ideologically hostile. The two most ambiguous nations being Ishmael and Midian (who also were mentioned the fewest times in the text). It may be suggested that the nations which are genealogically close are those nations which were conquered by Israel or the tributaries of the Israelites. This, however, can only be a partial explanation as both the Philistines and the Canaanites were also conquered by the Israelites yet they are genealogically distant. Even if the tributary aspect is part of the explanation, mythologically these nations would be even more problematic. Because being part of the Israelite empire they would almost be Israel. In this sense the genealogies can be considered to reflect historical reality.

	Edom	Amalek	Aram	Moav	Ammon	
Judges	1	3	1	1	3	
1 Samuel	1	3	1	1	2	
2 Samuel	1	1	2	1	3	
1 Kings	3	0	5	1	1	
2 Kings	3	0	7	3	1	
1 Chronicles	1	1	2	1	3	
2 Chronicles	6	0	3	1	3	
	16	8	21	9	16	70 (74)
Percent of Whole*	23% (22)	11% (11)	30% (28)	13% (12)	23% (22)	

Mean interactions including Midian and Ishmael: 13.6 (19%)
Mean interaction without Midian and Ishmael: 14 (20%)

* ( ) Including Midian (1 mention in Judges) and Ishmael
(1 in Judges and 2 in 2 Chronicles)

Figure 13. *Ideological History of Nations Genealogically Close to Israel*

8.11. *Those Nations Genealogically Distant*

The Canaanites and the Philistines are the two genealogically distant nations which are ideologically significant. Both are placed at great genealogical distance from the Israelites and both are descendants from Ham, through Canaan and Mitzraim respectively. As descendants of Ham, both are ideologically strongly negative (due to the sin of Ham mentioned in Gen. 9.20-29). Canaan is specifically singled out in the text as ideologically negative. Ham is described throughout the text as 'the father of Canaan'.

8.12. *Canaanites*

The Canaanites were the inhabitants of Canaan prior to the Israelite settlement. They covered a territory that included Canaan and part of the Lebanon: western Palestine to Latakia. Knowledge about the Canaanites rests entirely upon testimony by other peoples, primarily biblical texts (Wiseman 1973: 29). Based on the study of Hebrew and

Phoenician, Canaanite language is considered to be a distinct language within the Northern Semitic family (Wiseman 1973: 34). Recent scholarship suggests that the Canaanites were an amalgam of different peoples, primarily Amorite (a nomadic people known to have sacked cities as far east as Babylonia, who began urbanization under the influence of Egyptian and Mesopotamian traders).

Throughout the five books of Moses, the Canaanites are described as a people who are to be disinherited by the Israelites. See, for example, Exod. 23.20-23; 33.1-3; 34.11-13; Num. 21.1-3; 33.50-56. In Deuteronomy 7 the Israelites are forbidden to marry the Canaanites. These are only a few examples of typically strongly negative texts. In Judges they are mentioned three times: ch. 1; 3.1-6; and ch. 4. The only other substantive texts mentioning the Canaanites are those describing the capture of Jerusalem: 2 Sam. 5.6-12 and 1 Chron. 11.4. The Canaanites appear to have little significance in the later texts.

8.13. *Philistines*
The Philistines were of different origin than the other peoples settled in and around Canaan. They were settled around the southern coast of Canaan, and are thought to have been descended from various peoples, described by the Egyptians as 'sea peoples'. The sea peoples are thought to have originated in the eastern Mediterranean. After an attempted invasion of Egypt, the Philistines were settled by the Egyptians, perhaps as a buffer state at the edge of their domain. They are thought to have arrived at about the same time as the Israelites and eventually became the rulers of five Canaanite kingdoms: Gaza, Ashdod, Ashkelon, Ekron and Gath (Noth 1966: 78).

The Philistines are mentioned in Genesis 20 and 26 (ideologically neutral). In Exod. 13.17 their presence is used to explain why the Israelites did not go up the coast in their invasion of Canaan. In Judges they are mentioned three times: 3.1-6, 3.31 and ch. 13 and following. In 1 Samuel they are portrayed as the main enemy of Israel and are involved in six wars with the Israelites: 4.1-11; 7.7-13; 13; 17; 28; 31 (1 Chronicles also mentions one of Saul's wars against the Philistines [ch. 10]). In 2 Samuel the Philistines were involved in three wars with David, and are among those nations subdued by David: 5; 8.12; 21.15-22. In 1 Kings there are two very brief mentions of sieges against a Philistine town (one verse each), 15.27 and 16.15. In 2 Kings the Philistines are again mentioned only briefly at 18.8. In 1 Chronicles the Philistines are mentioned on three occasions (once during the reign of

Saul, and twice during that of David): 10; 14.8-17; 20.4. They are mentioned twice in 2 Chronicles: 21.16; 26.6. Examining the trend shown in these texts, the Philistines appear to have been an enemy of short duration. Of the 22 texts, 16 occur prior to the reign of Solomon. Of the remaining texts, five out of six are brief one-verse notices. This may indicate that, after David's reign, the Philistines were no longer a political force which concerned the ideological historians.

Similarly, the Canaanites are only substantially mentioned in two places (describing the same event) after Judges. This may indicate that, at the time the texts were written, the Canaanites no longer existed as an independent people.

8.14. *Assyrians*

It may be argued that the Assyrians, descendants of Assur, are also ideologically negative given that they are mentioned nine times in 2 Kings and 2 Chronicles. The texts that describe their invasion place them in a negative light (see 2 Chron. 32). Yet their significance seems to have been of short duration. In long-term ideological history they play only a small role. Similarly the Egyptian's are not singled out (except in terms of marriages—which might have been an attack on the actions of Solomon and the other kings who made alliances with Egypt through marriage), for strong negative reaction in books other than Exodus. It is possible that the great empires were seen as analogous to forces of nature or pawns of God, rather than as equivalent to the nations with which Israel usually dealt. Thus, they were not developed, either genealogically or ideologically, in the same way. The other nations in the Table of Nations appear to be ideologically neutral in relation to Israel.

	Philistines	Canaanites	Assyrians
Judges	3	3	0
1 Samuel	7	0	0
2 Samuel	3	1	0
1 Kings	2	0	0
2 Kings	1	0	5
1 Chronicles	2	1	0
2 Chronicles	3	0	4
Total 35	21	5	9
Percent	60%	15%	25%

Figure 14. *Ideological History of Nations Genealogically Distant from Israel*

Figure 14 summarizes the ideological history of those nations genealogically distant from Israel. The Philistines, as stated above, undergo a clear change of pattern. Nearly 75 percent of their wars with Israel occur in or prior to 1 Kings. It is also interesting to note that the Canaanites were of little ideological importance after Judges. Ideological history of all nations examined is presented in Figure 15.

	Edom	Amal.	Moav	Ammon	Aram	Ish.	Can.	Phil.	Other
	16	8	9	16	21	3	5	21	20
									Mid. 1
									Egy. 4
									Assy. 9
									Bab. 4
									Arav 2
Judges	1	3	1	3	1	1	3	3	1
1 Sam.	1	3	1	2	1	0	0	7	0
2 Sam.	1	1	1	3	2	0	1	3	0
1 Kings	3	0	1	1	5	0	0	2	0
2 Kings	3	0	3	1	7	0	0	1	9
1 Chron.	1	1	1	3	2	0	1	2	0
2 Chron.	6	0	1	3	3	2	0	3	10
Percent	13%	7%	8%	13%	18%	2%	4%	18%	17%
Percent without									
Other	16%	8%	9%	16%	21%	3%	5%	21%	

Mean mentions including other: 13%
Mean percent negative mentions without other: 12%
Mean percent negative mentions with other: 11%
Mean percent negative mention, other divided into nations: 8%

Figure 15. *Ideological History of Israel and the Nations*

8.15. *Analysis*

There are two primary approaches to biblical genealogies: fragmentary and holistic. A majority of the analyses do not examine the nations included in the Table of Nations in regard to their placement in relation to Israel, but try instead to explain the categorization of nations within the table. As Oded points out, they often rely on the three criteria given in the text itself: 'ethnopolitical...linguistic...and geographic' (Oded

1986: 14).[1] Westermann, for example, uses historical and geographic criteria for placement (1984: 504-13). Where certain nations do not fit his pattern he exercises verbal and intellectual gymnastics to bring them back into line. Von Rad focuses on political relations as the primary criterion, stating, 'The Table of Nations does not reveal humanity according to race or according to language. Rather, these are nations that were politically or historically distinct from one another or related to one another' (1961: 141). In this light he explains the placement of Aram as Shem's youngest son because of the late date of the Aramean migration (Von Rad 1961: 142). Speiser views the organizational criteria as being geographical, linguistic and occasionally political (1964: 65-71).

All of these approaches may partially explain why specific nations are grouped together, though no one criterion explains all placements.[2] They also do not explain the placement of those nations in respect to Israel. Von Rad argues that they reflect political relations, yet he does not consider their political relations with the authors of the genealogies, namely the Israelites. The limited perspective of these approaches emerges from their underlying theory. They are concerned with fragments rather than the redacted whole. Thus, since Israel is not included in the Table of Nations, these approaches do not perceive it as part of a broader scheme of organization.

These fragmentary approaches miss the implications of the genealogical form. Westermann, in fact, ignores it stating, 'The genealogical pattern is only the form of presentation; it is not meant to indicate descent' (Westermann 1984: 504). A genealogy expresses the perception of social relationships of the society creating it. It is the genealogical position of Israel that must be explained, the positions of nations vis-à-vis other nations are of secondary concern.

Another problem with these approaches, especially those which focus

1. Oded argues that all three of these criteria must be abandoned. He presents examples which show the fallacies with each: concerning language, the cities of Mesopotamia, Canaan and Aram, should be linked, but should not be linked with Egypt and Cush; concerning ethnopolitics, there is no link between Elam and Aram; and similarly there is no geographic link between Lud and the other Shemite peoples (Oded 1986: 14-18).

2. The geographical explanation, for example, explains many of the placements, yet it does not explain the genealogical distance of the Philistines and the Canaanites from the Israelites. Like many of the nations genealogically close to Israel, Edom, Ammon, Moav and the Philistines and Canaanites lived in geographic proximity to Israel.

on historical relations or migrations as the criteria for classification, is the aspect of genealogical fluidity discussed above. If genealogies are fluid, one cannot assume that placement in the biblical version necessarily reflects placement in any earlier version.[1] The repetition of nations, even from the same documentary stratum, also suggests that placement was not based on firm 'ethnographic' traditions.

A more comprehensive approach is suggested by Johnson.[2] He argues that the genealogies of P and J serve as a charter to explain the political relations between Israel and its neighbors. He states, 'the tribal genealogies...reflect the degree of closeness felt by various elements within Israelite tribes to their neighbours at different periods of history' (Johnson 1969: 7). This approach is similar to Robertson-Smith's, still common in anthropological theory (Vansina 1985: 182). Johnson supports his approach with examples from other societies in the Middle East, yet he never closely examines the relations expressed in the biblical genealogies to prove his contention. If his approach is correct, then those nations closest genealogically to Israel also should be the closest ideologically.

In order to determine the merit of his approach, it is necessary to examine the ideological history of Israel's relations with these other nations to ascertain their ideological relation to Israel. Israel's ideological attitude toward its neighbors is presented above in this chapter, and is summarized in Figures 13, 14 and 15. Figure 16 portrays both genealogical and ideological relations. Nations which are ideologically negative are in italics. If Johnson is correct, these nations should be genealogically

---

1. Von Rad uses Aram as an example of the historical criterion for the organization of the genealogy. Yet his approach cannot explain the contradictory evidence about Aram's origins (found in Gen. 22). He can only explain it by assigning the two statements to separate documentary traditions. From a holistic approach it is necessary to explain why the contradictory traditions existed.

2. Another holistic interpretation of Gen. 10 is offered by Oded (1986). He suggests that the original nucleus of the text was an attempt to categorize all peoples according to a tripartite scheme: the children of Eber, the dwellers of city and kingdom, the father of the isles and Gentiles (Oded 1986: 30). There are several problems with his approach. (1) In order to arrive at his scheme he removes all of the fragments which have been added to the text, and is unable to explain why these fragments were added on. (2) His approach does not explain the function of the texts. It is difficult to understand, from the perspective of Israelite culture (which at the time of writing was settled with substantial urban centres), the meaning of this structure—he explains neither its cultural or theological role.

distant from Israel. On the contrary, those nations genealogically closest are ideologically most distant.

Thus, when the ideological relations between the Israelites and the nations are examined, it is difficult to support the thesis that the genealogy reflects the 'degree of closeness' between the Israelites and their neighbors. Figure 16 summarizes these relations. Of the nine nations that are ideologically significant, seven are in close genealogical proximity to Israel, and all seven are ideologically negative. The genealogies seem to reflect the opposite trend to that suggested by Johnson—namely the degree of hostility rather than the degree of closeness. In fact, genealogical closeness is inversely related to ideological closeness.

If the genealogy is examined in relation to the structure of Israelite myth this problem can be resolved.[1] Structuralist analysis suggests that the mythological system is attempting to deal with the problem of internal and external relations, or on another level, endogamy. Endogamy creates an unnatural distinction between people, that is, those who can be married and those who cannot be married. Where there is a clear boundary between the group and the outside tribe, there is no problem. This is because there is an apparent natural boundary between the two groups. It is with those groups which are closest that the crisis arises, because they are genealogically (and therefore perhaps qualitatively) almost part of the group. Those nations genealogically closest fall in a middle ground between 'people' and 'non-people'. In order to support the societal structure of endogamy, and therefore strengthen the logic, those nations closest also must be the most negative ideologically in order to lessen the crises created by their proximity.

The genealogies and the mythological system needed to resolve two competing trends. On the one hand, due to the underlying structure, a concept of one God developed, mirroring the concept of one people.

1. Genealogies also function on a second level. In a sense they both validate and are validated by the mythical system. They provide the myths with a concrete historical setting which 'proves' that the myths, and thereby the logic created through the myths, are true. What could be more concrete than a comprehensive list of fathers and sons, with numerical chronology provided. The genealogies provide a logic and proof through continuity, as if to say, 'If we can fit ourselves into this line of descent, since we exist so must the events and the idealogy portrayed'. The myth provides a setting for the genealogy, and argues that the genealogical relations are more than fortuitous: they are ordained by God. The existence of the genealogy, objective truth, proves that the myth is true.

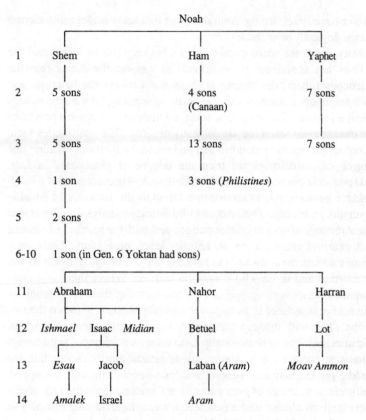

Figure 16. *Genealogical and Ideological Relations*

This God concept implied a single creation, and therefore a single humanity. On the other hand, the basic structural rule was endogamy, which suggests a qualitative difference between those people who can be married and those who cannot be married. This logic was further supported by the concept of the 'chosen people' which made Israel, on a spiritual level, qualitatively different from the other peoples.

In order to resolve these two competing trends there was a need for a genealogy to show where other nations break off, and to detail and emphasize the chosen line. Thus we find in the final text both linear and segmentary genealogies. As stated above, the linear genealogies focus on the chosen line, to the exclusion of any extraneous information (e.g., Seth's older brothers), while the segmentary lineages detail where the nations broke off from the chosen line. This, however, would not totally resolve the crisis, since some nations would be genealogically closer than others. In order to separate Israel from these close nations, they were shown to be ideologically distant.

Thus as the genealogy developed, both in narrative myth and in independent texts, ideological history emphasized the negative relations of those nations which were considered genealogically closest. It is possible that the change in genealogical position of Aram may be due to the change in ideological political relations between Aram and Israel. According to the texts detailed above, hostile relations (or perhaps any type of political relations) did not begin with the Arameans until the time of David. It is possible that the Arameans were originally genealogically distant (because they were structurally insignificant). As relations developed, a process of lessening the genealogical distance developed. The Arameans were linked with Abraham's relatives in Haran, with the term 'the Aramean' being added in key locations, for example, Laban being called 'the Aramean'. A later stage would be the addition of the name Aram onto Nahor's genealogy. Thus, as the Arameans became progressively more ideologically problematic, it was structurally useful to move them to a closer genealogical position.

The two other nations that are seen to be strongly negative, the Philistines and the Canaanites, must, however, be accounted for. In both cases there seems to be a lessening of ideological significance in the later texts. The Canaanites are hardly mentioned after Judges, and the Philistines, for the most part, receive only brief notices after 2 Samuel. Thus their placement in the genealogy may reflect the fact that, at the time of its composition, they were no longer qualitatively negative in Israelite society and thus would not adequately serve to emphasize the difference between Israel and its genealogical neighbors.

Why then are the Ishmaelite nations, and the nations descended from Keturah, either ideologically ambiguous or neutral? This distinction is made because the mothers of these two lines were not those of the main line. This suggests that descent from a common mother was mythologically significant. In three cases where concubines are mentioned (Keturah's status is unclear) there is clear separation from the other children. Thus Isaac and Ishmael are clearly distinguished, Amalek is separated from the other descendants of Esau, and Keturah's children are clearly distinguished from Sarah's.[1]

---

1. It should be noted that the Israelites were descended from four mothers, two official wives and two concubines. It is possible that these different mothers once

The genealogical importance of the mother, almost equal to the father, may be reflected in other biblical texts. In Genesis 20 Abraham states in order to justify calling Sarah his sister, 'Besides, she is indeed my sister, my father's daughter though not my mother's' (Gen. 20.12, M.I.13).[1] This indicates that had they also shared a mother he would have been unable to marry her, suggesting that descent through the mother was as important as through the father. A similar case is recorded in 2 Samuel, where the text appears to suggest that David's son Amnon could marry his sister Tamar (who had a different mother). This emphasis on both paternal and maternal lines fits into the logic of endogamy, which considers the origin of both lines significant. Thus both the lines of Ishmael and the Keturites (including the Midianites) are in a sense genealogically distant from the main line. Their genealogical position was not problematic and therefore ideologically ambiguous.

In the case of biblical material, the genealogies cannot be analyzed independently of the mythological structure. The genealogies are shaped by that structure and reflect its requirements. The mythological system creates (and is created by) and supports the logic of endogamy. This logic in turn organizes the world-view, and places Israel's neighbors in genealogical positions which best fit the needs of the system. The myth, however, contains an inner contradiction. It focuses on the one, but must explain the many. The problem is resolved through use of linear and segmentary genealogies, and through exploiting ideological distance to replace genealogical distance. In a sense Vansina is correct that genealogies reflect political relations; for biblical texts genealogical closeness is inversely related to political closeness. This material suggests that analogous material from other societies should also be analyzed in the context of those societies' mythological and political structures.

---

reflected differentiations in status within the tribes but there is no objective proof for this suggestion. In any case, the process of differentiation ceases once we reach Jacob and his sons, with the birth of the eponymous ancestors of the tribes.

1.   One of the three narratives in which it is claimed that the wife is actually a sister. See also Gen. 12.10 and 26.7.

Chapter 9

THE STRUCTURE OF RABBINIC THOUGHT (A)

This chapter is the first of two which analyze the midrashic interpretation and exegesis of Genesis. These chapters examine the midrashim that arise from the biblical texts about Abraham (Myth I) and *The Sacrifice of Isaac* (M.II.1). The analysis of *Genesis Rabbah* confines itself to texts that contain narrative elements, allude to narrative elements, or contain exegetical elements of structural significance.[1]

9.1. *Midrash*

Midrash, in its limited sense, refers to interpretations or expansions of words, verses or entire narratives from the Bible. It refers to either individual texts or collections of such texts (books). Midrashim are divided into two types: halachic and aggadic. Halachic midrash is concerned with deriving laws from the text and thus focuses primarily on Exodus through Deuteronomy. Aggadic midrash is concerned with any extra-legal area and draws its inspiration from all books of the Bible. Aggadah includes 'narratives, historical composition, poetry, speculation, genealogical records, fanciful interpretation...' (Goldin 1987: 109). The midrashim examined in this chapter and the following chapter are all aggadic.

Midrashic texts (compilations of midrashim) are further sub-divided into types. On the one hand, exegetical midrashim examine the biblical

---

1. Space does not permit a complete analysis of every text in either *Genesis Rabbah* or *Lekach Tov*. Discussion of texts deemed non-structurally significant are omitted from these chapters. An example of this type of text is presented here. This midrash explains Gen. 18.5: '"And I will fetch a bit of bread and you may refresh yourselves" (Gen. 18.5). Rabbi Isaac said: In the Torah, Prophets and Writings we find that it says that bread refreshes the heart (48.11).' The midrash continues by showing the connection between bread and refreshment. It also discusses whether angels were subject (like human beings) to the evil impulse. Although the text contains interesting elements, it neither adds to the narrative, nor develops or adds to the structural logic.

text verse by verse. *Genesis Rabbah* is an example of this type of midrash. Homiletical midrashim, on the other hand, deal with a general sermonic theme relating to a weekly Torah portion (a specific section of the Torah read each week in the synagogue) (Strack and Stemberger 1991: 261). No homiletical midrashim are examined here. Certain diachronically later midrashim are referred to as compilations (e.g., *Yalkut Shemone*). These midrashim contain collected selections of material from earlier midrashic books.

The rabbis used a variety of methods for interpreting the text. Several of these methods are illustrated below. One of the most common is 'creative philology'. The rabbis gave the words new vowels which could change their meaning, or divided larger words into smaller words or creatively derived ambiguous words. They also use puns and homonyms to expand the meaning of the text. The *Gezarah Shava* is another common method. This method makes analogies between two texts based on use of the same word. If the same word is present, information derived from one text can be applied to the second regardless of context (Strack and Stemberger 1991: 21). It should be noted that this was conscious creativity as the rabbis were fully aware of the plain meaning of the text. Both these and other methods were applied so that Scripture could answer problems which were not its original concern (Strack and Stemberger 1991: 259).

The analysis of the midrashic texts provides an opportunity to test structuralist theory. Although the midrashic texts are a very different type of source from the biblical text, including implicit myth and interpretation, the midrashic texts are versions of the myths told against the previous forms—both those of earlier rabbis and the biblical text itself. Each layer of diachronic development offers an opportunity to examine processes of transformation and continuity. The Bible and midrashic texts offer a perfect opportunity to study diachronic development. All levels of the development of the myths are preserved in contemporary documents. The texts analyzed provide four levels of diachronic development (illustrated in Figure 17). The analysis of these levels reveals mechanisms of transformation.

Genesis Rabbah was completed in the fourth and fifth century AD (Neusner 1985: ix). The text is composed of independent statements of rabbinic figures which interpret and develop material from Genesis. The interpretations are presented, on the narrative level, in a relatively logical order through which ideas are presented and developed. Much of the

Midrash haGadol (13th century)

Yalkut Shemone (13th century)

Lekach Tov (11th century)

Pirke deRabbi Eliezer (8th century)

Genesis Rabbah (4th century)

Bible

P

N

J

E

] = Synchronic Analysis

Figure 17. *Diachronic Levels of Hebrew Mythology*

material compiled in *Genesis Rabbah* may have originated prior to the fourth century, but for structuralist considerations discussed above in respect to the biblical text, the fourth century is considered the editorial present of the text. The historical context of *Genesis Rabbah* is the transformation of the Roman empire into a Christian empire, with the accompanying persecution of the Jewish community. *Genesis Rabbah* is a product of the Palestinian Jewish community. It is likely that Edom is portrayed in an especially negative manner in the texts due to its association with Rome and the Catholic Church. Ishmael, representing Arab power, is still ambiguous in *Genesis Rabbah*.

The nature of *Genesis Rabbah* makes it impossible, from a structuralist perspective, to look at the midrashic texts independently of biblical texts. This is partially due to the fragmentary nature of the texts and, more importantly, to the fact that the texts were inspired by the biblical texts. Rather than presenting the entire mythic structure, we find expansions and explanations of the original source material.[1] The texts in *Genesis Rabbah* develop or emphasize certain elements of underlying structure, but rely on the original sources for much of the structure. The midrashic texts develop similar oppositions to those found in the biblical text. These oppositions include variations on both the horizontal and vertical levels: Israel–Nations, divine fruitfulness–natural barrenness, father–son, and not transformed–transformed. *Genesis Rabbah* is examined in the context of biblical structure, focusing on those areas where the midrashic texts choose to transform, either qualitatively or in emphasis, the original Biblical structures.

9.2. *Abraham and the Fiery Furnace*[2]

This myth is a variation and expansion of M.I.1. It uses Gen. 11.28 as its starting point. The rabbis address the following question: 'How did Harran die?'[3] Since the death is mentioned, the implication of the text is that it must be significant (especially since he died unexpectedly before his father). The rabbis introduce two myths to answer this question. The myths develop three oppositions: between Abram and his father; between Abram and his brother; and within Abram himself, prior to rebirth and after rebirth.

> Var.I.1.A. (a) *Harran died in the presence of Terah his father* (Gen. 11.28).[4] Rabbi Hiyya said, 'Terah was a maker of idols. Once he went to another place, and gave Abraham charge of the store in his place.[5] A person would come to buy, and he (Abraham) would say to them, "how

1.   It is likely, however, that once these texts have been properly analyzed—first in the context of the biblical material—general statements about their overall structure can be made. In any case, my primary interest is in the diachronic mechanisms of transformation, which require analysis of the relationship between the biblical and midrashic structures.

2.   The text numbers are set up as follows: Var.(M) I.1.A1 where Var. = variation (midrashic expansion of Myth), M = Myth (original biblical text), the first two numbers (I.1) are the same as the myth of which the midrash is a variation, the capital letter indicates an independent variation, the final number indicates that it is a variation of a variation or that it is one of several variations on a single verse or word.

3.   Harran is one of Abraham's brothers, the other being Nahor.

4.   The biblical verse upon which the midrash is commenting is presented in italics.

5.   The names Abraham and Abram are used as found in the midrashic text. Usage does not always depend on the biblical text upon which the rabbis are commenting, that is, they use Abraham in a story which narratively occurs before his name was changed from Abram.

old are you?" He said to him (Abraham), "I am fifty years". He said to him, "Woe to him a man of fifty who bows to something but a day old". He (the man) was embarrassed and went away. Once a woman came to him with a bowl of flour, she said to him, "Take this and offer it before them". He took a stick and broke the idols, and placed the stick in the hand of the biggest idol. On the day his father returned, he (his father) said to him, "What have you done to these things". He (Abraham) said to him, "How can I hide it from you, one time a woman came with a bowl of flour and said to me, 'offer it to them'. This one (idol) said, 'I will eat first', and this one said, 'I will eat first'. Then the largest one arose and broke the other two with a stick". He (his father) said to him, "Why are you making fun of me? They have no thoughts". He (Abraham) said to him, "Do not your ears hear your mouth". He (his father) took him to Nimrod. (b) He (Nimrod) said to him, "We should bow to the fire". He (Abraham) said to him, "We should rather bow to water which extinguishes fire". He said to him, "We should bow to water". He said to him, "We should rather bow to clouds which carry water". He said to him, "We should bow to the clouds". He said to him, "We should rather bow to wind which disperses clouds". He said to him, "We should bow to wind". He said to him, "We should rather bow to men who withstand the wind". He (Nimrod) said to him, "You are bandying words with me. We will only worship fire. Behold I will cast you into the fire, let your God to whom you bow, come and save you from it!" Harran stood by undecided, he said to himself, "If Abram wins, I will say I believe according to Abram, and if Nimrod wins, I will say I believe according to Nimrod". When Abram went down into the furnace and came forth, he (Nimrod) said to him, "What do you believe?" He said to him, "I believe according to Abram". He seized him and cast him into the fire, his insides burned and he came forth and died in the presence of his father. Therefore it is written: Harran died in the presence of his father' (*Gen. R.* 38.13).

In the discussion of M.I.1 (*Abram Leaves Haran*) two levels of oppositions were distinguished: between Abraham and his father (and family); and between Abram (a) and Abram (b). The first of these oppositions is the primary focus of part (a), of *Abraham and the Fiery Furnace*. The biblical text did not explain why Abram had to leave his father's house, nor did it directly develop the opposition between Abram and his family. The midrash picks up the focus on Abram's father and strongly develops him in opposition to Abram.

The first half of the myth (a) develops the opposition between Abraham and his father. The opposition is developed on two levels: on the basis of belief, and on the basis of his father's actions. The text focuses on the absurdity of worshiping idols. It concludes with a statement by Abraham's father that he knows that idols cannot do such things (have thoughts), yet he persists in believing in and selling them. The opposition is further strengthened by his final act. He takes Abraham before Nimrod to be judged (and presumably punished). In effect his father is responsible for the (symbolic) sacrifice which is enacted in the second half of the myth. This opposition is also developed in part (b) through the discussion between Abraham and Nimrod. This myth emphasizes the distinction between Abraham and his family and Abraham and the rest of the world. He alone is chosen to understand the true nature of God.[1]

One common thread that runs through several texts in *Genesis Rabbah* is Abraham being placed in a fiery furnace by Nimrod. This myth is mentioned in several places but only fully developed here (part b). It has very little biblical support, that is, the narrative is never mentioned in Genesis. It is, however, tied to Gen. 15.7. The words אור כשדים can be translated as either 'Ur of the Chaldees' (a city in Mesopotamia), or a furnace (or fire) of the Chaldees.[2]

The myth seems related to other narratives of heroes being placed in furnaces and emerging alive, for example, Daniel, and its extended application suggests several possibilities. The tale could be part of the common mythic system, with possible application to any mythological figure; it could have originated in relation to Abraham and then been applied to other figures; or, it could have been originally applied to Shadrach, Meshach and Abednego, and later to Abraham. On a structural level, regardless of its origins, the fact that the narrative is found in relation to different figures, and in different places, suggests that it serves a key role in developing aspects of the underlying structure rather than merely a narrative device or an element of folklore. Repetitions are more likely to be structurally useful than merely fortuitous.

The fiery furnace evokes several related symbols or themes. First, there is the element of sacrifice. One type of sacrifice mentioned in biblical sources is sending a child through fire. Tied in with this theme is the possible association of Nimrod, the king who sends Abraham through the fire, with Abraham's father. In the biblical texts which describe this type of sacrifice the fathers are said to perform the sacrifice. Structurally, Nimrod may be seen as equivalent to Abraham in his

1. *Gen. R.* 39.1 presents another explanation for Abram's discovery of God. It is based on the concept that the earth must have a master (just as a building must have an owner.)

2. This play on words is found in *Gen. R.* 44.13.

attempt to sacrifice his son Isaac (this equivalence is discussed below).

Secondly, there is the analogous theme of symbolic death and rebirth. The furnace, the fiery pit, symbolizes death, which is often described as descent into the pit. Thirdly, the furnace also symbolizes miraculous rebirth, with the furnace standing for the non-human womb (based on the complex of symbols associated with the rebirth texts). In other biblical texts the element of sacrifice is closely tied to the themes of death and rebirth. This is most clearly presented in *The Sacrifice of Isaac*, but also in the murder of Abel by Cain. All three of these themes are elements of the underlying structure which are not emphasized (or not present) in the original biblical texts about Abraham.[1]

All three symbolic elements of the fiery furnace make aspects of the underlying structure more explicit. They create a myth which includes and ties together two major elements. The furnace is both the cancellation of natural birth (through death) and the source of divine birth (as a symbolic womb and vulva). The element of sacrifice is also added, with Nimrod—symbolically the father—removing Abraham (his son) from the natural pattern of descent, and thereby annulling his own role in the natural process.[2]

The second half of the myth (b) develops the second opposition, that is, between Abram (a) and Abram (b) seen in M.I.1. The primary aspect of this opposition is symbolic rebirth. In the biblical text the element of rebirth is subtly developed through use of words relating to birth and through words that allude to other rebirth texts. Thus in *Abram Leaves*

1. *Pirke deRabbi Eliezer* includes an interesting variation on the rebirth texts. It states that after Abram was born, the magicians of his land wanted to kill him. He was placed in a cave under the earth for thirteen years after which he emerged and spoke the holy language and accepted God. The text continues by describing two other trials: the fiery furnace and his leaving his father's house. All three of these texts are rebirth texts. The first two have autochthonous elements. The year thirteen is also significant. Traditionally it is the year in which a Jewish boy takes responsibility for himself in relation to God and the commandments. It is thus a symbolic birth unto responsibility (*PRE* 26.31a).

2. Nimrod should be seen as a mediator replacing Abraham's father in the sacrifice. Nimrod is both inside and outside—as king he is symbolic father but as descendant from Ham he is outside. His two facets as king and hunter also create the necessary dialectical opposition of King : Hunter :: Culture : Nature :: Inside : Outside. Thus Nimrod removes the possibly dangerous narrative element of parental sacrifice. In an analogous case, Abraham and Isaac, the ram likewise mediates the sacrifice and clouds the structure.

Haran (M.I.1) the words לך לך are used; these same words are found in
The Sacrifice of Isaac (M.II.1). In this variation of the myth, however,
the element of rebirth is brought to the fore.

Var.I.1.A is structurally equivalent to M.II.1 (*The Sacrifice of Isaac*).
The structural elements of *The Sacrifice of Isaac* were the father
(Abraham), the unknown young men (identified as Isaac's brothers), the
son (Isaac) and the mediator (the ram). The same elements, with the
exception of the ram, are found in *Abraham and the Fiery Furnace*: the
father (Terah), the son (Abram) and the brother (Harran). The mediator
is placed in a different position in the text. Nimrod replaces Terah in the
sacrifice (to lessen the apparent opposition between father and son).
Nimrod is structurally equivalent to Terah on a larger scale: Father :
Family :: King : Country. The action in the text is almost identical (with
one exception) to that in *The Sacrifice of Isaac*. The father (mediated by
Nimrod) takes the son to be sacrificed while the brother stands by. The
sacrifice in this case, however, is downward into the fire rather than
upward. As seen in the discussion of M.II.1 (*The Sacrifice of Isaac*) both
downward movement and upward movement are equated with death.[1]

The role of Harran is also significant. As opposed to the brothers who
are only implicitly present in *The Sacrifice of Isaac*, Harran (Abraham's
brother) is strongly developed. He enhances the opposition between
Abraham and his father's house on the horizontal level (whereas
previously it was only developed on the vertical level). Both his actions
and his fate strongly oppose him to Abraham. Of all the variations of
this type of text, this version is structurally one of the clearest.
Oppositions are strongly developed on the vertical and horizontal levels.

It should be noted, however, that the source for the 'peg', Gen. 15.7,
is found in texts dealing with substantially the same issues. In Genesis 15
we find the 'Covenant of the Pieces', in which God commands Abram
to cut in half a heifer, a she-goat, a ram, a turtle-dove and a pigeon, and
to make a bloody pathway between them. God promises Abram that he
will have descendants, who will become a nation and eventually inherit
the land. The pathway cut by Abram can be understood as being a
symbolic birth.[2] The association is strengthened by God's promises in
the covenant: Abram will have descendants and be the father of a nation.

This explanation is further clarified by the emphasis on barrenness

1.   It is possible that the sacrifice in the text is an upside down sacrifice. It is
upside down because Nimrod and his people had upside down beliefs.
2.   This is discussed in detail in relation to *The Covenant of Pieces* (M.I.5).

found in the beginning of the chapter. Throughout these texts there is a constant interplay between fruitfulness and barrenness. The fruitfulness always stems from God and the barrenness from human beings (sometimes found as barren fruitfulness, e.g., the birth of Ishmael).[1] There is a pattern of comparing divine birth (fruitful) with human birth (barren), which leads to a cultural emphasis on divine birth as the primary path of descent. This pattern is clearly related to that examined above (see Chapter 8) in relation to the genealogical position of Shem. In both cases, albeit through different routes, divine as opposed to natural birth is emphasized as the route of Israelite descent (or natural birth order). Israel stems from fruitfulness while the nations stem from barrenness.

The fiery furnace is also found in *Gen. R.* 39.3, a second variation of M.I.1 (Var.I.1.A1). This text develops two levels of structure. The first half emphasizes the distinction between Abram and his ancestors, describing him as qualitatively different from all other people. Abram is distinguished in two ways: he united the world, and he is distinguished by good deeds. The text states, 'No breasts suckled him in piety or good deeds'.[2] This develops the horizontal level of the structural opposition. The vertical level is developed in the second half, which alludes to the fiery furnace myth. The vertical level is also directly tied to God's command to Abram to leave his father's house, emphasizing that his departure was a symbolic rebirth.

It is significant that the fiery furnace is mentioned in conjunction with several myths, including Abraham's initial rebirth. It is also found in association with other rebirth texts. It is found twice regarding Genesis 17, *The Covenant of Pieces*: in *Gen. R.* 44.1 (Var.I.5.A) and 44.13 (Var.I.5.A1). The second of these texts reveals the exegetical peg, a play on the word Ur, taking it as 'furnace' rather than a place name. The position of the myth in conjunction with the biblical text emphasizes both its role as a rebirth text, and the role of the original biblical texts as rebirth myths.

The element of death and rebirth is expanded in *Gen. R.* 44.21

---

1. This pattern is only reversed in Gen. 3.14-22—though the pain felt at birth may be part of the cancellation of human birth.

2. This concept is also found in *Gen. R.* 39.4 (Var. I.1.B) in which Abraham is qualitatively distinguished from ten generations of his ancestors. It is also developed in a slightly different way in *Gen. R.* 39.10 (Var. I.1.B1). This text describes God as sifting through the generations in order to find Abraham. The generations (Abraham's ancestors) are likened to sand and Abraham to a pearl.

(Var.I.5.B). In effect the text turns the covenant of pieces into a fiery furnace. In the biblical text the path between the pieces became a burning furnace. The rabbis interpreted this furnace as representing hell, stating that God shows Abraham in the flame Gehenna (Hell). This can be understood as a symbolic death because, at least symbolically, Abraham travels to the world of the dead.

9.3. *Abraham and Terah*

These themes are also dealt with in Abraham and Terah. This text develops the vertical opposition, emphasizing the death of Terah prior to Abram's symbolic rebirth.

> Var.I.1.B. *God said to Abram: 'Go forth'* (Gen. 12.1). What is written prior to this matter? *'Terah died in Haran'* (Gen. 11.32). If the mathematics are considered, he should have lived another sixty-five years. Thus in the beginning you might explain: the wicked are called dead in their lifetimes. Because Abraham our father was afraid and said: 'I will go out and they will profane the name of God because of me saying: "He left his father and went from him in the time of his old age".' The Holy One Praised Be He said to him: 'לך לך (Go you out).[1] לך, You I free from (the commandment) honoring your father and mother, and I will never free any other (person) from honoring their father and mother. And that is not all, I will also anticipate (record) his death prior to your leaving.'[2] First, 'And Terah died in Haran', and then after it 'and God said to Abram go forth' (*Gen. R.* 39.7).

This text includes several interesting points which relate to the discussion of the fiery furnace. Like the fiery furnace, Abram's leaving his father's house can be seen as symbolic rebirth, and similarly it is caused by divine rather than human action. This text also uses several means to cancel the role of his 'natural' parents in this new conception. The first attempt is found in the statement 'The wicked are called dead in their lifetimes', making his father at least symbolically dead at the time of Abraham's 'birth'. The second attempt is more subtle: 'You I free from honoring your father and mother'. By removing this commandment, the text in effect argues that they are indeed not really his parents, because,

---

1.   This part of the midrash is 'pegged' on the word לך 'you' which is grammatically redundant—the word לך 'go out' already includes the you.

2.   The word מקדים translated here as 'anticipate' (meaning anticipate the report of) can also be translated as anticipate in time, that is, make the death earlier than originally stated.

if they had properly been his parents, God would not have released him.[1]

The third method relies on an alternative translation of the text: 'I will anticipate his death prior to your leaving'. This translation supports the earlier statement in the midrash that, even when alive the wicked are considered dead. Though Terah is alive, as far as God is concerned and as far as Abraham should be concerned he is dead. The text, however, can be taken as making an even stronger statement, God caused Terah to die (early) in order to prepare for Abraham's rebirth, and thereby annulling Abraham's parents role in the event. As above, this text creates the opposition of natural, human birth with divine rebirth, divine or cultural birth is emphasized.[2]

Gen. R. 39.9 (Var.I.1.C) emphasizes the relationship between Abram's exodus from Haran and *The Sacrifice of Isaac*. The midrashic equivalence is based on the introduction of each text by common words. In each case God tells Abram (Abraham) לך לך, 'go you'. This association of the two texts strengthens the structural identification of M.I.1 (*Abram Leaves Haran*) as a rebirth text.

9.4. *Origin of Israel and the Nations*

It is suggested that one aspect of the underlying structure is the logic of endogamy. The mythology creates a system in which endogamy, as opposed to perceived nature (unlimited marriage), is the natural and logical choice. In the above texts the primary dialectics appear to center around 'natural' birth and 'divine' birth, with the primary emphasis being on divine birth. Within the chosen line, the sexual reproductive roles of men and women are symbolically minimized in favor of the divine aspect. It seems likely that the texts are trying to create (or define) a qualitative difference between human beings, that is, those of divine origin and those of human origin.

This distinction is clearly stated in *Gen. R.* 39.11 (Var. I.1.D). This text states that from Noah arose seventy nations, yet from God only one.[3]

1. Although it is true that in several places in Genesis Abraham acts contrary to the commandments, and that in fact the commandments had not yet been given, it was a general rabbinic principle that Abraham was bound by the commandments. This is implied in this text. Abraham is not automatically freed from the commandment to honor father and mother, but rather must be freed from it by God.

2. Jacob Neusner translates this text in a similar way (1985: 63).

3. The Rabbis believed that there were seventy nations (other than Israel) in the world. This number is based on the nations listed in Gen. 10.

The text implies a clear qualitative difference between Israel and the other nations of the world. This difference is further emphasized later in the same text. It states, 'I have created thee (Abraham) to be a new creation, be fruitful and multiply'. This distinction is made in several texts comparing Abraham to his ancestors. *Gen. R.* 39.3 states that Abraham united the whole world and, further, that he had no one from whom to draw inspiration. He was *sui generis*. This theme is also found in 39.4 and 39.10.

9.5. *Abraham and Converts*
The position of converts is problematic in relation to the underlying structure. If the system is attempting to create a qualitative distinction between Israel and the nations, how could a non-Israelite become part of Israel; can the distinction be bridged? *Gen. R.* 39.14 deals with this question. It relies on the same exegesis as found in 39.11, built on the words אשר עשה, 'which he made'. The text states,

> Var.I.1.F. *And the souls which he had made in Haran* (Gen. 12.5). Rabbi Elazar said in the name of Rabbi Yossi ben Zimra: 'If all the fathers of the world gathered to create even one mosquito, they would not be able to throw into it a soul, and yet you say: "And the souls which he made". If these are the people he converted, it should say converted. Why does it say "made?" It teaches you, that he who brings a gentile near to God, it is as if he created him.'

The text resolves the problem by stating that the convert is a new creation, recreated upon his conversion. Thus rather than becoming a mediator, sharing characteristics of both sides, the convert is firmly taken into the Israelite camp. If converts had remained mediators, they would have blurred the boundaries within the system, creating possible crisis.

This transformation or rebirth from outside to inside is illustrated both in Talmudic law and current practice. The Talmud states that after a proselyte has converted, he is no longer related to his previous family. Thus, in spite of the laws against brother–sister incest, a proselyte could marry his sister (*b. Yeb.* 22a-23b). Effectively he is reborn. The element of rebirth is emphasized in modern Jewish practice. A proselyte, upon conversion, changes his name, and is said to be a son of Abraham and Sarah. In both these cases it is emphasized that the proselyte is recreated/reborn inside, and thus does not mediate between inside and outside.

9.6. *Abram in Egypt*[1]

Gen. R. 40.5 (Var.I.2.A) develops the mytheme of death and rebirth. This element was only implicit in the biblical text (*Wife/Sister 1*, M.I.2). The primary structural element developed in the biblical text was the transformation of wife into sister. This development involved a transformation (a rebirth) within Sarai.

> *And it came to pass when Abram came to Egypt, etc.* (Gen. 12.14). Now where was Sarai? (Seeing that she was not mentioned by the text). He had placed her in a box and locked her in it. When he arrived at the custom house, he (the officer) said, 'pay the toll'. He said, 'I will pay'. He replied, 'You are carrying garments'. He said, 'I will pay the toll for garments'. He said, 'You are carrying silk'. He replied, 'I will pay the toll for silk'. He replied, 'You are carrying gems'. He said, 'I will pay the toll for gems'. He replied, 'You cannot go through until you open the box and reveal to us the contents'.

It is possible to interpret this text as a symbolic death. Although in biblical times boxes or sarcophagi were not used, in the rabbinic period in Palestine they were used. Thus the box described in this text should be seen as a symbolic coffin. Therefore the descent to Egypt (in a box) is a symbolic death which prepares for Sarai's rebirth as Abram's sister.

Gen. R. 41.1 (Var.I.2.B) develops a variation on the mytheme of divine versus natural fruitfulness. The text compares Israel (the righteous) to both cedars and palm trees (based on biblical quotations). It then presents a story in which a certain palm tree does not bear fruit. An expert on palm trees reveals that the tree is pining for a certain other palm tree which is at a great distance. When the male tree is grafted to the female, the female bears fruit. The text explains the parable but concludes that the righteous only bear fruit when joined with God.

In the context of the wife/sister texts this text works on two levels. First, the tree can represent Sarah who is fruitless in respect to Pharaoh yet fruitful with Abraham. Secondly, it emphasizes (with the explanation) that even the righteous are fruitless without God—the divine element is necessary for Israel to bear fruit.

Gen. R. 41.2 (Var.I.2.C) is a second text which develops structural elements found in the biblical text. This text examines the question of

---

1.   In the discussion of the biblical text it was suggested that the three Wife/Sister texts were structurally analogous to the descent and ultimate exodus of the Israelites from Egypt. This element is directly stated in *PRE* 26.61a. It ties both the plagues and the wealth of *Wife/Sister 1* to those of the exodus.

how God plagued Pharaoh. In the discussion of *Wife/Sister 1* (M.I.2) I suggested that the plague was barrenness. This suggestion was based on the structural equivalence of *Wife/Sister 1* and *Wife/Sister 2* (M.1.12). Var.I.2.C develops the same analogy, stating that Pharaoh and Abimelech were plagued in the same way. The midrash bases this equivalence on the repetition of the same words by each text; they both include the words, 'For the sake of'.[1]

9.7. *Abraham and Lot*

The biblical text developed the opposition between Abram and Lot. In the previous biblical texts Lot mediated between Abram and the other nations. This mediation is transformed into opposition through the strife between the servants of Abram and Lot, and finally by their division of the land. The midrashic text further develops and strengthens the opposition between the two.

Gen. R. 41.5 (Var.I.3.A) places the blame for the strife firmly in Lot's camp. The text states, 'Abraham's cattle went out muzzled, while Lot's cattle went out without muzzles'.[2] This suggests a moral distinction between Lot's shepherds and Abraham's (and by implication between Lot and Abraham).[3] The text then rejects Lot by equating him with the Canaanites (who are structurally strongly negative). Lot's men claim that they are only taking what will be their master's, because he will inherit Abraham's property. This claim is rejected. God states that, although he will give the land to Abraham's seed, this will occur when the Canaanites (including Lot and his descendants) are uprooted from the land. Thus Lot is rejected as Abraham's inheritor and he is equally qualitatively negative through association with the Canaanites.

The opposition between Abraham and Lot is strongly developed in *Gen. R.* 41.6.3 (Var.I.3.A2). This text examines the use of the word 'separate' rather than 'depart'. It suggests that 'separate' is used because it contains the same letters as 'mule'.[4] The text continues, 'just as a mule

---

1. This analogy is based on a rabbinic principle of interpretation called *Gezera Shava*. This principle makes analogies between two texts in which identical words are used, implying that what is true of one is also true of the other (Mielziner 1968: 143).
2. Muzzles prevented the cattle from grazing in others' fields (Freeman 1939: 335).
3. *Gen. R.* 41.6.1 (Var.I.3.A1) suggests that the strife was also between Abraham and Lot.
4. 'Separate' in Hebrew is הפרד and 'mule' is פרדה. They both contain the same letters.

does not have seed, so it is not possible for this man to mix with the seed of Abraham'. This text works on two levels. On the one hand it recognizes Lot's role as a mediator. A mule mediates between a horse and an ass. The text, however, suggests that such mediation is barren. The text also emphasizes the opposition between Abraham and the other nations. They (represented by Lot) are associated with an animal which must not mix its seed with Abraham and his descendants.

The text further develops the opposition between Abraham and Lot, depicting Lot's attempt to cheat Abraham. Expanding Gen. 13.9 the midrash states, 'Lot said, "If you go to the left I will go to the right, If I go to the right you go to the left"'. The text concludes, stating that Lot would force Abraham to take the left. Each of these texts further emphasizes the opposition.[1]

Gen. R. 41.7 (Var.I.3.A3) develops the opposition in a second way. It emphasizes the sexually immoral nature of the area Lot chooses and suggests that Lot's choice was motivated by lust. R. Nahman bar Hanan (who is quoted by the text) suggests the analogy between Lot and lust. In Hebrew the name Lot is made up of letters found in the word for lust. R. Yose bar Haninah suggests that the entire verse is connected with sexual immorality (the midrash shows that three words used in the text can be found in texts about sexual immorality).

The midrash suggests that Lot's choice was motivated by a wish to separate from Abraham and from Abraham's God. The text states, '"And Lot journeyed east": He removed himself from the ancient of the world: "I want no part of Abraham or his God".' This interpretation is based on the word 'east'. In Hebrew, the words for 'east' and 'ancient' have the same letters (ק ד ם). Thus Lot opposes himself to Israel by rejecting Israel and Israel's God. All the midrashic texts examined in this section develop the same opposition as found in the biblical text. Lot is transformed from mediation to a position structural opposition, representing the nations.

9.8. *Sarah and Hagar*

There are several texts which examine Sarah's barrenness, and the associated role of Hagar. The first of these texts, 45.1 (Var.I.6.A), raises the question of the source of her barrenness. It offers three different possibilities: Sarah's fault, Abraham's fault, and both their fault. The text concludes that the fault was in both Abraham and Sarah. This

---

1. Neusner makes a similar point in his discussion of these texts (1985: 93).

emphasizes the denial of human fertility which is characteristic of biblical structure.

The role of God in Sarah's barrenness (and in her eventual fertility) is developed in *Gen. R.* 45.2 (Var. I.6.A1). The text states,

> And Sarah said to Abraham 'behold the Lord has prevented me, etc.' (Gen. 16.2). She said, 'I know the source of my barrenness. It is not as people say, "that she needs a charm, she needs an amulet". "Behold, the Lord has prevented me from bearing children".'

The text recognizes that Sarah's barrenness is unnatural. It is divine barrenness which can only be resolved by divine fertility.

The question of Sarah's infertility is also developed in opposition to Hagar's fertility in *Gen. R.* 45.4 (Var.I.6.C). The rabbis suggest that Hagar became pregnant on the first act of sexual intercourse. This is countered by the statement, 'a woman never gets pregnant the first time'. The rabbis objected to that by mentioning the daughters of Lot (who did become pregnant the first time). The text concludes that weeds grow faster than wheat. Hagar and the daughters of Lot (and their respective children) are compared to weeds, while Sarah and her descendants are compared to wheat.[1]

The rabbis use Sarah's quarrel with Hagar to emphasize the negative or dangerous characteristics of women. In *Gen. R.* 45.5 (Var.I.6.D) Sarah unfairly accuses Abraham of giving Hagar a child, but not giving her one. The text implies that it was Sarah's fault not Abraham's. The text suggests further, when she accused Abraham, that she scratched his face.

The strongest indictment, however, is found in part four of the text. The rabbis state that women are 'greedy, eavesdroppers, lazy and envious' and later include 'scratchers and talkative', and two final elements: 'they are thieves and run-abouts' (with the implication of sexual license). The text applies these adjectives to women throughout the Bible including Eve, Sarah and Rachel. In the chapters examining the biblical text it is shown that women were structurally dangerous. This was primarily due to the structure of Israelite society, that is, patrilineal (for the most part), segmentary and endogamous. Although, in rabbinic society, the matrilineal element was added (a Jew was defined

---

1. Hagar uses this fact (of her fruitfulness as opposed to Sarah's barrenness) against Sarah later on in the same text. The midrash uses this to oppose her (qualitatively) to Sarah and justify Hagar's expulsion from Abraham's camp.

as the child of a Jewish woman), the structural danger posed by women is retained and strengthened.

9.9. *Circumcision*[1]

It has already been suggested that circumcision, in the context of the covenant, is symbolic castration (symbolically removing the father as progenitor).[2] Circumcision serves also to distinguish Israel from the nations, and as a completion of the human being which is granted solely to Israel.[3] V.I.7.A, *Gen. R.* 39.11, develops this concept. It ties the Hebrew letter ה which is added to Abram's name, making it Abraham, to the covenant of circumcision. The text states,

> Rabbi Abahu said: 'see the heavens' is not written here (in the context of Gen. 15.5, the covenant of the pieces) but rather 'toward the heavens' (the text uses the accusative form of the noun which is created by the addition of a ה, i.e., השמימה rather than using a preposition and the more usual form of the noun השמים.) The Holy One Praised Be He said: 'with this ה I created this world, behold I add a ה and you shall be fruitful and multiply'.

The text continues by comparing the numerology (each Hebrew letter also had a numerical value, and words which had the same value were seen as being in some sense equivalent) of אברהם 'Abraham', and אברכך, 'And I shall bless you'. It concludes that, with the addition of the ה to Abram, the two words are numerically equivalent, and thus with the addition of the ה Abraham becomes a blessing.[4]

Secondly, this text is tied to circumcision on several levels. In parallel texts (in relation to Gen. 17) circumcision, completion, is tied to the

---

1. It should be noted that circumcision is to be considered as the structural equivalent of barrenness using the following equation: Circumcision : Barrenness :: Male : Female; Circumcision/Barrenness : Natural Fecundity :: Israel : Nations.

2. Circumcision is also symbolic sacrifice. *PRE* 29.65a states, 'everyone who brings his son for circumcision is similar to the High Priest bringing his meal offering and drink offering to the altar'. The connection with sacrifice is also developed later in the same chapter. It states that the blood put on the doors during the exodus from Egypt was the blood of circumcision. That blood is directly associated with the blood of the paschal lamb, the Passover sacrifice.

3. *PRE* 29.65b suggests that the uncircumcised defile like the dead: 'In their life time they (the uncircumcised) are like the dead'. It states further that only the prayers of Israel can reach God, because the dead cannot praise God.

4. The numerical value of אברם Abram is 243, while that of אברהם is 248. The letter ה had the value of 5, thus with the addition of the ה to Abram the name came to the value of 248.

addition of the ה. Without the ה the numerical value of Abram is 243. The rabbis believed that the body was composed of 248 limbs. Therefore Abram lacked five. With circumcision his body was completed, and therefore he merited the addition of the ה to his name to symbolize this completion. The midrash brings together the two covenants, that is, the original discussion of the ה is from Genesis 15 (M.I.5, *The Covenant of Pieces*) and the associated name change is in Genesis 17 (M.I.7, *The Covenant of Circumcision*).

On a structural level these covenants are also equivalent, and statements regarding one thus refers also to the other. The equation of the two covenants can therefore be made:

Circumcision = Blessing = Wholeness = Fruitfulness.

This is strengthened by the words in both covenants which emphasize that, although childless, Abram shall have a multitude of descendants (15.5 and 17.3). This is also included in the midrash itself: 'Be fruitful and multiply'. The midrash ties together the following oppositions: Natural Birth : Divine Birth :: Uncircumcised : Circumcised/Castrated :: Barrenness : Fruitfulness. These oppositions create the apparent paradox: divine birth implies castration which, in turn, implies fruitfulness.

These dialectical oppositions are further emphasized in *Gen. R.* 46.1 (Var.I.7.A1) and 46.2 (Var.I.7.A2).[1] *Gen. R.* 46.1 states,

> Thus spoke the Holy One Praised Be He to Abraham: there is no flaw in you save the foreskin, remove it and thereby remove the flaw, '*Walk before me and be thou whole hearted*' (Gen. 17.1).

The word used for flaw מום is used rabbinically to mean a blemish which makes something unfit for the altar or the priestly service. Thus with the removal of the foreskin, the distinction between Israel and the nations, Israel alone becomes fit for the service of God. Only Israel, by being less than whole, is truly whole.[2]

Gen. R. 46.2 (Var.I.7.A2) emphasizes the distinction between Ishmael (natural birth) and Isaac (divine birth). It states that Abraham was

1. The same concept is developed in *Gen. R.* 46.4 (Var.I.7.A3). In that text circumcision is tied to fruitfulness. The text emphasizes the distinction between natural and divine fruitfulness. Divine fruitfulness leads to exceeding fruitfulness.

2. The association of circumcision with wholeness is based on the verse quoted in the midrash. Gen. 17.1, 'walk before me and be thou whole hearted', introduces the covenant of circumcision. The Rabbis understood 'walk before me' as meaning, 'accept my covenant and be circumcised', and then you shall be whole hearted.

commanded regarding circumcision at the second covenant precisely so that Isaac would come from a 'holy drop', that he would come from circumcised rather than uncircumcised. Like *Gen. R.* 39.11 (see above, Var.I.7.A), this text develops the dialectical opposition: Ishmael : Isaac :: Nations : Israel :: Natural Birth : Divine Birth.

9.10. *Abram and Sarai versus Abraham and Sarah*
As mentioned above (see the discussion of M.I.7, *The Covenant of Circumcision*), Genesis 17 should be seen as the third stage in Abram's rebirth. The most obvious symbol of this rebirth is the change in names—from Abram to Abraham. The change in name occurs, however, not only to Abram but also to Sarai his wife. She too is symbolically reborn as Sarah. Abram and Sarai represent natural birth (with Ishmael being the product through the mediation of Hagar), while Abraham and Sarah represent cultural or divine birth: natural birth is barren, divine birth is fruitful.

The change in Abraham is highlighted by the status of Ishmael. Ishmael is born prior to the covenant, and is never considered worthy to carry on the line. His separateness is emphasized by the fact that his mother, unlike Sarah, is an outsider and a concubine. Once the covenant is cut, and Abram becomes Abraham, Isaac can be born.

This dialectical opposition is emphasized in *Gen. R.* 44.10 (Var.I.7.B). The text states,

> Abram said: '*Behold to me you have given no seed*' (Gen. 15.3). Rabbi Shmuel ben Rav Yitzhak said: 'The stars (astrology) came upon me and said to me: "Abram you will have no children". The Holy One Praised Be He said to him: "Let it be according to your words: Abram will have no children, Abraham will, Sarai will bear no children, Sarah will".'

This text emphasizes that the change in names, the rebirth, was of consequence, and that it allowed Abraham and Sarah to have Isaac who would carry on the divine blessing. It also highlights the difference between Isaac and Ishmael. Although Ishmael was born prior to the events narrated, Abraham says, 'I have no son'. Ishmael, natural birth, is considered no birth at all.[1]

---

1. In the biblical text Ishmael is at worst ambiguous. This position, however, begins to change in *Genesis Rabbah*. Several texts try to resolve the problems created by the texts which speak positively about Ishmael. Thus *Gen. R.* 47.5 (Var.I.7.A) suggests that God's blessing of Ishmael (Gen. 17.19-20) either did not actually refer to Ishmael or that it was limited in nature. Similarly the midrash consistently

One mytheme which is found throughout the biblical text is the denial
of Abraham's and Sarah's roles as parents. In *Abraham and the Three
Men* (M.I.8) this element was emphasized by the improbability of Sarah
or Abraham having a child naturally. This mytheme is developed in
several ways in *Genesis Rabbah. Gen. R.* 47.2 (Var.I.8.A) states that
God restored to Sarah her youth, thus making the birth the product of a
miracle.[1] Similarly *Gen. R.* 47.2 (Var.I.8.A1) states, 'She lacked an
ovary, the Holy one praised be, formed one for her'. Again the birth
depends on God's intervention. In a similar vein, *Gen. R.* 47.3.2
(Var.I.8.A2) emphasizes Abraham's surprise that a man of his age
should have a child. This is also developed in *Gen. R.* 48.16 (Var.I.8.A3)
in which the parental role of both Abraham and Sarah is denied.

9.11. *Abraham and Lot*

The rabbis emphasized Ishmael's negative characteristics (as well as
Esau's), and also strongly strengthened the structural distinction between
Abraham and Lot. *Gen. R.* 50.3.4 (Var.I.10.A) suggests that there were
five justices in Sodom, each named after a negative characteristic, for
example, 'False Principles'.[2] It states further that 'Lot was the chief
justice', linking him directly to their negative natures.

A second text (*Gen. R.* 50.4, Var.I.10.A1) attempts to distinguish Lot
from Abraham. It deals with a problem created by the biblical text in
which Lot seems to be equated with Abraham (Gen. 19.1-2). The
midrash takes each of the points of similarity and either inverts its
meaning or attributes it to Abraham. For example, they state that Lot
offered to wash the angels' feet after spending the night rather than
before (as Abraham had done). The rabbis attribute the filth (on the feet)
to the filth of idolatry and comment that Abraham was meticulous while
Lot was not. The text also concludes with a rejection of Lot's wife.

Another midrash (*Gen. R.* 50.11) picks up the fact that Lot lingered in
Sodom (Var.I.10.B).[3] The text suggests that there was one delay after

emphasizes the negative aspects of Esau (Edom) and its association with Rome.
    1. *Gen. R.* 48.16 (Var.I.8.A3) includes a similar statement about Abraham. This
fits with structuralist analysis of the original text M.I.8 in which it was suggested that
the roles of both Sarah and Abraham are equally denied.
    2. In *Pirke deRabbi Eliezer* the midrash compares Sodom to the world, stating
that the world will continue to exist for the sake of fifty righteous men. Effectively,
this extends the opposition between Abraham and Sodom to Abraham and the world
(*PRE* 25.58b).
    3. Based on Gen. 19.16.

another, and offers one reason for the delay: Lot's concern about his loss of wealth. This text emphasizes Lot's greed as well as his connections to the city and consequent wickedness. The same midrash also develops Lot's role as a mediator. The final section states,

> Lot said, before I went with Abraham, the Holy One praised be He looked at my deeds and the deeds of the people of my city. My deeds were more numerous than the deeds of my city. Now that I am going with Abraham, his deeds are many and I cannot stand his burning coal.

This text implies that, although Lot was good compared to his city, compared to Abraham he deserved to be destroyed. Lot mediates between Abraham and Sodom and, by implication, Abraham and the nations. *Gen. R.* 51.6 (Var.I.10.A2) returns to the theme of Lot's wickedness. It suggests that Lot was inextricably tied to all the wicked cities, having lived and lent money for interest in each of them.

The rabbis discuss Lot's incest with his daughters from two perspectives. On the one hand, they do not condemn the daughters, but emphasize the daughters' belief that all other people on earth had been destroyed. Thus their act is not necessarily negative (*Gen. R.* 51.8, Var.I.11.A). On the other hand, Lot is condemned. The text suggests that he knew (after the fact) what his elder daughter had done and thus could have stopped his younger daughter. In a second text (*Gen. R.* 51.9, Var.I.11.A1) the rabbis suggest that Lot lusted after his daughters and had previously been guilty of fornication.

The rabbis suggest that Lot's descendants took after him rather than his daughters. *Gen. R.* 51.10 (Var.I.11.A3) states that, although the daughters of Lot were virtuous, that is, the incest had virtuous motives, the Moabites acted for the sake of lust. Throughout both biblical and rabbinic texts, the Moabites are characterized as sexually uncontrolled. The text does, however, recognize the good which came from the union, that is, Ruth the Moabitess who is said to be the ancestor of David and the Messiah.

9.12. *Ishmael*

After the birth of Isaac, there are several texts which distinguish Ishmael from Isaac and justify his (and his mother's) expulsion from Abraham's camp. One text interprets the words 'making sport' (Gen. 21.9) in four different ways (*Gen. R.* 53.11, Var.I.13.A). It suggests that 'making sport' might mean fornication, idolatry, murder and claiming the inheritance (i.e., claiming to be the chosen descendant of Abraham).[1] The text ties Ishmael's expulsion to the fourth meaning. All four of these explanations emphasize the opposition between Isaac and Ishmael (although Isaac is not directly compared to him here).

In a later text, *Gen. R.* 53.15 (Var.I.13.B), the rabbis suggest that Ishmael grew in cruelty (making a pun on the Hebrew words רבה קשה). There are, however, several texts (also found in the compilations, see below) in which Ishmael is qualitatively ambiguous. These texts retain the ideological quality found in the biblical text.

9.13. *The Sacrifice of Isaac*

There are a number of texts which develop the exegesis of Genesis 22. The first two texts develop the opposition between Isaac and Ishmael. In section 55.1 (Var.II.1.A) *Genesis Rabbah* presents a discussion between Isaac and Ishmael in which they compete over who is more beloved.

Ishmael states that he was circumcised in his thirteenth year, Isaac counters that he was circumcised on the eighth day (as is prescribed by Jewish Law). Ishmael states that he is better because he could have protested against being circumcised while Isaac could not. Isaac responds that he would be willing to give to the Lord one of his limbs, to which God replies, 'Offer yourself to me as a sacrifice'. This midrash has an explicit opposition built into it which Isaac and Ishmael, with their argument, set up themselves. The final distinction is made when Isaac offers himself, and Ishmael has no response.[2] The text also adds a new element to Genesis 22. Isaac becomes an active participant rather than merely a passive one.

The second midrash (*Gen. R.* 55.7) similarly distinguishes between Isaac and Ishmael (Var.II.1.A1). Versions of this text are found in all the midrashim discussed. This text presents a discussion between God and

---

1.   *PRE* 30.66b expands this midrash. It presents a narrative in which Ishmael attempts to murder Isaac and attributes his expulsion to this attempt. The process begun in *Genesis Rabbah* is taken even further in *Pirke deRabbi Eliezer*. Ishmael is completely negative and becomes a literal trial to his father Abraham. The text continues by developing the opposition between Sarah and Hagar. It states that Sarah was destined to be Abraham's wife from the womb, where-as Hagar is only a handmaid. It states further that the expulsion was both from this world and the world to come. The text concludes by listing the negative things which the Ishmaelites will do to the Israelites in the future.

2.   An identical text is found in *b. Sanh.* 89b.

Abraham based on Gen. 22.2. The midrash focuses on the three terms which God uses to describe Isaac. It states,

> And He said to him: 'take...your son'; he said to him: 'which son'; he said to him: 'your only one'; he said to him: 'this is the only son of his mother and this is the only son of his mother'; He said to him: 'the one you love'; he said to Him: 'I love both'; He said to him: 'take Isaac'.

Although this midrash appears to equate Isaac and Ishmael, a subtle distinction is developed. On one level, like the above text, Isaac is identified as ideologically (+) regarding Ishmael because in the end Isaac is chosen rather than Ishmael. On a second level, no equation of Isaac and Ishmael is possible. It is God who describes Isaac using the three terms 'son', 'only one', and 'whom you love', and all Abraham's disclaimers of his special attachment to Isaac are no use. Ultimately the terms used by God can apply only to Isaac. By disclaiming them Abraham emphasizes them, and therefore strengthens the opposition between Isaac and Ishmael.[1]

---

1. The opposition between Isaac and Ishmael is developed in similar ways in *Pirke deRabbi Eliezer*. Here we find a similar midrash to that found in *Genesis Rabbah* with, however, several significant additions. The text is introduced by a statement that just prior to the events (of Gen. 22) Ishmael returns from the wilderness, thus making explicit his structural opposition to Isaac by bringing Ishmael in person into the myth. The midrash continues with an expansion of the first few verses of Gen. 22: the midrash portrays Abraham as bargaining with God, stating that each term might apply to either Isaac or Ishmael, until God finally singles Isaac out by name. The primary difference between this version and those found in other midrashim (see the version from *Genesis Rabbah* quoted above) relates to an additional way of distinguishing between Isaac and Ishmael which is introduced by Abraham. Abraham asks God, 'Which son, the one born prior to the circumcision or the one born after circumcision'. This emphasizes the importance of the covenant of circumcision, and Gen. 17 as a whole, in distinguishing between Isaac and Ishmael, developing the opposition: Prior to Circumcision : After Circumcision :: Natural : Divine. The force of this element as well as the other expansions of this part of the text emphasize the opposition between Isaac and Ishmael (and implicitly the opposition between Israel and the nations). This is further accentuated by the rationale given for Abraham's questions: Abraham's exceptional love for Isaac (*PRE* 31).

The second means of developing the opposition between Isaac and Ishmael is also found in several different midrashic texts. This text describes a discussion between Ishmael and Eliezer, who are identified as the two young men brought by Abraham to Mount Moriah. Ishmael tells Eliezer that with the upcoming sacrifice of Isaac, he will become Abraham's beneficiary. Eliezer challenges this, citing Ishmael's expulsion from Abraham's camp, stating that in fact he will inherit his master's property. At this

The text continues with an interesting association. It connects the sacrifice of Isaac with Abram's leaving his father's house. The rabbis observe that both texts include the words לֶךְ לְךָ, and further that in each case God uses three words to describe the point of transformation in the text. In Genesis 22 the three terms describe Isaac, who is structurally transformed from human origin to divine origin; while in Genesis 12 they describe Abram's father's house, which is structurally transformed from inside to outside. On a structural level both texts describe the process of divine rebirth.

Several texts in *Genesis Rabbah* focus on, and thus emphasize, the centrality of the sacrifice. This is seen in 56.6 (Var.II.1.B) where it states that the two (Abraham and Isaac) went together, the binder and the bound, the slaughterer and the slaughtered. In 56.12 (Var.II.1.B1) the text discusses whether Abraham drew even a drop of blood from Isaac. Both these and other texts, while not admitting actual sacrifice, continue to keep the possibility of sacrifice in the fore.

The final significant text in *Genesis Rabbah* is 56.19 (Var.II.1.C), which address the biblical statement that Abraham returned alone. The text offers the possibility that Isaac was sent to study Torah with Shem. This separation is one step away from death. Although mythologically Shem was still alive at the time of the Binding of Isaac, his yeshiva (school) has other worldly elements, emphasized by the fact that Shem lived ten generations before Abraham. Thus this text creates the

point a voice from God tells them that neither one nor the other will inherit. This text works on several levels. On the one hand, it inserts Ishmael and Eliezer into the myth, strengthening the opposition of Isaac to both of them as well as strengthening their structural equation, that Ishmael and Eliezer are structurally identical. The text therefore exactly corresponds with the structural analysis of the role of the young men in the biblical text and the projected identification of the two. And on the other hand, it strengthens the opposition by clearly stating that neither Ishmael or Eliezer shall inherit. Neither could take the place of Isaac as bearer of God's blessing (*PRE* 31).

This opposition is further developed on the spiritual level. Abraham asks Ishmael and Eliezer if they see any thing on the mountain. They say that they see nothing, whereas Isaac is said to have seen a pillar of fire. Abraham tells them to remain with the donkey—because just as the ass saw nothing, likewise you saw nothing. This ties into the opposition already developed: Ishmael and Eliezer, the products of natural birth, are equated with the ass, a product of nature; whereas Abraham and Isaac, products of divine birth, are equated with the divine. This text is also found in *Genesis Rabbah*, however, with one significant difference. In *Genesis Rabbah* (Var II.1.A2) the two young men are not identified as Ishmael and Eliezer (*Gen. R.* 56.2; *PRE* 31).

possibility of a death (and subsequent rebirth) without actually describing an actual sacrifice (and thus materially transforming the biblical text).[1]

The texts described in this chapter are typical of *Genesis Rabbah* as a whole. *Genesis Rabbah* tends to explore oppositions developed in the biblical text, without adding significant transformations or mediators. Of the texts only the Nimrod texts materially transformed the biblical text which they were interpreting, adding a significant narrative not found in Genesis. The narrative supplemented the biblical text rather than

---

1.   Whereas in *Genesis Rabbah* the only hint of the death of Isaac was that he went to study with Shem, in *Pirke deRabbi Eliezer* we find a clearer reference to death. Towards the end of the texts discussing Gen. 22 it states, 'When the sword touched Isaac's throat, terrified, his soul fled. Immediately (God's) his voice was heard from between the angels, and he said "do not lay your hand on the boy", thereupon his soul returned to his body... And Isaac knew of the resurrection of the dead from the Torah, that all the dead are destined to be resurrected' (*PRE* 31).

This text openly includes a death and resurrection, albeit in a short space of time. Although it might be thought that this merely refers to fainting or unconsciousness, the inclusion in the text of material referring to the future resurrection, implies that it was an example of that phenomenon. This ties into the logic discussed above, emphasizing the structural elements of both sacrifice and rebirth.

There are several texts in *Pirke deRabbi Eliezer* which develop the opposition of natural and divine birth, especially in regard to the denial of Sarah's parental role. These texts tie the death of Sarah directly to the sacrifice. Thus in ch. 32 the text presents the following story. After Satan found that he could not convince Abraham and Isaac to be unfaithful to God he went to Sarah. He told Sarah that Abraham had killed Isaac, thereupon Sarah died in grief. This text emphasizes a connection already built into the narrative structure, that is, it places the death of Sarah immediately after the Akedah and attributes her death directly to the Akedah. The death of Sarah, as suggested above, is part of logical structure in which the natural parents are progressively denied, leaving only the divine parent as the agent of the rebirth.

Pirke deRabbi Eliezer is much freer in regard to developing oppositions found in the biblical text. It clarifies and emphasizes connections made, that is, tying Sarah's death to the sacrifice, and the similar structural and narrative elements in Gen. 12, Abraham's first rebirth. It also expands upon the structural elements transforming the biblical text to emphasize the logical oppositions. It strengthens the opposition between Isaac and Ishmael through bringing Ishmael directly into the narrative. And it strengthens the element of sacrifice through including the death and resurrection of Isaac, albeit in a slightly weak form as Isaac dies of fright rather than actually being sacrificed. All the oppositions developed, however, remain consistent with those developed in the biblical text. They are also consistent with structuralist projections in regard to the development of the myth. For example, *Pirke deRabbi Eliezer* is congruent with the structural identification of Abraham's young men, identifying them as Ishmael and Eliezer.

transforming material in the Bible. Through its emphasis on death and rebirth, it highlighted structures already present in *Abram Leaves Haran* (M.I.1). It is also significant that the 'Fiery Furnace' narrative was alluded to specifically in relation to texts dealing with death and rebirth. The primary interest in these texts is the possible identification of Nimrod with Abraham's father, strengthening the symbolic connection with sacrifice and the associated denial of the parental role.

9.14. *Synthesis*

In the course of these reflections several dialectical oppositions have been identified. The oppositions are seen to be transformations or expansions of some of the oppositions found in the biblical text. The oppositions included that between father and son, between brothers, and between Israel and the nations. The midrash typically emphasized oppositions which were ambiguous or weak in the biblical text. The mythemes tend to become more sharply defined. Thus in the biblical text the mytheme 'Lot' serves several structural roles. In *Genesis Rabbah* his structural role is limited to a strongly negative one. Similarly Ishmael and Esau become strongly negative in *Genesis Rabbah*. *Genesis Rabbah* does not significantly transform structures ($s^{(3)}$) but rather seeks to clarify structures present in the original texts. This emphasizes the importance of analyzing *Genesis Rabbah* and related midrashic texts from a diachronic perspective, with the primary analysis seeking to determine where changes in structure occur and, perhaps more importantly, to isolate mechanisms of transformation which either cloud, clarify or mediate structure.

Chapter 10

THE STRUCTURE OF RABBINIC THOUGHT (B)

This chapter presents the final level of diachronic transformation examined in this volume. The discussion focuses on three texts: *Lekach Tov*, *Yalkut Shemone* and *Midrash haGadol*. These three texts, all compiled between the eleventh and thirteenth centuries, are from a group of texts collectively called Midrashic Compilations.[1]

Rather than introducing entirely new midrashic material, these texts collect related material from earlier texts. They are interesting from two perspectives. On the one hand, they reveal a process of selection. Thus, for example, although *Yalkut Shemone* includes many texts which are similar to *Genesis Rabbah*, in specific areas it disregards certain texts. Thus, regarding Ishmael it includes only a small selection of ambiguous texts (or positive texts) while including and enhancing the negative texts. On the other hand, the collections include a selection of diachronically more recent texts, and adapt and transform texts which develop structural elements in new directions.

These texts reveal several interesting transformations in emphasis. The texts about Ishmael betray the clearest transformation. Whereas in the biblical texts and in *Genesis Rabbah*, Ishmael remained an ambiguous figure, in the collections the trend is towards negative. This transformation is most likely tied to the rise of Islamic power (associated with Ishmael as ancestor of the Arabs). Other transformations occur regarding incest and the *Sacrifice of Isaac*.

---

1.   *Lekach Tov* was compiled in the eleventh century. The book is compiled from earlier midrashim, but the texts are reworked and supplemented by new interpretations (Strack and Stemberger 1991: 390). *Yalkut Shemone* was compiled in the thirteenth century. The book is compiled from over 50 midrashim. These texts have been corrected, combined and abbreviated by the author (Strack and Stemberger 1991: 383). *Midrash haGadol* was compiled in the thirteenth century. The author freely adapts texts from the full range of midrashic tradition (Strack and Stemberger 1991: 387).

10.1. *Abraham and the Fiery Furnace*[1]

Lekach Tov does not present a detailed version of this myth, but it is mentioned on several occasions and is thus known to the editor. One text provides an interesting transformation of the myth both in respect to the main actors and the death of Harran (Abraham's brother).

> Var.I.1.A2. *Harran died in the presence of Terah his father* (Gen. 11.28). Because up till that point no son had died prior to his father.[2] And this one, why did he die? (He died) through the events of the fiery furnace. When Abraham smashed the idols of Terah, they were jealous of him and cast him into the fiery furnace. Harran stood to start the fire and he burnt up in a blazing flame. Therefore it says that Harran died in the presence of Terah his father (*Lekach Tov* on Gen. 11.28).

This midrash transforms two related elements of the text. Rather than bringing in a mediator (Nimrod in other versions of the myth), this version only mentions Terah (Abraham's father) and Harran. Thus this version fits much more closely with the biblical narratives in which the father or brothers are usually the primary actors in the murder and sacrifice. This text contains all the key structural elements of the death/rebirth narratives. The father (or brother) places the son (Abram) into the pit. The son emerges from the pit and continues on alone. This is also emphasized in Harran's actions. He does not play a passive role. He actively starts the fire in the furnace.

The death of Harran is also significantly transformed. In the text examined in *Genesis Rabbah* (Var.I.1.A), Harran mediates between Abraham and the people of Ur (i.e., Nimrod and Terah). He suffers the same punishment as Abram, being placed in the fiery furnace, yet he does not really share Abram's beliefs. His death represents the barrenness of Ur's (the nations') beliefs and social system. In the text in *Lekach Tov* Harran is no longer a mediator. He is directly allied with those who seek Abram's death. Harran's death is their symbolic death (and barrenness) as opposed to Abram's rebirth (and promised divine fruitfulness).

Midrash haGadol on Gen. 11.28 (Var.I.1.A3) includes a slightly different variation on the death of Harran. After Abram withstood the

---

1.   *Yalkut Shemone* 62 and 77 presents the same version of the texts as did *Midrash Rabbah*.

2.   It should be noted that Harran is actually the second person to die prior to his father, Abel was the first. The Rabbis are referring to death caused by God rather than fellow humans.

flames, the magicians and sorcerers said, 'this one has a brother who is a great astrologer'. Because Abram was able to withstand the flames Harran's reputation is raised. In that moment God caused a spark to come from the fire and Harran was burned and died. In this version Harran is less culpable in the sacrifice/murder than in the version in *Lekach Tov*. He is, however, tarred with the same brush as the nations by being an astrologer. His death creates a second level of opposition, illustrated in the following equation: Abraham : Harran :: Israel : Nations :: Life : Death. If the furnace is accepted as a symbolic womb (based on the constellation of rebirth symbols discussed regarding M.I.1, M.I.5, M.I.7 etc.), then the equation can be completed by comparing two types of fertility. Abraham, and Israel, the products of divine fertility, are fruitful (alive), while Harran, and the nations, products of natural fertility, are barren (dead).

Although *Yalkut Shemone* does not significantly transform the fiery furnace narrative, it does contain other related narrative material found neither in *Genesis Rabbah* nor *Lekach Tov*.[1] It develops a variation of a narrative found in *Pirke deRabbi Eliezer*.[2]

> Var.I.1.A4 The first miracle, when he (Abram) was born all the great men of the kingdom and the magicians sought to kill him. He was placed in the ground for thirteen years. In all that time he did not see the sun or the moon. When he came forth he spoke in the Holy Language and hated idols. The second miracle, he was imprisoned in the prison for ten years... after which he was placed in the fiery furnace, and the King of Glory stretched forth his right hand and saved him. (*Yalkut Shemone* 77)

1.   See, however, *Yalkut Shemone* 77 for an interesting additional element. God, rather than an angel saves Abraham because just as God is unique Abraham is unique.

2.   This text is further expanded in *Midrash haGadol*. In its discussion of the words 'and Harran died before his father Terah', the text states that Abram's birth was predicted by Nimrod's astrologers, who also predicted that Abraham would inherit the world. They suggested that Nimrod imprison Abraham. Abraham's father hid him to prevent this. Upon his departure from the cave, Abraham knew of God and his service (*MHG* Gen. 11.28). This text does not transform any of the structural elements in the versions already discussed. It does add an additional element of opposition. Abraham is opposed to Nimrod who is to be dispossessed suggesting the equation: Israel : Nations :: Possessors : Dispossessed. The text continues with a version of the idol story found in *Genesis Rabbah*. As in the *Genesis Rabbah* version, the story concludes with Terah bringing Abraham before Nimrod for punishment, in effect making Terah culpable for the punishment.

This text contains several interesting elements. The first half of the narrative, the first miracle, adds a much clearer rebirth story for Abram. The earth, in the context of the other structural elements discussed regarding the biblical text, should be regarded as a symbolic womb. It seems to imply that Abraham came of autochthonous origin rather than human. This element is further emphasized by the number of years during which Abram stayed under the ground. Thirteen is the year at which a Jewish boy becomes an adult. Thus Abram is born an adult, possibly in opposition to all other people, knowing what an adult should know, the Holy Language, and that idols are false gods.

The second half of the text adds a second layer of death and rebirth to the fiery furnace narrative. I have already shown, in respect to Joseph, that a prison is a symbolic death. Thus it is likely that in the Abram myth, the prison also represents a symbolic death (especially as the original myth *Abram Leaves Haran* was shown to be a rebirth narrative). The mythemes of death and rebirth, which were only suggested in the original version of the narrative (*Abram Leaves Haran*, M.I.1), are developed in three different ways in *Yalkut Shemone*. This strongly emphasizes the structural role of the text, which relates to the different origin of Israel and the nations, and develops a clear structural opposition between Abram and both Terah (his father) and Harran (his brother).

In the discussion about *Genesis Rabbah* I suggested that the myth about the fiery furnace was found in conjunction with many of the texts in which the mytheme of death/rebirth was the central element. In all the midrashim this is alluded to in respect to Genesis 15, *The Covenant of the Pieces* (M.I.5). This fits in with the structuralist analysis of that text which suggested that it was structurally equivalent to *The Covenant of Circumcision* (M.I.7) and therefore a death/rebirth text. The clearest support for this interpretation is found in *Midrash haGadol* on Gen. 15.7 in which a complete version of the myth of the fiery furnace is presented.

10.2. *Abram and Terah*

Both *Lekach Tov* on Gen. 11.32 (Var.I.1.B2) and *Yalkut Shemone* 63 (Var.I.1.B3) examine the opposition between Abram and Terah in a similar way to *Genesis Rabbah*. As in Var.I.1.B, they ask, 'why is Terah's death mentioned prior to Abram's departure?' This question is especially significant, as the rabbis point out, because Terah was due sixty-five more years of life according to the ages listed in Genesis itself. *Lekach Tov* offers three different answers to this problem. The first two of these are already found in *Genesis Rabbah*.

The first explanation offered suggests that the wicked are called dead in their lifetimes. This explanation emphasizes the opposition between Abram and Terah (i.e., good versus wicked), while not contradicting the original text. The second explanation works in another direction: from the perspective of Abram rather than Terah. Abram was worried that he would transgress the obligation of a child to his parents, and further that people would profane the name of God by saying that God commanded him to abandon his father in his old age. Therefore God freed him from the command and postdated the announcement of Terah's death.

The word used in *Lekach Tov* to mean 'postdate', מוקדם, is a passive form, as opposed to that used in *Genesis Rabbah* and *Yalkut Shemone*. Those midrashim use מקדים which is an active causative form. מקדים can mean either anticipate or make early. Thus in *Lekach Tov* the first two explanations are symbolic deaths, while in *Genesis Rabbah* and *Yalkut Shemone* the second has the implication of actual death.

The final explanation in *Lekach Tov* is that, after Abram left him, Terah was as good as dead. This is similar to the other two in being a symbolic death. As stated regarding *Genesis Rabbah*, all three of these explanations, whether of symbolic or actual death, are tied to the structural meaning of the original text (M.I.1 *Abram Leaves Haran*), the divine birth (transformation) mytheme. One key element of the transformation mytheme was denial of parents. Thus the emphasis on Terah's death or symbolic death fits very well with the original structure.

10.3. *Abraham and Converts*
Yalkut Shemone 67 (Var.I.1.F1) and *Lekach Tov* (on Gen. 12.5) (Var.I.1.F2) both contain variations on the text found in *Genesis Rabbah* (Var.I.1.F). The text in *Yalkut Shemone* is almost identical with that in *Genesis Rabbah*.

> *And Abram took Sarai his wife etc.* If all the nations of the world gathered to create even one mosquito and to place into it a soul, and yet you say, 'the souls which they made in Harran'. Rather these are the proselytes which he converted. If they were converted why does it say made? It teaches that any one who brings near an unbeliever, the Torah considers it as if he made him.

The only significant difference lies in the conclusion of the text. Whereas *Genesis Rabbah* emphasizes the word ברא meaning 'created', *Yalkut Shemone* repeats the word עשה meaning 'made'. This transformation, though minor, weakens the structural role of the text.

Midrash haGadol (on Gen. 12.5) (Var.I.1.F3) includes an even weaker version. It states that the nations of the world could not create even a mosquito, but does not include the final statement, 'as if he created (or made) him'. The text, however, retains the basic structural equation of proselytes with new creations. These texts are tied to the concept that proselytes were symbolically divinely reborn or re-created upon their conversion. In *Genesis Rabbah* the word ברא emphasized this aspect. The word עשה is a weaker form of creation. Whereas ברא is usually associated with divine action, עשה also refers to human action.

A similar trend is found in *Lekach Tov* (on Gen. 12.5). The text there is much weaker. The texts in *Midrash haGadol*, *Genesis Rabbah* and *Yalkut Shemone* emphasize the possibility of creation through the discussion of the mosquito. This section of the text is absent from *Lekach Tov*. *Lekach Tov* states,

> Var.I.1.F2 *And Abram took Sarai his wife, Lot his brother's son, their property, and the souls which they had made in Harran* (Gen. 12.5). These are the proselytes. Rabbi Huniah said: 'Abraham converted the men and Sarah converted the women. They brought them under the wings of the Shechinah (the presence of God).[1] Therefore it says, whom they made, as if they created them.

Lekach Tov retains the word ברא but does not explicitly refer to actual creation. The position of proselytes is problematic in the structural logic. They are by definition not part of the genetic model which is basic to Israelite (Jewish) self definition.

In *Genesis Rabbah* this problem was resolved by a clear statement of re-creation which was structurally consistent with the mytheme of divine rebirth developed in the biblical text. In the three midrashim examined in this chapter, although the element of rebirth is weakened, it is retained. Two possible explanations suggest themselves to explain this weakening of the text. Whereas *Genesis Rabbah* was written just after a period where proselytizing was still possible, and therefore structurally problematic, *Midrash haGadol*, *Lekach Tov* and *Yalkut Shemone* were written in times and situations where proselytizing was unlikely, thus making the problem less structurally significant. It is also possible that the concept of re-creation would have conflicted with the philosophical movements in Judaism which were developing when the three latter midrashim were being edited.

---

1.   This discussion is also found in both *Genesis Rabbah* and *Yalkut Shemone*.

10.4. *Abram in Egypt*

All three texts (i.e., *Lekach Tov* [Var.I.2.A1], *Yalkut Shemone* [Var.I.2.A2] and *Midrash haGadol* [Var.I.2.A3]) emphasize the same elements as *Genesis Rabbah* in respect to *Wife/Sister 1*. *Lekach Tov 67* refers to the descent to Egypt (with Sarai in a box) but does not give the entire narrative. *Yalkut Shemone* on Gen. 12.14 and *Midrash haGadol* on Gen. 12.14 present the entire story in an identical form to that found in *Genesis Rabbah*. As discussed regarding *Genesis Rabbah*, the box may be a symbolic coffin. This interpretation is supported by the fact that the wife/sister texts are rebirth texts. Sarai is reborn as Abram's sister rather than wife.

Wife Sister 1 is also directly tied to the structurally equivalent narrative of Israel's descent into Egypt and its subsequent emergence. *Lekach Tov* includes an abbreviated list of the connection between the two narratives.

> Var.I.2.C1 *And it went well with Abram for her sake.* That which is said of Abraham is also said of Israel. About Abraham it is written: 'and there was famine in the land and Abram went down to Egypt'. And of Israel it is written: 'because the famine was heavy on the land and our fathers went down to Egypt'. About Abram it is written: 'And Abram became very heavy with goods, gold and silver'. And of Israel it is written: 'and he brought them forthwith and his tribes suffered no harm'.

Although this list is not as extensive as the list found in *Yalkut Shemone* (Var.I.2.C2) (which is basically identical with that found in *Genesis Rabbah*), it serves fundamentally the same purpose. Both emphasize the structural and narrative connections between the two events. *Midrash haGadol* on Gen. 12.17 (Var.1.2.C3) adds another element to this equation (also found in *Genesis Rabbah*), stating that Pharaoh was plagued on Pesach, the festival celebrating the exodus from Egypt. Just as the wife/sister texts transform Sarai, emphasized in the midrashim by her symbolic death and rebirth in the box, the Exodus texts transform Israel.

The more obvious connection between *Wife/Sister 1* and *Wife/Sister 2* is also developed in the midrashic collections. As in *Genesis Rabbah*, they (*Yalkut Shemone* on Gen. 12.15) make a *Gezarah Shavah*,[1] based on the words 'for the sake of', between the two texts. There appear to be no significant transformations in clouding or structure between the midrashic collections and *Genesis Rabbah* in respect to *Wife/Sister 1*.

1. See the discussion of *Genesis Rabbah* for an explanation of this exegetical principle.

10.5. *Division of the Land*
Both *Lekach Tov* (Var.I.3.A4) and *Yalkut Shemone* 70 (Var.I.3.A5)
include the same narrative as *Genesis Rabbah* (Var.I.3.A). They continue
the process by which Lot is transformed from a mediator into a position
of structural opposition to Abram. In all the texts examined this
transformation is effected through the conflict between Lot's and
Abram's servants, and the subsequent division of the land. The narrative
states (Var.I.3.A4),

> *There was conflict between the shepherds of Abram's flocks and the*
> *shepherds of Lot's flocks*: Rabbi Barchiya said in the name of Rabbi
> Yehudah son of Rabbi Simon, the beasts of Abraham our father were
> muzzled to prevent them from stealing, and those of Lot were not muzzled.
> The shepherds of Abraham said, 'is it permitted to steal?' The shepherds
> of Lot said, 'Abraham is a barren mule, he lacks seed. Tomorrow he will
> die and Lot his brother's son will inherit. Then we will eat what is his'.
> The Holy One Praised Be He said, 'Unto your seed will I give this land, at
> which time, when the seven nations are uprooted from the land' (*Lekach
> Tov* on Gen. 13.7).[1]

This text distinguishes between both the servants of Lot and Abram, and
between Lot and Abram themselves. The behavior of Lot's servants is
clearly negative. They are stealing from the natives of the land, who still
have rights prior to being uprooted in the future. They are also making
the unwarranted assumption that their master will be Abram's inheritor.
Abram, however, is also distinguished in a positive way. God specifically
states that Abram (and his line) is chosen rather than Lot.

The text in *Lekach Tov*, however, is weaker than that found in
Genesis Rabbah. In that text Lot and his descendants are equated with
the Canaanites; this equation is omitted from *Lekach Tov*. *Yalkut
Shemone* includes all the same elements in this text as *Genesis Rabbah*.

A second text in *Lekach Tov* also strongly condemns Lot. This text
(on Gen. 13.6, Var.I.3.A6) introduces Ps. 125.3: 'The rod of wickedness
shall not rest upon the lot of the righteous'. The text interprets this verse
to refer to Lot as the wicked who cannot dwell with the righteous, that
is, Abram. (The midrash makes a pun on the word שבט, meaning 'dwell',

---

1. A very short version of this text is found in *Midrash haGadol*. In that text
when Lot (or his men) are confronted with the accusation that they are stealing, they
refuse to accept the criticism. The text concludes with a reinterpretation of Abram's
words to mean, 'do not be a transgressor'. This text is structurally equivalent to the
more complete versions.

used in Genesis, and שבט, meaning 'rod', used in the psalm).

This general pattern of condemnation is also found in *Lekach Tov* on Gen. 13.9 (Var.I.3.A7). This text summarizes *Gen. R.* 41.3 (Var.I.3.A2), making the analogy between Lot and a mule as the basis for forbidding Lot's descendants from mixing their seed with Abraham's. This text ironically inverts *Lekach Tov* on Gen. 13.7, in which Lot's shepherds called Abram a mule. The two texts oppose the two types of fertility. Abram's apparent barrenness is transformed into divine fruitfulness, while Lot's human fruitfulness is as barren as a mule.[1]

Like *Genesis Rabbah*, *Lekach Tov* emphasizes Lot's immorality. It relates many aspects of Lot's choice to sexual perversion.[2] The most obvious connection is on the first words of Gen. 13.10: 'and Lot lifted up his eyes'. These words are also found in respect to Hamor just prior to his rape of Dinah, and also in the text about Potiphar's wife (Gen. 49.7).

Another text from *Lekach Tov* on Gen. 13.11 (Var.I.3.A8) suggests that Lot, by separating himself from Abram, was as good as dead. 'Anyone who separates himself from the righteous separates himself from his life'. This midrash concludes with a similar text to *Gen. R.* 41.7 (Var.I.3.A3) in which Lot separates himself from both Abram and Abram's God. The final sentence, 'a complete separation was between them, "neither an Ammonite nor a Moabite shall come into the congregation of the Lord"', is not found in *Genesis Rabbah*.

This verse makes explicit the structural role of the entire section. If Lot was a mediator then the structural position of his descendants would be ambiguous; they too would mediate. The problem is compounded by their genealogical closeness to Abram's line. Thus, by rejecting Lot, and making him ideologically negative, his descendants, the Moabites and Ammonites, are also rejected.[3]

10.6. *Sarah and Hagar*

Lekach Tov (based on Gen. 16.1) (Var.I.6.A2) offers a variety of different possibilities for Sarai's barrenness. One text suggests that God withheld children in order to test Abram's and Sarai's faith (God tests righteous people). This creates an immediate opposition to Hagar and

---

1.   Both *Lekach Tov* and *Yalkut Shemone* include texts similar to the second half of Var.I.3.A2. In both cases Lot is depicted as the villain.

2.   A sort version of this is also found in *Midrash haGadol* on Gen. 13.10.

3.   Texts which are part of this general structure are also discussed in the section on incest below.

the other peoples who bear children immediately. The opposition to
Hagar is directly implied by the text. The statement is made in interpretation of the text about Hagar, and Hagar is mentioned in the next
section of the same midrash. Hagar represents the nations and natural
fertility on two levels. She is constantly referred to as 'the Egyptian
Handmaid', emphasizing that she is 'outside'. In several midrashic texts
she is said to be the daughter of Pharaoh and therefore may represent
Egypt and the other nations.

In a second text, *Lekach Tov* (on Gen. 16.2, Var.I.6.A3) emphasizes
that it is God who is causing Sarai's infertility. This text is similar to (but
stronger than) *Gen. R.* 45.2 (Var.I.6.A1).

> *Sarai said unto Abram, behold the Lord has prevented me from conceiving.*
> Sarah[1] said: 'I know the source of my trouble. It is not because of charms,
> and it is not because I need amulets, rather the Lord has prevented me from
> conceiving'.

This text emphasizes that none of the methods or mechanisms of natural
childbirth will succeed. The only possibility of her bearing a child is
through divine intervention.

The opposition between Sarai and Hagar is clearly developed in
Lekach Tov on Gen. 16.3 (Var.I.6.A4).

> Matrons would come to see how Sarah was. Hagar would say to them,
> 'Sarah, my mistress is not the same in secret as she appears in public. She
> appears to be a righteous woman but she is not one. If she were a
> righteous woman why did she not conceive for so many years, while I
> conceived in a single night'.

This text works on two levels. On one level Hagar is depicted as a
disloyal servant. The text emphasizes that Hagar is Sarai's servant, yet
Hagar clearly fails to give her the respect to which she is entitled. On the
second level Hagar condemns herself with her own words. The midrash
developed the concept that the righteous are afflicted. Therefore, Sarah's
righteousness is proved precisely by her barrenness, while Hagar's
immediate fertility condemns her. The text emphasizes the equation:
Righteousness = Barrenness = Divine Fertility (+), Immorality =
Apparent Fruitfulness = (Real) Barrenness (–).

Lekach Tov (on Gen. 16.5, Var.I.6.D1), however, also emphasizes
Sarah's negative role in the affair.

---

1.   The midrashic text uses the name Sarah in its exegesis of the verses.

> Sarah was meant to live as long as Abraham (i.e., 120 years). But because
> she said, *let God judge between me and between you* (Gen. 16.5), her
> years were lessened by 38.

Neusner suggests that Sarah's crime in this text is that she brought litigation against Abram (implied by the words 'Let the Lord judge between me and thee') (Neusner 1985: 150). This suggestion is supported by a text from *Yalkut Shemone* 79 (on Gen. 16.5, Var.I.6.D2). The midrash states,

> Rabbi Hannan said, one who brings his fellow to litigation he is punished
> first, as it says: *And Sarai said to Abram, my wrong be upon thee* (Gen.
> 16.5). It is also written: And Abraham mourned for Sarah and wept for her
> (Gen. 23.2)…Three things evoke the sins of a man: an unsafe wall, selfish
> prayer, and bringing litigation against ones fellow.[1]

The first half of the text links Sarah's early death (i.e., prior to Abraham's) to her words to him, and the second half links it to litigation.

Although this and similar texts suggest that the element of danger posed by the wife is characteristic of the biblical text, *Lekach Tov* does not develop this theme to the same degree as either the Bible or *Genesis Rabbah*. *Yalkut Shemone* (on Gen. 16.5) does allude to the criticisms of women found in *Genesis Rabbah*. It does not, however, present these criticisms in full. There seems to be a general trend in the compilations away from emphasis on the ambiguous and dangerous position of the wife. This is found regarding the lessening of emphasis on danger found here and also in the clouding of the incest texts discussed below. It is likely that with the restrictions forced upon the Jewish community of the Middle Ages (imposed by the outside) to marry within, the need to emphasize the mythemes relating to endogamy was lessened. The structure, however, is not materially transformed because endogamy remained a fundamental building block of Jewish culture.

10.7. *Circumcision*
Although *Lekach Tov* does not include the same midrashim as *Genesis Rabbah*, tying circumcision directly to the addition of an additional letter to Abram's name (see discussion of Var.I.7.A), it strongly emphasizes the importance of circumcision by including a lengthy discussion of its laws.[2]

---

1. A similar text is found in *Midrash haGadol* on Gen. 16.5.
2. This discussion is placed between the discussion of Gen. 17.13 and Gen. 17.14.

Midrash haGadol on Gen. 17.1 (Var.I.7.A3) states that God offered
Abram the command of circumcision, and that if Abram had refused,
God would have returned the world to chaos. This midrash uses a pun
on the name El Shadai similar to one found below (Var.I.7.A4). God
would say ד׳ (enough) to the world. The same text concludes with the
words: 'without the blood of the covenant (of circumcision) the world
would not exist'. This implies that the world exists for the sake of and
by means of Israel, the people of the covenant.

Lekach Tov includes texts which use circumcision to create opposition
between Ishmael and Isaac.[1] A similar though weaker version of the text
was discussed in the chapter on *Genesis Rabbah*. *Lekach Tov* states,

> Var.I.7.A4 *And it came to pass when Abram was ninety-nine years old*
> *that the Lord revealed himself to Abram*. The Holy One Praised Be He
> wanted to distinguish between Ishmael and Isaac, therefore he placed
> circumcision prior to the birth of Isaac. *And He said to him I am El*
> *Shadai*. I am the one who said ד׳ 'enough' to my world. I am he who said
> 'enough' to the foreskin. *Walk before me and be perfect*. All the time that
> you have a foreskin you are imperfect. Another explanation: *And be*
> *perfect*. Now Abram is your name and it shall be Abraham. Let the name
> of Abraham our father be whole, because Abraham (i.e., the numerology
> of) is equivalent to the number of limbs in the body.

This text suggests that Isaac, the chosen son, is the product of a more perfect father. The fact of Abraham's circumcision qualitatively distinguishes
Isaac from Ishmael. Israel (Isaac) as opposed to the nations (Ishmael) is
the product of circumcision. The text also ties circumcision to the creation
of the world. This is found in the two uses of the word 'enough'. In the
first case 'enough' ended the first phase of creation, in the second
'enough' led to the perfection of creation through circumcision. This last
interpretation is emphasized in the third section of the text in which
Abram's perfection is tied to his circumcision.[2] The last section of the
text ties Abram's rebirth, his change of name, with his circumcision.

The effect of this rebirth is developed in *Lekach Tov* on Gen. 17.1
(Var.I.7.B1). God tells Abram that Abram and Sarai will not conceive,
Abraham and Sarah will. This text emphasizes that, with their rebirth,

---

1.   A text in *Midrash haGadol* discusses Ishmael's circumcision. It states that
Ishmael was circumcised against his will, and therefore he is implicitly separated from
Isaac and his descendants (in spite of being circumcised).
2.   This is also emphasized in *Midrash haGadol* on Gen. 17.1. The text states,
'Abraham our father was not called perfect until he had been circumcised'.

Abraham and Sarah are transformed and fit to carry the divine seed. They are also opposed to the nations. Unlike the nations, Israel's fate is not found in the stars (this is also more clearly stated in the parallel text in *Midrash haGadol* on Gen. 15.5 [Var.I.7.B2]). They can control their fate through prayer, repentance and acts of righteousness.

As in *Genesis Rabbah* there are several texts which are tied to the denial of Abraham and Sarah giving birth according to the natural order (and the consequent denial of human sexuality). One such text is *Lekach Tov* on Gen. 18.11.

> Var.I.8.A4 *Abraham and Sarah were old.* Rabbi Isaac said, they were old and their youth was restored to them.[1]

Thus, Isaac's birth was the product of a double transformation. Not only were Abram and Sarai symbolically reborn as Abraham and Sarah, they were also transformed from old to young. A similar text is found in *Lekach Tov* on Gen. 21.1 (Var.I.8.A5). The text asks, 'how did God remember Sarah?' It concludes that he blessed her with lactation—something physically unlikely for a woman of ninety years.

The next text also emphasizes the miraculous nature of the birth (*Lekach Tov* on Gen. 21.2 [Var.I.8.A6]). It states that Isaac was born at midday in order that the whole world should know that Sarah had given birth. This mytheme is also found in *Yalkut Shemone. Yalkut Shemone* 92 (Var.I.8.A7) suggests that God remembered Sarah, Rachel and Hannah (all mothers of chosen children) on Rosh Hashanah. Rosh Hashanah commemorates the creation of the world, thus in effect the association suggests that their births were similarly new creations. The cumulative effect of these and related texts is to emphasize the miraculous nature of the birth (and therefore the origins of Israel) as opposed to natural childbirth (the origin of the nations).

Yalkut Shemone 93 (Var.I.8.A8) greatly increases the miracles surrounding Isaac's birth. The text initially suggests that God stopped up the wombs of all the women of the earth because they denied the possibility of Sarah giving birth. This element is tied to an opposition between natural and divine fruitfulness. The women's barrenness represents the barrenness of natural birth, as opposed to the fruitfulness of divine birth represented by Sarah. This opposition is also developed in the second half of the text. God made abundant milk flow from Sarah's

---

1. *Midrash haGadol* on Gen. 18.11 goes even further suggesting that God returned them from old age to childhood.

breasts. Sarah allowed the children of pious mothers to drink of it (becoming symbolically their mother). These children became the proselytes who are called children of Abraham and Sarah.

A further text from *Yalkut Shemone* 93 tells that Abraham gave a feast to celebrate Isaac's birth (Var.I.8.A9). All the people were telling each other that Abraham and Sarah could not have been the parents, and that they must have picked Isaac up in the market. God puts a stop to this by making Sarah's breasts overflow with milk to feed all the children present, yet they still talked of Abraham and Sarah's age. So God made Isaac look exactly like Abraham so all could see that he was the father. These texts emphasize the unlikely nature of the birth and thereby the divine element. The final element also suggests a structural identification of Abraham with Isaac. They were identical because both were part of the chosen line and mythologically represent Israel.

10.8. *Abraham and Lot*

As in *Genesis Rabbah*, the compilations continue the process by which Lot is distinguished from Abraham. In *The Division of the Land* (above in this chapter) the process whereby Lot is transformed from mediator to direct opposition is discussed. In the texts describing the destruction of Sodom and Gomorrah this process is continued.

Lekach Tov on Gen. 19.1 (Var I.10.C) introduces a qualitative opposition between Abraham and Lot. It asks, why are the angels called men when they met Abraham and called angels when they met Lot? Rabbi Levi responds: Abraham was strong so he could recognize who they were, while Lot was not so they needed to appear to him as angels. Thus although Lot merits being saved, he is weak compared to Abraham.

The same text also compares Lot's and Abraham's actions. It states that, while Lot stood for the angels, Abraham ran to greet them. This emphasizes an essential point. Although Abraham's and Lot's actions appear similar—suggesting that they are structurally equivalent— Abraham's actions are portrayed as consistently qualitatively better. As in *Genesis Rabbah*, Lot is also condemned by being appointed chief justice of Sodom, an unjust city.

Lot is also described as unwilling to leave Sodom. *Lekach Tov* on Genesis 19.16 (Var.I.10.B1) suggests that there was one hesitation after another and attributes this to Lot's worry about his property, gold and silver.[1] The rabbis introduce a quotation from Ecclesiastes to condemn

---

1. See also *Yalkut Shemone* 84.

Lot's actions: 'There is a grievous evil which I have seen under the sun, that is, wealth kept by its owner to his hurt' (Eccl. 5.12). Thus, although Lot is saved from destruction, he remains distinctly connected to the cities and their wickedness. This link is also found in his choice to remain in the valley. He chose to dwell in Zoar rather than go to Abraham in the mountains. The text states that Zoar was not destroyed merely because it was founded a year later than Sodom, and thus had one year's fewer sins. Zoar was not more moral than Sodom, it was only younger.

Lekach Tov on Gen. 19.19 (Var.I.10.A3) also includes an expanded version of Var.I.10.A2. Both versions emphasize that although Lot was better than the people of the cities, compared to Abraham his merit counted for nothing. In these texts Lot retains his role as mediator suggesting the following equation: Abraham's righteousness is greater than Lot's, and Lot's righteousness is greater than the nations, therefore Abraham's is greater than the nations (Abraham : Lot :: Lot : Nations :: Abraham : Nations).

10.9. *Incest*

Incest is one of the key areas of transformations between the Midrashic Collections and *Genesis Rabbah*. In *Genesis Rabbah* (and in the biblical text) incest, whether half-brother and half-sister (Abraham and Sarah) or father/daughter (Lot and his daughters), was not mythologically problematic. In fact it resolved the structural problem of the wife by bringing her inside. In *Lekach Tov*, however, structure is clouded.

The primary case of incest in the text examined is between Abraham and Sarah. In *Wife/Sister 2* it was stated that Sarah was Abraham's sister, albeit of a different mother. This pattern of marriage was similar to the possible marriage of Amnon and Tamar (also discussed regarding *Wife/Sister 2*). In several midrashim it is suggested that Iscah, Abraham's niece, was Sarah, and thus she was his classificatory sister rather than an actual sister. Freeman suggests that *Gen. R.* 38.14 (Var.I.12.A) alludes to this relationship (1939: 312). The text, however, makes no such allusion. Rather, it implies that Abram was married to Sarai at the time of Iscah's birth, and further that her birth was an unfavorable criticism of Sarai who could not give birth. In the discussion of Abraham's relationship to Sarah regarding *Wife/Sister 2*, she is never connected with Iscah. Thus *Genesis Rabbah* preserves the incestuous relationship found in the biblical text.

This, however, is not the case in the Midrashic Compilations. In both *Lekach Tov* and *Midrash haGadol* the relationship is explicitly stated.

Lekach Tov on Gen. 11.29 states, 'Rav said, "Iscah is Sarah"'. It suggests further that she was called Iscah because she was a prophetess (Iscah means 'to look'). This point is further emphasized in the midrashic texts which interpret *Wife/Sister 2*. In *Lekach Tov* on Gen. 20.12 (Var.I.12.A1) Abraham states that Sarah was called his sister; she was actually his brother's daughter. *Yalkut Shemone* follows a similar pattern. Regarding Gen. 11.29, it states that Iscah is Sarah (cited in the name of Rabbi Yitzhak rather than Rav). It also presents similar interpretations of her name. In the discussion of Genesis 20, Abraham states that she was his sister according to the customs of his home. These cases suggest that the culture which produced the Midrashic Collections was uncomfortable with the mytheme of incest, and thus the structure was clouded at the points where such a relationship was mentioned.

This pattern is also found in respect of the second case of incest in the texts discussed, *Lot and his Daughters*. In the biblical text neither Lot nor his daughters are condemned for their incestuous relationship. This pattern is slightly transformed in *Genesis Rabbah*. *Gen. R.* 51.8 suggests that Lot was negligent in respect of the second daughter because he must have known when his elder daughter got up in the morning. There is, however, no direct criticism. In *Lekach Tov* on Gen. 19.33 (Var.I.11.A4), however, the criticism is clearly spelled out. It states that Lot must have known of his elder daughter's presence when he awoke in the morning, and further that he should not have allowed himself to become drunk on the second night. It suggests that Lot's licentious nature was the reason that Moabite and Ammonite women are allowed to be proselytes, while Moabite and Ammonite men are not. The criticism is echoed in several subsequent texts. *Lekach Tov* on Gen. 20.1 (Var.I.11.A5) is one such text. It states, 'Abraham went from there, why did he go? Because of Lot's bad reputation. They were saying: Lot, Abraham's brother's son had intercourse with his daughters.'

Yalkut Shemone 86 has a lengthy discussion of Lot and his daughters. Initially it includes the same text as *Genesis Rabbah*, which only implicitly condemns Lot. In a later section of the same text (Var.I.11.A6) it unfavorably compares Lot with his daughters. They are described as righteous (because they were acting for the sake of heaven), while he is described as wicked (because he was acting for the sake of sin). The text concludes with a discussion of whether it was Lot or his daughters who had carnal appetites, and concludes that it was Lot.

Thus the Lot texts confirm the suggestion that there is a transformation in attitude towards incest. In the biblical text incest is structurally acceptable. In *Genesis Rabbah* the transformation is found with respect to father–daughter incest but not regarding brother–sister incest. In the compilations, however, neither father–daughter incest nor brother–sister incest is acceptable, and both are condemned or strongly clouded.

10.10. *Ishmael*
Lekach Tov includes several texts condemning Ishmael similar to those in *Genesis Rabbah*. *Lekach Tov* on Gen. 21.9 (Var.I.13.A1) includes the same elements as *Gen. R.* 53.11, accusing Ishmael of forbidden sexual relations, idol worship, and murder. The text also includes a final narrative. It describes Ishmael as luring Isaac into the fields and shooting arrows at him. Ishmael is also opposed to Isaac through God's choice. *Lekach Tov* on Gen. 21.10 emphasizes that Ishmael should not inherit with Isaac, because Isaac rather than Ishmael is chosen by God.

Unlike *Genesis Rabbah*, however, *Lekach Tov* goes even further in condemning Ishmael. It discusses why God answered Ishmael after he was expelled from Abraham's household, suggesting that God answered him not for his own merit, but rather because he was ill. God answered him for his condition at that moment, even though he was destined to kill Israel (from thirst). This text emphasizes that, although God spoke to Ishmael in the desert, he is in fact (in the long term) negative, not ambiguous. This reflects a transformation from both the biblical text and *Genesis Rabbah*. In both of those texts Ishmael was ambiguous rather than negative. It is likely that this transformation occurred because of Ishmael's association with the Arabs and therefore with Islamic power. *Lekach Tov* was compiled after the Islamic conquest of many of the major centers of Jewish communal life.

Yalkut Shemone also includes a variety of texts which condemn Ishmael. *Yalkut Shemone* 93 states,

> Var.I.13.A2: In the future the Holy One Praised be He will hold a feast for the righteous...after they have eaten and drunk they will give the cup to Abraham to do the grace after meals. He will say, I cannot do the blessing because Ishmael came from me. He will say to Isaac do the blessing. Isaac will say, I cannot bless because Esau came from me. He will say to Jacob, do the blessing. Jacob will say, I cannot do the blessing because I married two sisters while both were alive. (The text continues with each person stating something negative about himself until it arrives at David who does the blessing.)

The part of the midrash relevant to our discussion is the equation of Ishmael with Esau and the other negative elements listed. In this text Ishmael is again negative rather than ambiguous. *Yalkut Shemone* 94 (Var.I.13.A3) includes the same condemnations of Ishmael found in *Lekach Tov* and *Genesis Rabbah*. Regarding each element the text describes Ishmael's actions. Thus, for example, in respect to forbidden sexual relations the text states that Sarah saw Ishmael committing adultery. An even more extended version of this discussion is found in *Midrash haGadol* on Gen. 21.9 (Var.I.13.A4). The text in *Yalkut Shemone* also includes both the narrative of Ishmael's shooting arrows at Isaac and a more explicit variation on Ishmael's attempt to murder Isaac. In this text no doubt remains. It states specifically that Ishmael intended to kill Isaac (whereas the previous texts only suggested that he aimed his bow at Isaac).

The midrash uses this story to explain the biblical text 'and the matter was evil in Abraham's eyes'. The plain meaning of the verse is that Abraham was upset at loosing Ishmael, reflecting the ambiguous position of Ishmael in the biblical text. In *Yalkut Shemone*, however, the words can refer to Ishmael's attempt at killing Isaac. The same text also explicitly ties Abraham's anger to Ishmael's presumption, stating that Abraham was angered by Ishmael's assumption that he would be given the inheritance of the first-born. Both texts remove one of the ambiguous elements about Ishmael and firmly oppose him to Isaac and thereby to Israel.

Yalkut Shemone (Var.I.13.C) (and *Midrash haGadol* [Var.1.13.C1]) does, however, contain some ambiguous (or even positive) texts about Ishmael. One text describes Ishmael's and Hagar's exile in the desert. Hagar is portrayed as praying to her own gods while Ishmael prays to Abraham's God. The text continues by describing two visits by Abraham to Ishmael. On the first visit Ishmael's first wife refuses to give Abraham any food. At Abraham's suggestion, Ishmael sends her away. On his second visit Ishmael's second wife gives Abraham food and drink. Abraham blesses her and her children. This text describes Ishmael as separate from Isaac, that is, separate from Israel. In all cases where the two are together, Ishmael is negatively opposed to Isaac.

It is significant, however, that the final text about Ishmael in *Yalkut Shemone* (Var.I.13.B1) is negative. It repeats the midrash found in *Gen. R.* 53.15 emphasizing that Ishmael grew in cruelty. Aside from the ambiguous texts, most texts in *Yalkut Shemone* are strongly negative regarding Ishmael. The change in attitude toward Ishmael is similar to that found in *Lekach Tov*. Like *Lekach Tov*, *Yalkut Shemone* was compiled after the rise of Islamic power.

10.11. *The Sacrifice of Isaac*

The oppositions found in the *Sacrifice of Isaac* (M.II.1) are developed in a variety of way in later midrashic texts. In the biblical text two primary questions or ambiguities were addressed, centering on the identification of the two young men who travelled with Abraham and Isaac, and on the sacrifice itself. Structuralist analysis of the biblical text suggested answers to both these questions. In the diachronic layers examined thus far, *Genesis Rabbah* and *Pirke deRabbi Eliezer*, the answers found are exactly in agreement with structuralist projections. Similar patterns are found below in respect to the Midrashic Collections.

The opposition developed between Isaac and Ishmael remains consistent with the earlier texts. *Lekach Tov* on Gen. 22.1 includes a similar text to *Gen. R.* 55.1 (Var.II.1.A), but introduces a subtle transformation. In *Genesis Rabbah* Isaac offers initially a single limb. In *Lekach Tov* (Var.II.1.A3) he immediately offers to allow himself to be sacrificed. This fits in with a trend in the compilations to make Isaac a full partner in the sacrifice (*Lekach Tov* on *VaYerah*, Gen. 22.1). The midrash also develops the opposition between Ishmael and Isaac. Ishmael is satisfied merely to have been circumcised against his will, while Isaac is willing to offer his life to God. As in the other versions of this myth, Ishmael has (and can have) no response. Both *Lekach Tov* (Var.II.1.A4) and *Yalkut Shemone* 98 (Var.II.1.A5) also include texts similar to Var.II.1.A2, with little or no distinction from *Genesis Rabbah*.[1] *Lekach Tov* compares the two young men who went with Abraham to animals.

> *He saw the place from afar.* What did he see? He saw a cloud attached to the mountain. He asked Isaac 'do you see anything?' He said, 'I see a cloud attached to the mountain'. He said to his servants, 'do you see any thing?' They said, 'we see nothing'. He said to them, 'Stay here with the ass, you are similar to the ass. Just as the ass does not see, so you do not see' (*Lekach Tov* on *VaYerah*, Gen. 22.4).[2]

This text is similar to that in *Pirke deRabbi Eliezer*. The primary difference is that in *Lekach Tov* the two servants are not identified (at least in this text). The text, however, still works in the same way. The

---

1. See also *Midrash haGadol* on *VaYerah*, Gen. 22.3 (Var.II.1.A6).
2. See also *Yalkut Shemone* 100.

two servants represent the products of natural birth who are blind to God's presence (represented by the cloud). They are equated with the ass who is also blind. The servants are opposed to Abraham and Isaac, products of divine birth, who in going up to God (as opposed to staying with the ass) are equated with the divine.

Yalkut Shemone 98 includes an identification of the two men as Ishmael and Eliezer.[1] As stated above, in respect of *Pirke deRabbi Eliezer*, this fits well with the predictions of structuralist analysis. The two unknown young men in Genesis 22 fill a structurally equivalent role to Joseph's brothers in *The Murder of Joseph* and thus were provisionally identified as Ishmael and Eliezer. *Yalkut Shemone* supports this identification. This same text emphasizes the opposition between Isaac and Ishmael. Ishmael and Eliezer are depicted as discussing who will inherit in Isaac's place after he has been sacrificed. Ishmael claims that he as eldest son will inherit. Eliezer suggests that he will be the one, as Ishmael has already been expelled. The spirit of God answers them saying, 'neither one nor the other will inherit'. This text emphasizes that neither Ishmael nor Eliezer are fit to carry on the chosen line (*Yalkut Shemone* 98).

Structuralist analysis of the biblical text suggested that the sacrifice was the center of the structural message of the text, and that although narratively Isaac was not sacrificed, structurally he was. The death of Isaac is developed in several ways in the midrashic compilations. Midrashim from all periods emphasize the description of the events leading up to the sacrifice. They describe how Abraham placed Isaac on the wood (*Tan.* on *VaYerah*). They describe the discussion between Abraham and Isaac, often making Isaac a full participant in the events (*PRE* 31, *MHG* on *VaYerah*, Gen. 22.8 [Var.II.1.B2]). This element of full participation is emphasized in *Yalkut Shemone*. The text states,

> (Var.II.1.B3) The two of them came to the place, and the two of them brought the stones, and the two of them brought the fire and the two of them brought the wood…(Isaac says to Abraham) Father quickly do the will of your creator. Burn me well and bring my ashes to my mother… (*Yalkut Shemone* 101).

These elements focus the mythological center on the sacrifice, emphasizing the logical possibility of sacrifice.

The logical possibility of sacrifice is focused on in several midrashim in which Abraham and Isaac discuss the outcome of the sacrifice. For

---

1. *Midrash haGadol* includes a similar identification.

example, in *Midrash haGadol* (Var.II.1.D) Isaac asks Abraham not to tell Sarah when she is on a wall in case she falls and dies (*MHG* on *VaYerah*, Gen. 22.11). This both focuses on the possibility of the sacrifice occurring, and creates logical connections between the death of Sarah and the sacrifice. It is primarily regarding the sacrifice that significant transformations or developments are found.

In *Yalkut Shemone* 101 Rabbi Yehudah states,

> (Var.II.1.C1) When the sword cut his throat, Isaac's soul fled. When he heard his voice from between the two cherubim saying: do not send your hand against the boy, Isaac's soul returned to his body…and Isaac knew that it was the future of the dead to be resurrected.

This text presents a clear statement of death and resurrection. A second text in *Yalkut Shemone* 101 (Var.II.1.C2) suggests that Isaac was actually burned. It states that the smell of the smoke of Isaac reached God and caused God to revive Isaac and bless him in this world and the next. In a text from *Midrash haGadol* (Var.II.1.C3), the death and resurrection are emphasized by a midrash which states that Isaac spent three years in Paradise before returning to his home. A similar possibility is suggested in *Lekach Tov* (Var.II.1.C4), in which Abraham sends Isaac to study with Shem (who was born ten generations earlier than Abraham). *Midrash haGadol* also directly ties Abraham's returning alone to the death of Sarah. Sarah dies when she sees that Abraham arrives without Isaac (*MHG* on Gen. 22.19). In *Lekach Tov* the text states that Isaac died and was revived by dew drops of resurrection (*Lekach Tov* on *VaYetzeh*, Gen. 31.42). In *Shibbole ha-Leket*, a thirteenth-century text, Isaac was reduced to dust and ashes, after which he was the revived by God who used life-giving dew.[1] Thus in these later texts the trend begun with the Bible and *Genesis Rabbah* finds its logical conclusion. The structure develops from a suggestion of sacrifice in the biblical text, to a literal sacrifice and resurrection in the midrashic texts.

Yalkut Shemone (Var.II.1.C) ties *The Sacrifice of Isaac* to *The Murder of Abel*. It states that the altar which Abraham used was the same altar used by Cain and Abel (*Yalkut Shemone* 101). These narratives are structurally equivalent, dealing with the death and rebirth of the chosen person or line. The association between the two myths emphasizes the possibility of Isaac's death.

The midrashic texts also turn their attention to the mediator (i.e., the

---

1. This text is quoted in Spiegel 1979: 33.

ram), attributing to it all types of miraculous connections. One interesting text in *Midrash haGadol* (Var.II.1.E) states that the ram's name was Isaac (*MHG* on *VaYerah*, Gen. 22.13). This text highlights the connection of the mediator with Isaac. The closer the ram is to Isaac, the greater its potential as mediator. In connecting the ram with miraculous events, the aspect of mediation is weighted in favor of the divine aspect of Isaac. Thus in several texts the ram is said to be resurrected, emphasizing the logical possibility of Isaac's resurrection. In other texts the ram is said to be taken from Gan Eden—Paradise—also being Isaac's temporary home (*Yalkut Shemone* 101 [Var.II.1.E1]). In the same text the ram is tied to events throughout Israelite history. Its horns were blown on Mount Sinai when the Ten Commandments were given, and were used by David to make his harp and so on. The ram is said to have been created during the six days of creation. All these texts emphasize the miraculous aspect of the ram. They strengthen the identification of the ram with Isaac by bringing it closer to the divine side of the equation (Isaac after sacrifice). In another text the identification of Isaac and the ram is even closer. Isaac's soul, upon departing his body, is said to have been transferred to the ram (*Yalkut Reubbeni* 200). These texts strengthen the ram as a mediator, and by strengthening its identification with Isaac, strengthen the logical possibility that he too was sacrificed.

10.12. *Synthesis*

This discussion of the midrashic collections reveals transformations at several levels of the myth. The various mythemes receive different emphasis in these texts than in the earlier texts. Other elements are clouded, and mediators are added or removed from the myth to strengthen the structure. Figure 18 charts the development of the mythemes through the diachronic development of the myths. The midrashim use two main methods for developing these transformations. The majority of the texts use interpretation or explanation. They use words of the text to provide pegs for all types of interpretations, or they explain these words in the context of their understanding of the myth. The second method which they use is addition of narrative material. This is found throughout the texts. The text of the fiery furnace is added to clarify the structures implicit in *Abram Leaves Haran* (M.I.1), and the story of Ishmael's attempt on Isaac's life is used to transform Ishmael from an ambiguous to a negative figure.

Transformations in the myths occur on two levels: emphasis and clouding. Transformation on the level of emphasis is found in most of the myths examined. The analogous examples of Lot and Ishmael are cases in point. In the biblical text both characters had ambiguous or mediatory characteristics. In *Genesis Rabbah* the process of transformation began. Regarding Lot, a clear pattern is developed by which he is moved from a position of mediation to a negative figure. This transformation is effected by emphasizing Lot's choice of the valley—connected in all the texts to sexual perversion, and through expanding the narrative regarding the conflict between Lot's shepherds and those of Abraham. This process is continued in the collections and enhanced by a discussion of who was to blame for the incestuous relations between Lot and his daughters.

Diachronic development					
Compilations 1100–1300 AD	–	– –/+	–	– –/+	+
Pirke deRabbi Eliezer 700–800 AD	+	–/+	– –/+	– –/+	++/–
Talmud Bavli 600–			– –/+	–/+	
Genesis Rabbah 400–500 AD	+	+	– –/+	–/+	+/–
Bible	+	+	–/+	+/–	–/+
Mytheme	Incest	Danger	Lot	Ishmael	Sacrifice

Figure 18. *Diachronic Development of Key Mythemes*

The texts about Ishmael reveal a similar process. In *Genesis Rabbah* the ambiguous texts occur in similar numbers to the negative texts. In the compilations, however, there is a strong trend in the negative direction. The texts attribute to Ishmael all types of crimes, and even suggest that he attempted to kill Isaac. The transformation is completed in *Yalkut Shemone* in which even Abraham's anger at loosing Ishmael is turned around and aimed at Ishmael. It is likely that this process of transformation is related to the growth of Islamic power. Just as Christian (and Roman) power was identified and condemned through Edom and Esau, Ishmael is used to reflect attitudes about the Islamic world.

The texts about incest move in the opposite direction. These texts increase the clouding of this mytheme. Whereas in the biblical text and *Genesis Rabbah* mythological incest was not problematic (i.e., it was culturally acceptable), in the compilations it is clearly not acceptable. In both texts which include incestuous elements the incest is rejected. In the case of Abraham and Sarah the incestuous relationship is denied. Sarah is said to be Iscah, Abraham's niece, rather than his sister. Regarding Lot and his daughters, Lot is condemned for the relationship. It must be noted that although the mytheme is transformed it is retained in a weakened form. It is likely that this transformation is tied to a change in cultural patterns. When the biblical text and *Genesis Rabbah* were being written there was no external force enforcing endogamy, thus all the texts which strongly emphasized the need to marry as closely as possible would be necessary to maintain the system. When the collections were produced there was external enforcement to remain in the community, and thus emphasis on endogamy was no longer structurally necessary and those texts directly associated with endogamy could be more clouded.

This suggestion is supported by the associated transformation in the perception of women. Although the Midrashic Collections retain the element of danger, it is not emphasized to the same degree as in either the biblical text or *Genesis Rabbah*. The mytheme of danger is tied directly to endogamy—with the woman by definition representing the outside. If endogamy no longer needs to be emphasized, then the danger posed by women equally no longer needs to be emphasized.

The texts relating to the sacrifice of Isaac, as well as the marginaliza-tion of Ishmael and Lot, reveal the area emphasized in place of endogamy. These texts are tied to two mythemes: opposition to other nations and rebirth. These two elements are tied to the logic of chosenness. Israel is qualitatively distinguished from the other nations on the human level through ideologically negative texts about the nations (a process seen clearly regarding the genealogies), and on the divine level through divine rebirth. Israel is chosen both on the human level and on the divine. This new emphasis is seen most clearly in the texts relating to the *Sacrifice of Isaac*. Isaac and therefore Israel are not only symbolically resurrected, they are actually resurrected.

Transformation in emphasis is found with respect to *The Sacrifice of Isaac*. In the early texts the question of sacrifice is left to the realm of logical possibility rather than actuality, while in the later texts Isaac actually dies and is reborn. It is possible that historical events led to the sacrifice being perceived as less problematic and thus textually acceptable.[1] The death of Isaac was, however, structurally acceptable and implicit even in the biblical texts.

Another kind of transformation occurs on the level of mediation. This type of transformation is seen with respect to the position of Nimrod between Terah and Abram, and with respect to the transformation within the Lot mytheme. It is seen most clearly in relation to the ram in *The Sacrifice of Isaac*. In the later texts (and to some extent in the earlier texts) the ram is much more closely identified with Isaac than in the biblical text, strengthening its role as mediator, and strengthening the logical structure.

The transformations all work in the same direction. Regarding incest and the danger of women, the transformation is related to reduced internal division. Inside becomes absolute rather than relative. In the biblical text the system was based on ever smaller circles mirroring the segmentary opposition structure of Israelite culture. In the midrashic texts the emphasis on segmentation is removed and replaced by emphasized boundaries between inside and outside.

The transformation in the incest mytheme is supported by the transformation regarding Lot and Ishmael as well as that of *The Sacrifice of Isaac*. All three of these transformations strengthen the external boundaries. Ishmael and Lot are removed from mediating positions and placed firmly outside. Through this transformation the distinction between Israel and the nations is strengthened. Equally, the actual sacrifice emphasizes Israel's divine origin and distinction from the nations, because through Isaac, Israel is divinely reborn, while the nations are products of natural birth. The emphasis on actual divine rebirth also strengthens the logic of chosenness (the flip side of endogamy) which would have been problematic in periods in which the Jews were reduced to an unwanted, unaccepted minority.

In this journey through the diachronic development of the myths about Abraham, several consistent oppositions have been presented. The oppositions are seen to center on the symbolic sacrifice and rebirth developed in both the fiery furnace narratives and in *The Sacrifice of Isaac*. As the text developed over time, and the aspect of sacrifice and rebirth became less culturally problematic, it was made progressively more explicit in the text. Thus the fiery furnace narrative is expanded and enhanced (transforming implicit rebirth into actual rebirth) and the sacrifice of Isaac moves from symbolic to actual. The sacrifice/rebirth

---

1. See, for example, Spiegel 1979 where this question is examined in detail.

functions on a structural level to emphasize the distinction between natural birth and divine birth, and through that distinction the opposition of the nations to Israel. This opposition was supported by two related oppositions also developed in the midrashic texts. First, between Abraham and Lot, and between Ishmael and Isaac, which created ideological distance to supplement genealogical distance. Secondly, the denial of human parenthood in favor of divine paternity. These oppositions serve to create a logic by which endogamy/chosenness is perceived as the natural and logical choice, and it is precisely the role of mythology to prove that cultural choices are also natural choices.

Chapter 11

THE STRUCTURE OF HEBREW THOUGHT

This chapter synthesizes the material examined in the previous chapters. The first section presents the mythemes found in the text. These mythemes are divided into two types: horizontal and vertical. The horizontal mythemes include: the opposition between brothers, the opposition between inside and outside (especially regarding women), and the opposition between Israel and the nations. Vertical mythemes include oppositions within the chosen line, for example, father son. Both the synchronic presentation and the diachronic development of these elements are analyzed. Two other mythemes are also analyzed. These—the structural role of women in the text and incest—are examined independently of the other mythemes. They undergo a clear process of transformation (between biblical and rabbinic texts), which is revealed by diachronic analysis.

The second section examines several theoretical questions. It discusses the methods of clouding and transformation found in the texts, focusing on mediation, inversion and doubling. Theoretical expectations of the analysis are also queried. Are all four biblical textual strata structurally consistent? What types of transformation and continuity are found between biblical and rabbinic texts? I also discuss the structural significance of diachronic development within the text and its relation to synchronic structure (see §2.10 regarding the work of T. Turner).

Finally, the chapter examines the relevance of this research to anthropology and biblical studies and introduces questions for future study. Are the structures found in the myth also present, as suggested by structuralist theory, in other elements of Israelite culture? Preliminary analysis, presented below, of specific areas of Israelite social structure and ritual suggests that the structure is found at all levels of Israelite culture. These areas include 'existential ritual', time, geography, biology and social structure. What is the relationship between early Christian myth and biblical and rabbinic structure? Is the relationship characterized by continuity or transformation? On a broader anthropological level, to what extent do these structures continue to work today in modern Jewish culture?

11.1. *Horizontal and Vertical Oppositions*

The analysis highlights opposition on several levels. The primary opposition works on two levels: horizontal and vertical (best understood by using a genealogical metaphor: horizontal is within a generation and vertical is between generations). The horizontal level is found in almost every text. The most common example of this type of opposition is that between brothers. This is clearly developed in the myths about Joseph, especially in *The Murder of Joseph* (where Joseph's brothers are opposed to him through Joseph's dreams, their father's preference, divine favor, and through their attempted murder of him). It is also found in the conflict between Jacob and Esau, which becomes the eternal conflict of Israel and Edom (an opposition prefigured in the prophecy just prior to the birth of Jacob and Esau), as well as in the opposition between Isaac and Ishmael.

In the texts the brothers represent different nations. Thus Ishmael and Esau represent the Ishmaelites and Edomites, while the patriarch's are structurally equivalent to Israel. The opposition between brothers is effectively the opposition between nations. This structural association of brothers with nations is also clearly developed in Genesis 10, the Table of Nations. This element is emphasized in the rabbinic texts where there is a clear association between Esau and Rome, and Ishmael and Islam.

The horizontal level is also seen in the opposition of inside to outside developed in respect of the wives of Abraham and Isaac (as well as other marginal figures including Lot and Hagar). As in the case of brothers, the opposition is ultimately between 'inside Israel' and 'outside Israel'. The horizontal level expresses the opposition between Israel and the nations. This opposition is also developed in the genealogies (see Chapter 8). Segmentary genealogies express the division of nations on the horizontal level, which is always expressed in terms of brothers (e.g., the descendants of Shem, Ham and Yaphet).

This opposition serves to create ideological distance to resolve a paradox implicit in Israelite mythology. The system posits a single creation and therefore a single humanity, yet it also posits distinction between human beings which is the basis of endogamy. By suggesting that, even at the lowest level, brothers can be qualitatively distinguished, it presents the logical possibility that such distinctions can (and should) be made on all levels of humanity. The horizontal level can be expressed in the equations found in Figure 19.

(1) Brother (chosen) : Brother :: Israel : Nations :: Inside : Outside

(2) Genealogical closeness is inversely related to ideological closeness

Figure 19. *Structural Equations for Horizontal Oppositions*

This logic is also the basis for the structure of the genealogies in Genesis and in their rabbinic expansions. In accordance with the first half of the paradox, all nations are descended from a single couple, and in accordance with the second half, those nations which are closest are qualitatively the most negative, and therefore ideologically distant. The genealogies also express the vertical level in the pedigrees. They indicate the passage of the divine choice from father to son, down to Jacob and his descendants.

The vertical level is represented in each myth. It is found with respect to M.I.1 *Abram Leaves Haran*, M.I.5 *The Covenant of Pieces*, M.I.7 *The Covenant of Circumcision*, M.II.1 *The Sacrifice of Isaac*, M.III.10 *Jacob Wrestles with an Angel*, M.III.12 *The Covenant at Beth El*, and M.IV.3 *The Murder of Joseph* (among many others) and their corresponding rabbinic interpretations. The primary element of the vertical opposition is the denial of human birth in favor of divine rebirth. It also develops the opposition of father to son, in which the divine seed is passed from one generation to the next. These texts emphasize the structural impossibility of the divine seed being carried by more than one line. The primary oppositions on the vertical level focus on the denial of the natural parents, or on death and rebirth.

Barrenness (denial of sexual role) should not be seen as the sole preserve of women in the biblical text since the role of the father is also denied. In these texts both the father and mother are unable to produce the chosen line without divine intervention. Although it is women who are called 'barren', the sexual potency of the father is also denied: his age is emphasized, he is symbolically castrated. The structural logic of the myth is the denial of the human element in Israelite birth.

In several of the myths these two aspects (denial of human fruitfulness and divine rebirth) are developed together. Thus in the texts about Abraham's rebirth, there is also a denial of human fertility. This denial is found in statements emphasizing Abraham's childlessness, Sarah's barrenness and Abraham's circumcision. It is also developed in the rabbinic texts which focused on the need for divine intervention in Isaac's birth, and on the human perception that it was impossible for Sarah (and Abraham) to have a child. In the *Sacrifice of Isaac*, while Isaac is symbolically (or actually) reborn, he is structurally distinguished from Abraham (who attempts to sacrifice him), and Sarah's role as mother is denied since she dies prior or during his symbolic birth. Both elements are progressively highlighted. As the myth develops diachronically, Abraham sacrifices Isaac, and Sarah's death is directly tied to Isaac's death.

Divine birth and transformation from human descent to divine descent are the keys to this mytheme. All figures who carry the divine seed are symbolically (or actually) reborn. The myths use a variety of mechanisms to develop this structure: mediators are added, either at the level of sacrifice or divine birth, and the transformation is sometimes suggested by a change of name. The weakest version of the mytheme is found with respect to Adam and Eve, and Noah. Adam and Eve are created and live in the garden, yet are expelled, as in a birth, into the world. Similarly, Noah and his sons enter the re-created world from their symbolic womb, the ark. The strongest version of the myth is the murder of Abel, who is structurally replaced by Seth. In the rabbinic texts each version is strengthened with respect to the symbolic death and rebirth. The relationships between the various biblical versions of this mytheme are illustrated in Figure 20.

(–)Weak   (+)Strong

V. 2, V. 6   —   I.1   —   III.10   —   I.7   —   II.1   —   IV.2   —   V. 3

Figure 20. *Synchronic Development of the Sacrifice Mytheme*

The denial of human fruitfulness emphasizes divine fruitfulness and thereby the divine origin of Israel. This element is carried into Israelite ritual in which all men are circumcised. Effectively all Israelite men are divinely transformed (reborn). This aspect of divine origin is integrated with the horizontal oppositions. On the horizontal level ideological distance is emphasized. When combined with the vertical level, in which Israel is removed from the human pattern of descent, genealogical distance is added. Israel (as opposed to the nations) is the product of divine fruitfulness, rather than natural or human fruitfulness. Thus both levels, vertical and horizontal, resolve the paradox through creation of distance, and by doing so strengthen the logic of endogamy. This is illustrated in Figure 21.

(3) Son : Father :: Father : Son (R) :: Barren : Fruitful :: Human : Divine

(1*+ 3) Father : Son (R) :: Brother : Brother (C) :: Barren : Fruitful :: Human : Divine :: Nations : Israel

(3) = Vertical Oppositions (1) = Horizontal Oppositions

(R) = reborn
(C) = chosen

* '1' is the equation presented in Figure 20.

Figure 21. *Structural Equation of Vertical and Horizontal Oppositions*

11.2. *Women in Biblical Texts*[1]

In order to understand the position of women in biblical society, it is necessary to chart the basic elements of that society. Israelite society is characterized by three related structures, endogamy is the most basic. The texts examined reveal a strong preference or rule in favor of endogamy. In the other biblical texts there is a legal presumption of endogamy. Within the Israelite system marriage is directed inward (mythologically concluding with brother–sister marriage). This inward force is supported by the second element of Israelite culture: segmentary opposition.[2] Like endogamy, segmentary opposition supports the preference to marry as close as possible. This is due to the implied opposition and segmentation which begins at the lowest levels. Segmentary opposition also creates points of opposition between brothers, emphasized by the land tenure system.[3] The third element of the system is an emphasis on patrilineal descent and patrilocality. All three of these elements work to create an ambiguous role for the wife. By definition

1. The following two mythemes are initially discussed in regard to their biblical configurations, and then in §11.4 in their rabbinic transformations.
2. Using the definition presented by Barth (1981).
3. The biblical text suggests a system in which land was held by the tribe and subdivided to smaller family units. Thus brothers would be in direct competition for the same limited resource (which would be sub-divided between them).

(according to the rules of incest), she comes from outside the immediate family and therefore comes from a unit in opposition to the husband's family (even, and perhaps especially, if she comes from his close kin).[1]

The opposition between inside and outside is the structural center of the texts dealing with women in the biblical and rabbinic texts. All the texts include at least one of the following mythemes: transformation of outside to inside, and danger. The first of these mythemes is the primary element of the three wife/sister texts. In each of these texts the wife, who is structurally outside, mythologically becomes sister, who is inside. The narrative creates a structural problem. The patriarch (inside) must get a wife from outside because there are no inside women available. The text attempts to resolve this crisis by bringing the wife relatively inside through making her part of the patriarch's extended family (FBD). Yet this does not completely resolve the crisis; the wife although relatively inside still retains an element of outside. Thus these three texts, mythologically bring the wives even closer. In two of the texts *Wife/Sister 1* and *Wife/Sister 3*, the myth raises the structural possibility that they are sisters. In *Wife/Sister 2* the possibility becomes reality in Abraham's statement that Sarah is indeed his sister. Wives become sisters thereby resolving the structural crisis.

Within the three biblical variations of the text, there is a varying degree of clouding. The structure is clearest in *Wife/Sister 2*, where all the structural elements are openly developed. The structure is built on five elements: (1) Sarah starts as wife; (2) she is called sister, creating the mythological possibility that this is so; (3) she is taken by a local king as wife leading to barrenness; (4) she is returned to her husband, after which he becomes wealthy (divine favor) and she is fruitful (divine fruitfulness); and (5) she is identified as actually being his sister. In the second version of the text, *Wife/Sister 1*, only elements 1 through 4 are present. The barrenness of Pharaoh's wives is not openly expressed. The final version of the text, *Wife/Sister 3*, includes only 1, 2 and 4.

---

1. Lindholm suggests a similar explanation for the ambiguous (and dangerous) position of women among the Swat Pathan. He states, 'The repulsiveness of women is linked to the conundrum they pose in the social structure as foci of the contradiction between the necessity of exchanging women and the social ideal of the self sufficient nuclear family' (Lindholm 1982: 148). Both in Israelite and Swat Pathan culture women mediate two forces. Incest pushing outward and endogamy and segmentation pushing inward. By representing the contradiction they are ambiguous and dangerous.

The wife/sister texts contain a second element which is characteristic of texts dealing with women, that of danger. In the introduction of all three wife/sister texts a mythological equation is developed: Wife = Danger = Outside, and Sister = Safety = Inside. The wife is dangerous because she is outside and she can only become safe by being brought inside. The three wife/sister texts add a second level to the equation: barrenness and fruitfulness. When they are taken as wives by the local king, who represent 'the nations', they are barren, yet when they are wives of their 'brother' Israel they are fruitful. Thus the complete equation for the wife/sister texts is:

$$\text{Wife} = \text{Danger} = \text{Outside} = \text{Barren}$$
$$\text{Sister} = \text{Safety} = \text{Inside} = \text{Fruitful}$$

A fourth text examining both aspects of the role of women is *Jacob Marries Rachel and Leah*, in which the problem of inside/outside is resolved in a different way. Jacob marries the elder daughter first. She is structurally equivalent to both the concubines of Abraham and the chosen wife. She is not Jacob's chosen partner, yet she comes from the appropriate family in Harran. By becoming his wife, Leah's 'inside' elements are emphasized. Due to the structure developed in the wife/sister texts, she is structurally almost his sister. In marrying Rebekah, he marries structurally inside because she is his sister's sister.[1]

Jacob Marries Rachel and Leah also includes the element of danger. In that text, however, the element is embodied in the person of Laban (Rachel and Leah's father). Laban represents both the danger of outside and that of affinal kin who, although relatively inside, are still outside in respect to the man's immediate family. Rachel herself also contains an element of danger. In *Jacob Returns to Canaan 1*, Rachel steals her father's household gods. This text reveals two sides of the danger posed by women. Women create danger regarding the relations between families: Jacob is pursued by Laban. They also create danger within the family by bringing in elements from the outside.

Women are also perceived as dangerous within the family in a second respect: they create conflict and form alliances within the family which may disrupt it. This type of danger is found in several texts. Conflict is

---

1. The levirate works in the same way. Once two families are allied, joined by marriage, they are both almost inside in respect to each other. In order to preserve this tie it is logical that upon the death of a brother his younger brother would take his wife, who is in effect his sister (see *Judah and Tamar*).

endemic throughout the texts about Rachel and Leah, and their conflict is carried down to the next generation in the conflicts between Jacob's sons. This type of conflict is also found in the two texts in which Sarah exiles Hagar. Alliances and divisions are most clearly developed in *Jacob Steals the Blessing*, in which Rebekah is allied with Jacob against Isaac and Esau.

In several texts the sexual aspect of women is highlighted as dangerous. It is possible that Eve's taking the apple represents this type of danger. Although this text is not usually thus interpreted in Jewish tradition, several elements suggest that it is correct. The serpent, at least in Freudian terms, has phallic connotations, and the result of eating the apple is that Adam and Eve recognize that they are naked, that is, they become sexually aware. This element is found in three texts in Chapter 6. In the *Rape of Dinah* the text implicitly suggests that Dinah was being, at the least, sexually provocative, leading to a destructive war. In *Judah and Tamar*, Tamar's disguise as a prostitute (although narratively justified) emphasizes the negative uncontrolled aspect of female sexuality as well as introducing dangerous elements from the outside: Tamar is described as a sacred prostitute. The wife of Potiphar is the final exemplar of this danger. Her uncontrolled sexuality leads to Joseph's false imprisonment.

Women are thus structurally problematic on two levels. On one level women are dangerous because they represent uncontrolled sexuality (their sexual role makes them necessary and thus is problematic). This kind of sexuality is dangerous both to the family (as seen in Judah and Tamar) and to the ideology of endogamy since it recognizes no rules, boundaries or distinctions. Danger is also developed in *The Rape of Dinah* and *Joseph and Potiphar's Wife*. On the second level women are dangerous in representing the outside. Both within the narrative and this system, women must be brought in either from outside the people (mythologically) or outside the family (culturally). Both cases are problematic regarding the logic of endogamy. The narrative problem is apparent, the myth contradicts the structural logic. The cultural problem is less clear. Wives are taken within the people and thus are culturally acceptable. The structure of the system, however, when extended to its logical conclusion creates a system of concentric circles where ultimately the immediate family is inside and all else is outside: incest is the logical conclusion of this structure. In line with the logic of endogamy, the text unwittingly displays a clear hostility and suspicion against affinal kin.

This hostility is similar to that found in many Arab societies today.[1] The structural equation including the element of women is: Israel : Nations :: Sisters : Wives :: Safety : Danger :: Men : Women.

11.3. *Incest*

Incest is the logical outcome of endogamy (while incest prohibitions are the inverse of endogamy, forcing ego to look outward rather than inward). This logical conclusion is a mythical and structural rather than a cultural conclusion. Israelite society, at least as portrayed in the legal texts of the Bible, had clear and comprehensive laws against incest. These laws were further extended in rabbinic texts, fitting the pattern regarding incest discussed in 11.4. The laws regarding incest and those of endogamy pull in opposite directions; together they create boundaries and fill the alliance function. Endogamy, if taken to its logical conclusion in the Israelite system, would create a completely segmented society. The incest prohibitions force marriages and thereby alliances outside the immediate family.

The analysis indicates that, upon marriage, a fictitious tie is created between families, bringing both 'inside' relative to each other. This is illustrated in the incest laws (see Chapter 2).[2] It is also reflected in the obligation of levirate which seeks to maintain the alliance between families upon the death of the husband if no issue was produced to maintain the link. Prohibited relations are found in the consanguinial line, and upon marriage are extended to the affinal line. By forbidding the

1. See Mernissi 1975: part 1.
2. The Bible includes two main enumerations of incest prohibitions: in Leviticus and Deuteronomy. Deuteronomic prohibition is against both a paternal or maternal sister, mother and stepmother. In relation to ego's affinal kin the mother-in-law is also prohibited (Deut. 27.15-26). This is considered by some scholars to be the oldest set of incest laws in the biblical text (Plaut 1981: 1514).
The Levitical code is the most comprehensive of those found in the Bible (Lev. 18.6-18). Leviticus extends the prohibitions concerning consanguinial and affinal kin. The prohibited relations included: son's daughter, daughter's daughter, father's sister, mother's sister, father's brother's wife, and brother's wife. Verses 17 and 18 deal with women who ego could not marry at the same time. These included: a woman and her daughter, or a woman and her grandchildren, and two sisters (because by marrying one, a kin relationship is created with the other).
In Lev. 18.8 the prohibition against ego's stepmother is stated in terms of ego's relation with her husband: 'It is the nakedness of your father'. Thus lying with the father's wife is seen as tantamount to lying with the father and thus doubly forbidden.

wife's family as possible wives for the husband, the wife's family is placed into a fictitious blood relationship with the husband's family. His wife's sisters, in effect, become his sisters.

Several texts which have been discussed above center on incestuous relationships. The three wife/sister texts create, at the very least, the structural possibility of incest. Other texts which deal with incest are *Lot and his Daughters* and *Judah and Tamar*. In these cases the incestuous relationships, although culturally prohibited, are mythologically positive. I suggest that incest resolved the problem of inside/outside and is the logical extension of endogamy, strongly supporting that logic. Other texts which contain positive incestuous elements include the myths about Adam and Eve, and Jacob and his two wives.

In two texts the incestuous relationship is negative: *Reuben Sleeps with his Father's Concubine* and its parallel *Reuben and the Mandrakes* (M.III.7). The incest found here, effectively mother–son, is mythologically negative. The condemnation, however, is not necessarily tied to the incest, but is associated with trespass on the father's rights. In the blessing Reuben is criticized not for incest but for 'going into his father's bed' (assuming the rights of inheritor before his father's death). The same logic is found in the levirate. A man is forbidden to marry a brother's wife while he lives, but permitted (or obliged) to do so upon his death.

The second text which is mythologically negative is the *Sin of Ham*. In that text, however, the incestuous relationship is inverted, being homosexual incest. By definition, homosexual incest is barren. This serves the opposite mythological function to heterosexual incest, which leads to fruitfulness. Inside plus inside (the incestuous relation) engenders divine fruitfulness.

11.4. *Structure and Transformation*

The structure ($s^{(3)}$) of biblical thought is developed through a set of related oppositions. The structures developed in these oppositions are found consistently throughout Genesis. There appears to be no structural distinction between the material which emerges from different textual strata. The oppositions which characterize biblical structure include: Inside/Outside, Divine Fertility/Natural Fertility, Israel/Nations, and God/Humans. These oppositions (a few of a larger structurally equivalent set) relate to many aspects of Israelite culture and ideology; they all create distinct boundaries between ideal types. Israel is as fundamentally distinct from the nations as God is distinct from humankind. Oppositions with the same structural logic are also developed with respect to creation and the animal world.

Within this structure of oppositions, the role of mediator (on a structural level as opposed to the narrative level which is examined below) and its ideological value are essential. The mediator can have three different values: positive, negative or neutral. In a system (perhaps exogamous) in which the mediator is positive, the boundaries between the two entities are ambiguous. The mediator bridges the gap between the two, creating the possibility that the two are structurally equivalent. This type of mediation, for example, would enable an exogamous culture to naturalize requirements of exogamy, lessening the ideological distance between the exchanging groups. In a system where the mediator is negative, the gap between the pair of opposing elements is emphasized clarifying the boundaries, because it is logically impossible and negative to bridge the gap. The structure ($s^{(2)}$ and $s^{(3)}$) of Israelite culture (an endogamous system) is characterized by negative mediators and therefore impermeable boundaries. This suggestion is confirmed by Mary Douglas. She develops a similar argument in *Implicit Meanings*. She presents three cultures—the Hebrews, the Karam and the Lele—which exemplify the three types of mediation. The Hebrews have negative, the Karam ambivalent or neutral, and the Lele have positive mediators. In each case the ideological value of the mediator is directly related to the attitude toward exchange (Douglas 1975: 306).

The opposition of inside to outside, especially regarding the structural role of incest, also supports the logic of endogamy. The discussion of several biblical texts (*Wife/Sister 1–3* etc.) demonstrates that incest is used to overcome the problematic position of the wife in respect to the three structures of Israelite culture: endogamy, segmentary opposition and patrilineal descent. The women who are brought in from the outside contain elements of both inside and outside, and therefore cloud the distinction between the two. They are problematic and negative. The wife is transformed into sister or mother (or conversely the mother or daughter is transformed into wife) in order not to blur the boundaries. If she had remained 'wife', she would remain a mediator which was not acceptable in the Israelite system.

Both basic sets of mythemes, the distinctness of Israel (sacrifice, rebirth) and endogamy (incest, danger), are transformed in opposing ways in the rabbinic texts. Incest, which was mythologically acceptable in the Bible, is de-emphasized. In the rabbinic texts all possible incestuous relations are clouded. This transformation is coupled with a corresponding reduction of danger regarding women. I suggest that this transformation is tied to a change in the Jewish community's cultural position. Internal enforcement of endogamy was no longer needed in the Middle Ages because of external constraints. The community was often forced to live in enclosed areas and forbidden (while remaining Jewish) from marrying either Christians or Muslims. Thus the emphasis on incest was no longer needed to support endogamy because endogamy was no longer culturally problematic. The segmentary aspect of the culture was reduced in two ways: first, by opposition from the outside (in Northern Europe often in the form of violent attacks and oppressive laws), which encouraged communal unity; secondly, the Jewish mode of production changed from land based agriculture (with land as a limited resource) to a trade economy, reducing competition and segmentation of kin. Thus the position of women was no longer as ambiguous as in biblical times.

It is likely that the element of danger was de-emphasized for another reason. In biblical society the primary principle of descent was patrilineal. In rabbinic society (and today) there is a significant matrilineal element. Though property and status descend through the father, membership in the people descends through the mother. Thus in rabbinic society the woman is necessarily inside and therefore is no longer structurally dangerous. This change in pattern of descent is first found in rabbinic law in the second century (Seltzer 1987: 127).[1]

The mytheme of rebirth is also transformed in medieval times. It is emphasized rather than de-emphasized. This mytheme is associated with the qualitative distinction between Israel and the other nations. It accentuates the fact that Israel is of divine birth and rebirth, while the nations are of natural birth. It is likely that this element was transformed in response to persecution. Under the Christian and Islamic regimes of the Middle Ages, the problem of chosenness rather than that of endogamy comes to the fore (Israel was not obviously chosen). Thus the mythemes which cloud or emphasize the qualitative distinction of Israel (apart from material circumstance) are strengthened.

This transformation is also reflected in the ideological position of Ishmael and the Ishmaelites. In order to emphasize the distinctness of Israel, all remaining mediators are removed. Thus Ishmael and Lot are both transformed from ambiguous to negative. Ishmael is also

1. None of the explanations for the change are convincing. They include problems in determining paternity or influence of Roman law.

transformed in response to political changes. The biblical text and *Genesis Rabbah* were written prior to the rise of Islamic power, the compilations (in which the transformation in Ishmael is most evident) were written after.

11.5. *Analysis of the Structure of the Four Strata*

Any analysis of biblical material must consider source-critical analysis.[1] That type of analysis challenges some of the assumptions of my research. This is especially evident in its basic supposition that the texts from which Genesis was created can be distinguished as independent cultural sources (basically untransformed by the redaction process). According to structuralist theory the biblical text should be regarded as a synchronic whole. This is due both to the editorial process which created the biblical text, and to the fact that all the sources emerged from the same cultural context. In order to test this theoretical supposition Figure 22 charts the oppositions developed by each source. It is clear from the chart that all oppositions and mythemes are present in all four strata. This suggests that it is correct to view the four strata as a synchronic whole.[2] This also suggests that source criticism and similar fragmentary analyses reveal only one layer of meaning and can be supplemented by holistic analysis.

---

1. Source criticism is one methodology which has been applied to biblical material. Although Fohrer is not the most recent advocate of this approach and some aspects of his approach have been challenged, he provides a comprehensive analysis of Genesis as a whole which allows us to test the findings of structuralist analysis against those of source criticism. Other methodologies include form criticism, which focuses on the development of individual units and the genres into which they fit (emphasizing their social context) (see Westermann 1984), and the traditio-historical method of Rendtorff (1985). Essentially, Rendtorff synthesizes the insights of the two other approaches. He examines the development of independent units and the genres presented in the text, and also discusses the editorial process by which the text was created. He assigns the 'authors' of source criticism a primarily editorial role (Rendtorff 1985: 157-63). Neither form criticism nor traditio-historical methodology challenges the findings of this volume as texts in Genesis from all genres can be shown to develop the same sets of structural relationships.

2. It should be noted that, as several of the texts contain more than one stratum, those texts will be cited under each stratum which is present.

	J	E	P	N
Brother/Brother	9	8	6	6
Incest	4	3	1	5
Israel/Nations	12	10	10	14
Death/Rebirth	8	8	4	4
Inside/Outside re Women/Danger	10	7	5	8
Denial of Natural Birth/Parents	7	7	5	4

Figure 22. *The Mythemes Found in the Four Textual Strata*

11.6. *Mechanisms of Transformations*
In the texts analyzed there were two primary methods of clouding the structure: mediation and inversion. Mediation is used in a variety of ways. In the *Sacrifice of Isaac* the mediator (the ram) replaced Isaac in the sacrifice (possibly because child sacrifice by a Patriarch was culturally, though not structurally, problematic). Similarly, in *The Murder of Abel*, Seth replaced Abel in the rebirth. In one case the mytheme of sacrifice was clouded, and in the second that of rebirth.

Mediation also bridged other gaps. In *The Murder of Joseph* the culpability of the brothers in the murder is lessened by the imposition of mediators. The primary mediators in that text were the Ishmaelites and the Midianites. They stood structurally between the Israelites and the Egyptians, and thus were the best conduit to bring Joseph to Egypt. The sons of the concubines also functioned as mediators in that text. As children of the concubines, rather than the primary wives, they were relatively outside and therefore functioned to lessen the blame attributed to the chosen line. Eliezer was used in a similar way (to the Midianites and Ishmaelites) in *The Wooing of Rebekah*. He bridged the gap between inside and outside and was thus the best messenger to bring Isaac a wife from the outside (and to begin the process of transforming her into inside.)

In these cases and other examples found in the texts the mediators share certain characteristic elements. Mediators are able to bridge boundaries because they share elements from both sides. For example, the ram in *The Sacrifice of Isaac* was both given by God and, as an animal, was a product of nature. It mediated between Isaac before and after his rebirth. Prior to his rebirth Isaac was a product of natural fertility and after his rebirth a product of divine fertility, matched by the two aspects of the ram. The ram and other mediators cloud the structure by covering up the distinction between the two sides.

The second mechanism which is found in several texts is inversion. In several texts (e.g., *The Murder of Joseph* in comparison to *The Sacrifice of Isaac*) all the structural elements are inverted, thus preserving the relationships between the elements ($s^{(2)}$). They suggest a general rule of structural inversion: where elements are inverted all elements will be equally inverted. This is illustrated in the following equation in which capital letters represent the original structure and small letters the inverted structure: $A : B :: a^{-i} : b^{-i}$.

A similar equation is suggested for the final type of clouding found in Genesis, that is, doubling. This mechanism is found throughout the texts about Joseph. In those texts every structural element (as well as most narrative elements) were doubled. This suggests the structural principle: where structural elements are doubled, all elements will be equally doubled, illustrated in the equation: $A : B :: a^2 : b^2$. It is further proposed that, where structural elements are transformed in any way, all elements will be similarly transformed in order to preserve their structural relationships. This is expressed in the equation: $A : B :: a^t : b^t$.

Identical mechanisms of transformation are also found in the diachronic (time) development of the myths. One of the primary mechanisms found was the transformation of mediators and in some cases the imposition of new mediators. In other cases mediators were removed to emphasize the structural elements. Thus the ram in *The Sacrifice of Isaac* is removed or transformed and, in the fiery furnace texts, Nimrod is added to mediate between Abram and his father. Other mechanisms included addition of new narrative material (e.g., the fiery furnace myth) and clouding of oppositions clear in the biblical text (especially regarding incest). These mechanisms are seen to respond, on the narrative level, to cultural changes.

11.7. *Diachronic Development within the Myth*
Diachronic analysis of the text, from a theoretical perspective, reveals both consistency and flexibility. Two areas of flexibility are discussed above: incest (endogamy) and rebirth (chosenness). Both these and related transformations occur on the level of $s^{(3)}$. The underlying structural elements are found throughout biblical and rabbinic myth. Different elements, however, are highlighted by changes in clouding or emphasis.

The diachronic transformations in the presentation of structure examined here reveal an important contribution of diachronic analysis to structuralist theory. It *v*.ows that structure (at the level of emphasis and clouding) is affected, diachronically, by external events and changes. This was suggested by Lévi-Strauss in respect to the movement across geographic time, especially with respect to changes in available material foci for symbols. (See Lévi-Strauss's *Mythologiques* 1969, 1973, 1981). Each community would use the symbols which were close to hand and familiar. As nature changed (in space) new elements were substituted for symbolic elements no longer available.

The transformations in Israelite/rabbinic culture, however, are on a different level. They reflect actual changes in meaning ($s^{(3)}$), while those examined by Lévi-Strauss relate to transformations in communication and meaning. The diachronic transformations examined here reflect political transformations and cultural transformations.

This type of surface transformation suggests a possibility for integrating both Leach's (1969, 1983) and Prewitt's (1990) analyses with that undertaken here. Both introduce short-term conscious political considerations as determining underlying structure. If conscious political changes affect surface structure rather than underlying structure, then it is likely that their analyses are of surface transformations rather than underlying structure.

As suggested by T. Turner (1977, 1985), diachronic transformation also works on an inter-textual level. One of the clearest examples of this is in the Abraham myths. As the myths developed, the structural position of all the characters was developed. Abraham himself is transformed from outside to inside. In *The Covenant of Circumcision* (M.I.7) he is reborn and can therefore carry the divine seed and pass it on to his son. The structures developed in M.I.7 depend on those transformed earlier in the myth. Likewise, the structural positions of both Lot and Sarah are transformed diachronically within the text, allowing them to fill their necessary structural functions at the conclusion of the text.

This was also seen on a broader scale regarding the development of Israel. In the narratively earlier texts brothers were always structurally opposed, with the divine seed usually passing to the younger son. On the synchronic level this mytheme is found even in the final texts in Genesis (i.e., regarding Joseph and his brothers). On the diachronic level, however, this process of horizontal opposition reaches its conclusion with Jacob. All Jacob's sons are structurally inside (effectively twelve is one). Mediators and other structural elements support this new structure. Thus one level of the structure recognizes this diachronic narrative development while on the synchronic level it is not recognized. Analysis of both levels is necessary for the complete structuralist analysis of a mythological system.

Analysis of diachronic transformation within synchronic mythological texts emphasizes the importance of T. Turner's (1977) contribution to structuralist theory. Synchronic analysis reveals one level of the cultural grammar. It highlights the rules governing the formation of oppositions in the system. Diachronic (historical) analysis reveals a second equally important layer. With respect to the biblical text, synchronic analysis reveals the mythemes of endogamy, chosenness and so forth, and their relationship to each other. Diachronic analysis (comparing biblical myth and rabbinic myth) suggests that, at the time the Bible was written, endogamy was more structurally problematic than chosenness (a situation which is inverted in the rabbinic texts).

Both levels of diachronic transformation emphasize the importance of holistic analysis as opposed to the more fragmentary methodology applied by Leach, Pitt-Rivers and source critics. A single text, out of its synchronic and diachronic context, may reveal only a small clouded fragment of that grammar, or a substantially transformed element of the grammar. Only by examining each text in the context of its synchronic system as a whole can its place in the overall structure be understood. Holistic analysis is also necessary in order to appreciate the types of developments in structure suggested by T. Turner. Although fragmentary analyses may reveal some aspect of the function of the myth (e.g., particular political ends), they do not reveal underlying structure.

11.8. *Structural Meaning of Direction and Geography*

Directions are structurally significant. East is consistently a negative direction, occasionally in opposition to west. In the early chapters of Genesis east represents the descent of humanity into degradation. Thus, after killing Abel, Cain moves east and founds a city, making the city and the life descended from it ideologically negative. The men in the Tower of Babel myth continue this process, moving east before they build their doomed city. This element is also found in *The Division of the Land*. Lot chooses the east bank of the Jordan, settling in the corrupt cities of the rift valley. This is opposed to Abraham who settles in the west, on the land promised him and his descendants by God. The direction west is also portrayed as ideologically positive in *Abram Leaves Haran* (M.I.1) in which Abram moves westward to the land chosen by God. Most of the nations mentioned in the biblical text lived to the east of Israel. Thus the opposition East : West is structurally equivalent to Nations : Israel.

The directions north and south are also structurally significant. If the movement in the texts is charted, it is seen that certain events occur in specific directions. Wives are always brought from the north and taken south. In effect they are brought from the outside (north) and made inside (south). Thus the equation for the four directions: north and east = negative; south and west = positive.

Geography also has structural significance. It is divided into a series of concentric circles, which are qualitatively more positive as the series moves towards its center. In Exodus, Leviticus and Numbers this geographic center moves, being centered on the camp, yet the structure is constant. The Israelite camp is logically opposed to the rest of the world, the enclosure of the tent of meeting is opposed to the camp, the tent of meeting to the enclosure, and the ark of the covenant to the tent of meeting.[1]

Once the Israelites were (narratively) settled in Canaan, as first seen in Deuteronomy, the concentric circles have a fixed center. The land of Canaan is distinguished from the rest of the world as the land promised by God to Abraham. Jerusalem is distinguished in Deuteronomy (though not by name) as the chosen city. The Temple is the center of Jerusalem, and the Holy of Holies is the center of the temple. In both the camp and the settled model the center is progressively forbidden. The unclean were forbidden from entering the camp, women were forbidden from entering the enclosure, only the Levites and priests were allowed to enter the tent, and only the High Priest was allowed to approach the Ark. Similarly, Canaan was the land of the Israelites, Judah that of the tribe of Judah (one of the mythologically chosen lines), women were not permitted into the Temple enclosure (nor were handicapped people), only the priests and Levites were permitted in the Temple, and only the High Priest in the Holy of Holies.

---

1. Prewitt suggests that the tribes are also arranged in qualitative order in the camp (1990: 54).

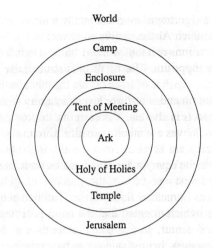

Figure 23. *Structure of Israelite Geography*

11.9. *Structural Elements in Other Areas of Israelite Society*

Preliminary analysis indicates that the structure ($s^{(2)}$) which underlies the mythological system is also present in other areas of Israelite culture. The Israelite understanding and categorization of geographic direction and geography is presented above. The same pattern is also found with respect to the organization of Israelite society.[1] Israel was distinct from the nations, having divinely given laws not given to the other nations (nor were the other nations expected to follow them). The Levites were distinct from the rest of the Israelites through service in the Temple, and the Cohanim (once part of the Levites) were separated by their priestly function. The Cohanim had their own laws which were not binding for the rest of Israel, and in some cases were opposite to the laws binding everyone else.[2]

In addition, similar structures are found in several 'existential rituals', which affect thought because they are constantly present, rather than through large public ceremonies. Circumcision should be considered primarily an existential ritual because the fact of circumcision was structurally more significant than the actual operation. The role of

1. This is also suggested by Mary Douglas. She argues: High Priest : People (common Israelites) :: Clean : Unclean :: Humans : Animals :: Israel : Nations (1978: 312).

2. See also Jenson 1992 for a detailed discussion of similar structures in regard to the priestly cult.

circumcision as a sign of the covenant and as a means of distinguishing Israel from the nations was the significant element.

The ritual of circumcision worked in a second way, through interaction with the myth. The myth of circumcision is structurally associated with the sacrifice of Isaac (as are the other birth/rebirth texts). Thus circumcision functions on three levels: as a sign of the covenant, as a denial of human fertility (and therefore, in the context of rebirth, a denial of parents), and as a symbolic sacrifice. Circumcision as a ritual is the symbolic sacrifice and rebirth of the child. If the two elements are joined together, then the myth and ritual can be understood as follows. Prior to circumcision the boy is the product of natural birth and therefore part of his immediate family alone. Through being circumcised the role of the parents is denied and the child is reborn as a cultural entity (of divine descent), part of Israel rather than a natural being. A similar interpretation of circumcision in another culture is found in *From Blessing to Violence* (Bloch 1986: 80-82).

The food laws are another example of this type of 'ritual'. They come into force any time a Jew (or Israelite) eats,[1] and were foreshadowed in the texts about the flood, in which there is an opposition between pure and impure animals. This opposition is developed into a set of specific rules which categorize all animals into two opposing categories: *kosher* and *treif* (non-*kosher*).[2] As the *kosher* animals (called 'pure' in the Noah text) are also the only animals fit to be sacrificed to God, it is likely that they can be considered qualitatively 'better' than non-*kosher* animals. Thus this logic of animals mirrors that of human beings: *Kosher* : *Treif* :: Israel : Nations.[3]

---

1. The relationship between taxonomies and social structure has been pointed out by Lévi-Strauss (1966) and by Bulmer (1967) and Tambiah (1969).

2. Mary Douglas presents the logic behind this categorization in *Purity and Danger* (1966). The primary flaw of the discussion in that text is that she fails to show how the logic fits into the structures of Israelite culture as a whole. In *Implicit Meanings* (1975), however, Douglas ties the system to social structure. She focuses on the problem of the mediator (those animals which do not fit the logical categories); why are some mediators positive and some negative? She concludes that, in those systems which are open to exchange with other human groups, the mediator will be positive (because human boundaries are permeable). In those societies which are suspicious of exchange, the mediators are negative because they imply that the boundaries are non-existent (Douglas 1975: 289).

3. Mary Douglas suggests the following equation: Animals : Humans :: Nations : Israel (Douglas 1975: 312). This opposition has also been observed in M.V.1 *Creation*.

The same structural problems found in human society are also found in the animal world. The structural crisis revolved around nations which were too close, that is the nations which mediated between Israel and the world. The crisis was resolved by imposition of ideological distance. These nations were ideologically the most negative. Similarly, in the animal world, the animals which mediated or blurred the existence of boundaries were structurally problematic; they suggested that the boundaries in fact did not exist. Like the mediating nations, the mediating animals are ideologically distinguished as negative. Thus, the pig which shares characteristics of both sides, being cloven hoofed but not a ruminant, was ideologically emphasized in order to create ideological distance in the place of biological distance (Douglas 1984: 55). The pig was negative not because it was unknown and infrequently eaten, but rather because it was well known and frequently eaten.[1]

In Chapter 7 (M.5.1) it was noted that time shared the same structure. In that text the seventh day, Shabbat, was qualitatively distinguished from the remainder of the week. Shabbat was the only day given a name, the other days were called by number. Similarly, Shabbat is blessed and distinguished by God from the rest of the week. On a broader scale the seventh year, the sabbatical year, and the fiftieth (after seven times seven years) were also qualitatively distinguished from other years.[2]

The biblical text also includes a set of laws concerned with mixing categories. A variety of different types of mixtures are forbidden. Mixture of cloth made of plants (e.g, cotton) and animals (e.g., wool) were forbidden (though it was permitted to the High Priest). It was forbidden for animals of different kinds to be yoked together. Sexual contact between man and beast was also forbidden. Most of these examples pro-

However, in suggesting that animals were not used to 'represent differentiation in their society', she ignores the flexibility of symbols. The divisions within the animal world represent the divisions in human society.

1.   Mary Douglas concludes her discussion of abominations in Leviticus by stating, 'The dietary laws would have been like signs which at every turn inspired meditation on the oneness, purity and completeness of God' (1966: 57). She stops one step too early. She ties neither the God concept (i.e., the oneness of God) nor the categorization of animals to deeper sociological questions.

2.   In rabbinic texts this pattern is played out on an even broader stage; the distinction between this world and the world to come. They make a clear analogy between the Shabbat and the world to come. Thus the equation Shabbat : Weekdays :: World to Come : This World :: Israel : Nations is implied in their texts.

vide no qualitative distinction between the categories, they are merely two distinct groupings. These laws support the structural logic which suggests that by definition different types cannot be mixed. Unlike the food laws, however, they do not develop the logic of Israel : Nations.

This discussion indicates that the structural pattern developed in the mythological texts is found in many other constructs of Israelite culture. It is likely that similar structures will also be found in other cultural constructs. This supports the theoretical supposition that, as part of the naturalization process, the same logic will be present in all cultural forms.

11.10. *Last Words*

This research contributes to both biblical studies and anthropology. The contributions to biblical analysis are in three areas. The first challenges the nature of mainstream biblical study. Various schools of source and textual criticism primarily use fragmentary analysis, seeking to determine the origin (and authorship) of individual fragments. Structuralist theory suggests that, when the fragments are edited or redacted, their structure and perhaps narrative elements would be transformed to fit the structures of the editor, thus all fragments would betray identical structure. This is supported by the ethnographic evidence presented here. The analysis reveals that all four strata include the same mythemes and are thus structurally and culturally indistinguishable. This supports the use of holistic analysis of text found in the literary school of biblical study. Holistic analysis and structuralist analysis examine one aspect of the mythic system. Other approaches, for example, functionalist and source critical, examine other equally significant levels. Use of one methodology does not preclude the importance or application of other methodologies.

The second contribution to biblical studies is ethnographic. This study presents the structures of biblical thought and demonstrates their use in understanding a wide range of textual material. The patterns of Israelite thought are based on dialectical opposition with positive and negative value placed on each half of the opposition. Mediators in the Israelite system are negative. The analysis shows that all the myths in Genesis include the same types of oppositions and can be explained based on those oppositions.

The third area of interest to biblical scholarship lies on the diachronic level. The analysis demonstrates both transformation and continuity between biblical and rabbinic cultures and suggests that diachronically later material can confirm the results of structuralist analysis. Thus, midrashic texts that include an actual sacrifice confirm structuralist speculation about the biblical text (e.g., *The Sacrifice of Isaac*). The contributions on the anthropological level are equally wide ranging. Ethnographically, the analysis adds to the understanding of Israelite culture. It also provides a framework by which previous structuralist and non-structuralist analyses can be contextualized. The research also emphasizes the importance of analysis of informants' explanations on the same basis as the original mythological material. The rabbinic explanations, for example, are as mythologically based and structured as are the narrative biblical texts. The rabbinic statements are essentially implicit myth, the analysis here confirms that implicit myth is structurally equivalent to explicit myth.[1] Although they appear as explanations, they are not anthropological, they are part of the mythic system and must be examined as such. What is interesting in the material studied is that diachronically later exegesis and narrative material usually reveals structural elements that were only implicit in the original text.

Regarding the interpretation of ritual, Hugh-Jones and Leach state, 'what is symbolized in ritual can only be understood with reference to what is "said" in myth, the message being conveyed...by the structural patterns embedded in the myth' (Hugh-Jones 1979: 255).[2] Although both myth and ritual must be analyzed in a broader context, either can be the starting point. The structures embodied in ritual can elucidate those in myth. This approach to ritual is also somewhat different to that applied by Lévi-Strauss. He suggests that rituals and myths work in opposite directions. Myths create disunity while rituals attempt to recreate unity. This study suggests that the two are alternative modes of development and presentation of structure, thereby working in the same direction, as suggested by Hugh-Jones (1979: 260). Analysis of biblical ritual supports this proposal. Both biblical myth and biblical ritual manipulate symbols (by differing means) for the same structural ends. Thus, for example, the structural relations created by the laws of *kashrut*

1.   Theoretical discussion of this equivalence is found in Hugh-Jones (1979), Lévi-Strauss (1981) and V. Turner (1969). Hugh-Jones also makes the same point in respect to exegesis. He states, 'Native explanations...should be treated as part of the data to be explained and not as anthropological explanations in their own right' (1979: 254).
2.   Leach, however, states, 'In such cases...ritual is incomprehensible without a knowledge of the myth, but the details of the myth are incomprehensible without a knowledge of the ritual' (Leach 1982: 6). This proposition should be generalized to include all myth and ritual.

(food) are identical with those developed in the mythic system. The comprehensiveness of structure in all aspects of culture is also suggested by the analysis of social structure, geography and time. Each of these areas is characterized by the same underlying structure.

On a theoretical level, the importance of both synchronic and diachronic analysis is demonstrated. Synchronic analysis refers to the methodology of Lévi-Strauss. It seeks to discover overall patterns of logic which transcend the narrative development of the myth. Diachronic analysis works on two levels. Within a synchronic text, it examines the development of structural elements within the diachronic progression of the narrative (based on T. Turner's approach). The second level is concerned with the transformations in structural elements over time, it compares structure and the presentation of structure in diachronically distinct texts. On the textual level, both contribute to the structural grammar of the system. This analysis presents the mechanisms of transformation on both the synchronic and diachronic development of the myth.

The textual material analyzed in this book emphasizes the importance of diachronic analysis as well as synchronic analysis. Such analysis is necessary to present and evaluate the dynamism within a given system. It is also possible that this dynamism is linked to different aspects of self-perception, especially regarding that of cultural dynamism. It is possible that the structure of those societies which perceive themselves as dynamic, would also be dynamic. That of societies which perceive themselves as static, would change at a slower pace. Clearly most societies would range between these two ideal types. This dynamism, however, far from limiting useful structuralist analysis, in fact adds to the scope of the analysis.

One aspect of the pervasiveness of structure is tied to the naturalization process. It is suggested that one of the aims of myth and ritual is to naturalize the structural logic. The extension of similar structures to all aspects of Israelite culture, and the associated extension to the similar structures of categorization to perception of nature, support this suggestion. Rather than suggesting a nature–culture dialectic, the approach taken here suggests that the role of myth is to make culture appear natural, clouding any distinction between the two. Nature as the handmaiden of culture proves that culture is natural and therefore true.

This work has implications not only for structuralist theory and biblical and rabbinic studies, it also has implications (which need to be developed through future research) regarding the birth of Christianity and the relation of Christian myth to Jewish myth. One important avenue of research is a comparative analysis of biblical structure and New Testament structure. This question is important to understanding the relationship of rabbinic culture and early Christian culture, and their respective relationship with biblical culture (are they complementary offshoots of biblical culture, or does one or the other include significant areas of transformation?). A second avenue regards understanding the nature of the Jewish community in the modern world. It is possible that certain structural elements examined here still retain power within that community. These structures are reflected in many aspects of intra-communal policy. Most Jewish communities today perceive two fundamental challenges: intermarriage and assimilation. The challenge of intermarriage is directly tied to endogamy and Jewish self-perception. Even in families which are fully integrated into American (or English) society, and are non-practicing religiously, there is a strong negative feeling and reaction against intermarriage. Assimilation challenges the fabric of distinctiveness which is the reverse side of endogamy. It is portrayed in Jewish thought as one of the greatest dangers to the community and is linked with the destruction and loss of Judaism. It is also likely that much of the challenge that Progressive forms of Judaism create for Orthodoxy is due to the perception of Progressive Jews as mediators and therefore negative. It is also possible that some aspects of the State of Israel's self-perception emerge from such structures. In order to test such proposals, however, one major question must be answered: how is structure transformed when two cultures are merged to the extent that the Jewish community in Western Europe and the United States is merged with its host cultures? These questions and proposals open the major avenues of future research suggested by this volume.

BIBLIOGRAPHY

Ackerman, J.S.
    1982   'Joseph, Judah, and Jacob', in Gros Louis 1982.
Ackroyd, P.
    1991   *The Chronicler in his Age* (Sheffield: JSOT Press).
Aharoni, Y.
    1979   *The Land of the Bible* (London: Burns & Oates).
Alter, R.
    1981   *The Art of Biblical Narrative* (New York: Basic Books).
Andriolo, K.
    1973   'A Structural Analysis of Genealogy and Worldview in the Old Testament', *American Anthropologist* 75: 1657-69.
Aycock, D.
    1992   'Potiphar's Wife: Prelude to a Structural Exegesis', *Man* 27.3: 475-94.
Bar-Efrat, S.
    1979   *The Art of the Biblical Story* (Sheffield: Almond Press).
    1980   'Some Observations on the Analysis of Structure in Biblical Narrative', *VT* 30: 154-73.
Barnes, J.A.
    1947   'The Collection of Genealogies', *Rhodes-Livingstone Journal* 5: 48-55.
Barr, J.
    1959   'The Meaning of Mythology', *VT* 9: 1-10.
Barth, F.
    1981   *Process and Form in Social Life* (London: Routledge & Kegan Paul).
Barth, L.M.
    1983   *An Analysis of Vatican 30* (Cincinnati: Hebrew Union College Press).
Barthes, R.
    1972   *Mythologies* (trans. A. Lavers; New York: Hill & Wang).
Bartlett, J.R.
    1973   'The Moabites and the Edomites', in Wiseman 1973.
Beltz, W.
    1983   *God and the Gods: Myths of the Bible* (New York: Pelican Books).
Biddle, M.E.
    1990   'The "Endangered Ancestress" and Blessing for the Nations', *JBL* 109: 599-611.
Blenkinsopp, J.
    1991   'Temple and Society in Achaemenid Judah', in Davies 1991.

Blumenberg, H.
1985   *Work on Myth* (trans. R. Wallace; Cambridge, MA: MIT Press).
Bock, P.
1988   *Rethinking Psychological Anthropology* (New York: Freeman).
Bohannan, L.
1952   'A Genealogical Charter', *Africa* 22: 301-15.
Bright, J.
1972   *A History of Israel* (Philadelphia: Westminster Press).
Bryan, D.T.
1987   'A Reevaluation of Gen 4 and 5 in Light of Recent Studies in Genea-
        logical Fluidity', *ZAW* 99.2: 180-88.
Buber, S. (ed.)
1960   *Tanhumah* (Vilna: Romm).
1987   *Lekach Tov* (Jerusalem: Hotzaat H. Vegeshel).
Bulmer, R.
1967   'Why is the Cassowary not a Bird? A Problem of Zoological Taxonomy
        among the Karam of the New Guinea Highlands', *Man* NS 2.
Campbell, J.
1968   *The Masks of God* (Norwich: The Viking Press): I–IV.
1988   *Myths, Dreams, and Religion* (Dallas: Spring Publications).
Carmichael, C.M.
1982   'Forbidden Mixtures', *VT* 32.4: 394-415.
Carroll, M.
1985   'Genesis Restructured', in Lang 1985.
Cassirer, E.
1946   *The Myth of the State* (New Haven: Yale University Press).
1955   *The Philosophy of Symbolic Forms*. II. *Mythical Thought* (New Haven:
        Yale University Press).
Cassuto, U.
1961a   *The Documentary Hypothesis* (Jerusalem: Hebrew University Press).
1961b   *Commentary on Genesis I* (Jerusalem: Hebrew University Press).
1961c   *Commentary on Genesis II* (Jerusalem: Hebrew University Press).
Clifford, J.
1983   *Person and Myth* (Berkeley: University of California Press).
Cunnison, I.
1966   *Baggara Arabs* (Oxford: Oxford University Press).
Culler, J.
1975   *Structuralist Poetics* (Ithaca: Cornell University Press).
Culley, R.C.
1976   *Studies in the Structure of Hebrew Narrative* (Philadelphia: Scholars
        Press).
1979   *Perspectives on Old Testament Narrative* (Missoula, MT: Scholars
        Press).
Davies, P.R.
1991   *Second Temple Studies: 1. Persian Period* (Sheffield: JSOT Press).
Dolgin, J., *et al.*
1977   *Symbolic Anthropology: A Reader in the Study of Symbols and
        Meaning* (New York: Columbia University Press).

Dolgin, J., and J. Magdoff
    1977   'The Invisible Event', in Dolgin *et al.* 1977.
Donaldson, M.E.
    1981   'Kinship Theory in the Patriarchal Narratives: The Case of the Barren Wife', *JAAR* 49: 77-87.
Douglas, M.
    1966   *Purity and Danger: An Analysis of Concepts of Pollution and Taboo* (London: Ark).
    1975   *Implicit Meanings: Essays in Anthropology* (London: Routledge & Kegan Paul).
Durkheim, E.
    1926   *The Elementary Forms of the Religious Life* (New York: The Free Press).
Dundes, A.
    1962   'Earth-driver: Creation of the Mythopoeic Male', *American Anthropologist* 64: 1032-51.
Edelheit, J.
    1983   'Children of Mixed Marriage: A Non-Lineal Approach', *Journal of Reform Judaism* 30: 34-42.
Eliade, M.
    1964   *Myth and Reality* (trans. W.R. Trask; London: George Allen & Unwin).
    1971   *The Myth of the Eternal Return* (Princeton, NJ: Princeton University Press).
Emerton, J.A.
    1976   'An Examination of A Recent Structuralist Interpretation of Genesis XXXVIII', *VT* 26: 79-98.
Eph'al, I.
    1982   *The Ancient Arabs* (Jerusalem: Magnes Press).
Evans-Pritchard, E.E.
    1940   *The Nuer* (Oxford: Oxford University Press).
Finkelstein, J.J.
    1963   'The Antideluvian Kings: A University of California Tablet', *JCS* 17: 39-51.
Firth, R.
    1973   *Symbols Public and Private* (Ithaca, NY: Cornell University Press).
Fisch, H
    1979   'A Structuralist Approach to the Stories of Ruth and Boaz', *Beth Mikra* 24: 260-65.
    1982   'Ruth and the Structure of Covenant History', *VT* 32: 425-37.
Fohrer, G.
    1986   *Introduction to the Old Testament* (Slough: SPCK).
Fortes, M.
    1967   *The Dynamics of Clanship among the Tallensi* (London: Oxford University Press).
    1969   *Kinship and Social Order* (Chicago: University of Chicago Press).
Foucault, M.
    1973   *The Order of Things* (New York: Doubleday).

Freeman, H.
1939   *Midrash Rabbah Vol. 1 (Genesis)* (London: Soncino).
Freud, S.
1959   *Collected Papers* (New York: Basic Books): V.
Frezer, J.
1958   *The Golden Bough* (New York: Macmillan).
Friedlander, G.
1981   *Perke de Rabbi Eliezar* (New York: Sepher-Hermon Press).
Frye, N.
1963   *Fables of Identity* (New York: Harcourt Brace & World).
Gaster, T.
1950   *Thespis* (New York: Harper & Row).
1969   *Myth, Legend, and Custom in the Old Testament* (London: Gerald Duckworth).
Gesenius, W.
1846   *Gesenius's Hebrew and Chaldee Lexicon to the Old Testament Scriptures* (trans. S. Tregelles; London: Samuel Bagster & Sons).
Gillman, N.
1990   *Sacred Fragments: Recovering Theology for the Modern Jew* (New York: JTS).
Ginsberg, L.
1968   *The Legends of the Jews (Seven Volumes)* (Philadelphia: Jewish Publication Society of America).
Goldin, J.
1977   'The Youngest Son or Where Does Genesis 38 Belong', *JBL* 96: 27-44.
1987   'Midrash and Aggadah', in Seltzer 1987a.
Goody, J. (ed.)
1975   *Literacy in Traditional Societies* (Cambridge: Cambridge University Press).
Goody, J., and I. Watt
1975   'The Consequences of Literacy', in Goody 1975.
Gottwald, N.K.
1979   *The Tribes of Yahweh* (London: SCM Press).
Gould, S.J.
1977   *Ontogeny and Phylogeny* (Cambridge, MA: Harvard University Press).
Greenberg, M.
1977   'The Use of the Ancient Versions for Interpreting the Hebrew Text', in J.A. Emerton *et al.* (eds.), *Congress Volume, Göttingen 1977* (Leiden: Brill): 131-48.
Gros Louis, K.R.R. (ed.)
1982   *Literary Interpretations of Biblical Narratives* (Nashville; Abingdon Press): III.
Hallpike, C.R.
1979   'Social Hair', in Lessa and Vogt 1979.
Hason, R.
1990   'לוח העמים' ('The Table of Nations'), *Beth Mikra* 123: 359-61.

Hayes, E., and T. Hayes
    1970   *Claude Lévi-Strauss: The Anthropologist as Hero* (Cambridge, MA: MIT Press).
Heaton, E.W.
    1987   *The Hebrew Kingdoms* (Oxford: Oxford University Press).
Hendel, R.S.
    1987   'Of Demigods and the Deluge: Towards an Interpretation of Genesis 6:1-4', *JBL* 106: 13-26.
Hiat, P., and B. Zlotowitz
    1983   'Biblical and Rabbinic Sources on Patrilineal Descent', *Journal of Reform Judaism* 30.1: 43-48.
Hill, J.D. (ed.)
    1988   *Rethinking History and Myth* (Chicago: University of Illinois Press).
Hoglund, K.
    1991   'The Achaemenid Context', in Davies 1991.
Hooke, S.H.
    1933   *Myth and Ritual* (London: Oxford University Press).
Hopkins, K.
    1982   'Brother-Sister Marriage in Roman Egypt', *Comparative Studies in Society and History* 22: 303-54.
Hugh-Jones, S.
    1979   *The Palm and the Pleides: Initiation and Cosmolody in Northwest Amazonia* (Cambridge: Cambridge University Press).
Hyman, D., and I. Shiloni (eds.)
    1973   *Yalkut Shemone* (Jerusalem: Mossad Harev Kook).
Hymes, H.
    1977   'The "Wife" who "Goes Out" Like a Man: Reinterpretation of a Clackamas Chinook Myth', in Dolgin *et al.* 1977.
Jacobs, M.
    1976   'Animals and God-man-nature in the Old Testament', *The Jewish Journal of Sociology* 18.2: 141-54.
Jacoby, M.
    1994   'Who was the First Deborah? The Puzzle of Genesis 35.8', *Journal of Progressive Judaism* 2: 5-14.
Jacopin, P.-Y.
    1988   'The Structure of Myth, or the Yukuna Invention of Speech', *Cultural Anthropology* 3(2).
Jagersma, H.
    1982   *A History of Israel in the Old Testament Period* (London: SCM Press).
Jenson, P.
    1992   *Graded Holiness* (Sheffield: JSOT Press).
Jobling, D.
    1978   *The Sense of Biblical Narrative: Structural Analysis in the Hebrew Bible* (Sheffield: JSOT Press): I.
    1986   *The Sense of Biblical Narrative: Structural Analysis in the Hebrew Bible* (Sheffield: JSOT Press): II.

Johnson, M.D.
  1969   *The Purpose of Biblical Genealogies* (Cambridge: Cambridge
             University Press).
Jung, C.G., and C. Kerenyi
  1951   *Introduction to a Science of Mythology* (London: Pantheon Press).
Kirk, G.S.
  1970   *Myth: Its Meaning and Functions in Ancient and Other Cultures*
             (Cambridge: Cambridge University Press).
Klausner, J.
  1975   'The Economy of Judea in the Period of The Second Temple', in
             M.A. Yonah, *The World History of the Jewish People* (New Brunswick:
             Rutgers University Press): VII.
Kluckholn, C.
  1979   'Myths and Rituals: A General Theory', in Lessa and Vogt 1979.
Kunin, S.
  1994a   'Perilous Wives and (Relatively) Safe Sisters', *Journal of Progressive
             Judaism* 2: 15-34.
  1994b   'The Death of Isaac: Structuralist Analysis of Genesis 32', *JSOT* 64:
             57-81.
Lang, B. (ed.)
  1985   *Anthropological Approaches to the Old Testament* (London: SPCK).
Leach, E.
  1954   *Political Systems of Highland Burma* (London: Bell).
  1958   'Magical Hair', *Journal of the Royal Anthropological Institute* 88.2:
             147-64.
  1961   *Rethinking Anthropology* (London: Athlone Press).
Leach, E. (ed.)
  1967   *The Structural Study of Myth and Totemism* (London: Tavistock
             Publications).
  1969   *Genesis as Myth* (London: Jonathan Cape).
  1970   'Lévi-Strauss in the Garden of Eden: An Examination of Some Recent
             Developments in the Analysis of Myth', in *Claude Lévi-Strauss: The
             Anthropologist as Hero* (Cambridge, MA: MIT Press).
  1982   'Introduction', in M.I. Steblin-Kamenskij, *Myth: The Icelandic Sagas
             and Eddas* (Ann Arbor: Karoma).
Leach, E., and A. Aycock
  1983   *Structuralist Interpretations of Biblical Myth* (Cambridge: Cambridge
             University Press).
Lessa, W.A., and E.Z. Vogt (eds.)
  1979   *Reader in Comparative Religion* (New York: Harper & Row).
Lévi-Strauss, C.
  1963   *Structural Anthropology* (New York: Basic Books): I.
  1966   *The Savage Mind* (Chicago: The University of Chicago Press).
  1969a   *The Raw and the Cooked* (New York: Harper & Row).
  1969b   *The Elementary Structures of Kinship* (Boston: Beacon Press).
  1973   *From Honey to Ashes* (Chicago: The University of Chicago Press).
  1976   *Structural Anthropology* (New York: Basic Books): II.
  1978   *The Origin of Table Manners* (New York: Harper & Row).

1981   *The Naked Man* (New York: Harper & Row).

1985   *The View from Afar* (New York: Basic Books).

1988   *The Jealous Potter* (Chicago: University of Chicago Press).

Lindholm, C.

1982   *Generosity and Jealousy: The Swat Pukhtun of Northern Pakistan* (New York: Columbia University Press).

Malinowski, B.

1926   *Myth in Primitive Psychology* (London: W.W. Norton).

1954   *Magic, Science and Religion* (New York: Anchor Books).

1961   *Argonauts of the Western Pacific* (New York: Dutton).

Manisha, R.

1975   'The Oedipus Complex and the Bengali Family in India', in T. Williams (ed.), *Psychological Anthropology* (The Hague: Mouton).

Margulies, M. (ed.)

1947   *Midrash HaGadol* (Jerusalem: Mossad Harev Kook).

Mars, L.

1984   'What Was Onan's Crime', *Journal of the Society for Comparative Study of Society and History* 26: 429-39.

McKane, W.

1979   *Studies in the Patriarchal Narratives* (Edinburgh: Handsel Press).

Mendenhall, G.E.

1970   *The Tenth Generation: The Origins of Biblical Tradition* (Baltimore: The Johns Hopkins University Press).

Mernissi, F.

1975   *Beyond the Veil* (New York: John Wiley & Sons).

Middleton, J. (ed.)

1967a   *Myth and Cosmos* (New York: Natural History Press).

1967b   'Some Social Aspects of Lugbara Myth', in Middleton 1967a.

Mielziner, M.

1968   *Introduction to the Talmud* (New York: Bloch).

Moore, S.F.

1967   "Descent and Symbolic Filiation', in Middleton 1967a.

Moye, R.

1990   'In the Beginning: Myth and History in Genesis and Exodus', *JBL* 109: 577-98.

Murphy, R., and L. Kasdan

1959   'The Structure of Parallel Cousin Marriage', *American Anthropologist* 61: 17-29.

Neusner, J.

1985   *Genesis Rabbah: The Judaic Commentary to the Book of Genesis* (3 vols.; Atlanta: Scholars Press).

Noth, M.

1960   *The History of Israel* (New York: Harper & Row).

1966   *The Old Testament World* (London: A. & C. Black).

Oded, B.

1986   'The Table of Nations (Gen 10)—A Socio-Cultural Approach', *ZAW* 98: 14-31.

Oden, R.A., Jr
   1979a   'Method in the Study of Near Eastern Myths', *Religion* 9 (Autumn): 182-96.
   1979b   ' "The Contendings of Horus and Seth" (Chester Beatty Papyrus No. 1): A Structural Interpretation', *HR* 18.4: 352-69.
   1983   'Jacob as Father, Husband, and Nephew: Kinship Studies and the Patriarchal Narratives', *JBL* 102: 189-205.
Pace, D.
   1983   *Claude Lévi-Strauss: The Bearer of Ashes* (Boston: ARK).
Peters, E.
   1960   'The Proliferation of Lineage Segments in Cyrenaica', *Journal of the Royal Anthropological Institute* 90: 29-53.
Pirke deRabbi Eliezer
   1983   (Jerusalem: Hozaat Siferim Eshkol). Not a critical edition.
Pitt-Rivers, J.
   1977   *The Fate of Shechem or the Politics of Sex* (Cambridge: Cambridge University Press).
Plaut, W.G.
   1981   *The Torah: A Modern Commentary* (New York: UAHC).
Polzin, R.
   1977   *Biblical Structuralism* (Philadelphia: Fortress Press).
Prewitt, T.J.
   1981   'Kinship Structures and the Genesis Genealogies', *JNES* 40: 87-98.
   1990   *The Elusive Covenant: A Structural-Semiotic Reading of Genesis* (Bloomington: University of Indiana Press).
Rad, G. von
   1961   *Genesis* (OTL; London: SCM Press).
Rendtorff, R.
   1985   *The Old Testament: An Introduction* (Trowbridge, SCM Press).
Richards, A.I.
   1960   'Social Mechanisms for the Transfer of Political Rights in Some African Tribes', *Journal of the Royal Anthropological Institute* 90: 175-90.
Robertson Smith, W.
   1956   *The Religion of the Semites* (New York: A. & C. Black).
Rogerson, J.W.
   1978   *Anthropology and the Old Testament* (Oxford: Basil Blackwell).
Sahlins, M.
   1985   *Islands of History* (Chicago: University of Chicago Press).
Saussure, F. de
   1959   *Course in General Linguistics* (London: Peter Owen).
Schapera, I.
   1985   'The Sin of Cain', in Lang 1985.
Scholes, R.
   1974   *Structuralism in Literature: An Introduction* (New Haven: Yale University Press).
Seltzer, R.M. (ed.)
   1987a   *Judaism: A People and its History* (New York: Macmillan).

1987b 'The Jewish People', in Seltzer 1987a.
Shaver, J.
1989 *Torah and the Chronicler's History Work* (Atlanta: Scholars Press).
Simmons, J.
1954 'The Table of Nations (Genesis X): Its General Structure and Meaning', *Old Testament Studies* 10: 154-84.
Speiser, E.A.
1953 'The Wife Sister Motif in the Patriarchal Narratives', in A. Altmann (ed.), *Biblical and Other Studies* (Cambridge, MA: Harvard University Press).
1964 *Genesis* (AB; Garden City, NY: Doubleday).
Sperber, D.
1975 *Rethinking Symbolism* (Cambridge: Cambridge University Press).
1979 'Claude Lévi-Strauss', in Sturrock 1979.
Spiegel, S.
1979 *The Last Trial* (New York: Behrman House).
Spiro, M.E.
1982 *Oedipus in the Trobriands* (Chicago: University of Chicago Press).
1987 *Culture and Human Nature* (Chicago: University of Chicago Press).
Soggin, J.A.
1984 *A History of Israel* (London, SCM Press).
Steinberg, N.
1991 'Alliance or Descent', *JSOT* 51: 45-55.
Steiner, F.
1985 'Enslavement and the Early Hebrew Lineage', in Lang 1985.
Stordalen, T.
1992 'Man, Soul, Garden', *JSOT* 53: 3-25.
Strack, H.L., and G. Stemberger
1991 *Introduction to the Talmud and Midrash* (Edinburgh: T. & T. Clark).
Strenski, I.
1987 *Four Theories of Myth in Twentieth-Century History* (London: Macmillan).
Sturrock, J. (ed.)
1979 *Structuralism and Since: From Lévi-Strauss to Derrida* (Oxford: Oxford University Press).
Tambiah, S.J.
1969 'The Magic Power of Words', *Man* NS 3.
Theodor, J., and C. Albeck (eds.)
1965 *Bereshit Rabbah* (Jerusalem: Wahrmann Books).
Torrey, C.
1970 *Ezra Studies* (New York: Ktav).
Turner, T.
1977 'Narrative Structure and Mythopoesis: A Critique and Reformulation of Structuralist Concepts of Myth, Narrative and Poetics', *Arethusa* 10.1: 103-63.
1985 'Animal Symbolism, Totemism and the Structure of Myth', in G. Urton (ed.), *Animal Myths and Metaphors in South America* (Salt Lake City: University of Utah Press).

1988   '*Commentary*: Ethno-Ethnohistory: Myth and History in Native South American Representations of Contact with Western Society', in Hill 1988.

Turner, V.
1969   *The Ritual Process; Structura and Anti-Structure* (London: Aldine).

Tylor, E.B.
1889   'On a Method of Investigating the Development of Institutions: Applied to Laws of Marriage and Descent', *Journal of the Anthropological Institute* 18: 245-72.

Van Seters, J.
1975   *Abraham in History and Tradition* (New Haven: Yale University Press).

Vansina, J.
1985   *Oral Tradition as History* (London: Currey).

Vawter, B.
1977   *On Genesis* (New York: Doubleday).

Vermes, G.
1975   *Post-Biblical Jewish Studies* (Leiden: Brill).

Wagner, R.
1981   *The Invention of Culture* (Chicago: University of Chicago Press).

Wander, N.
1981   'Structure, Contradiction, and "Resolution" in Mythology: Father's Brother's Daughter Marriage and Treatment of Women in Genesis 11–50', *JANESCU* 13: 75-99.

Westermann, C.
1984   *Genesis 1–11* (Minneapolis: SPCK).

White, H.
1979   'A Theory of the Surface Structure of the Biblical Narrative', *USQR* 34: 159-73.

Wilson, R.R.
1977   *Genealogy and History in the Biblical World* (New Haven: Yale University Press).

Wiseman, D.J.
1973   *Peoples of Old Testament Times* (Oxford: Oxford University Press).

INDEXES

INDEX OF REFERENCES

HEBREW BIBLE

Genesis					
1–11	27	10.8-19	182	17	76, 95, 96, 98, 102, 221-23, 227
1	163	10.22	184, 190		
1.1–2.4	163	11	101, 162		
2.3	106	11.1-9	176	17.1	222
2.5–3.24	165	11.10	184	17.3	222
2.18	165	11.28	208, 232	17.17	97
2.21	165	11.32	214	17.19-20	223
3	100	12–50	27	18.1-15	77
3.14-22	213	12	28, 63, 65, 98, 100, 229	18.5	205
3.24	166	12.1-9	63	18.11	78
4	100	12.1	214	18.12	78
4.1-22	166	12.5	65, 216	18.16-33	79
4.1	184	12.10–13.4	65	19	27, 28
4.17-22	182, 183	12.10	204	19.1-28	80
4.23-24	169	12.14	217	19.1-2	224
4.25-26	166	13.4-5	69	19.16	224
4.26	183	13.5-18	69	19.29-38	82
5.1-28	182	13.7-11	69	19.30-38	192
5.3	184	13.9	219	20	28, 29, 65-67, 83, 95, 196, 204
5.22	169	13.11	69		
5.32	110	13.12-18	69		
6	100	14	70	20.12	84, 204
6.1-4	170	15	72, 96, 98, 100, 102, 212, 222, 234	21	56
6.5–9.19	171			21.1-21	86
9.6	171			21.1	97
9.20-29	195			21.9	225
9.20-28	173	15.3	223	21.12	87
9.21-25	158	15.5	221, 222	21.13	87
10	50, 55, 133, 181, 182, 185, 200, 215	15.7	210, 212, 234	21.22-24	88
		16	74, 123	22	64, 95, 96, 99-103, 181, 200, 226-28
		16.1	189		
10.1-8	182	16.11-13	189	22.1–23.2	94

22.2	95, 227	34.22	137	*Leviticus*	
22.6	96	35.1-20	131	18.6-23	174
22.20-24	184	35.21-22	139	18.6-18	158, 265
23	89	35.29	132	18.8	265
23.20	89	36.1-43	186	18.17	265
24	103	36.12	188	18.18	265
24.2	104, 158	36.20	184	20.24	59
24.55	104	37	100-103,		
25	98, 99, 104,		141	*Numbers*	
	186	37.2	145	13.29	188
25.1-18	90	37.24	146	20.14-21	186, 187
25.1-6	191	37.28	145	21.1-3	196
25.1-5	184	37.35	146	22.4	190
25.6	90	37.36	145	22.7	190
25.12-16	184	38	147	23.7	191
25.15	189	39	145, 150	24.17	193
25.19-26	105	39.7	138	24.18	186
25.22	113	40	153	24.20	188
25.23	99, 186	41	151, 154	24.21-22	183
25.25-34	113	41.42	153	25	60, 190
25.30	114	41.50	152	25.1-18	190
25.32	113	42	155	25.1-3	193
26	28, 65, 196	44.1-47.27	155	31	190
26.1-17	107	46.8-27	184	33.50-56	196
26.7	204	47.28-49.33	157	36	56
26.34-35	115, 186	47.29	158		
27	114	48	100	*Deuteronomy*	
27.1-28.9	116	48.6	158	2	193
27.12-14	118	48.11	205	2.1-7	187
28.5	191	48.15	158	2.8-13	192
28.10-22	119	49	140	2.19	194
29-31	191	49.4	140	7	196
29.1-30	120	49.10	143	7.3	60
29.31-35	122	49.27	143	7.6	59
30.1-13	122	50	159	9.4-5	59
30.14-24	124			14.2	59
30.25-43	125	*Exodus*		18.9	59
31.1-21	125	2.18	183	21.15	56
31.22-54	127	9-10	60	23.4	193, 194
32	100	9.12	60	23.8	187
32.1-3	127	10.11-44	60	25.13-19	188
32.4-33	128	13.17	196	27.15-26	265
32.31	129	15.15	186, 193		
32.33	17	19.5	59	*Judges*	
34	136	23.20-23	196	1	196
34.1	138	33.1-3	196	3.1-6	196
34.2	136	34.11-13	196	3.7-11	187
34.13	137			3.12-30	193

3.13	188, 194	16.22	140	*Psalms*	
3.31	196	21.15-22	196	83	187, 189,
4	196				190, 193
4.11	183	*1 Kings*		83.6	189, 193
5	55	1–9	193	83.7	189, 194
6.1-6	188	2.13-25	140	83.9	190
6.3	189	11	60	125.3	238
6.8	190	11.1-12	194		
6.33	188	11.14-25	187	*Ecclesiastes*	
10.6-18	194	11.14-22	187	5.12	245
10.6	191	11.23	191		
11.4-15	194	14.24	59	*Ezra*	
11.17	187	15.16-23	191	9	53
12	55	15.27	196	9.1-2	193
13	196	16.15	196	10	53, 60
19	27, 28	20.1-21	191		
		20.26-43	191	*1 Chronicles*	
1 Samuel		22.1-38	191	2.55	183
4.1-11	196			8.11	194
7.7-13	196			10	196, 197
8.14	187	*2 Kings*		11.4	196
13	196	1.1	193	14.8-17	197
14.47	187, 193,	3.4-27	193	18.11	189
	194	3.4	187	18.12-13	187
14.48	188	6.8-21	191	19	191
15	188	6.24–7.20	191	20.4	197
15.1-35	188	8.12	194		
17	196	8.20-22	187	*2 Chronicles*	
28	196	10	194	15	191
30	188	11	194	18	191
31	196	12.18-20	191	20	191
		13.3-8	191	20.1-30	187
2 Samuel		13.22-25	191	21.8-10	187
5	196	14.7	187	21.16	189, 197
5.6-12	196	15.37	191	25.11-14	187
8.2	193	16.5-20	191	26.6	197
8.3	191	16.6	187	26.7	187, 189
8.5	191	18.8	196	28.17	187
8.12	189, 196	24.2-3	193	32	197
10.6-19	191	*Hosea*			
13	56	2.17	156		

RABBINIC WRITINGS

Talmuds		*b. Sanh.*		*b. Suk.*	
b. Pes.		89	226	52	150
41	41				

b. Yeb.		56.2	228	17.1	242
22–23	216	56.6	228	18.11	243
		56.12	228	21.9	248
Midrashim		56.19	228	22.3	249
Gen R.				22.8	250
38.13	209	*Lekach Tov Gen.*		22.11	251
38.14	245	11.29	246	22.13	252
39.1	210	11.32	234	22.19	251
39.3	213, 216	12.5	235, 236		
39.4	213, 216	13.6	238	*PRE*	
39.7	214	13.7	238, 239	25.58	224
39.9	215	13.9	239	26.31	211
39.10	213, 216	13.10	239	26.61	217
39.11	215, 216,	13.11	239	29.65	221
	221, 223	16.1	239	30.66	226
39.14	216	16.2	240	31	227-29, 250
40.5	217	16.3	240	32	229
41.1	217	16.5	240, 241		
41.2	217	17.1	242	*PRE Gen.*	
41.3	239	17.13	241	22	250
41.6.3	218	17.14	241		
41.7	219, 239	18.11	243	*Yal. Reub.*	
44.1	213	19.1	244	200	252
44.10	223	19.16	244		
44.13	210, 213	19.19	245	*Yal. Shem.*	
44.21	213	19.33	246	62	232
45.1	219	20.1	246	63	234
45.2	220, 240	20.12	246	67	235
45.4	220	21.1	243	70	238
45.5	220	21.2	243	77	232, 233
46.1	222	21.9	247	79	241
46.2	222	21.10	247	86	246
46.4	222	22.1	249	92	243
47.2	224	22.4	249	93	243, 244,
47.3.2	224	31.42	251		247
47.5	223	49.7	239	98	249, 250
48.16	224			100	249
50.3.4	224	*Midrash haGadol*		101	250-52
50.4	224	597	132		
50.11	224			*Yal. Shem. Gen.*	
51.6	225	*Midrash haGadol Gen.*		11.29	246
51.8	225, 246	11.28	233	12.14	237
51.9	225	12.5	236	12.15	237
51.10	225	12.14	237	16.5	241
53.11	225, 247	12.17	237	20	246
53.15	226, 248	13.10	239		
55.1	226, 249	15.5	243		
55.7	226	16.5	241		

INDEX OF AUTHORS

Ackroyd, P. 52
Aycock, D. 11, 14, 16, 25, 45, 67, 81, 82, 88, 168

Barnes, J.A. 180
Barr, J. 40
Barth, F. 261
Barthes, R. 42
Bartlett, J.R. 186
Beltz, W. 25, 29, 31
Biddle, M.E. 66
Blenkinsopp, J. 52, 55, 57
Blumenberg, H. 37
Bohannan, L. 179
Bright, J. 174, 186, 194
Bryan, D.T. 183
Bulmer, R. 276

Campell, J. 35
Carmicheal, C.M. 148
Carroll, M. 15, 163, 167
Cassirer, E. 31, 32
Cunnison, I. 179, 180

Dolgin, J. 43
Donaldson, M.E. 49
Douglas, M. 15, 16, 267, 275-77
Dundes, A. 33
Durkheim, E. 19, 25, 30

Eliade, M. 36, 37
Emerton, J.A. 45-48
Evans-Pritchard, E. 179, 180

Finkelstein, J.J. 184
Firth, R. 19
Fohrer, G. 29, 44, 65, 69, 70, 79, 80,

83, 169, 173, 176, 269
Fortes, M. 179, 180
Freeman, H. 218, 245
Freud, S. 30, 32
Frezer, J. 25, 31

Gaster, T. 30
Gesenius, W. 141
Gillman, N. 26, 36
Goldin, J. 205
Goody, J. 178, 181
Gottwald, N.K. 55, 174, 182, 186
Gould, S.J. 33
Graves, R. 29, 31

Hallpike, C.R. 107
Hiat, P. 53, 54
Hill, J. 22
Hoglund, K. 53
Hooke, S.H. 30
Hopkins, K. 68
Houseman, A.E. 37
Hugh-Jones, S. 42, 279
Hymes, H. 39

Jacoby, M. 123, 132
Jacopin, P.Y. 19
Jenson, P. 275
Johnson, M.D. 182, 185, 191, 200
Jung, C.G. 31-35

Kasdan, L. 84
Kerenyi, C. 31-34
Kirk, G.S. 40
Klausner, J. 52, 53
Kluckholn, C. 30
Kunin, S. 66, 103

Leach, E. 11, 14-16, 22, 25, 27, 28, 45-
     48, 50, 66, 67, 82, 133, 163, 168,
     272, 273, 279
Lévi-Strauss, C. 11-19, 21-23, 25, 31,
     34, 36-45, 163, 272, 276, 279,
     280
Lindholm, C. 262

Magdoff, J. 43
Malinowski, B. 36, 37, 143
Manisha, R. 33
Mars, L. 16, 148
Mendenhall, G.E. 56, 174
Mernissi, F. 265
Middleton, J. 19, 26
Mielziner, M. 218
Moore, S.F. 30
Moye, R. 27, 41
Murphy, R. 84

Neusner, J. 206, 215, 219, 241
Noth, M. 188, 189, 192

Oded, B. 198-200
Oden, R.A., Jr 25, 28, 29, 49

Pace, D. 19, 20, 22-24
Peters, E. 180
Pitt-Rivers, J. 16, 25-28, 44, 49, 50, 56,
     57, 139, 273
Plaut, W.G. 265
Prewitt, T. 14, 15, 133, 137-39, 142-
     44, 157, 272, 274

Rad, G. von 199, 200
Rendtorff, R. 55, 269
Richards, A.I. 178, 179

Robertson Smith, W. 31, 200

Sahlins, M. 41
Saussure, F. de 20
Schapera, I. 16, 168
Seltzer, R.M. 268
Speiser, E.A. 191, 199
Sperber, D. 11, 12
Spiegel, S. 251, 255
Spiro, M.E. 31, 33
Steinberg, N. 49, 65
Steiner, F. 157, 158
Stemberger, G. 206, 231
Stordalen, T. 165
Strack, H.L. 206, 231
Strenski, I. 31, 32, 37
Sturrock, J. 20

Tambiah, S.J. 276
Torrey, C. 58, 59
Turner, T. 11-13, 19, 21, 22, 41-44,
     93, 134, 258, 272, 273, 280
Turner, V. 279
Tylor, E.B. 23

Vansina, J. 178, 180, 200
Vawter, B. 148

Wagner, R. 11, 19, 40
Wander, N. 84, 105, 106
Watt, I. 178, 181
Westermann, C. 184, 199, 269
Wilson, R.R. 178, 181, 183, 184
Wiseman, D.J. 191, 192, 195, 196

Zlotowitz, B. 53, 54

JOURNAL FOR THE STUDY OF THE OLD TESTAMENT

Supplement Series

80 THE NATHAN NARRATIVES
Gwilym H. Jones

81 ANTI-COVENANT:
COUNTER-READING WOMEN'S LIVES IN THE HEBREW BIBLE
Edited by Mieke Bal

82 RHETORIC AND BIBLICAL INTERPRETATION
Dale Patrick & Allen Scult

83 THE EARTH AND THE WATERS IN GENESIS 1 AND 2:
A LINGUISTIC INVESTIGATION
David Toshio Tsumura

84 INTO THE HANDS OF THE LIVING GOD
Lyle Eslinger

85 FROM CARMEL TO HOREB:
ELIJAH IN CRISIS
Alan J. Hauser & Russell Gregory

86 THE SYNTAX OF THE VERB IN CLASSICAL HEBREW PROSE
Alviero Niccacci
Translated by W.G.E. Watson

87 THE BIBLE IN THREE DIMENSIONS:
ESSAYS IN CELEBRATION OF FORTY YEARS OF BIBLICAL STUDIES
IN THE UNIVERSITY OF SHEFFIELD
Edited by David J.A. Clines, Stephen E. Fowl & Stanley E. Porter

88 THE PERSUASIVE APPEAL OF THE CHRONICLER:
A RHETORICAL ANALYSIS
Rodney K. Duke

89 THE PROBLEM OF THE PROCESS OF TRANSMISSION
IN THE PENTATEUCH
Rolf Rendtorff
Translated by John J. Scullion

90 BIBLICAL HEBREW IN TRANSITION:
THE LANGUAGE OF THE BOOK OF EZEKIEL
Mark F. Rooker

91 THE IDEOLOGY OF RITUAL:
SPACE, TIME AND STATUS IN THE PRIESTLY THEOLOGY
Frank H. Gorman, Jr

92 ON HUMOUR AND THE COMIC IN THE HEBREW BIBLE
Edited by Yehuda T. Radday & Athalya Brenner

93 JOSHUA 24 AS POETIC NARRATIVE
William T. Koopmans

94   WHAT DOES EVE DO TO HELP?
AND OTHER READERLY QUESTIONS TO THE OLD TESTAMENT
David J.A. Clines

95   GOD SAVES:
LESSONS FROM THE ELISHA STORIES
Rick Dale Moore

96   ANNOUNCEMENTS OF PLOT IN GENESIS
Laurence A. Turner

97   THE UNITY OF THE TWELVE
Paul R. House

98   ANCIENT CONQUEST ACCOUNTS:
A STUDY IN ANCIENT NEAR EASTERN AND BIBLICAL HISTORY WRITING
K. Lawson Younger, Jr

99   WEALTH AND POVERTY IN THE BOOK OF PROVERBS
R.N. Whybray

100   A TRIBUTE TO GEZA VERMES:
ESSAYS ON JEWISH AND CHRISTIAN
LITERATURE AND HISTORY
Edited by Philip R. Davies & Richard T. White

101   THE CHRONICLER IN HIS AGE
Peter R. Ackroyd

102   THE PRAYERS OF DAVID (PSALMS 51–72):
STUDIES IN THE PSALTER, II
Michael Goulder

103   THE SOCIOLOGY OF POTTERY IN ANCIENT PALESTINE:
THE CERAMIC INDUSTRY AND THE DIFFUSION OF CERAMIC STYLE
IN THE BRONZE AND IRON AGES
Bryant G. Wood

104   PSALM STRUCTURES:
A STUDY OF PSALMS WITH REFRAINS
Paul R. Raabe

105   RE-ESTABLISHING JUSTICE
Pietro Bovati

106   GRADED HOLINESS:
A KEY TO THE PRIESTLY CONCEPTION OF THE WORLD
Philip Jenson

107   THE ALIEN IN ISRAELITE LAW
Christiana van Houten

108   THE FORGING OF ISRAEL:
IRON TECHNOLOGY, SYMBOLISM AND TRADITION IN ANCIENT SOCIETY
Paula M. McNutt

109   SCRIBES AND SCHOOLS IN MONARCHIC JUDAH:
A SOCIO-ARCHAEOLOGICAL APPROACH
David Jamieson-Drake

110 THE CANAANITES AND THEIR LAND:
THE TRADITION OF THE CANAANITES
Niels Peter Lemche

111 YAHWEH AND THE SUN:
THE BIBLICAL AND ARCHAEOLOGICAL EVIDENCE
J. Glen Taylor

112 WISDOM IN REVOLT:
METAPHORICAL THEOLOGY IN THE BOOK OF JOB
Leo G. Perdue

113 PROPERTY AND THE FAMILY IN BIBLICAL LAW
Raymond Westbrook

114 A TRADITIONAL QUEST:
ESSAYS IN HONOUR OF LOUIS JACOBS
Edited by Dan Cohn-Sherbok

115 I HAVE BUILT YOU AN EXALTED HOUSE:
TEMPLE BUILDING IN THE BIBLE IN LIGHT OF MESOPOTAMIAN
AND NORTHWEST SEMITIC WRITINGS
Victor Hurowitz

116 NARRATIVE AND NOVELLA IN SAMUEL:
STUDIES BY HUGO GRESSMANN AND OTHER SCHOLARS 1906–1923
Translated by David E. Orton
Edited by David M. Gunn

117 SECOND TEMPLE STUDIES:
1. PERSIAN PERIOD
Edited by Philip R. Davies

118 SEEING AND HEARING GOD WITH THE PSALMS:
THE PROPHETIC LITURGY FROM THE SECOND TEMPLE IN JERUSALEM
Raymond Jacques Tournay
Translated by J. Edward Crowley

119 TELLING QUEEN MICHAL'S STORY:
AN EXPERIMENT IN COMPARATIVE INTERPRETATION
Edited by David J.A. Clines & Tamara C. Eskenazi

120 THE REFORMING KINGS:
CULT AND SOCIETY IN FIRST TEMPLE JUDAH
Richard H. Lowery

121 KING SAUL IN THE HISTORIOGRAPHY OF JUDAH
Diana Vikander Edelman

122 IMAGES OF EMPIRE
Edited by Loveday Alexander

123 JUDAHITE BURIAL PRACTICES AND BELIEFS ABOUT THE DEAD
Elizabeth Bloch-Smith

124 LAW AND IDEOLOGY IN MONARCHIC ISRAEL
Edited by Baruch Halpern & Deborah W. Hobson

125 PRIESTHOOD AND CULT IN ANCIENT ISRAEL
Edited by Gary A. Anderson & Saul M. Olyan

126   W.M.L. DE WETTE, FOUNDER OF MODERN BIBLICAL CRITICISM:
      AN INTELLECTUAL BIOGRAPHY
      John W. Rogerson
127   THE FABRIC OF HISTORY:
      TEXT, ARTIFACT AND ISRAEL'S PAST
      Edited by Diana Vikander Edelman
128   BIBLICAL SOUND AND SENSE:
      POETIC SOUND PATTERNS IN PROVERBS 10–29
      Thomas P. McCreesh
129   THE ARAMAIC OF DANIEL IN THE LIGHT OF OLD ARAMAIC
      Zdravko Stefanovic
130   STRUCTURE AND THE BOOK OF ZECHARIAH
      Michael Butterworth
131   FORMS OF DEFORMITY:
      A MOTIF-INDEX OF ABNORMALITIES, DEFORMITIES AND DISABILITIES
      IN TRADITIONAL JEWISH LITERATURE
      Lynn Holden
132   CONTEXTS FOR AMOS:
      PROPHETIC POETICS IN LATIN AMERICAN PERSPECTIVE
      Mark Daniel Carroll R.
133   THE FORSAKEN FIRSTBORN:
      A STUDY OF A RECURRENT MOTIF IN THE PATRIARCHAL NARRATIVES
      Roger Syrén
135   ISRAEL IN EGYPT:
      A READING OF EXODUS 1–2
      G.F. Davies
136   A WALK THROUGH THE GARDEN:
      BIBLICAL, ICONOGRAPHICAL AND LITERARY IMAGES OF EDEN
      Edited by P. Morris & D. Sawyer
137   JUSTICE AND RIGHTEOUSNESS:
      BIBLICAL THEMES AND THEIR INFLUENCE
      Edited by H. Graf Reventlow & Y. Hoffman
138   TEXT AS PRETEXT:
      ESSAYS IN HONOUR OF ROBERT DAVIDSON
      Edited by R.P. Carroll
139   PSALM AND STORY:
      INSET HYMNS IN HEBREW NARRATIVE
      J.W. Watts
140   PURITY AND MONOTHEISM:
      CLEAN AND UNCLEAN ANIMALS IN BIBLICAL LAW
      Walter Houston
141   DEBT SLAVERY IN ISRAEL AND THE ANCIENT NEAR EAST
      Gregory C. Chirichigno

142 DIVINATION IN ANCIENT ISRAEL AND ITS NEAR EASTERN ENVIRONMENT:
A SOCIO-HISTORICAL INVESTIGATION
Frederick H. Cryer
143 THE NEW LITERARY CRITICISM AND THE HEBREW BIBLE
David J.A. Clines & J. Cheryl Exum
144 LANGUAGE, IMAGERY AND STRUCTURE IN THE PROPHETIC WRITINGS
Philip R. Davies & David J.A. Clines
145 THE SPEECHES OF MICAH:
A RHETORICAL-HISTORICAL ANALYSIS
Charles S. Shaw
146 THE HISTORY OF ANCIENT PALESTINE FROM THE PALAEOLITHIC PERIOD
TO ALEXANDER'S CONQUEST
Gösta W. Ahlström
147 VOWS IN THE HEBREW BIBLE AND THE ANCIENT NEAR EAST
Tony W. Cartledge
148 IN SEARCH OF 'ANCIENT ISRAEL'
Philip R. Davies
149 PRIESTS, PROPHETS AND SCRIBES:
ESSAYS ON THE FORMATION AND HERITAGE OF SECOND TEMPLE
JUDAISM IN HONOUR OF JOSEPH BLENKINSOPP
Eugene Ulrich, John W. Wright, Robert P. Carroll & Philip R. Davies (eds)
150 TRADITION AND INNOVATION IN HAGGAI AND ZECHARIAH 1–8
Janet A. Tollington
151 THE CITIZEN-TEMPLE COMMUNITY
J.P. Weinberg
152 UNDERSTANDING POETS AND PROPHETS:
ESSAYS IN HONOUR OF GEORGE WISHART ANDERSON
A.G. Auld
153 THE PSALMS AND THEIR READERS:
INTERPRETIVE STRATEGIES FOR PSALM 18
D.K. Berry
154 MINHAH LE-NAHUM:
BIBLICAL AND OTHER STUDIES PRESENTED TO NAHUM M. SARNA IN
HONOUR OF HIS 70TH BIRTHDAY
M. Brettler and M. Fishbane (eds)
155 LAND TENURE AND THE BIBLICAL JUBILEE:
DISCOVERING A MORAL WORLD-VIEW THROUGH THE SOCIOLOGY
OF KNOWLEDGE
Jeffrey A. Fager
156 THE LORD'S SONG:
THE BASIS, FUNCTION AND SIGNIFICANCE OF CHORAL MUSIC
IN CHRONICLES
J.E. Kleinig
157 THE WORD HESED IN THE HEBREW BIBLE
G.R. Clark

158 IN THE WILDERNESS
     Mary Douglas
159 THE SHAPE AND SHAPING OF THE PSALTER
     J. Clinton McCann
160 KING AND CULTUS IN CHRONICLES:
     WORSHIP AND THE REINTERPRETATION OF HISTORY
     William Riley
161 THE MOSES TRADITION
     George W. Coats
162 OF PROPHET'S VISIONS AND THE WISDOM OF SAGES:
     ESSAYS IN HONOUR OF R. NORMAN WHYBRAY ON HIS
     SEVENTIETH BIRTHDAY
     Heather A. McKay and David J.A. Clines
163 FRAGMENTED WOMEN:
     FEMINIST (SUB)VERSIONS OF BIBLICAL NARRATIVES
     J. Cheryl Exum
164 HOUSE OF GOD OR HOUSE OF DAVID:
     THE RHETORIC OF 2 SAMUEL 7
     Lyle Eslinger
166 THE ARAMAIC BIBLE:
     TARGUMS IN THEIR HISTORICAL CONTEXT
     Edited by D.R.G. Beattie & M.J. McNamara
167 SECOND ZECHARIAH AND THE DEUTERONOMIC SCHOOL
     Raymond F. Person
168 THE COMPOSITION OF THE BOOK OF PROVERBS
     R.N. Whybray
169 EDOM, ISRAEL'S BROTHER AND ANTAGONIST:
     THE ROLE OF EDOM IN BIBLICAL PROPHECY AND STORY
     Bert Dicou
170 TRADITIONAL TECHNIQUES IN CLASSICAL HEBREW VERSE
     Wilfred G.E. Watson
171 POLITICS AND THEOPOLITICS IN THE BIBLE AND POSTBIBLICAL
     LITERATURE
     Edited by Y. Hoffman & H. Graf Reventlow
172 AN INTRODUCTION TO BIBLICAL ARCHAEOLOGY
     Volkmar Fritz
173 HISTORY AND INTERPRETATION:
     ESSAYS IN HONOUR OF JOHN H. HAYES
     Edited by M. Patrick Graham, William P. Brown & Jeffrey K. Kuan
174 'THE BOOK OF THE COVENANT':
     A LITERARY APPROACH
     Joe M. Sprinkle
175 SECOND TEMPLE STUDIES:
     2. TEMPLE AND COMMUNITY IN THE PERSIAN PERIOD
     Edited by Tamara C. Eskenazi & Kent H. Richards

176 STUDIES IN BIBLICAL LAW:
     FROM THE HEBREW BIBLE TO THE DEAD SEA SCROLLS
     Gershon Brin
177 TEXT-LINGUISTICS AND BIBLICAL HEBREW:
     AN EXAMINATION OF METHODOLOGIES
     David Allan Dawson
178 BETWEEN SHEOL AND TEMPLE:
     A STUDY OF THE MOTIF STRUCTURE AND FUNCTION OF THE I-PSALMS
     Martin R. Hauge
179 TIME AND PLACE IN DEUTERONOMY
     James G. McConville and John G. Millar
180 THE SEARCH FOR QUOTATION:
     VERBAL PARALLELS IN THE PROPHETS
     Richard Schultz
181 THEORY AND METHOD IN BIBLICAL AND CUNEIFORM LAW
     Edited by Bernard M. Levinson
182 STUDIES IN THE HISTORY OF TRADITION:
     MARTIN NOTH'S ÜBERLIEFERUNGSGESCHICHTLICHE STUDIEN
     AFTER FIFTY YEARS
     Edited by Steven L. McKenzie & M. Patrick Graham
183 THE RELIGION OF THE SEMITES:
     LECTURES ON THE RELIGION OF THE SEMITES (SECOND AND THIRD
     SERIES) BY WILLIAM ROBERTSON SMITH
     Edited by John Day
184 PURSUING THE TEXT:
     STUDIES IN HONOUR OF BEN ZION WACHOLDER ON THE OCCASION
     OF HIS SEVENTIETH BIRTHDAY
     Edited by John C. Reeves & John Kampen
185 THE LOGIC OF INCEST:
     A STRUCTURALIST ANALYSIS OF HEBREW MYTHOLOGY
     Seth Daniel Kunin